MARKETING 97/98

Nineteenth Edition

Editor

John E. Richardson
Pepperdine University

Dr. John E. Richardson is associate professor of Management in The George L. Graziadio School of Business and Management at Pepperdine University. He is president of his own consulting firm and has consulted with organizations such as Bell and Howell, Dayton-Hudson, Epson, and the U.S. Navy as well as with various service, nonprofit, and franchise organizations. Dr. Richardson is a member of the American Marketing Association, the American Management Association, the Society for Business Ethics, and Beta Gamma Sigma honorary business fraternity.

A Library of Information from the Public Press

Dushkin Publishing Group/Brown & Benchmark Publishers
Sluice Dock, Guilford, Connecticut 06437

The Annual Editions Series

ANNUAL EDITIONS is a series of over 65 volumes designed to provide the reader with convenient, low-cost access to a wide range of current, carefully selected articles from some of the most important magazines, newspapers, and journals published today. ANNUAL EDITIONS are updated on an annual basis through a continuous monitoring of over 300 periodical sources. All ANNUAL EDITIONS have a number of features that are designed to make them particularly useful, including topic guides, annotated tables of contents, unit overviews, and indexes. For the teacher using ANNUAL EDITIONS in the classroom, an Instructor's Resource Guide with test questions is available for each volume.

VOLUMES AVAILABLE

Abnormal Psychology
Adolescent Psychology
Africa
Aging
American Foreign Policy
American Government
American History, Pre-Civil War
American History, Post-Civil War
American Public Policy
Anthropology
Archaeology
Biopsychology
Business Ethics
Child Growth and Development
China
Comparative Politics
Computers in Education
Computers in Society
Criminal Justice
Criminology
Developing World
Deviant Behavior
Drugs, Society, and Behavior
Dying, Death, and Bereavement

Early Childhood Education
Economics
Educating Exceptional Children
Education
Educational Psychology
Environment
Geography
Global Issues
Health
Human Development
Human Resources
Human Sexuality
India and South Asia
International Business
Japan and the Pacific Rim
Latin America
Life Management
Macroeconomics
Management
Marketing
Marriage and Family
Mass Media
Microeconomics

Middle East and the
    Islamic World
Multicultural Education
Nutrition
Personal Growth and Behavior
Physical Anthropology
Psychology
Public Administration
Race and Ethnic Relations
Russia, the Eurasian Republics,
    and Central/Eastern Europe
Social Problems
Social Psychology
Sociology
State and Local Government
Urban Society
Western Civilization,
    Pre-Reformation
Western Civilization,
    Post-Reformation
Western Europe
World History, Pre-Modern
World History, Modern
World Politics

Cataloging in Publication Data
Main entry under title: Annual Editions: Marketing. 1997/98.
        1. Marketing—Periodicals. 2. Marketing—Social aspects—Periodicals.
3. Marketing management—Periodicals. I. Richardson, John, comp. II. Title: Marketing.
HF5415.A642   658.8'005   73-78578   ISBN 0-697-37316-9
ISSN 0730-2606

Nineteenth Edition

Cover image © 1996 PhotoDisc, Inc.

Printed in the United States of America

 Printed on Recycled Paper

Editors/Advisory Board

Staff

To the Reader

In publishing ANNUAL EDITIONS we recognize the enormous role played by the magazines, newspapers, and journals of the *public press* in providing current, first-rate educational information in a broad spectrum of interest areas. Many of these articles are appropriate for students, researchers, and professionals seeking accurate, current material to help bridge the gap between principles and theories and the real world. These articles, however, become more useful for study when those of lasting value are carefully *collected, organized, indexed,* and *reproduced* in a *low-cost format,* which provides easy and permanent access when the material is needed. That is the role played by ANNUAL EDITIONS. Under the direction of each volume's *academic editor,* who is an expert in the subject area, and with the guidance of an *Advisory Board,* each year we seek to provide in each ANNUAL EDITION a current, well-balanced, carefully selected collection of the best of the public press for your study and enjoyment. We think that you will find this volume useful, and we hope that you will take a moment to let us know what you think.

The 1990s are proving to be an exciting and challenging time for the American business community. Recent dramatic social, economic, and technological changes have become an important part of the present marketplace. These changes—accompanied by increasing domestic and foreign competition—are leading a wide array of companies and industries toward the realization that better marketing must become a top priority now to assure their future success.

How does the marketing manager respond to this growing challenge? How does the marketing student apply marketing theory to the real-world practice? Many reach for *The Wall Street Journal, Business Week, Fortune,* and other well-known sources of business information. There, specific industry and company strategies are discussed and analyzed, marketing principles are often reaffirmed by real occurrences, and textbook theories are supported or challenged by current events.

The articles reprinted in this edition of *Annual Editions: Marketing 97/98* have been carefully chosen from numerous different public press sources to provide current information on marketing in the world today. Within these pages you will find articles that address marketing theory and application in a wide range of industries, from automobiles to health care, and from computers to transportation. In addition, the selections reveal how several firms interpret and utilize marketing principles in their daily operations and corporate planning.

The volume contains a number of features designed to make it useful for marketing students, re-searchers, and professionals. These include the *Industry/Company Guide,* which is particularly helpful when seeking information about specific corporations; a *Topic Guide* to locate articles on specific marketing subjects; the *Table of Contents abstracts,* which summarize each article and highlight key concepts; a *Glossary* of key marketing terms; and a comprehensive *Index.*

The articles are organized into four units. Selections that focus on similar issues are concentrated into subsections within the broader units. Each unit is preceded by an overview, which provides background for informed reading of the articles, emphasizes critical issues, and presents *Challenge Questions* focusing on major themes running throughout the selections.

This is the 19th edition of *Annual Editions: Marketing.* Since the first edition in the mid-1970s, the efforts of many individuals have contributed toward its success. We think this is by far the most useful collection of material available for the marketing student. We are anxious to know what you think. What are your opinions? What are your recommendations? Please take a moment to complete and return the *Article Rating Form* on the last page of this volume. Any book can be improved, and this one will continue to be, annually.

John E. Richardson

John E. Richardson

Contents

UNIT 1

Marketing in the 1990s and Beyond

Fourteen selections examine the current and future status of marketing, the marketing concept, service marketing, and marketing ethics.

The concepts in bold italics are developed in the article. For further expansion please refer to the Topic Guide, the Glossary, and the Index.

The concepts in bold italics are developed in the article. For further expansion please refer to the Topic Guide, the Glossary, and the Index.

UNIT 2

Research, Markets, and Consumer Behavior

Eight selections provide an analysis of consumer demographics and lifestyles, the growth and maturation of markets, and the need for market research and planning.

The concepts in bold italics are developed in the article. For further expansion please refer to the Topic Guide, the Glossary, and the Index.

UNIT 3

Developing and Implementing Marketing Strategies

Sixteen selections analyze factors that affect the development and implementation of marketing strategies.

The concepts in bold italics are developed in the article. For further expansion please refer to the Topic Guide, the Glossary, and the Index.

The concepts in bold italics are developed in the article. For further expansion please refer to the Topic Guide, the Glossary, and the Index.

UNIT 4

Global Marketing

Four selections discuss the increasing globalization of markets, trends in world trade, and increasing foreign competition.

Topic Guide

This topic guide suggests how the selections in this book relate to topics of traditional concern to students and professionals involved with the study of marketing. It is useful for locating articles that relate to each other for reading and research. The guide is arranged alphabetically according to topic. Articles may, of course, treat topics that do not appear in the topic guide. In turn, entries in the topic guide do not necessarily constitute a comprehensive listing of all the contents of each selection.

TOPIC AREA	TREATED IN	TOPIC AREA	TREATED IN
Advertising	1. Future of Marketing 4. Sensitive Groups and Social Issues 13. Marketing and Ethics 14. New Hucksterism 15. Frontiers of Psychographics 20. Scouting for Souls 36. Talk of the Town 37. 'Net Effect	Distribution Planning and Strategies	3. New Marketplace 8. Leader of the Pack 24. Win the Market 28. Ten Timeless Truths about Pricing 32. Retailers with a Future 33. Selling the Superstores 34. Target "Micromarkets" Its Way to Success 42. Whole New World
Brands and Branding	2. New Gold Rush? 4. Sensitive Groups and Social Issues 9. Relationship Marketing 15. Frontiers of Psychographics 21. Consumer Behavior 25. What's in a Brand? 27. Flops 28. Ten Timeless Truths about Pricing 31. Your Secret Weapon 33. Selling the Superstores 38. First, Green Stamps. Now, Coupons? 39. Beware the Pitfalls of Global Marketing	Economic Environment	10. Service Is Everybody's Business 16. Database Marketing 18. Generations Quiz 21. Consumer Behavior 26. How to Tell Fads from Trends 40. Isolationism in a Global Economy 41. Hot Markets Overseas
		Exporting	39. Beware the Pitfalls of Global Marketing 40. Isolationism in a Global Economy 41. Hot Markets Overseas
Competition	2. New Gold Rush? 8. Leader of the Pack 21. Consumer Behavior 23. The Very Model of a Modern Marketing Plan 24. Win the Market 26. How to Tell Fads from Trends 27. Flops 30. More to Offer than Price 31. Your Secret Weapon 32. Retailers with a Future 33. Selling the Superstores 34. Target "Micromarkets" Its Way to Success 40. Isolationism in a Global Economy 41. Hot Markets Overseas	Focus Group	4. Sensitive Groups and Social Issues 7. How to Keep Your Customers 8. Leader of the Pack 15. Frontiers of Psychographics 35. Death and Rebirth of the Salesman 39. Beware the Pitfalls of Global Marketing
		Franchising	10. Service Is Everybody's Business 29. Stuck! 33. Selling the Superstores 35. Death and Rebirth of the Salesman
		Global Markets	1. Future of Marketing 2. New Gold Rush? 6. Happiness Isn't Everything 28. Ten Timeless Truths about Pricing 29. Stuck! 39. Beware the Pitfalls of Global Marketing 40. Isolationism in a Global Economy 41. Hot Markets Overseas 42. Whole New World
Consumer Demographics/ Consumer Behavior	1. Future of Marketing 3. New Marketplace 4. Sensitive Groups and Social Issues 7. How to Keep Your Customers 8. Leader of the Pack 9. Relationship Marketing 12. Learning from Customer Defections 15. Frontiers of Psychographics 16. Database Marketing 17. Beginner's Guide to Demographics 18. Generations Quiz 19. Making Generational Marketing Come of Age 20. Scouting for Souls 21. Consumer Behavior 22. Penetrating Purchaser Personalities 25. What's in a Brand? 34. Target "Micromarkets" Its Way to Success 35. Death and Rebirth of the Salesman	Innovation	14. New Hucksterism 15. Frontiers of Psychographics 30. More to Offer than Price 37. 'Net Effect

TOPIC AREA	TREATED IN	TOPIC AREA	TREATED IN
Market Segmentation	16. Database Marketing 17. Beginner's Guide to Demographics 18. Generations Quiz 19. Making Generational Marketing Come of Age 21. Consumer Behavior 22. Penetrating Purchaser Personalities 26. How to Tell Fads from Trends 30. More to Offer than Price 31. Your Secret Weapon 34. Target "Micromarkets" Its Way to Success	**Marketing Planning and Strategies**	4. Sensitive Groups and Social Issues 9. Relationship Marketing 19. Making Generational Marketing Come of Age 22. Penetrating Purchaser Personalities 23. The Very Model of a Modern Marketing Plan 24. Win the Market 26. How to Tell Fads from Trends 34. Target "Micromarkets" Its Way to Success 39. Beware the Pitfalls of Global Marketing
Market Share	8. Leader of the Pack 9. Relationship Marketing 25. What's in a Brand? 28. Ten Timeless Truths about Pricing 35. Death and Rebirth of the Salesman	**Marketing Research**	5. Marketing Myopia 6. Happiness Isn't Everything 7. How to Keep Your Customers 12. Learning from Customer Defections 13. Marketing and Ethics 15. Frontiers of Psychographics 16. Database Marketing 19. Making Generational Marketing Come of Age 21. Consumer Behavior 22. Penetrating Purchaser Personalities 27. Flops 39. Beware the Pitfalls of Global Marketing
Marketing and the Computer/ Technology	1. Future of Marketing 2. New Gold Rush? 14. New Hucksterism 15. Frontiers of Psychographics 16. Database Marketing 17. Beginner's Guide to Demographics 23. The Very Model of a Modern Marketing Plan 34. Target "Micromarkets" Its Way to Success 37. 'Net Effect 42. Whole New World		
		Mass Marketing	2. New Gold Rush? 12. Learning from Customer Defections 16. Database Marketing 17. Beginner's Guide to Demographics 19. Making Generational Marketing Come of Age 33. Selling the Superstores
Marketing Concept	5. Marketing Myopia 6. Happiness Isn't Everything 7. How to Keep Your Customers 8. Leader of the Pack 9. Relationship Marketing 11. 'My Lawyer Sent Me Flowers' 26. How to Tell Fads from Trends 27. Flops 28. Ten Timeless Truths about Pricing 31. Your Secret Weapon 34. Target "Micromarkets" Its Way to Success 35. Death and Rebirth of the Salesman 36. Talk of the Town	**New Product Introductions**	3. New Marketplace 9. Relationship Marketing 26. How to Tell Fads from Trends 27. Flops 33. Selling the Superstores 38. First, Green Stamps. Now, Coupons?
		Packaging	15. Frontiers of Psychographics 23. The Very Model of a Modern Marketing Plan 33. Selling the Superstores 38. First, Green Stamps. Now, Coupons? 39. Beware the Pitfalls of Global Marketing
Marketing Ethics and Social Responsibility	4. Sensitive Groups and Social Issues 8. Leader of the Pack 13. Marketing and Ethics 14. New Hucksterism 30. More to Offer than Price	**Personal Selling**	11. 'My Lawyer Sent Me Flowers' 36. Talk of the Town
Marketing Mix	13. Marketing and Ethics 22. Penetrating Purchaser Personalities 23. The Very Model of a Modern Marketing Plan 24. Win the Market	**Price Competition**	22. Penetrating Purchaser Personalities 26. How to Tell Fads from Trends 28. Ten Timeless Truths about Pricing 29. Stuck! 30. More to Offer than Price 31. Your Secret Weapon

TOPIC AREA	TREATED IN	TOPIC AREA	TREATED IN
Price Planning and Strategy	3. New Marketplace 12. Learning from Customer Defections 13. Marketing and Ethics 22. Penetrating Purchaser Personalities 24. Win the Market 27. Flops 28. Ten Timeless Truths about Pricing 29. Stuck! 30. More to Offer than Price 31. Your Secret Weapon 39. Beware the Pitfalls of Global Marketing	**Sales Management**	6. Happiness Isn't Everything 10. Service Is Everybody's Business 22. Penetrating Purchaser Personalities 23. The Very Model of a Modern Marketing Plan
Product Differentiation/ Product Positioning	10. Service Is Everybody's Business 23. The Very Model of a Modern Marketing Plan 24. Win the Market 25. What's in a Brand? 26. How to Tell Fads from Trends 31. Your Secret Weapon	**Sales Promotion**	8. Leader of the Pack 9. Relationship Marketing 14. New Hucksterism 29. Stuck! 33. Selling the Superstores 35. Death and Rebirth of the Salesman 36. Talk of the Town 38. First, Green Stamps. Now, Coupons?
Product Life-Cycle	13. Marketing and Ethics 27. Flops	**Services Marketing**	3. New Marketplace 7. How to Keep Your Customers 8. Leader of the Pack 10. Service Is Everybody's Business 11. 'My Lawyer Sent Me Flowers' 12. Learning from Customer Defections 22. Penetrating Purchaser Personalities 30. More to Offer than Price 31. Your Secret Weapon 32. Retailers with a Future 36. Talk of the Town 37. 'New Effect 41. Hot Markets Overseas
Product Planning and Development	13. Marketing and Ethics 21. Consumer Behavior 25. What's in a Brand? 26. How to Tell Fads from Trends 27. Flops 33. Selling the Superstores 34. Target "Micromarkets" Its Way to Success 36. Talk of the Town 41. Hot Markets Overseas		
		Social Marketing	3. New Marketplace 4. Sensitive Groups and Social Issues
Promotion Planning and Development	13. Marketing and Ethics 35. Death and Rebirth of the Salesman 36. Talk of the Town 37. 'Net Effect 39. Beware the Pitfalls of Global Marketing	**Target Marketing**	9. Relationship Marketing 17. Beginner's Guide to Demographics 19. Making Generational Marketing Come of Age 20. Scouting for Souls 21. Consumer Behavior 23. The Very Model of a Modern Marketing Plan 29. Stuck! 31. Your Secret Weapon
Psychographics	15. Frontiers of Psychographics 17. Beginner's Guide to Demographics		
Public Relations	1. Future of Marketing 9. Relationship Marketing 30. More to Offer than Price	**Telemarketing**	16. Database Marketing
		Test Marketing	27. Flops 38. First, Green Stamps. Now, Coupons? 39. Beware the Pitfalls of Global Marketing
Relationship Marketing	2. New Gold Rush? 4. Sensitive Groups and Social Issues 7. How to Keep Your Customers	**Wholesaling**	33. Selling the Superstores 35. Death and Rebirth of the Salesman
Retailing	9. Relationship Marketing 16. Database Marketing 32. Retailers with a Future 33. Selling the Superstores 35. Death and Rebirth of the Salesman 38. First, Green Stamps. Now, Coupons? 42. Whole New World		

Industry/Company Guide

This guide was prepared to provide an easy index to the many industries and companies discussed in detail in the 42 selections included in *Annual Editions: Marketing 97/98*. It should prove useful when researching specific interests.

INDUSTRIES

COMPANIES AND DIVISIONS

Marketing in the 1990s and Beyond

- Changing Perspectives (Articles 1–4)
- The Marketing Concept (Articles 5–9)
- Services and Social Marketing (Articles 10–12)
- Marketing Ethics and Social Responsibility (Articles 13 and 14)

If we want to know what a business is we must start with its purpose. . . . There is only one valid definition of business purpose: to create a customer. What business thinks it produces is not of first importance—especially not to the future of the business or to its success. What the customer thinks he is buying, what he considers "value" is decisive—it determines what a business is, what it produces, and whether it will prosper.

—Peter Drucker, The Practice of Management

When Peter Drucker penned these words in 1954, American industry was just awakening to the realization that marketing would play an important role in the future success of businesses. The ensuing years have seen an increasing number of firms in highly competitive areas—particularly in the consumer goods industry—adopt a more sophisticated customer orientation and an integrated marketing focus.

The dramatic economic and social changes of the last decade have stirred companies in an even broader range of industries—from banking and air travel to communications—to the realization that marketing will provide them with their cutting edge. Demographic and lifestyle changes have splintered mass, homogeneous markets into many markets, each with different needs and interests. Deregulation has made once-protected industries vulnerable to the vagaries of competition. Vast and rapid technological changes are making an increasing number of products and services obsolete. Intense international competition and the growth of truly global markets have many firms looking well beyond their national boundaries.

Indeed, it appears that during the 1990s marketing has taken on a new significance—and not just within the industrial sector. Social institutions of all kinds, which had thought themselves exempt from the pressures of the marketplace, are also beginning to recognize the need for marketing in the management of their affairs. Colleges and universities, charities, museums, symphony orchestras, and even hospitals are beginning to give attention to the marketing concept—to provide what the consumer wants to buy.

The selections in this unit are grouped into four areas. Their purposes are to provide current perspectives on marketing, discuss differing views of the marketing concept, analyze the use of marketing by social institutions and nonprofit organizations, and examine the ethical and social responsibilities of marketing.

The four articles in the first subsection provide significant clues about salient approaches and issues that marketers in the 1990s need to address in order to reach, promote, and sell their products in ways that meet the product and service expectations of consumers.

The five selections addressing the marketing concept include Theodore Levitt's now-classic "Marketing Myopia," which first appeared in the *Harvard Business Review* in 1960. This version includes the author's retrospective commentary, written in 1975, in which he discusses how shortsightedness can make management unable to recognize that there is no such thing as a growth industry. The next two articles cover the importance of differentiating between customer satisfaction and customer loyalty. "Leader of the Pack" provides a concrete example of an entrepreneur successfully using creative customer-winning tactics. "Relationship Marketing: Positioning for the Future" reveals how developing a continuous relationship with consumers across a family of related products and services can help create more effective and efficient ways of reaching consumers.

In the Services and Social Marketing subsection, the three articles delineate how quality products and exemplary customer service will be the essential determinants for business survival in the 1990s.

In the final subsection, a careful look is taken at the strategic process and practice of incorporating ethics and social responsibility into the marketplace. "Marketing and Ethics" provides a basic background for understanding critical areas of ethical concern for marketing. "The New Hucksterism" reveals some subtle and controversial ways advertising has been woven into our culture.

Looking Ahead: Challenge Questions

Dramatic changes are occurring in the marketing of products and services. What social and economic trends do you believe are most significant today, and how do you think these will affect marketing in the future?

Theodore Levitt suggests that, as times change, the marketing concept must be reinterpreted. Given the varied perspectives of the other articles in this unit, what do you think this reinterpretation will entail?

"The New Hucksterism" reveals how stealth advertising is creeping into a culture saturated with logos and pitches. Do you see the forms of advertising discussed in this article to be problematic? Why or why not?

In the present competitive business arena, is it possible for marketers to behave ethically in the environment and still survive and prosper? What suggestions can you give that could be incorporated into the marketing strategy for firms that want to be both ethical and successful?

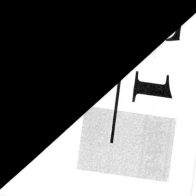

The Future Of Marketing

WHAT EVERY MARKETER SHOULD KNOW ABOUT BEING ONLINE

Address by, BOB WEHLING, *Senior Vice President Advertising, The Proctor & Gamble Company*
Delivered to the World Federation of Advertisers, Sydney, Australia, October 31, 1995

Over the next half hour or so, we're going to have some fun. We're going to take a test drive — at warp speed — down the information superhighway.

Our destination is the future: the future of marketing, actually, a future where smart marketers will be surfing across the internet into the homes of billions of consumers in hundreds of countries, at the speed of light.

We'll be driving by the virtual storefronts of companies that are already creating this future. Pay attention. Because when our trip is finished, you'll be ready for more than a test drive. You'll be ready to get wired into this exciting future yourself. I know, because that's exactly what happened to me — and to a lot of us at Procter & Gamble — after we took this trip.

Preparing for the New Media Future

Before we get started, let me give you just a little background.

There's been a lot of hype about the Information Superhighway for several years now. P&G got into the fray a year and a half ago when our chairman, Ed Artzt, gave a watershed speech to the American Association of Advertising Agencies.

Here's a brief clip that captures the essence of what he had to say.

"From where we stand today, we can't be sure that ad-supported TV programming will have a future in the world being created — a world of video-on-demand, pay-per-view, and subscription television.

If that happens, if advertising is no longer needed to pay most of the cost of home entertainment, then advertisers like us will have a hard time achieving the reach and frequency we need to support our brands."

That talk created quite a stir. Dick Hopple at DMB&B called it "a seminal speech for the industry." Advertising Age, the New York Times, the Wall Street Journal, and the Financial Times all covered the talk extensively. It was truly a wake-up call that got the industry moving.

The first thing that happened was the creation of CASIE, an industry coalition led by senior advertiser and agency executives from the Four A's and the Association of National Advertisers.

They got to work in several areas. They kicked off a legislative and regulatory game plan both to protect ad-supported broad-reach television and to ensure advertiser access to new media.

They started work to establish common technical standards for new media. The lack of standards is one of the biggest barriers to advertiser participation in new media. Currently, applications developed for one new media provider cannot be used on another, without the advertiser incurring significant reauthoring costs.

But, perhaps most important, they did an inventory of new media research, looking at which new media technologies were closest to commercialization and how their emergence would likely affect consumer behavior.

The Future of Marketing

The most valuable learning that has come from this research is that the technologies that had seemed most imminent when Ed gave his speech — interactive TV, pay-per-view movies, video game channels — are being eclipsed by computer-based media.

This has happened principally because the economics of building and operating interactive TV systems are out of line with what consumers will pay. And furthermore, while only a few thousand households currently have access to interactive TV, more than 20 million people are on the internet today — and that number is growing fast.

As a result, the internet is now positioned to influence the future of marketing as much as — and maybe even more than — any other medium we've ever known.

The internet originated in the early '70s as a network to connect university, military and defense contractors. It was an information sharing tool that was never intended for broad public use. But throughout the '70s, as its capabilities were expanded, the network grew.

Then, in 1993, two things happened that dramatically accelerated the net's growth. First, the World Wide Web was created. The Web is the graphical portion of the internet. And, at

From *Vital Speeches of the Day,* January 1, 1996, pp. 170-173. © 1996 by City Publishing Company, Inc. Reprinted by permission.

about the same time, the first, easy-to-use navigation tools were developed. Together, these two breakthroughs turned the internet — or, more specifically, the Web — into a medium that consumers were attracted to and could find their way around.

As a result, the Web has grown — and continues to grow — at extraordinary rates. The number of web sites is doubling every 53 days — that's growth of about 50% per month. Today, millions of consumers are "surfing" the net through online commercial services, like America Online and Prodigy, and through direct connections with navigators such as Netscape.

This is unprecedented. As the Economist pointed out recently, "no communications medium or consumer electronics technology has ever grown as quickly — not the fax machine, not even the PC. At this rate, within two years, the citizens of cyberspace will outnumber all but the largest nations."

What does all this frenetic activity mean for us, as marketers? It means that an entirely new form of marketing — interactive, online marketing — is emerging as a breakthrough way to sell products and services to consumers.

Unprecedented Opportunities for Marketers

There are different types of marketing opportunities online. The most common, on the Web, are corporate sites, or home pages. A home page is a company's online storefront. It's a place where consumers go for product and corporate information. At a minimum, a company's home page can be an extremely effective public relations tool. At its best, a web site captures the personality of the company and presents such useful information and services that consumers not only visit but return again and again.

Another opportunity is "webvertising" — banner ads placed inside editorial or other content in Web-based media. What makes these banner ads so effective is that, by clicking on them, a reader can jump instantly to the marketer's own site.

This is a technology called "hyperlinking." And it works not only for banner ads, but even for straight editorial. For example, the Economist did an article about the internet earlier this year. In the online version of that article, a reader interested in a particular example — say, this reference to Zima beer — could simply click on the word "Zima" and, in an instant, be taken directly to the Zima home page.

No other marketing medium can accomplish this. It elevates the power of right-time marketing to an unparalleled level.

There's one additional marketing niche that's just beginning to evolve on the Web, and that's sponsored programming.

The most common programming right now are celebrity interviews. Oldsmobile, for example, features online discussions with a range of celebrities as a way to attract consumers to its corporate site.

But an even more innovative form of content is the virtual magazine — which, at its best, is far more than an electronic version of a print publication. HotWIRED is a good example. It's a highly-interactive journal of online culture that incorporates banner ads and commercially-supported hyperlinks throughout its editorial. In fact, they reportedly made $2 million in ad revenue last year from these kinds of placements — and you can bet they're just getting started.

As you can see, these are far ranging and very significant new marketing opportunities. Now, to be clear, mass media isn't going away. There will always be a need for the reach and frequency of mass advertising. But online marketing represents the next generation of advertising — and smart marketers are already using it as a powerful new way to create con-

sumer awareness, to stimulate trial, even to sell their products and services.

P&G On the Net

At P&G, we're just getting online. We launched an experimental web site in Germany about five months ago. This site includes information about P&G, it announces employment opportunities and, most important, it contains information about a few of our brands.

For example, consumers can request a handy dispenser for our leading laundry detergent brand, Ariel, and find solutions to common laundry problems. As you can see, this first experiment is pretty basic.

We made our second — and somewhat more sophisticated — venture onto the net just two weeks ago, with our new WordSlam site tied to the U.S. introduction of Hugo, the new Hugo Boss men's fragrance.

This site is an integral part of our product launch and publicity campaign. The selling line for this new fragrance is, "Don't imitate...innovate."

The Hugo page builds on this theme with the first online Spoken Word poetry contest. Spoken Word competitions are a hot trend among Generation Xers and this unique site should attract young "surfers" from around the world. While they're visiting, we'll give them a chance to learn about the new Hugo line of products. We'll invite them to join in online forums and chats with celebrity guests. And we'll provide links to other sites, as well.

We're planning to expand our Web presence over the next several months. One prototype we're experimenting with is for our leading laundry brand in the U.S. We call it the Tide Stain Detective. If you spill red wine on your favorite cotton shirt, you can ask the Tide Stain Detective how to get it out. And he'll give you a fast — and proven — solution. This is the kind of value-added information consumers want, which builds loyalty to our brand.

It's premature for me to talk much more about our plans, but — as we take our test drive into the future — I can tell you some of what we've learned over the past few months while we've prepared to expand our presence on the Web.

So let's get going. We see six core benefits of marketing online.

Instant Access to the World

First, the net is global. It reaches consumers in literally every part of the world. It's hard to get a precise number of users, but we know that there are somewhere between five and six million host computers that provide Web access to at least 20 million consumers in over 100 countries.

The distribution is very uneven — 90% of the host computers are in North America and Western Europe — but interest and access is growing around the world.

For example, there are now over 300,000 host computers in Asia/Pacific. In fact, Australia is the third most wired country in the world. In terms of the number of computer hosts per 1,000 people, Australia ranks behind only Finland and the U.S.

In Central and South America, there are only 16,000 hosts — but that's more than double the number that existed just a year ago.

One major restriction to the Web's global growth is language. The net is principally an English-language medium today, which makes it inaccessible to non-English-speaking users. But smart, global marketers like IBM are changing that by providing multi-lingual sites.

IBM offers a unique feature called Planetwide. By clicking

on Japan, for example, a user can get information about IBM, its products or its operations in Japan — in Japanese. Or in Italian. Or Spanish.

More than any other I've come across, the IBM site demonstrates conclusively that this is truly a global medium. There is no other medium that enables you not just to reach but to interact with consumers in virtually every country on earth — if you do it right.

And its global reach is not just for the IBMs of the world. Because the price of entry onto the Web is relatively low, a corner flower shop, for example, has the potential to become a global flower powerhouse virtually overnight with the right kind of approach.

Unprecedented Depth of Sale

Second benefit: online marketing is self-selective. You know the consumers who visit your site are interested. They want to know more about your products. Not only does this help identify your highest-potential consumers, it permits a depth of sale that no other medium can provide.

Auto makers have been among the first companies to tap this potential. Virtually every major car company is online today: Ford, General Motors, Toyota, Nissan, Honda, Mitsubishi. They provide a world of information, from a lineup of models to lists of options to comprehensive dealer directories.

But the best among them, from what I've seen, is the Chrysler Technology Center. You can get all kinds of information on Chrysler — the company's environmental record, its financial performance, you can even chat with CEO Bob Eaton.

But most interesting, you can look at cars.

Want to see the cars of the future? Go to the Technology section and look at concept cars. For example, the Plymouth Back Pack — a part utility, part pickup and part sporty coupe that's likely to be a real hit with young buyers.

Or you can go to the showroom and look at the latest cars on the market today. If you're in the market for a Jeep, you've got your choice of three models. Click on the Jeep Grand Cherokee and you can look at the vehicle, pull down specs, compare it feature-by-feature to its main competitors — even read reviews from the auto press.

And that's not all: soon you'll be able to custom price the Jeep of your dreams — or the Chrysler or the Dodge or the Eagle. Choose the features you want and the system will automatically calculate the suggested retail price and even tell you what your monthly payment will be.

Together, these features are the perfect right-time marketing tool: they give you the chance to reach consumers who are interested — when they're interested.

Opportunities to Engage

The third benefit of online marketing is that it is interactive. It enables you to engage consumers in a way that no other medium can. The Chrysler site I just mentioned is one good example. Another is American Express ExpressNet on America Online.

You can apply for a card, check your account status, pull down photos of exciting travel locations, plan a trip and even make reservations. If you're travelling to Asia and want to know what's happening in Beijing this week, you can choose from sports to shopping to restaurants and nightlife. You can order a customized Fodor's travel guide that helps ensure you get to see and do exactly what you want to do no matter where you go.

Whether you're planning a trip or charting your expenses after one, ExpressNet puts you in charge. And reminds you that, no matter where you're going or where you've been, you can always count on American Express.

Fully Integrated Marketing

The fourth benefit is that online marketing is fully integrated. It combines the activities of every marketing discipline, from advertising to PR to direct mail.

Sony, for example, uses its web site to promote new products, from CDs to movies to electronics. It's even being used as a sampling device.

Click on Wiretap and check out the CD from Mariah Carey, one of the biggest recording artists in the U.S. You can even sample the video of her #1 hit, Fantasy.

You can find out where she's touring, enter a contest for a "Fantasy" weekend in New York, or win tickets to her live TV special.

This is truly integrated marketing. There is no other medium in which you can integrate so many different marketing tools at once.

Marketing One-to-One

The fifth benefit of being online is the medium's unique one-to-one marketing capability. This is the most important loyalty-building benefit of online marketing, because it gives you the ability to establish enduring relationships with individual consumers.

McDonald's McFamily, on America Online, is a good example. This site reinforces the idea of McDonald's as a parent's best friend. Parents can get information on the latest Happy Meal or nutritional information about McDonald's products.

But even more valuable is the community McDonald's has created. For not only can parents talk directly to McDonald's, they can also talk with experts and with each other on a whole range of parenting issues — from how to keep the family healthy and safe to how they can spend more quality time with their kids.

McDonald's has proven the benefits of relationship marketing through a number of direct mail programs they've used in recent years. And they believe the interactivity of online marketing will make it even easier to build relationships with consumers. In fact, the level of relationship building they're achieving online would have been almost impossible to create even two or three years ago.

The Virtual Store

Finally, there is one last and very important benefit: you can sell.

A great example of this is right here in Australia — the Flag network of hotels, inns, resorts and apartments. Flag is Australia's largest independent accommodation group with properties in Australia, New Zealand, Papua New Guinea, Fiji, Western Somoa as well as the U.S. and the U.K.

They make it easy to stay at a Flag hotel or inn. A traveler can navigate by map to any of the 450 facilities in the Flag network. If you're on your way to Australia, simply click on the region — say New South Wales — and the city — perhaps Sydney — and you're ready to select your hotel.

You can pull down details and ratings of every Flag hotel in the area and, once you've made a decision, enter your reservation.

Flag will confirm within 24 hours, either by phone or e-mail — whichever you request.

There are other benefits of being online, as well. But these six are the most important, because they demonstrate that everything we do to build consumer loyalty is affected by this new medium: from awareness to trial to purchase and repurchase. It is a major step forward in the evolution of marketing.

Next Steps: Tapping the Net's Potential

The key question, is how do we tap the full potential of this exciting new medium? How do we make it a global bonanza for advertising and a rich source of entertainment, information and community for consumers?

To do this, we have to resolve a number of issues — from the security of online transactions to consumer privacy. But there are a a few things, in particular, that I would urge you to focus on most.

Measuring Online Effectiveness

As an industry, we need to establish clear, broadly-accepted standards for measuring the cost effectiveness of the net versus other media.

All the examples I've just shared demonstrate that the Web can be a highly-effective marketing medium. But, for it to become a truly valuable tool for the industry, it must also be highly-efficient. And we need accurate, reliable measures to guage that efficiency. CASIE has provided a good starting point. Just a month ago, they presented a set of guiding principles for measurement that I strongly endorse. We have copies of the executive summary in the back, but let me just mention the highlights.

First, audience measurement of interactive media should be directly comparable to the measures used for other media. This is fundamental to the reliability of audience research.

Second, audience measurements should be taken by objective third-party research suppliers and not by the medium being measured. What little measurement there is today rarely follows this principle.

And one more: interactive media research standards must be set by a broad representation of the advertising industry, including advertisers, agencies, media, research companies and industry groups.

In all, CASIE has developed 11 guiding principles. We need to use them to establish clear measurement standards as quickly as possible.

I've been told by some of our agencies that it may take three to five years to iron out the measurement issue. That's too long. We need to do it by next year so we can begin building on and justifying our investments in this new medium.

This is a global issue and it needs broad, global leadership from the advertising industry. So today, I'm calling for the WFA to join forces with CASIE to accelerate the creation and adoption of measurement standards for interactive media.

By this time next year, at the '96 WFA conference, I'd like to see the WFA and CASIE jointly endorse a set of broadly accepted standards that will enable us to measure and compare the effectiveness of interactive media in any part of the world.

Getting Up Close and Personal

In addition to this industry-wide effort, there are a few important things that I encourage you to do as individual advertisers.

First, get up close and personal with the internet.

Any advertising professional who hasn't been online should get online. You simply cannot appreciate the potential of this medium until you've "surfed" it yourself.

In fact, seeing first hand how limited the current online efforts are will convince you that, even if you're not online to-

day, you're not that far behind. No one out there — even the best, like those I've mentioned here today — is very far out in front at this point. Now is the time to get online. Not just to catch up but to jump ahead. It's a big opportunity.

Another thing you can do, when you get back home, is to be sure that your governments are not establishing regulations that will inhibit the growth of this medium or advertiser access to it. If that's happening, it is in your interest to try to change it. This is as strategic a public policy issue as any advertiser will face.

Six Questions to Ask Before You Go Online

Now, if you go away from this meeting thinking that Wehling's talk was interesting, but I'm not sure it has anything to do with me, I encourage you to think about it harder. Think about what the Economist said recently: "As a new medium with almost no distribution costs, the internet has the potential to reshape the media world, letting new competitors in and forcing established giants to evolve or die." That's a pretty clear call to action, in my book.

If, on the other hand, you go away from here fired up about the potential of this new medium — convinced that you've seen the future and it works — then I have some parting advice for you.

The key to winning online is content. That's true for any marketing medium, and it is especially true for the internet. And what's important to remember about online content is that it's not just a matter of piping a 30-second ad over the internet or converting printed materials into electronic form. It requires a fundamentally different approach.

My suggestion is to start with the six benefits I listed earlier. They should provide a valuable framework to guide your thinking. Take a look at your marketing messages and at how you're delivering them today. Then ask yourself six questions:

1. How can I make my message global?
2. How can I offer such useful and interesting content that consumers will come back to my site again and again?
3. How can I make it interactive?
4. How can I fully integrate the full range of marketing disciplines into the delivery of my message?
5. How can I make my message more compelling by using the net's one-to-one capability? And,
6. How can I use this technology to sell my products?

I think you'll find that the answers to these questions will provide a creative blueprint as you think about how to tap the full potential of the net.

Find a Way to Get Online

The key is: find a way to get online. Experiment, Learn about it. Get prepared. You may ultimately decide it's not right for your business. But make it an informed decision.

In fact, I echo what the Economist had to say. I believe that — over the long term — marketers who remain unprepared for the sea-change we're about to experience won't survive. Marketers who understand the implications and get ahead of the curve will not only survive, they'll thrive. They'll emerge more competitive than ever and they'll build relationships with consumers that are deeper and more enduring than any we can create today.

The future of marketing is bright and the smartest among us are going to take tremendous advantage of that potential. I encourage you to be among the leaders.

Thanks for the chance to talk with you today. I look forward to seeing you online.

THE NEW GOLD RUSH?

CATHERINE ROMANO

Catherine Romano is Management Review's staff editor. Her e-mail address is amapubs@aol.com.

The greatest technological invention of the 20th century was supposed to be the television. When first introduced, the picture box was going to replace the radio, and years later its sister entertainment vehicle, the VCR, was expected to put a substantial dent in movie attendance. Industry pundits predicted that the role of the television would far exceed the domain of entertainment and enter a realm where banking from home and ordering from a touch-tone screen would be de rigueur.

That reality never really materialized, and television's futuristic possibilities have been cast aside in favor of the computer. The PC, with penetration in 35 percent of American households, is the gateway to the Internet, the crux of the information superhighway. The Internet, which started in 1969 as a network of computers for government and academia, has mushroomed into a vehicle for information, entertainment and commerce.

In fact, companies are eyeing the Internet and the World Wide Web, a hypertext browsing and searching system on the Internet that links multimedia files and graphics, as an untapped marketing gold mine that will create new opportunities well into the millennium. The graphics and linking capabilities of the Web have sent companies flooding the Net at rates reminiscent of the 1849 Gold Rush.

Roughly 20 million to 30 million people are on the Internet, and the number is growing by as much as 15 percent a month. Add to that the number of people who will gain access through the upstart Microsoft Network and the constant daily flow of newbies (computer parlance for novice Internet users), and there could be as many as 500 million users by 2000. Rumors (mostly unsubstantiated) abound that those companies which don't get on the Internet soon will fade from existence by early next decade.

A Virtual Future

"It's the platform for the future. People don't want to be left out," says Sharon Pinder, Internet program manager for GE Information Services (GEIS). The charge is being led, not unexpectedly, by computer and software companies and financial and insurance-related firms.

There are compelling reasons for companies to establish a home page on the Web. "It gives you the opportunity to develop a pres-

> ## BRIEFCASE
>
> **Marketing on the Internet marries the needs of consumers with the ever-evolving cybertechnology. The result: companies go electronic to communicate with their customers, create an awareness of their product and, perhaps, make a profit.**

ence with the customer," says Julia Lommatzch, an internal consultant at a firm called marketing 1:1 in Stamford, Conn. For this reason, GE is very strict about maintaining a constant image on its home page. "Anything marketed under the brand of GE must have the look and the feel of the company. You don't want to cause confusion by everyone going out there and doing their own thing," explains Pinder.

MCI (http://www.mci.com) presents such a unified image that it ties its television advertisements into its home page. The fictional Gramercy Press shows up on the Web, providing the latest on the publishing company and providing a way for browsers to learn more about MCI.

Lommatzch points to Zima, the clear malt beverage unit of Coors, as a company that is striving to build a solid relationship with its consumers. "Zima's Tribe Z campaign is building a relationship with customers, and that's a success. By building a relationship and knowing Zima is a good product, consumers don't have to second-guess their choice," explains Lommatzch.

Zima's (http://www.zima.com) goal is to position its alcoholic beverage as the brand of choice among the "wired generation." Its page features the life of a 20-something named Duncan in the electronic version of a Taster's Choice commercial. The goal is to keep people coming back for each weekly installment, a key factor in successful on-line marketing.

Once a user is hooked on Zima's page, Zima hopes to further its relationship with its users through Tribe Z. To join Tribe Z, users give the pertinent demographic information, which is every marketer's dream, and then get to enter the clubhouse, where they can interact with other Zima drinkers. To make the experi-

So far, there hasn't been overwhelming proof that there is gold in Cyberspace.

ence more participatory, Tribe Z members vote on such things as the club logo.

This relationship building is designed to foster a sense of community among consumers with the same interests or tastes. Lommatzch has even heard of a virtual quilting bee. The women exchange patterns and information online, finish their sections individually and then complete the final quilt together.

The Internet's ease of use and users' strong opinions have turned the medium into a virtual focus group. "If you do something they don't like, they'll let you know," says Pinder. Click on the link that says, "Please give us your comments," and a visitor to the GEIS home page (http://www.ge.com/geis) automatically moves to an e-mail form, preaddressed to Pinder.

Indeed, getting on the Internet is not for the faint of heart. "Everyone on the Net feels they own a piece of it. If they see a brand they're not happy about, they're going to tell you about it," explains Linda McCutcheon, the director of advertising, sales and marketing for Time Inc., whose home on the Internet, Pathfinder (http://www.timeinc.com), is one of the most visited sites.

And while Pathfinder, with its glossy magazine sites, is popular because of its size and subject matter, the Internet affords smaller companies a major strategic advantage —equal access to customers. Windham Hill, a record company in

"Everyone on the Net feels they own a piece of it. If they see a brand they're not happy about, they're going to tell you about it."

—Linda McCutcheon, Time Inc.

Menlo Park, Calif. (http://www.windham.com), garnered a 94 percent response rate for a recent survey. In fact, larger companies are more likely to go overboard with large, unnecessary graphics. Their corporate vanity could annoy users who may not have the computer speed—and patience—to easily download the complex images.

Digital Dynamics

At the very least, digital marketing broadens product awareness. But using the Internet can also have very tangible effects on marketing. Len Keeler, author of *Cybermarketing* (AMACOM, 1995), illustrates how going electronic can improve the marketing function:

• **Stretching the marketing budget.** Catalogs, brochures and directories don't have to be printed, stored or distributed; those ever-increasing costs are eliminated by technology. Pinder at GEIS estimates that just putting its phone directory on an internal Web would save about $100,000 in 1995.

• **Saving time.** Information is available immediately in the office or in the field. There's no waiting for printing or mailing. Customers can get answers quickly.

• **Offering customers another way to buy.** Customers like control, and the more choices they have in either product or process, the better.

• **Satisfying information-hungry consumers.** Today's buyers want to know everything before they make a decision, and this is the ideal forum for them to find all the information they think they need. "Consumers want choice and access to content, communication, and products and services — information to guide their decision making," says William B. Clausen Jr., an advertising manager at AT&T.

• **Encouraging international reach.** That Web page is out there, and what works in New York will also have to float in London. "The Internet is a new communications medium that is helping to squeeze out cross-cultural differences," explains Keeler.

• **Lowering barriers to entry.** Even though a larger company can spend more money creating a Web page, a small company can still make a good impression if it presents the right images. A small business is on equal footing with a larger company on the Net. "You have to get over the paradigm that bigger is better," says Steve Yastrow, vice president of Resort Marketing at Hyatt Hotels Corp. (http://www.travelweb.com/hyatt.html.).

Fool's Gold?

Another paradigm that must be shattered is that the Net is designed to make money *now*. So far, there hasn't been overwhelming proof that there is gold in Cyberspace. "Too many people are looking at the Net as a medium for making money, and that's wrong. People believe that if there's not a lot of cash transactions going on, it's not a success as a marketing tool. That's patently ridiculous," says Keeler.

"Because of the rapid growth rate and the increasing number of people who are first-time users and people who have become hooked, the jury is still out on how successful you can be," says Pinder. Because it provides electronic commerce solutions to clients, GEIS feels it is uniquely positioned to turn a profit on the Internet. Other companies just laugh at the projections that electronic commerce will reach $650 billion by 2000. "Sales are much less than activity, but that will change," sums up Roy Gattinella, Windham Hill's marketer.

For now, making money on the Internet is being limited by the perception that transmitting financial data is unsafe, that an enterprising hacker could capitalize on the credit card numbers being sent via the Internet. "In the mind of the consumer, [the ability to transmit financial information] is not available yet. If the Web site has the right software and the latest Netscape browser, it's just as secure as giving credit card numbers over the phone," says Keeler.

"You can encrypt data on the Internet and have it arrive at the service and unencrypt it at that stage," says Cathy Medich, executive director of CommerceNet, a Menlo Park, Calif., consortium that is determining the infrastructure necessary to facilitate electronic commerce. The catch? The software necessary to secure transactions has only been available since the beginning of the year, and people are just starting to get access to it. Also, security systems outside the United States are not as tight, thereby prohibiting truly international electronic commerce.

CommerceNet is also currently working on a public key certificate, a digital document that will authenticate the parties involved. It includes a public key that is used to encrypt and decrypt documents. What is missing, however, is the infrastructure to check these certificates. "When dealing on-line, anyone can be sitting at your PC and saying that they are you. We need a public and private key to verify who they are," says Medich.

Until consumers more readily accept the ability to safely encrypt credit card numbers, companies must offer other means of purchasing, including 800 numbers for consumers to call and place an order. Iang Jeon, director of electronic marketing for Fidelity Investments (http://www.fid-inv.com), says that Fidelity plans to do on-line transactions eventually. In fact, he says, "We'll get there probably sooner than people are forecasting."

The freedom to conduct transactions on-line used to be the distinct advantage the commercial on-line providers, CompuServe, Prodigy and America Online, had over the unregulated Internet. But since more commercial providers now offer Internet access, they are vulnerable to the same security issues.

Overall, the private services are more secure for transactions, but it is more expensive for a company to provide as robust a site as they can on the Internet. Windham Hill's co-nundrum is that it sells more products via its America Online page, but it cannot afford to make it as grand as its Internet site.

Conspicuous by Absence

What's usually missing in a discussion about marketing on the Internet is old-fashioned selling. The Internet has revolutionized the way marketing is conducted. The emphasis is on creating a relationship with an individual, not selling en masse.

"If you approach the Web with the first objective of selling and making money, you will almost always fall on your face," says John Klug, chairman of the Customer Communications Group in Denver. "The classic business return on investment will fall flat."

In marketing, especially advertising, the ROI mind-set has always been one of mass communication, where the more people who would see a message the better. Klug compares that method of communications to WWII fliers. "That's like B-52 bombers dropping leaflets in the sky, indiscriminately over the population with relatively little knowledge or interest in who was hit by or who read the leaflets," says Klug.

That type of attack also doesn't take into account that we're not a homogeneous nation, but instead, a nation of tribes. And each tribe demands its own message. "You can't think of males 18 to 34. You can't talk to them as a mass; you have to dialogue with them one to one," says Hyatt's Yastrow.

Consumers have become cynical and they're tired of searching through messages to find the information that is relevant to them. To avoid turning off potential customers, companies can tailor messages to targeted consumers and measure individual hits to the site. Internet providers can get a good idea of

SUPERHIGHWAY LINGO

Address: Internet addresses use three main extensions: .com, .edu and .gov to designate commercial sites, educational institutions and governmental agencies.

Browser: Software for navigating the Web.

FAQ, or frequently asked questions: Answers to the common questions of new on-line users. Always look here first, if you're new.

Home page: A company's preliminary page of information on the Web.

HTML, or Hypertext mark-up language: The computer language used to write and edit Web documents. Hypertexts provide links from one document to another.

Netiquette: Customs and generally accepted rules for being online.

World Wide Web, Web, WWW: A hypertext browsing and searching system on the Internet that allows linked multimedia files and graphics.

15

who is visiting their sites. "There's limited information but still more than you could get from a profile of subscribers of a publication," says Lommatzch.

This, of course, leaves digital marketers reliant on the customer to seek out information (read: advertising) on products and services. Companies cannot bombard consumers with junk mail—it's too easy for recipients to filter out or delete unread mail. Consumers will not tolerate junk mail. They're paying for the time they spend on-line and they don't want to waste their time on unsolicited mail.

Triangle of Success

In the past, the marketing function was simply to persuade the audience that the product in question was a worthwhile purchase. These days, according to Klug, marketing on the Internet will only be successful if practitioners turn their advertising into an opportunity to inform, communicate and entertain their audiences.

• **Inform.** This is the closest purpose to traditional marketing, but it has evolved into an entirely new creature. It's no longer about repackaging already existing product information; the minimum requirement is providing value-added service.

"It can't simply be a corporate backgrounder in Cyberspace. Focus on what it means for the end-user," says Jeon at Fidelity Investments. In addition to answers about investment basics, the

Fidelity Investments Information Center provides an on-line worksheet to select mutual funds based on goals and investment experience, a college savings planner and a demonstration of Fidelity's proprietary trading software.

• **Communicate.** It's imperative that this medium be interactive and that it facilitate conversations between audience members. "Every company has a community of people whose interests intersect concerning that particular economic activity," says Klug. Alamo's site (http://www.freeways.comm) allows visitors to reserve cars, get detailed directions, talk to Alamo and exchange information with other travelers.

This freedom in communications opens up a company to negative public relations. News of a flaw in Intel's Pentium chip spread like wildfire on Internet on-line discussion groups last year. Dell Computer has employees whose job it is to cruise the Internet looking for negative comments and follow up to resolve them.

"Companies are discovering that while it might be uncomfortable or downright frightening, it is better to get that stuff out where it can be addressed rather than trying to pretend it doesn't exist," says Klug.

• **Entertain.** "The Internet is the ultimate zappable media. You can click from Web page to Web page," says Klug. In order to keep people interested and coming back, Web pages have to be entertaining and they have to be updated constantly. Luckily, there aren't the production and distribution costs associated with keeping the Web pages fresh as there are with publishing a magazine.

"To get your message across, you have to blur the lines between advertising and entertainment, information and advertising. You have to create 'entermercials,' 'edutainment' that speaks to consumer interests," says Clausen at AT&T.

If a Tree Falls...

"The goal is to let people know you're out there and let them come to you," says Jeon at Fidelity. But considering there are more than 118,000 commercial domains on the Internet, you can't just take the chance that those unfamiliar with your address will happen upon it.

Instead, marketers engage in intricate strategies of planting seeds and herding consumers to their sites. Seeding is the strategic placement of a company's banner or icon to attract users to the site. Herding is the strategic purchase of a banner to attract a target audi-

---

WORKBOOK

Advertising is only one component of marketing on the Internet, but if that's the route you want to take, Len Keeler suggests these tips in *Cybermarketing* (AMACOM, 1995):

☑ **Get comfortable with the on-line culture.** Become an on-line user before you try to do business on the Internet. You'll instinctively know how to be a better on-line businessperson.

☑ **Play it straight.** Craft your message carefully; stick to the facts and avoid exaggeration and hype.

☑ **Mind your Netiquette.** Advertise only where it's appropriate; don't intrude where your message won't be welcome; and follow the rules of the road.

☑ **Overcome resistance.** Offer something extra, such as added information, interactivity or benefits that will repay users for the time they invested in your ad.

☑ **Don't forget your marketing basics.** Set your objectives, give readers a reason to buy, use testimonials, stick with it and keep testing. In short, follow the rules for a traditional marketing campaign.

ence. The goal in either case is to create links between your content and other providers who might have traffic you would like to draw into your site. "The biggest drawback to reciprocal arrangements is they take time," says G. M. O'Connell, a founding partner of interactive marketing company Modem Media. "Once they're in place, you want to make sure the information you're pointing to doesn't change in a way that is bad for you."

Attracting traffic can even be low-tech. Fidelity makes sure its Uniform Resource Locator (URL, or address) is on all its advertising. Zima prints the URL directly on the bottle.

Testing the Waters

Some companies are not up to making the giant leap to put their own page on the Web but still want to get their feet wet, while other companies choose to capitalize on the traffic at popular sites. In these instances, the method of choice is advertising, which is not too different from advertising in traditional venues. For instance, both AT&T and Zima advertised on *HotWired*'s site. Seven percent of Pathfinder screens have advertisements from other companies.

Advertising on Pathfinder can cost from $3,000 every three months to $30,000 a quarter, depending on the position of the ad. *HotWired* charges $15,000 a pop for four-week ad slots.

The cost of running your own site varies greatly, depending on the type of hardware and telecommunications used. Basic connection services range from $12 to $20 a month. A T-1 telecommunications connection, the highest speed available, would raise the ante to approximately $1,000 per month. Some of the larger companies have spent millions creating their presence, but others have done it with less than $10,000. Companies that choose to hire a full-time staffer to manage their content must add salary to the cost.

Whichever way a company decides to go, Klug offers this analogy to marketers: Getting on the Internet is like riding a bike. Either you can read a manual on how to do it or you can get on and pedal. "This is not a medium you can intellectualize. You can't write research reports about it. You just have to get on and ride."

MATT FOSTER

Is the traditional marketplace falling apart? More people now are skipping the downtown shopping trip and using catalogs, home computers, cable TV, and other forums to buy what they need.

The New Marketplace

Edith Weiner
Arnold Brown

About the Authors

Edith Weiner and Arnold Brown are president and chairman, respectively, of Weiner, Edrich, Brown, Inc., 200 East 33rd Street, Suite 9I, New York, New York 10016. Telephone 212/889-7007; fax 212/679-0628. They are co-authors of several future-oriented books, including *Office Biology* (MasterMedia, 1993), which is available from the Futurist Bookstore for $12.95 ($11.95 for Society members) cat. no. B-1696.

Not too long ago, if you wanted a new briefcase, you would look for one in either a department store or a luggage shop. Today, you can just as easily make your purchase at a flea market, from a street vendor, from a mail-order catalog, from a direct-mail offer, through a TV shopping service, or via your computer shopping database.

Concerned about your health? Aside from your traditional annual physical and health-club membership, you can visit a spa, adopt one or more of the hundreds of do-it-yourself diets, utilize home exercise and diagnostic equipment, buy instructional videotapes, subscribe to any or all of the dozens of health magazines on the market, or consult a homeopath, a nutritionist, or any of dozens of nontraditional practitioners.

Consumers are increasingly seeking out new sources for goods and services; that is no longer news. What is news is that they are *bypassing* traditional delivery channels—corner drugstores, doctors' offices, the mass media—in their search for quality, savings, convenience, and personal fit in all products and services. This movement to cut out the traditional middleman, so to speak, is part of a massive socioeconomic phenomenon known as *disintermediation.*

Disintermediation is fueled by people's intense and widening desire to feel more in control. Most people occasionally feel helpless and victimized. But in the marketplace, you can be a king or a queen—your ability to choose gives you power.

Consuming Control

Consumers often alter their marketplace behavior, but they are not necessarily seeking novelty. Very often they want gratification that comes from feeling in control. Some factors feeding this desire for control are:

• Advances in communications and information technology that are constantly and drastically reducing the cost of information.

• Substantially higher levels of education.

• Availability of more information through expanded media.

• A widespread distrust of experts—and of authority in general.

• A strong consumer-advocacy movement.

• A resistance to arbitrary pricing practices.

All of this, in the words of consumer-trends analyst Daniel Yankelovich, has resulted in a significant change in the nature of the consumer from uninformed and passive to informed and adversarial.

In effect, the consumer demands

Reprinted with permission from *The Futurist*, May/June 1995, pp. 12-16. © 1995 by the World Future Society, 7910 Woodmont Avenue, Suite 450, Bethesda, MD 20814.

alternatives. When there aren't choices, consumers will help create them by finding substitute products and services, thus becoming willing customers for creative entrepreneurs. Hundreds of thousands of new firms respond quickly to consumer needs and bring thousands of innovations and alternatives to the delivery of goods and services. This is true whether marketing to individuals or marketing to businesses.

Leading Us to Bypass

What is behind this booming growth in the trend toward bypassing traditional markets?

1. Time. Time has become an important consumer issue. Growing numbers of working women, overworked executives, and moonlighters are among the people who are increasingly willing to pay more money for things that save them time. Companies that handle household chores such as gardening, auto maintenance, and housecleaning are proliferating. Food companies have lost billions of dollars to fast-food chains over the years and are trying to recapture these dollars by providing supermarkets with prepared meals. Door-to-door sales are being replaced by catalogs that consumers can thumb through at their convenience. The ability to deliver goods and services when and where the customer chooses is crucial to success in the new marketplace.

2. Demographic changes. Significant demographic developments have also fostered demand—and opportunities—for new products and new marketplace-delivery modes. These developments include the aging of society (and increased diversity among the elderly), more working mothers, latchkey children, more temporary and part-time workers, sizable immigrant populations from Asia and Latin America (representing cultural and linguistic challenges to traditional marketing practices), and regionalism (grounded in ethnic, "grass roots," community, and recreational diversity).

3. Product proliferation. Shoppers are overwhelmed with new products and services that are vying for their disposable income. More than 4,000 new supermarket and drugstore products a year flood the market.

Retailers have to decide how to allocate shelf space, with the result that many consumers may never get to see a lot of the new products.

No wonder, then, that hundreds of new distribution channels and outlets are springing up every month, from discount stores and warehouses to upscale boutiques and home delivery, from specialty dealers to hypermarkets. And consumers have generally not only responded well to the alternatives, they have come to expect and demand the diversity.

4. Proliferation of information. The proliferation of media, and of advertisements in and on media, has created a background of constant noise, out of which consumers increasingly select only those messages of direct interest to them. The consumer is no longer the passive recipient of advertising that marketers were used to in the past. Now, consumers control what gets through to them and what doesn't. As Grateful Dead lyricist and infotech guru John Perry Barlow says (and this is a profound insight into the modern world), "In an information economy, attention is the monetary unit."

Today's producers and sellers are competing in a mature, overstocked, intensely competitive environment where products and advertisements look too much alike—a serious problem in an increasingly splintered marketplace. With shelf space and consumers' attention at a premium, the shots are now being called not by the producer but by the consumer and by the distributor who is oriented to what is new.

Catalogs, toll-free numbers, discounters, and one-stop convenience centers all have become part of the marketing vernacular. And all have become part of the consumer's expectations. Taken to their extremes, these delivery channels give us a clue to future possibilities.

In-home systems such as TV, computers, and catalogs provide *portability* of time and place, *convenience* of use, *relaxation, solitude,* and *time savings.*

Catalogs were the major retailing revolution of the 1980s. In the future, catalogs will carry increasing amounts of advertising, thus disintermediating other forms of media. Catalogs will also find their way to consumers through novel distribution channels

(Catalog Cash is a combination of several catalogs supporting a frequent-buyer program introduced at nine ShopRite Supermarkets). Another trend is video catalogs in kiosks in retail stores or in malls (Florsheim and Levi Strauss & Co. are early pioneers in this phenomenon).

Out-of-store sales now account for up to a third of all retail sales. To compete, stores must try to match the convenience and time savings offered by direct marketing. A major breakthrough before the end of the decade may be scanning systems that enable shoppers to check themselves out, thus avoiding the major disadvantage of in-store shopping—waiting on line to pay.

Shopping for Services

Consumers are demanding control over other areas of the marketplace as well, including professional services. Doctors, lawyers, and other professionals have lost their monopoly on their areas of specialty. The "defrocking of the professional priesthoods" has been a result of better-informed consumers, much higher costs of services, communications and computing technologies available to large segments of the public, and competition from within and outside the professions.

Professional services have become retail businesses, as more consumers accept storefront dentistry, optometry, and legal services. In the coming years, we will see more mall and storefront hearing specialists, foot doctors, divorce consultants, will preparers, self-diagnostic machinery, and so on. Temporary agencies for legal services are also springing up, staffed by an ample and less-costly supply of unemployed or underemployed attorneys. Individuals and businesses alike will increasingly secure legal services through temps.

A prime example of the disintermediation of professions is healthcare delivery. Despite cautions by the American Medical Association, more Americans flock to chiropractors (about 11 million a year now), as well as acupuncturists, midwives, and health-care providers in other countries for disease treatments not sanctioned in the United States. When insurance companies began requiring that a second opinion be rendered before costly medical treatment could be undertaken, many consumers applauded, for it undermined the absolute authority of the doctor.

Other trends to watch in health and well-being delivery:

• Hospital services will be completely segmented into lifestyle-oriented, convenience, and contractual facilities.

• Consumers will use videos and computer databases to select advisers, caregivers, and health services.

• Cable TV shows and videocassettes on counseling, exercise, health maintenance, and therapy will gain popularity.

• Home-diagnostic equipment and testing will become more elaborate.

• Drug advertising will increasingly be directed to consumers rather than doctors.

• Pharmacists will prescribe drugs and doctors will sell drugs.

• Health technicians and para-professionals of all kinds will see their roles expand.

One industry that has already capitalized on the public's demand for autonomy over professional services is publishing. Do-it-yourself books for medical, accounting, and legal affairs capture growing amounts of shelf space and consumer dollars. Even medical reference books are finding markets beyond physicians and pharmacists. The *Physician's Desk Reference* (PDR) on prescription-drug information is "often found in household libraries, and consumer sales continue to grow year after

year," says Thomas F. Rice, PDR general manager. "The PDR's popularity reflects the increased responsibility patients are taking for their health in partnership with their doctors."

Consumer Power Beyond the Marketplace

The consumer's power to break down, or disintermediate, the marketplace is also reaching into less-obvious arenas, such as:

• **Travel.** Retail businesses that can provide global and exotic experiences closer to home will thrive beyond the 1990s. Customers are seeking more ways to obtain novel and exotic experiences without having to travel. Supermarket chains are expanding once-small gourmet sections into major areas offering foreign delicacies. Shops that mainly feature cultural artifacts (arts, crafts, clothing) from around the world do well, as does safari-based imagery. Restaurants, too, are finding profits in simulating ethnic and foreign environments.

In the next century, technology will be able to further create simulated experience—vicarious vacations and experiences that satisfy consumer demands. Virtual reality incorporating holographic projections, total-surround audiovisual systems, mind-altering techniques, and enclosed chambers such as flight simulators are all examples of what will be available to create multiple trips and environments in or close to home.

• **Energy.** Utilities are also chal-

lenged by newly empowered consumers. Cogeneration, which allows utility customers to use their homes' waste heat to create electricity, is expected to grow rapidly. By the year 2000, electricity output from cogeneration could double in the United States, producing 6% of the nation's electricity (about the output of 50 average-size nuclear power plants). Some states now allow at least some customers to shop for cheaper energy. This beginning of the end of power-company monopoly will spread even more rapidly.

• **Government services.** Government has customers, too, and these customers have the power to disintermediate. The school-choice movement, for example, is a manifestation of the customer's insistence on the right to choose. Privatization is another manifestation.

• **Nonprofit organizations.** In the nonprofit sector, traditional trade and professional associations are finding that their increasingly fragmented constituencies are creating alternatives to focus on or advance their own subsets of issues. In the insurance business, for example, some large companies have formed new organizations to lobby for their particular interests, breaking the cohesiveness of the industry. The American urge to associate has taken on an aspect of impermanence. The constituents keep getting ahead of the association, which finds itself, if it can't keep up, bypassed.

New voluntary organizations in philanthropy spring up all the time

Storefront optometry is commonplace among "disintermediated" professional services. Soon, such shops will be joined by storefront divorce consultants, foot doctors, and other specialists.

No time to travel? India, El Salvador, and many other exotic locales may be as close as your neighborhood restaurant.

By Nicholas Imparato and Oren Harari

Squeezing the Middleman

New technology is forcing insurance brokers and other "middlemen" to innovate.

In July of 1993, six managers from around the country are in the San Francisco corporate offices of insurance broker Sedgwick James, talking about improving service quality. Suddenly they are hit broadside with a message they never anticipated. President Don Morford is challenging not only their conception of quality, but the entire service mix of the company as well. He agrees that quality improvements in current services and operations are called for, but argues that what is defined as quality today within Sedgwick might be undermined by advances in information technology that could eliminate 30% of Sedgwick's market within five years.

"Customers would just as soon eliminate brokers," he explains. "They see middlemen as a value-detracting cost factor. Right now, two groups of people want us out of business: the client and the insurance company. Technology will give them the means to do exactly that. We can spend all the time we want on improving current services, but if those services become obsolete, we are doing little more than improving the quality of buggy whips."

A few managers are skeptical. Their group sales are solid, as are the net written premium volume and net income figures of the company as a whole. But Morford is relentless. He begins to tick off potential lost chunks of business, suggesting that client institutions in the future will use their own computer power to scan a compre-hensive database and select an optimal insurance package for themselves, in the process cutting out as many people as possible in the distribution chain.

Warming to his theme of technology-as-competition, Morford cites airlines' concerns that teleconferencing technology will be so effective by the next decade that significantly fewer business people will need to fly as often as they do today. Further, he notes, travel agents are beginning to realize that advances in information technology are such that many of their current services can be duplicated by cost-conscious customers who can access the same database and come to their own informed conclusions.

Catching on to Morford's argument, one manager observes that overnight mail carriers have already lost significant domestic market share to technologies such as faxes and on-line services. Another manager chimes in, pointing out that mass retailers are already cutting out middlemen by installing electronic data interchanges (EDI) that connect point-of-sale information directly with suppliers.

Inevitably, the discussion homes in on a sobering reality: From EDI and shared databases to phone and television retailing, the trends lean relentlessly toward diminishing the distance between vendor and customer. For a broker, or any middleman, the time bomb is ticking.

Morford's charge is clear: If responsiveness and quality are to mean anything, they must include responsiveness and quality for tomorrow's customer, who will have entirely new demands and an increasing number of choices. Morford is encouraging his people to "look a customer ahead" because the alternative holds no place for today's insurance broker; even high-quality obsolete services are still obsolete.

At the end of the discussion, an energized group begins to redefine Sedgwick's services to include fast, customized solutions to clients' emerging business problems, new kinds of value-adding information, new specialized niche services, and significant improvements in personalized customer service across all Sedgwick offices.

From the vantage point of Morford's vision, the bottom line was clear: Sedgwick James must embrace new market realities—providing services that tomorrow's clients will not be able to obtain on their own. By doing so, Sedgwick will be positioned for success tomorrow.

About the Authors

Nicholas Imparato and Oren Harari are professors at the McLaren School of Business, University of San Francisco.

This article is excerpted, with permission of the publisher, from *Jumping the Curve: Innovation and Strategic Choice in an Age of Transition* by Nicholas Imparato and Oren Harari. Copyright © 1994 by Jossey-Bass Inc., Publishers, 350 Sansome Street, San Francisco, California 94104. Telephone 415/433-1767. 324 pages.

to address causes that existing organizations are seen as improperly ignoring. And they offer products through catalogs, open retail outlets, and market cause-related wares. And so it goes.

Strategies for the New Marketplace

Disintermediation is all-pervasive—it affects *every* sector—and it can't be stopped. In the 1980s, most producers tried to protect the status quo through rapid competitive scrambling and stepped-up lobbying. Success in the 1990s and beyond will require recognizing and capitalizing on this phenomenon, and not resisting it or reacting too swiftly.

It will be ever more important to remember the people side of the equation. When companies attempt to enter new markets via piggybacking additional goods and services on existing delivery channels, one of the sources of difficulty is the assump-tion that the existing sales and service force can perform equally well with the additional offerings. For example, if you want to start selling computers, don't take them to appliance stores and expect the sales and service people to know how to sell and give advice on them.

A disintermediated market also needs new approaches to market analysis. Niche marketing, for example, isn't what it used to be. Today's niche markets are big enough to have qualified as mass markets a few decades ago: There are more than 3 million women business owners—a small percentage of the population, but a large market for suppliers of products and services to small business. When poorly served or ignored by traditional channels providing goods and services, these large numbers have defected to alternative sources.

Demographic analysis, too, is changing. For years, blind acceptance of a category of consumer called 55-and-older prevented marketers from clearly seeing that there were distinct market groups in the older ages—groups with very different needs. Demographic profiles may tell a company how old its customer is. But how old does the customer *think* she is? The 65-year-old who perceives herself to be 48 will participate differently in the marketplace from the 65-year-old who thinks of herself as nearing life's end. This is critical for financial services, clothing manufacturers, health-care deliverers, and others.

Finally, consider what *really* should be asked in market research. In a time of disintermediation, it is imperative to be one step ahead of both competition and marketplace. Good market research will articulate what the public is thinking but cannot quite articulate for itself.

Sensitive Groups and Social Issues

Are You Marketing Correct?

Bart Macchiette and Abhijit Roy

Bart Macchiette is Associate Professor in the Department of Business, Hyde Hall, Plymouth State College, Plymouth, USA and Abhijit Roy is a Doctoral Student in Marketing at Boston University, Boston, MA, USA.

Allegiance among members of sensitive groups has become a critical factor for marketers in the 1990s. Increasingly, media have reflected the criticism, anxiety, and overt demands from groups such as African and native Americans, the gay population and working women. The mainstream concerns of these groups regard marketing techniques—the way they are portrayed in advertising and the nature of the products targeted toward them. These controversies have consistently occupied center stage in national publicity, reflecting a highly volatile environment for marketers targeting such "sensitive groups".

A series of sociological, economic and other external variables have collectively created an atmosphere that warrants extreme caution and deliberation in considering social issues inherent in marketing plans. This is especially significant when the products, promotional techniques or target audiences are under current public scrutiny.

This article provides a profile of factors that may have spawned an emerging era of socially-conscious marketing. It offers a typology of "sensitive groups", and identifies dubious promotional techniques. Guidelines and proactive strategies for avoiding ethical crises are also presented, and the concept of "marketing correctness" is explored.

An Emerging Era of Social Issues

So far, the 1990s have witnessed some major changes in consumer attitudes, buying motives and product-related values that reflect the heightened influence of social issues in the American marketplace.

Several factors in the market environment have synergized to create a new arena of competition, whereby social responsibility has become a salient means of product differentiation, and an effective instrument for developing brand equity. The growth of cause-related marketing programs exemplifies this trend. Through examining the reasons for the emergence of social issues in marketing, the ramifications of this development become strikingly clear. Strongly embedded in these social issues is the need for considering the concept of group sensitivity.

Causes for Focus on Social Issues

Changing Market Factors/Consumer Apathy

Recent trends generally portray a frustrated consumer, economically squeezed by high living costs, disillusioned with poor product quality and inferior service. More importantly, a consistent barrage of new products has resulted in an overwhelming choice of brands, many of which are perceptually identical and lacking in unique innovations. In 1975, the average supermarket carried 9,000 items; by 1992, the number was 30,000, with more than 3,000 brands introduced each year (*The Economist*, 1992). The influence of product parity and proliferation has been further exacerbated by a major shift from traditional advertising to sales promotion emphasizing coupons and price reductions.

Evidence of Consumer Discontent

These developments have had a definite influence on consumer behavior. First, there has been an across-the-board erosion of brand loyalty. Of promotional dollars expended, 70 percent is being spent to push products

From *Journal of Consumer Marketing*, Vol. 11, No. 4, 1994, pp. 57-66. © 1994 by MCB University Press. Reprinted by permission.

through the retail channel. A major reason for people not having the same brand loyalties as in the past is that manufacturers have decreased the amount of advertising behind their brands (Alsop, 1990).

Second, consumers are demonstrating a growing sense of apathy toward advertising as an "institution". A recent US poll suggests that 72 percent of the nation believes few, if any, of the ads they see on TV or in print (Mandese, 1991). These findings are in stark contrast to the primary goal of most advertisers: to make credible claims that will encourage consumers to buy their products. Consumer discontent is further supported by the legislative attacks on Madison Avenue, and an unprecedented number of bills are before Congress relevant to marketing and advertising practices (*Business Week*, 1990).

Third, consumer anxiety is evidenced by a general disillusionment with shopping. The "shop till you drop" attitude has not totally disappeared, but shopping is not the leisure time activity it was in the recent past. Nearly one-third of respondents in a recent *Wall Street Journal* poll revealed that they "do not enjoy at all" window shopping or browsing (Schwandel, 1989). While they have less time to shop, they also feel stressed in facing parity products, and lower quality merchandise at exorbitant prices.

Changing Demographics and Cultural Values

Another major change in the marketplace, augmenting the focus on social responsibility, relates to changing demographics. Currently, close to one-third of the nation largely consists of baby boomers, many of whom are jaded in the aftermath of the turbulent 1960s, where concerns about civil righters, anti-marketing and the environment have been lying dormant for two decades. These late baby boomers have, for the most part, satisfied their material needs, but are spiritually frustrated with meaningless product differentiation and redundant promotional claims. Their anger has been vented in part by adopting cause-related marketing programs, and embracing the "green consumer movement". Many boomers are searching for self-actualization, and are increasingly influenced in discriminating between brands of similar quality based on environmental and social concerns.

A related demographic factor is the growth of cultural diversity and minorities in America. For example, there are now twice as many Asians as in 1980, up 40 percent or more in most states but Hawaii (where they represent 60 percent of the population), and the US takes in approximately one million immigrants a year. During the 1980s, all minorities increased by 30 percent to 60 million, including Asians, Hispanics, blacks, and American Indians (*Kiplinger*, 1991). These new consumers demand representation,

attention and acceptance from the marketing community. Portraying these groups as being highly visible, mainstream Americans create distinct opportunities to penetrate these markets.

Shift in Consumer Values: "Me" to "We"

Perhaps the foremost cause for the focus on social issues and sensitive groups is due to societal and cultural change. The movement toward a sense of moral stability has indeed replaced the previous materialistic mentality and the "me" orientation of the 1980s. Social responsibility, cause-related marketing, and environmental concerns now portend the cultural direction of the 1990s. People are longing for some permanent and transcendent sense of values (Fisher, 1990).

The shift to this "we" orientation is further evidenced by an unprecedented growth in support groups in America, totaling over 500,000 and attended by 15 million people per week. The number of self-help groups has nearly quadrupled over the last ten years (*Newsweek*, 1990). These are people literally helping others with similar problems. For each support group member, several significant others probably share in moral support. Again, the notion of sensitive groups creates real opportunities for knowledgeable marketers.

Consumer Anxiety Translates into Focus on Sensitive Groups

Thus, changing values are shaping new consumption patterns and purchasing motives throughout America. Consumers have responded to "green marketers" at varying rates. Yet, in a recent survey, over 93 percent of those surveyed consider protecting the environment a very important factor in their decision to purchase a product (Manly, 1992). Marketers are also becoming much more critical of social issues related to marketing and sensitive groups. There is a heightened awareness of what is being marketed, how and to whom. The consequences of marketing efforts on the individual consumer, target group and society are currently the focus of public scrutiny (Uehling, 1991) and are creating a national orientation toward social issues in marketing.

Boycotts are expected to reach unparalleled heights in the decade of the nineties (Putnam, 1993). This is due to the increasing propensity of sensitive groups to respond to the notions of political correctness, environmental and ethical issues as they relate to marketing techniques. For example, consumers have recently responded through boycotts of cosmetic companies engaged in animal testing. Animal rights groups have virtually crippled the fur trading industry. The previous boycott against the sale of Nestlé's infant formula in the Third World has been reinstituted. American consumers are still sensitive toward companies doing business with South Africa. Tuna companies were forced by environmental rights groups to respond to the dolphin crisis. Currently, the resurgence of "Made in America" has become a major influence in the marketplace. Television violence and its effect on children continues to be a burning issue.

The focus here is on social issues as they relate to marketing techniques involving the concept of sensitive groups. Basically, these are consumers who are responsive to social issues, or who perceive themselves to be disadvantaged by various marketing techniques. For example, the concept of "status vulnerability" has been utilized to explain the opposition to targeting African-Americans, as well as women and young people, for inherently damaging products such as alcohol and cigarettes (Spratten, 1991).

The Nature of Sensitive Groups

The term "sensitive group", then, refers to a segment of the population generally perceived as being disadvantaged, vulnerable, discriminated against, or involved in social issues which consequently influence their consumer behavior. Admittedly, the concept is provocative, subjective and often influenced by contemporary media events which popularize a particular issue and bring national attention to the sensitive group. Thus, the degree of sensitivity is affected by the extent of media attention generated from consumer advocates, regulatory agencies, support groups, and the public at large. For example, recent concern about gays in the military has been translated into a focus on this group as a viable market segment and created ethical debates associated with targeting this group.

Problems of Group Isolation and Mutual Exclusivity

A strong argument can be made to suggest that all consumers, at some point, are members of a sensitive group. This is either by choice of lifestyle, situational circumstance, life cycle, or demographics. For example, one might be born into an impoverished community or with a physical disadvantage. Children are categorically "sensitive", due to their lack of information-processing skills and lack of maturity. Middle age may bring divorce, loss of loved ones, unemployment, or disability. Elderly consumers face debilitating health and vulnerability to being overly trustful to marketing ploys. This perspective also suggests that a large variance of intensity exists in terms of group sen-

sitivity. This is a function of the consumer's situation and the marketing environment at a particular point in time.

It is also important to recognize that consumers may belong to several sensitive groups simultaneously and that they are not mutually exclusive. While identifying subsegments of sensitive groups may prose problems for marketers, aggregating these markets in terms of unmet needs may also create unique opportunities. This entails gathering groups with high probabilities of being "sensitive" consumers along several different dimensions.

Group Sensitivity Is Product Related

In a marketing context, sensitive groups may also be product related. For example, an elderly consumer may have extreme competence in discerning product categories with which she or he has had a life's worth of vocational consumption experience. Yet, the same person may be vulnerable to life-saving communication beepers which may use high-powered fear appeals through telemarketing, and may be unscrupulously overpriced. Thus, products considered to be legitimate when targeting one group, may not be perceived as being socially responsible when targeting other sensitive groups. The question of promoting cigarettes to children is another case in point.

Sensitive Groups may Have Life Cycles

This hypothesis can be construed in two ways. The first view is that people transcent group sensitivity merely by living out normal life spans. Thus, there is an important temporal dimension to the concept of sensitivity. For example, permanently disabled individuals will face their inevitable problems longer than those facing temporary unemployment.

The second view is that some sensitive groups and social issues experience a life cycle. This results from the media collectively popularizing a particular group and social issue. Often, national talk shows, newspaper and other media events will focus on a specific social issue related to a sensitive group. Eventually, a new issue will engage the public's attention and the cycle may repeat.

Proposed Typology of Sensitive Groups

Despite the lack of mutual exclusivity, it is important to provide a general means of categorizing the source and nature of various sensitive groups. The following typology identifies the primary sources from which groups derive their sensitivity.

In examining these groups, one should not only consider the perceptions of sensitive group members, but also attitudes of the public at large concerning related social issues. This most often exerts the real pressure on marketers for social responsibility and remedial action.

Culturally Dictated Sensitive Groups

These groups elicit a high impact media profile and, despite fluctuations in the intensity of public awareness, have captured the nation's attention and invite public scrutiny for an *enduring* period of time. They are usually associated with specific social issues.

In the last decade, the nation has embraced such sensitive groups as abused children, starvation in the Third World, subjects of sexual abuse, and victims of terminal illness. More recently, the homeless, gays and sexually harassed women have received acknowledgment from the general public, which has a heightened awareness of such issues.

Specific demographic groups are included. Children, the elderly and people of color are subcultures illustrating the notion of culturally-dictated sensitive groups. Many traditional means of segmenting markets can be used to identify these groups.

Situationally Influenced Sensitive Groups

These groups result from *temporary* environmental or personal circumstances which place the consumer in a sensitive group for a period of time. Divorce, temporary unemployment, family death or other circumstances can create a situation of consumer vulnerability. An example would be the controversy surrounding the "Smoking Joe" cartoon character. Many critics feel that he is easily recognized by children which may motivate them to start smoking. Similar allegations have been made against malt liquor marketers targeting low income African-Americans (*Wall Street Journal*, 1993).

Recently, a slender model nicknamed "Skeleton" appeared in a magazine ad for Diet Sprite. An advocacy group, BAM—an acronym for Boycott Anorexic Marketing—accused the company of encouraging starvation diets (Bass, 1994). Since specific advertising campaigns have a limited life, these are considered *situationally sensitive issues*. The broader question of advertising's collective influence on children and ethnic minorities in terms of alcohol and tobacco consumption, would represent a *culturally dictated sensitive issue.*

Marketing-generated Sensitive Groups

This term refers to groups that become vulnerable as the result of promotional strategies conceived and executed by marketers. Those groups are usually created through marketing innovation. Children are a particularly vulnerable population. Cartoon characters such as Little Mermaid, Smurfs and Ninja Turtles are examples of marketing-generated products that have translated into segments of young consumers who are very brand loyal to these promotionally conceived characters. The controversy surrounding "Barbie" doll as a role model for pre-teen girls falls into this category (Leo, 1992). Licensing agreements allow thousands of manufacturers to utilize the characters as promotional leverage for selling a wide array of products. "Product-based programming" is an example of an ethical issue for marketing-generated sensitive groups. This refers to the notion that children may not distinguish actual programming from product-related ads that sponsor the show; i.e. ads for Ninja Turtle dolls, embedded in the Ninja Turtle TV program.

Issue-driven Sensitive Groups

Unlike the above-mentioned categories, these consumers need only to be sympathetic to cause-related or social issues, rather than being an actual member of a vulnerable group. These are defined as groups of consumers responding to social issues through observable changes in their purchasing behavior. "True-blue" green consumers, rain forest advocates, and members of other cause-related marketing groups are suitable examples.

Managerial Implications

The New Marketing Culture

The current cultural milieu accenting political correctness has become a critical factor in marketing management. Recent evidence suggests that marketers take great risk by ignoring the potential reactions caused by various interpretations of their marketing actions by concerned publics. Not only have boycotts increased dramatically in the last few years, but also other means of collective action to deter and publicly damage incorrect or socially irresponsible marketers have arisen. These actions can depreciate a brand's equity and tarnish a well-established corporate image.

Consequences of Ignoring Social Responsibility: Damned Brands

If adequate analysis and foresight is absent from the marketing plan, the result may well be a "damned brand". This is a brand that, owing to a lack of foreseeing social response from a sensitive group, has received such negative publicity that the product is dropped for the sake of preserving brand equity and corporate image. Such adverse public reaction can arise from social issues relating to questionable products and promotional techniques, which are interpreted as exploitation of a particular sensitive group.

Given the adversarial climate towards marketers, caution should be taken to pre-empt the launching of a "damned brand", or initiating a new promotional campaign that might create a negative public image. Certain products invite public scrutiny because of their inherently injurious nature or ethical controversies may surround marketing campaigns targeting sensitive groups. Companies have been forced to "bail out" and abandon their efforts when such negative publicity (regardless of its legitimacy) has surfaced. Brands such as Uptown and Dakota cigarettes and Power Master malt liquor became "damned" by the allegations of exploitation in reference to African-American consumers (*Business and Society Review,* 1992).

Advertising and Media Considerations

Currently, the issue of political correctness has created great controversy in the advertising industry, as its influence is direct and inescapable. Many advertisers face the dilemma of sacrificing humor, creativity and effectiveness for mediocrity owing to the constraints imposed by the prospect of attack from special interest groups. Some advertising professionals refer to America as a "New Age Fundamentalist State" whereby their advertising execution must walk a fine line between radical right religious groups and politically correct "police" representing sensitive groups. Copy writers feel stifled because they cannot portray ethnic dialects, use humor and create "break through" advertising without the threat of retribution from special interest groups. Conversely, special interest groups (often opinion leaders for large sensitive groups), know full well the power and strategic use of the media. Through criticizing advertising campaigns, the media become a conduit for their cause and a *de facto* spokesperson for the group.

Problems and social issues of sensitive groups, in and of themselves, are not noteworthy. However, once they are reflected through the boycott of a product associated with a nationally-known marketing campaign, for example, the issue becomes news and the cause becomes anchored to a tangible item about which the public is highly aware. With increasing frequency, the news media have focussed on the controversies surrounding marketing advertising and its negative portrayal or influence on sensitive groups. From the bizarre to the perhaps legitimate, the sensitive group/marketing issue phenomenon has become a major factor for marketing managers in the 1990s, as the media remain poised and ready for special interest groups to be heard, and later endorsed. These groups could never afford the promotion which is generated from the publicity associated with these social debates. Ironically, in many such cases, the marketer benefits from the experience when the majority of public opinion interprets the accusation as absurd. This is an area relatively unresearched, yet the need for identifying proactive propositions as guidelines are quite obvious—marketers cannot portray ethnic dialects, or use humor without the threat of retribution. Thus, it is important to identify some general proactive propositions as guidelines for avoiding the crisis of a "damned brand".

Proactive Strategies for Corporate Social Responsibility

Increasingly, addressing the subject of corporate social responsibility has become recognized as being vitally important to marketers (Gatten, 1991). The heightened concern about, and public awareness of, social issues has provided strong initiatives for the development of corporate social responsibility as a market-driven phenomenon. Employees do not want to work for companies looking for a social conscience, nor do consumers want to buy from companies that pollute the environment. Social responsibility can only become a reality if managers become moral instead of amoral or immoral (Carroll, 1991). A heightened concern and awareness of social issues has provided incentives for corporate social responsibility to be fully integrated into a systematic agenda within the marketing system, and aggressively implemented within marketing plans. With highly commendable companies such as IBM, Merck, Levi Strauss, and Cummins engine, American business is only now on the verge of seriously analyzing corporate social policy issues and how they influence business performance (Hutton, 1992). What, then, are some philosophical guidelines for marketers pursuing this task?

What Is Marketing Correctness?

In the last four years, the national debate over "political correctness" has emerged from college campuses and has migrated into the business environment. The central focus encompassed issues relating to vulnerable populations, multiculturalism and speech codes as they relate to gender, race and class (Taylor, 1993). Primarily, the movement involved challenging traditional views and social norms as related to these groups. Soon these principles were applied to the corporate world, concentrating mostly on environmental issues and marketing to sensitive groups.

Thus, the term "marketing correct" refers to the process of establishing a social responsibility policy as a fully integrated, systematic component of the marketing program, carefully incorporated into each promotional plan. Inherent in the philosophy of marketing correctness is the idea that social responsibility has become a salient attribute and a fruitful means of product differentiation. It is not an arbitrary "give away" program, but should enhance profitability, build brand equity and more clearly define product positioning in the marketplace.

The level of commitment to social responsibility is dictated by several factors, including the nature of the product, target market, corporate culture and mission statement. Companies selling tobacco and alcohol through inner city billboards, or handguns to women, obviously must answer to a higher sense of social responsibility because of the inherent controversy surrounding these products and sensitivity to their target markets.

Ben and Jerry's and the Body Shop, for example, are totally committed to social responsibility, in that it is deeply embedded in their mission statements and is a significant component of their corporate image. This is not to imply that all companies should be totally consumed by the subject, but that they should strive for new perspective. Marketing correctness implies an awareness of how social responsibility can be incorporated into the marketing mix.

Integrating Social Responsibility into the Marketing Program

The development of a social responsibility program requires research, sensitivity and commitment from all levels in the marketing team. It should be consumer driven. Cultural diversity implies not only differences in language and lifestyle, but also temperament, perceptions and values intimately linked to consumer behavior. Knowledge of these differences can provide rich insights for product development, positioning strategy and promotional appeals.

Many customized training programs, video tapes series and other learning tools are available, replete with vignettes revealing cultural misunderstandings, and illustrating how managers, employees and sales personnel can better deal with these unique differences (Bahls, 1994). Many small business programs, in-

cluding college seminars, the urban league and Chambers of Commerce, bring academicians, business professionals and community leaders together to discuss multicultural issues.

Contemporary periodicals offer rich insights into ethnic subculture and sensitive groups, often providing excellent cases of successful strategic planning from a myriad diverse companies. It is helpful for marketers to absorb the culture of their target markets through reading magazines, newspapers and viewing their popular films and television programs. Participating in community affairs and tracking relevant global issues is also suggested.

Concept testing, focus group studies and constant tracking of consumer attitudes is a critical component of social responsibility policy. Often with incredible haste, an issue can develop which draws a particular industry practice, promotional technique or product attribute into the limelight of public scrutiny. Companies devoid of a crisis management program and contingency plan are at great risk in this volatile marketing environment. It is prudent to be prepared for the unexpected with systematic alternative measures, a central source of communicators, and pre-established decision-making authority. Finally, it is wise to establish an interactive communications network and constructive liaison with opinion leaders of special interest groups representing the target markets that might react negatively to a particular market plan. Involving members of such groups in developing the plan, or alerting special interest group leaders concerning campaign concepts and the logic behind them, serves as an "inoculation effect", and can desensitize potentially damaging issues. Overall, a successful social policy program is predicated on awareness of cultural diversity, sensitive groups and their special interests; research on contemporary and potentially relevant social issues; a creative search for regional and cause-related marketing, preparedness for crisis; and common sense. Specific guidelines for proactive strategies are offered below:

(1) Establish corporate social responsibility as a component of a firm's marketing information system

(2) Introduce sensitive group and social issue research in the earliest stages of the new product development process

(3) Specifically, establish a model for tracking public attitudes and perceptions of relevant social issues and sensitive groups

(4) Consider alternative means of utilizing social policy to build brand equity and enhance relationship marketing with sensitive groups

(5) Utilize concept testing and focus groups among consumers representing targeted sensitive groups

(6) Develop an ethical rationale and defensive strategies prior to the introduction of a marketing plan

(7) Seek to gain endorsements from opinion leaders and respected celebrities within these groups

(8) Have a crisis management program intact and consider the crucial linkages of public relations and publicity to corporate social responsibility programs

(9) Consider optimizing the use of interactive marketing, and video news releases to enhance the use of CSR projects

(10) Examine opportunities with sensitive groups for socially-oriented, cause-related marketing programs and environmental issues.

Conclusion

It is very probable that America's concern with social responsibility will continue to create problems and opportunities for marketers targeting sensitive groups. Anticipating and incorporating these issues into a systematic social responsibility program is essential for competing in the 1990s. Social issues, cultural diversity, environmental concerns and cause-related marketing are becoming a central focus in many areas of consumer decision making. They represent great potential for product positioning and building brand equity among a growing number of socially responsible consumers. While product quality, value and service still reign supreme, the new era of competition asks—"Are You Marketing Correct?".

References

Alsop, R. (1990), "Brand Loyalty is Rarely Blind Loyalty", *Wall Street Journal*.

Bahls, J. (1994), "Culture Shock America's Face Is Changing—Are You Prepared?", *Entrepreneur*, February, pp. 66–72.

Bass, A. (1994), " 'Anorexic Marketing' Faces Boycott", *Blobe Globe*, April 25, pp. 1 and 16.

Carroll, A. B. (1991), "The Pyramid of Corporate Social Responsibility: Toward the Moral Management of Organizational Stakeholders", *Business Horizons*, July–August, pp. 39–48.

"Consumers Are Getting Mad, Mad, Mad, Mad at Mad Ave" (1990), *Business Week*, April 30, pp. 70–2.

"Critics Shoot at New Colt 45 Campaign" (1993), *Wall Street Journal*, February 17, p. B-1.

Fisher, N. B. (1990), "What Consumers Want in the 1990's", *Fortune*, January 29, pp. 108–10, 112.

Gatten, C. (1991), "Social Issues Guide Consumer Buying", *Marketing News*, December 9, p. 4.

Hutton, B. (1992), "Conference to Examine Corporate Social Policy", *Marketing News*, January 6.

Leo, J. (1992), "The Indignation of Barbie", *US News and World Report*, October 12, p. 25.

Mandese, J. (1991), "Poll: Ads Strain Credibility", *Advertising Age*, December 16, p. 4.

Manly, L. (1992), "It Doesn't Pay to Go Green When Consumers Are Seeing Red", *Adweek*, March 23, pp. 32–3.

"Marketing to Minorities—Distilling the Truth about Alcohol Ads" (1992), *Business and Society Review Symposium*, Fall, pp. 12–17.

"The Party's Over" (1992), *The Economist*, February 1, pp. 69–76.

Putnam, T. (1993), "Boycotts Are Busting Out All Over", *Business and Society Review*, Spring, pp. 47–51.

Schwandel, F. (1989), "Shoppers' Blues: The Thrill is Gone—Dropouts Cite Poor Service, Tight Schedules", *Wall Street Journal*, October 13, pp. B1, B2.

Sharkey, B. (1993), "Sound and Fury", *Adweek*, April 12, p. 21.

Spratten, T. (1991), "The Controversy over Targeting Black Consumers in Cigarette Advertising: Racial/Ethnic and Ethical Issues", *Academy of Marketing Sciences Proceedings*, pp. 249–53.

Taylor, J. (1993), "Are You Politically Correct?", in Beckwith, F. J. and Bauman, M. (Eds), *Are You Politically Correct? Debating America's Cultural Standards*, Promenthus Books, Buffalo, NY.

The Kiplinger Washington Letter (1991), December 27.

Uehling, M. D. (1991), "All-American Apathy", *American Demographics*, November, pp. 30–5.

"Unite and Conquer: America Is Crazy for Support Groups. Or Maybe Support Groups Keep America from Going Crazy" (1990), *Newsweek*, February 9, pp. 50–5.

Marketing myopia
(With Retrospective Commentary)

Shortsighted managements often fail to recognize that in fact there is no such thing as a growth industry

Theodore Levitt

At the time of the article's publication, Theodore Levitt was lecturer in business administration at the Harvard Business School. He is the author of several books, including The Third Sector: New Tactics for a Responsive Society *(1973) and* Marketing for Business Growth *(1974).*

How can a company ensure its continued growth? In 1960 "Marketing Myopia" answered that question in a new and challenging way by urging organizations to define their industries broadly to take advantage of growth opportunities. Using the archetype of the railroads, Mr. Levitt showed how they declined inevitably as technology advanced because they defined themselves too narrowly. To continue growing, companies must ascertain and act on their customers' needs and desires, not bank on the presumptive longevity of their products. The success of the article testifies to the validity of its message. It has been widely quoted and anthologized, and HBR has sold more than 265,000 reprints of it. The author of 14 subsequent articles in HBR, Mr. Levitt is one of the magazine's most prolific contributors. In a retrospective commentary, he considers the use and misuse that have been made of "Marketing Myopia," describing its many interpretations and hypothesizing about its success.

Every major industry was once a growth industry. But some that are now riding a wave of growth enthusiasm are very much in the shadow of decline. Others which are thought of as seasoned growth industries have actually stopped growing. In every case the reason growth is threatened, slowed, or stopped is *not* because the market is saturated. It is because there has been a failure of management.

Fateful purposes: The failure is at the top. The executives responsible for it, in the last analysis, are those who deal with broad aims and policies. Thus:

□

The railroads did not stop growing because the need for passenger and freight transportation declined. That grew. The railroads are in trouble today not because the need was filled by others (cars, trucks, airplanes, even telephones), but because it was *not* filled by the railroads themselves. They let others take customers away from them because they assumed themselves to be in the railroad business rather than in the transportation business. The reason they defined their industry wrong was because they were railroad-oriented instead of transportation-oriented; they were product-oriented instead of customer-oriented.

□

Hollywood barely escaped being totally ravished by television. Actually, all the established film companies went through drastic reorganizations. Some simply disappeared. All of them got into trouble not because of TV's inroads but because of their own myopia. As with the railroads, Hollywood defined its business incorrectly. It thought it was in the movie business when it was actually in the entertainment business. "Movies" implied a specific, limited product. This produced a fatuous contentment which from the beginning led producers to view TV as a threat. Hollywood scorned and rejected TV when it should have welcomed it as an opportunity—an opportunity to expand the entertainment business.

Today TV is a bigger business than the old narrowly defined movie business ever was. Had Hollywood been customer-oriented (providing entertainment), rather then product-oriented (making movies), would it have gone through the fiscal purgatory that it did? I doubt it. What ultimately saved Hollywood and accounted for its recent resurgence was the wave of new young writers, producers, and directors whose previous successes in television had decimated the old movie companies and toppled the big movie moguls.

There are other less obvious examples of industries that have been and are now endangering their futures by improperly defining their purposes. I shall discuss some in detail later and analyze the kind of policies that lead to trouble. Right now it may help to show what a thoroughly customer-oriented management *can* do to keep a growth industry growing, even after the obvious opportunities have been exhausted; and here there are two examples that have been around for a long time. They are nylon and glass—specifically, E. I. duPont de Nemours & Company and Corning Glass Works.

Both companies have great technical competence. Their product orientation is unquestioned. But this alone does not explain their success. After all, who was more pridefully product-oriented and product-conscious than the erstwhile New England textile companies that have been so thoroughly massacred? The DuPonts and the Cornings have succeeded not primarily because of their product or research orientation but because they have been thoroughly customer-oriented also. It is constant watchfulness for opportunities to apply their technical know-how to the creation of customer-satisfying uses which accounts for their prodigious output of successful new products. Without a very sophisticated eye on the customer, most of their new products might have been wrong, their sales methods useless.

Aluminum has also continued to be a growth industry, thanks to the efforts of two wartime-created companies which deliberately set about creating new customer-satisfying uses. Without Kaiser Aluminum & Chemical Corporation and Reynolds Metals Company, the total demand for aluminum today would be vastly less.

Error of analysis: Some may argue that it is foolish to set the railroads off against aluminum or the movies off against glass. Are not aluminum and glass naturally so versatile that the industries are bound to have more growth opportunities than the railroads and movies? This view commits precisely the error I have been talking about. It defines an industry, or a product, or a cluster of know-how so narrowly as to guarantee its premature senescence. When we mention "railroads," we should make sure we mean "transportation." As transporters, the railroads still have a good chance for very considerable growth. They are not limited to the railroad business as such (though in my opinion rail transportation is potentially a much stronger transportation medium than is generally believed).

What the railroads lack is not opportunity, but some of the same managerial imaginativeness and audacity that made them great. Even an amateur like Jacques Barzun can see what is lacking when he says:

"I grieve to see the most advanced physical and social organization of the last century go down in shabby disgrace for lack of the same comprehensive imagination that built it up. [What is lacking is] the will of the companies to survive and to satisfy the public by inventiveness and skill." [1]

Shadow of obsolescence

It is impossible to mention a single major industry that did not at one time qualify for the magic appellation of "growth industry." In each case its assumed strength lay in the apparently unchallenged superiority of its product. There appeared to be no effective substitute for it. It was itself a runaway substitute for the product it so triumphantly replaced. Yet one after another of these celebrated industries has come under a shadow. Let us look briefly at a few more of them, this time taking examples that have so far received a little less attention:

☐

Dry cleaning—This was once a growth industry with lavish prospects. In an age of wool garments, imagine being finally able to get them safely and easily clean. The boom was on.

Yet here we are 30 years after the boom started and the industry is in trouble. Where has the competition come from? From a better way of cleaning? No. It has come from synthetic fibers and chemical additives that have cut the need for dry cleaning. But this is only the beginning. Lurking in the wings and ready to make chemical dry cleaning totally obsolescent is that powerful magician, ultrasonics.

☐

Electric utilities— This is another one of those supposedly "no-substitute"

1. Jacques Barzun, "Trains and the Mind of Man," *Holiday*, February 1960, p. 21.

products that has been enthroned on a pedestal of invincible growth. When the incandescent lamp came along, kerosene lights were finished. Later the water wheel and the steam engine were cut to ribbons by the flexibility, reliability, simplicity, and just plain easy availability of electric motors. The prosperity of electric utilities continues to wax extravagant as the home is converted into a museum of electric gadgetry. How can anybody miss by investing in utilities, with no competition, nothing but growth ahead?

But a second look is not quite so comforting. A score of nonutility companies are well advanced toward developing a powerful chemical fuel cell which could sit in some hidden closet of every home silently ticking off electric power. The electric lines that vulgarize so many neighborhoods will be eliminated. So will the endless demolition of streets and service interruptions during storms. Also on the horizon is solar energy, again pioneered by nonutility companies.

Who says that the utilities have no competition? They may be natural monopolies now, but tomorrow they may be natural deaths. To avoid this prospect, they too will have to develop fuel cells, solar energy, and other power sources. To survive, they themselves will have to plot the obsolescence of what now produces their livelihood.

☐

Grocery stores—Many people find it hard to realize that there ever was a thriving establishment known as the "corner grocery store." The supermarket has taken over with a powerful effectiveness. Yet the big food chains of the 1930s narrowly escaped being completely wiped out by the aggressive expansion of independent supermarkets. The first genuine supermarket was opened in 1930, in Jamaica, Long Island. By 1933 supermarkets were thriving in California, Ohio, Pennsylvania, and elsewhere. Yet the established chains pompously ignored them. When they chose to notice them, it was with such derisive descriptions as "cheapy," "horse-and-buggy," "cracker-barrel storekeeping," and "unethical opportunists."

The executive of one big chain announced at the time that he found it "hard to believe that people will drive for miles to shop for foods and sacrifice the personal service chains have perfected and to which Mrs. Consumer is accustomed."[2] As late as 1936, the National Wholesale Grocers convention and the New Jersey Retail Grocers Association said there was nothing to fear. They said that the supers' narrow appeal to the price buyer limited the size of their market. They had to draw from miles around. When imitators came, there would be wholesale liquidations as volume fell. The current high sales of the supers was said to be partly due to their novelty. Basically people wanted convenient neighborhood grocers. If the neighborhood stores "cooperate with their suppliers, pay attention to their costs, and improve their service," they would be able to weather the competition until it blew over.[3]

It never blew over. The chains discovered that survival required going into the supermarket business. This meant the wholesale destruction of their huge investments in corner store sites and in established distribution and merchandising methods. The companies with "the courage of their convictions" resolutely stuck to the corner store philosophy. They kept their pride but lost their shirts.

Self-deceiving cycle: But memories are short. For example, it is hard for people who today confidently hail the twin messiahs of electronics and chemicals to see how things could possibly go wrong with these galloping industries. They probably also cannot see how a reasonably sensible businessman could have been as myopic as the famous Boston millionaire who 50 years ago unintentionally sentenced his heirs to poverty by stipulating that his entire estate be forever invested exclusively in electric streetcar securities. His posthumous declaration, "There will always be a big demand for efficient urban transportation," is no consolation to his heirs who sustain life by

pumping gasoline at automobile filling stations.

Yet, in a casual survey I recently took among a group of intelligent business executives, nearly half agreed that it would be hard to hurt their heirs by tying their estates forever to the electronics industry. When I then confronted them with the Boston streetcar example, they chorused unanimously, "That's different!" But is it? Is not the basic situation identical?

In truth, *there is no such thing* as a growth industry, I believe. There are only companies organized and operated to create and capitalize on growth opportunities. Industries that assume themselves to be riding some automatic growth escalator invariably descend into stagnation. The history of every dead and dying "growth" industry shows a self-deceiving cycle of bountiful expansion and undetected decay. There are four conditions which usually guarantee this cycle:

1
The belief that growth is assured by an expanding and more affluent population.
2
The belief that there is no competitive substitute for the industry's major product.
3
Too much faith in mass production and in the advantages of rapidly declining unit costs as output rises.
4
Preoccupation with a product that lends itself to carefully controlled scientific experimentation, improvement, and manufacturing cost reduction.

I should like now to begin examining each of these conditions in some detail. To build my case as boldly as possible, I shall illustrate the points with reference to three industries—petroleum, automobiles, and electronics—particularly petroleum, because it spans more years and more vicissitudes. Not only do these three have excellent reputations with the general public and also enjoy the confidence of sophisticated investors, but their managements have become known for progressive thinking in areas like financial control, product research, and

management training. If obsolescence can cripple even these industries, it can happen anywhere.

Population myth

The belief that profits are assured by an expanding and more affluent population is dear to the heart of every industry. It takes the edge off the apprehensions everybody understandably feels about the future. If consumers are multiplying and also buying more of your product or service, you can face the future with considerably more comfort than if the market is shrinking. An expanding market keeps the manufacturer from having to think very hard or imaginatively. If thinking is an intellectual response to a problem, then the absence of a problem leads to the absence of thinking. If your product has an automatically expanding market, then you will not give much thought to how to expand it.

One of the most interesting examples of this is provided by the petroleum industry. Probably our oldest growth industry, it has an enviable record. While there are some current apprehensions about its growth rate, the industry itself tends to be optimistic.

But I believe it can be demonstrated that it is undergoing a fundamental yet typical change. It is not only ceasing to be a growth industry, but may actually be a declining one, relative to other business. Although there is widespread unawareness of it, I believe that within 25 years the oil industry may find itself in much the same position of retrospective glory that the railroads are now in. Despite its pioneering work in developing and applying the present-value method of investment evaluation, in employee relations, and in working with backward countries, the petroleum business is a distressing example of how complacency and wrongheadedness can stubbornly convert opportunity into near disaster.

One of the characteristics of this and other industries that have believed very strongly in the beneficial consequences of an expanding population, while at the same time being indus-

2. For more details see M. M. Zimmerman, *The Super Market: A Revolution in Distribution* (New York, McGraw-Hill Book Company, Inc., 1955), p. 48.

3. Ibid., pp. 45–47.

tries with a generic product for which there has appeared to be no competitive substitute, is that the individual companies have sought to outdo their competitors by improving on what they are already doing. This makes sense, of course, if one assumes that sales are tied to the country's population strings, because the customer can compare products only on a feature-by-feature basis. I believe it is significant, for example, that not since John D. Rockefeller sent free kerosene lamps to China has the oil industry done anything really outstanding to create a demand for its product. Not even in product improvement has it showered itself with eminence. The greatest single improvement—namely, the development of tetraethyl lead—came from outside the industry, specifically from General Motors and DuPont. The big contributions made by the industry itself are confined to the technology of oil exploration, production, and refining.

Asking for trouble: In other words, the industry's efforts have focused on improving the *efficiency* of getting and making its product, not really on improving the generic product or its marketing. Moreover, its chief product has continuously been defined in the narrowest possible terms, namely, gasoline, not energy, fuel, or transportation. This attitude has helped assure that:

O

Major improvements in gasoline quality tend not to originate in the oil industry. Also, the development of superior alternative fuels comes from outside the oil industry, as will be shown later.

O

Major innovations in automobile fuel marketing are originated by small new oil companies that are not primarily preoccupied with production or refining. These are the companies that have been responsible for the rapidly expanding multipump gasoline stations, with their successful emphasis on large and clean layouts, rapid and efficient driveway service, and quality gasoline at low prices.

Thus, the oil industry is asking for trouble from outsiders. Sooner or later, in this land of hungry inventors and entrepreneurs, a threat is sure to come. The possibilities of this will become more apparent when we turn to the next dangerous belief of many managements. For the sake of continuity, because this second belief is tied closely to the first, I shall continue with the same example.

Idea of indispensability: The petroleum industry is pretty much persuaded that there is no competitive substitute for its major product, gasoline—or if there is, that it will continue to be a derivative of crude oil, such as diesel fuel or kerosene jet fuel.

There is a lot of automatic wishful thinking in this assumption. The trouble is that most refining companies own huge amounts of crude oil reserves. These have value only if there is a market for products into which oil can be converted—hence the tenacious belief in the continuing competitive superiority of automobile fuels made from crude oil.

This idea persists despite all historic evidence against it. The evidence not only shows that oil has never been a superior product for any purpose for very long, but it also shows that the oil industry has never really been a growth industry. It has been a succession of different businesses that have gone through the usual historic cycles of growth, maturity, and decay. Its overall survival is owed to a series of miraculous escapes from total obsolescence, of last-minute and unexpected reprieves from total disaster reminiscent of the Perils of Pauline.

Perils of petroleum: I shall sketch in only the main episodes.

First, crude oil was largely a patent medicine. But even before that fad ran out, demand was greatly expanded by the use of oil in kerosene lamps. The prospect of lighting the world's lamps gave rise to an extravagant promise of growth. The prospects were similar to those the industry now holds for gasoline in other parts of the world. It can hardly wait for the underdeveloped nations to get a car in every garage.

In the days of the kerosene lamp, the oil companies competed with each other and against gaslight by trying to improve the illuminating characteristics of kerosene. Then suddenly the impossible happened. Edison invented a light which was totally nondependent on crude oil. Had it not been for the growing use of kerosene in space heaters, the incandescent lamp would have completely finished oil as a growth industry at that time. Oil would have been good for little else than axle grease.

Then disaster and reprieve struck again. Two great innovations occurred, neither originating in the oil industry. The successful development of coal-burning domestic central-heating systems made the space heater obsolescent. While the industry reeled, along came its most magnificent boost yet —the internal combustion engine, also invented by outsiders. Then when the prodigious expansion for gasoline finally began to level off in the 1920s, along came the miraculous escape of a central oil heater. Once again, the escape was provided by an outsider's invention and development. And when that market weakened, wartime demand for aviation fuel came to the rescue. After the war the expansion of civilian aviation, the dieselization of railroads, and the explosive demand for cars and trucks kept the industry's growth in high gear.

Meanwhile, centralized oil heating— whose boom potential had only recently been proclaimed—ran into severe competition from natural gas. While the oil companies themselves owned the gas that now competed with their oil, the industry did not originate the natural gas revolution, nor has it to this day greatly profited from its gas ownership. The gas revolution was made by newly formed transmission companies that marketed the product with an aggressive ardor. They started a magnificent new industry, first against the advice and then against the resistance of the oil companies.

By all the logic of the situation, the oil companies themselves should have made the gas revolution. They not only owned the gas; they also were the only people experienced in handling, scrubbing, and using it, the only people experienced in pipeline technology and transmission, and they understood heating problems. But, partly because they knew that natural gas would compete with their own sale of heating oil, the oil companies poohpoohed the potentials of gas.

The revolution was finally started by oil pipeline executives who, unable to persuade their own companies to go into gas, quit and organized the spectacularly successful gas transmission companies. Even after their success became painfully evident to the oil companies, the latter did not go into gas transmission. The multibillion dollar business which should have been theirs went to others. As in the past, the industry was blinded by its narrow preoccupation with a specific product and the value of its reserves. It paid little or no attention to its customers' basic needs and preferences.

The postwar years have not witnessed any change. Immediately after World War II the oil industry was greatly encouraged about its future by the rapid expansion of demand for its traditional line of products. In 1950 most companies projected annual rates of domestic expansion of around 6% through at least 1975. Though the ratio of crude oil reserves to demand in the Free World was about 20 to 1, with 10 to 1 being usually considered a reasonable working ratio in the United States, booming demand sent oil men searching for more without sufficient regard to what the future really promised. In 1952 they "hit" in the Middle East; the ratio skyrocketed to 42 to 1. If gross additions to reserves continue at the average rate of the past five years (37 billion barrels annually), then by 1970 the reserve ratio will be up to 45 to 1. This abundance of oil has weakened crude and product prices all over the world.

Uncertain future: Management cannot find much consolation today in the rapidly expanding petrochemical industry, another oil-using idea that did not originate in the leading firms. The total United States production of petrochemicals is equivalent to about 2% (by volume) of the demand for all petroleum products. Although the petrochemical industry is now expected to grow by about 10% per year, this will not offset other drains on

the growth of crude oil consumption. Furthermore, while petrochemical products are many and growing, it is well to remember that there are nonpetroleum sources of the basic raw material, such as coal. Besides, a lot of plastics can be produced with relatively little oil. A 50,000-barrel-per-day oil refinery is now considered the absolute minimum size for efficiency. But a 5,000-barrel-per-day chemical plant is a giant operation.

Oil has never been a continuously strong growth industry. It has grown by fits and starts, always miraculously saved by innovations and developments not of its own making. The reason it has not grown in a smooth progression is that each time it thought it had a superior product safe from the possibility of competitive substitutes, the product turned out to be inferior and notoriously subject to obsolescence. Until now, gasoline (for motor fuel, anyhow) has escaped this fate. But, as we shall see later, it too may be on its last legs.

The point of all this is that there is no guarantee against product obsolescence. If a company's own research does not make it obsolete, another's will. Unless an industry is especially lucky, as oil has been until now, it can easily go down in a sea of red figures—just as the railroads have, as the buggy whip manufacturers have, as the corner grocery chains have, as most of the big movie companies have, and indeed as many other industries have.

The best way for a firm to be lucky is to make its own luck. That requires knowing what makes a business successful. One of the greatest enemies of this knowledge is mass production.

Production pressures

Mass-production industries are impelled by a great drive to produce all they can. The prospect of steeply declining unit costs as output rises is more than most companies can usually resist. The profit possibilities look spectacular. All effort focuses on production. The result is that marketing gets neglected.

John Kenneth Galbraith contends that just the opposite occurs.[4] Output is so prodigious that all effort concentrates on trying to get rid of it. He says this accounts for singing commercials, desecration of the countryside with advertising signs, and other wasteful and vulgar practices. Galbraith has a finger on something real, but he misses the strategic point. Mass production does indeed generate great pressure to "move" the product. But what usually gets emphasized is selling, not marketing. Marketing, being a more sophisticated and complex process, gets ignored.

The difference between marketing and selling is more than semantic. Selling focuses on the needs of the seller, marketing on the needs of the buyer. Selling is preoccupied with the seller's need to convert his product into cash, marketing with the idea of satisfying the needs of the customer by means of the product and the whole cluster of things associated with creating, delivering, and finally consuming it.

In some industries the enticements of full mass production have been so powerful that for many years top management in effect has told the sales departments, "You get rid of it; we'll worry about profits." By contrast, a truly marketing-minded firm tries to create value-satisfying goods and services that consumers will want to buy. What it offers for sale includes not only the generic product or service, but also how it is made available to the customer, in what form, when, under what conditions, and at what terms of trade. Most important, what it offers for sale is determined not by the seller but by the buyer. The seller takes his cues from the buyer in such a way that the product becomes a consequence of the marketing effort, not vice versa.

Lag in Detroit: This may sound like an elementary rule of business, but that does not keep it from being violated wholesale. It is certainly more violated than honored. Take the automobile industry.

4. *The Affluent Society* (Boston, Houghton Mifflin Company, 1958), pp. 152-160.

Here mass production is most famous, most honored, and has the greatest impact on the entire society. The industry has hitched its fortune to the relentless requirements of the annual model change, a policy that makes customer orientation an especially urgent necessity. Consequently the auto companies annually spend millions of dollars on consumer research. But the fact that the new compact cars are selling so well in their first year indicates that Detroit's vast researches have for a long time failed to reveal what the customer really wanted. Detroit was not persuaded that he wanted anything different from what he had been getting until it lost millions of customers to other small car manufacturers.

How could this unbelievable lag behind consumer wants have been perpetuated so long? Why did not research reveal consumer preferences before consumers' buying decisions themselves revealed the facts? Is that not what consumer research is for—to find out before the fact what is going to happen? The answer is that Detroit never really researched the customer's wants. It only researched his preferences between the kinds of things which it had already decided to offer him. For Detroit is mainly product-oriented, not customer-oriented. To the extent that the customer is recognized as having needs that the manufacturer should try to satisfy, Detroit usually acts as if the job can be done entirely by product changes. Occasionally attention gets paid to financing, too, but that is done more in order to sell than to enable the customer to buy.

As for taking care of other customer needs, there is not enough being done to write about. The areas of the greatest unsatisfied needs are ignored, or at best get stepchild attention. These are at the point of sale and on the matter of automotive repair and maintenance. Detroit views these problem areas as being of secondary importance. That is underscored by the fact that the retailing and servicing ends of this industry are neither owned and operated nor controlled by the manufacturers. Once the car is produced, things are pretty much in the dealer's inadequate hands. Illustrative of Detroit's arm's-length attitude is the fact that, while servicing holds enormous sales-stimulating, profit-building opportunities, only 57 of Chevrolet's 7,000 dealers provide night maintenance service.

Motorists repeatedly express their dissatisfaction with servicing and their apprehensions about buying cars under the present selling setup. The anxieties and problems they encounter during the auto buying and maintenance processes are probably more intense and widespread today than 30 years ago. Yet the automobile companies do not *seem* to listen to or take their cues from the anguished consumer. If they do listen, it must be through the filter of their own preoccupation with production. The marketing effort is still viewed as a necessary consequence of the product, not vice versa, as it should be. That is the legacy of mass production, with its parochial view that profit resides essentially in low-cost full production.

What Ford put first: The profit lure of mass production obviously has a place in the plans and strategy of business management, but it must always *follow* hard thinking about the customer. This is one of the most important lessons that we can learn from the contradictory behavior of Henry Ford. In a sense Ford was both the most brilliant and the most senseless marketer in American history. He was senseless because he refused to give the customer anything but a black car. He was brilliant because he fashioned a production system designed to fit market needs. We habitually celebrate him for the wrong reason, his production genius. His real genius was marketing. We think he was able to cut his selling price and therefore sell millions of $500 cars because his invention of the assembly line had reduced the costs. Actually he invented the assembly line because he had concluded that at $500 he could sell millions of cars. Mass production was the *result* not the cause of his low prices.

Ford repeatedly emphasized this point, but a nation of production-oriented business managers refuses to hear the great lesson he taught. Here is his operating philosophy as he expressed it succinctly:

"Our policy is to reduce the price, extend the operations, and improve the article. You will notice that the reduction of price comes first. We have never considered any costs as fixed. Therefore we first reduce the price to the point where we believe more sales will result. Then we go ahead and try to make the prices. We do not bother about the costs. The new price forces the costs down. The more usual way is to take the costs and then determine the price; and although that method may be scientific in the narrow sense, it is not scientific in the broad sense, because what earthly use is it to know the cost if it tells you that you cannot manufacture at a price at which the article can be sold? But more to the point is the fact that, although one may calculate what a cost is, and of course all of our costs are carefully calculated, no one knows what a cost ought to be. One of the ways of discovering ... is to name a price so low as to force everybody in the place to the highest point of efficiency. The low price makes everybody dig for profits. We make more discoveries concerning manufacturing and selling under this forced method than by any method of leisurely investigation." [5]

Product provincialism: The tantalizing profit possibilities of low unit production costs may be the most seriously self-deceiving attitude that can afflict a company, particularly a "growth" company where an apparently assured expansion of demand already tends to undermine a proper concern for the importance of marketing and the customer.

The usual result of this narrow preoccupation with so-called concrete matters is that instead of growing, the industry declines. It usually means that the product fails to adapt to the constantly changing patterns of consumer needs and tastes, to new and modified marketing institutions and practices, or to product developments in competing or complementary industries. The industry has its eyes so firmly on its own specific product that it does not see how it is being made obsolete.

5. Henry Ford, *My Life and Work* (New York, Doubleday, Page & Company, 1923), pp. 146-147.

The classical example of this is the buggy whip industry. No amount of product improvement could stave off its death sentence. But had the industry defined itself as being in the transportation business rather than the buggy whip business, it might have survived. It would have done what survival always entails, that is, changing. Even if it had only defined its business as providing a stimulant or catalyst to an energy source, it might have survived by becoming a manufacturer of, say, fanbelts or air cleaners.

What may some day be a still more classical example is, again, the oil industry. Having let others steal marvelous opportunities from it (e.g., natural gas, as already mentioned, missile fuels, and jet engine lubricants), one would expect it to have taken steps never to let that happen again. But this is not the case. We are now getting extraordinary new developments in fuel systems specifically designed to power automobiles. Not only are these developments concentrated in firms outside the petroleum industry, but petroleum is almost systematically ignoring them, securely content in its wedded bliss to oil. It is the story of the kerosene lamp versus the incandescent lamp all over again. Oil is trying to improve hydrocarbon fuels rather than develop *any* fuels best suited to the needs of their users, whether or not made in different ways and with different raw materials from oil.

Here are some things which nonpetroleum companies are working on:

☐

Over a dozen such firms now have advanced working models of energy systems which, when perfected, will replace the internal combustion engine and eliminate the demand for gasoline. The superior merit of each of these systems is their elimination of frequent, time-consuming, and irritating refueling stops. Most of these systems are fuel cells designed to create electrical energy directly from chemicals without combustion. Most of them use chemicals that are not derived from oil, generally hydrogen and oxygen.

☐

Several other companies have advanced models of electric storage batteries designed to power automobiles. One of these is an aircraft producer that is working jointly with several electric utility companies. The latter hope to use off-peak generating capacity to supply overnight plug-in battery regeneration. Another company, also using the battery approach, is a medium-size electronics firm with extensive small-battery experience that it developed in connection with its work on hearing aids. It is collaborating with an automobile manufacturer. Recent improvements arising from the need for high-powered miniature power storage plants in rockets have put us within reach of a relatively small battery capable of withstanding great overloads or surges of power. Germanium diode applications and batteries using sintered-plate and nickel-cadmium techniques promise to make a revolution in our energy sources.

☐

Solar energy conversion systems are also getting increasing attention. One usually cautious Detroit auto executive recently ventured that solar-powered cars might be common by 1980.

As for the oil companies, they are more or less "watching developments," as one research director put it to me. A few are doing a bit of research on fuel cells, but almost always confined to developing cells powered by hydrocarbon chemicals. None of them are enthusiastically researching fuel cells, batteries, or solar power plants. None of them are spending a fraction as much on research in these profoundly important areas as they are on the usual run-of-the-mill things like reducing combustion chamber deposit in gasoline engines. One major integrated petroleum company recently took a tentative look at the fuel cell and concluded that although "the companies actively working on it indicate a belief in ultimate success . . . the timing and magnitude of its impact are too remote to warrant recognition in our forecasts."

One might, of course, ask: Why should the oil companies do anything different? Would not chemical fuel cells, batteries, or solar energy kill the present product lines? The answer is that they would indeed, and that is precisely the reason for the oil firms having to develop these power units before their competitors, so they will not be companies without an industry.

Management might be more likely to do what is needed for its own preservation if it thought of itself as being in the energy business. But even that would not be enough if it persists in imprisoning itself in the narrow grip of its tight product orientation. It has to think of itself as taking care of customer needs, not finding, refining, or even selling oil. Once it genuinely thinks of its business as taking care of people's transportation needs, nothing can stop it from creating its own extravagantly profitable growth.

'Creative destruction': Since words are cheap and deeds are dear, it may be appropriate to indicate what this kind of thinking involves and leads to. Let us start at the beginning—the customer. It can be shown that motorists strongly dislike the bother, delay, and experience of buying gasoline. People actually do not buy gasoline. They cannot see it, taste it, feel it, appreciate it, or really test it. What they buy is the right to continue driving their cars. The gas station is like a tax collector to whom people are compelled to pay a periodic toll as the price of using their cars. This makes the gas station a basically unpopular institution. It can never be made popular or pleasant, only less unpopular, less unpleasant.

To reduce its unpopularity completely means eliminating it. Nobody likes a tax collector, not even a pleasantly cheerful one. Nobody likes to interrupt a trip to buy a phantom product, not even from a handsome Adonis or a seductive Venus. Hence, companies that are working on exotic fuel substitutes which will eliminate the need for frequent refueling are heading directly into the outstretched arms of the irritated motorist. They are riding a wave of inevitability, not because they are creating something which is technologically superior or more sophisticated, but because they are satisfying a powerful customer need. They are also eliminating noxious odors and air pollution.

Once the petroleum companies recognize the customer-satisfying logic of what another power system can do, they will see that they have no more choice about working on an efficient, long-lasting fuel (or some way of delivering present fuels without bothering the motorist) than the big food chains had a choice about going into the supermarket business, or the vacuum tube companies had a choice about making semiconductors. For their own good the oil firms will have to destroy their own highly profitable assets. No amount of wishful thinking can save them from the necessity of engaging in this form of "creative destruction."

I phrase the need as strongly as this because I think management must make quite an effort to break itself loose from conventional ways. It is all too easy in this day and age for a company or industry to let its sense of purpose become dominated by the economies of full production and to develop a dangerously lopsided product orientation. In short, if management lets itself drift, it invariably drifts in the direction of thinking of itself as producing goods and services, not customer satisfactions. While it probably will not descend to the depths of telling its salesmen, "You get rid of it; we'll worry about profits," it can, without knowing it, be practicing precisely that formula for withering decay. The historic fate of one growth industry after another has been its suicidal product provincialism.

Dangers of R&D

Another big danger to a firm's continued growth arises when top management is wholly transfixed by the profit possibilities of technical research and development. To illustrate I shall turn first to a new industry—electronics—and then return once more to the oil companies. By comparing a fresh example with a familiar one, I hope to emphasize the prevalence and insidiousness of a hazardous way of thinking.

Marketing shortchanged: In the case of electronics, the greatest danger which faces the glamorous new companies in this field is not that they do not pay enough attention to research and development, but that they pay *too much* attention to it. And the fact that the fastest growing electronics firms owe their eminence to their heavy emphasis on technical research is completely beside the point. They have vaulted to affluence on a sudden crest of unusually strong general receptiveness to new technical ideas. Also, their success has been shaped in the virtually guaranteed market of military subsidies and by military orders that in many cases actually preceded the existence of facilities to make the products. Their expansion has, in other words, been almost totally devoid of marketing effort.

Thus, they are growing up under conditions that come dangerously close to creating the illusion that a superior product will sell itself. Having created a successful company by making a superior product, it is not surprising that management continues to be oriented toward the product rather than the people who consume it. It develops the philosophy that continued growth is a matter of continued product innovation and improvement.

A number of other factors tend to strengthen and sustain this belief:

1

Because electronic products are highly complex and sophisticated, managements become top-heavy with engineers and scientists. This creates a selective bias in favor of research and production at the expense of marketing. The organization tends to view itself as making things rather than satisfying customer needs. Marketing gets treated as a residual activity, "something else" that must be done once the vital job of product creation and production is completed.

2

To this bias in favor of product research, development, and production is added the bias in favor of dealing with controllable variables. Engineers and scientists are at home in the world of concrete things like machines, test tubes, production lines, and even balance sheets. The abstractions to which they feel kindly are those which are testable or manipulatable in the laboratory, or, if not testable, then functional, such as Euclid's axioms. In short, the managements of the new glamour-growth companies tend to favor those business activities which lend themselves to careful study, experimentation, and control—the hard, practical realities of the lab, the shop, the books.

What gets shortchanged are the realities of the *market*. Consumers are unpredictable, varied, fickle, stupid, shortsighted, stubborn, and generally bothersome. This is not what the engineer-managers say, but deep down in their consciousness it is what they believe. And this accounts for their concentrating on what they know and what they can control, namely, product research, engineering, and production. The emphasis on production becomes particularly attractive when the product can be made at declining unit costs. There is no more inviting way of making money than by running the plant full blast.

Today the top-heavy science-engineering-production orientation of so many electronics companies works reasonably well because they are pushing into new frontiers in which the armed services have pioneered virtually assured markets. The companies are in the felicitous position of having to fill, not find markets; of not having to discover what the customer needs and wants, but of having the customer voluntarily come forward with specific new product demands. If a team of consultants had been assigned specifically to design a business situation calculated to prevent the emergence and development of a customer-oriented marketing viewpoint, it could not have produced anything better than the conditions just described.

Stepchild treatment: The oil industry is a stunning example of how science, technology, and mass production can divert an entire group of companies from their main task. To the extent the consumer is studied at all (which is not much), the focus is forever on getting information which is designed to help the oil companies improve what they are now doing. They try to discover more convincing advertising themes, more effective sales promotional drives, what the market shares of the various companies are, what people like or dislike about service station dealers and oil companies, and so forth. Nobody seems as interested in probing deeply into the basic human needs that the industry might be trying to satisfy as in probing into the basic properties of the raw material that the companies work with in trying to deliver customer satisfactions.

Basic questions about customers and markets seldom get asked. The latter occupy a stepchild status. They are recognized as existing, as having to be taken care of, but not worth very much real thought or dedicated attention. Nobody gets as excited about the customers in his own backyard as about the oil in the Sahara Desert. Nothing illustrates better the neglect of marketing than its treatment in the industry press.

The centennial issue of the *American Petroleum Institute Quarterly*, published in 1959 to celebrate the discovery of oil in Titusville, Pennsylvania, contained 21 feature articles proclaiming the industry's greatness. Only one of these talked about its achievements in marketing, and that was only a pictorial record of how service station architecture has changed. The issue also contained a special section on "New Horizons," which was devoted to showing the magnificent role oil would play in America's future. Every reference was ebulliently optimistic, never implying once that oil might have some hard competition. Even the reference to atomic energy was a cheerful catalogue of how oil would help make atomic energy a success. There was not a single apprehension that the oil industry's affluence might be threatened or a suggestion that one "new horizon" might include new and better ways of serving oil's present customers.

But the most revealing example of the stepchild treatment that marketing gets was still another special series of short articles on "The Revolutionary Potential of Electronics." Under that heading this list of articles appeared in the table of contents:

○
"In the Search for Oil"
○
"In Production Operations"
○
"In Refinery Processes"

○
"In Pipeline Operations"

Significantly, every one of the industry's major functional areas is listed, *except* marketing. Why? Either it is believed that electronics holds no revolutionary potential for petroleum marketing (which is palpably wrong), or the editors forgot to discuss marketing (which is more likely, and illustrates its stepchild status).

The order in which the four functional areas are listed also betrays the alienation of the oil industry from the consumer. The industry is implicitly defined as beginning with the search for oil and ending with its distribution from the refinery. But the truth is, it seems to me, that the industry begins with the needs of the customer for its products. From that primal position its definition moves steadily backstream to areas of progressively lesser importance, until it finally comes to rest at the "search for oil."

Beginning & end: The view that an industry is a customer-satisfying process, not a goods-producing process, is vital for all businessmen to understand. An industry begins with the customer and his needs, not with a patent, a raw material, or a selling skill. Given the customer's needs, the industry develops backwards, first concerning itself with the physical *delivery* of customer satisfactions. Then it moves back further to *creating* the things by which these satisfactions are in part achieved. How these materials are created is a matter of indifference to the customer, hence the particular form of manufacturing, processing, or what-have-you cannot be considered as a vital aspect of the industry. Finally, the industry moves back still further to *finding* the raw materials necessary for making its products.

The irony of some industries oriented toward technical research and development is that the scientists who occupy the high executive positions are totally unscientific when it comes to defining their companies' overall needs and purposes. They violate the first two rules of the scientific method —being aware of and defining their companies' problems, and then devel-

oping testable hypotheses about solving them. They are scientific only about the convenient things, such as laboratory and product experiments.

The reason that the customer (and the satisfaction of his deepest needs) is not considered as being "the problem" is not because there is any certain belief that no such problem exists, but because an organizational lifetime has conditioned management to look in the opposite direction. Marketing is a stepchild.

I do not mean that selling is ignored. Far from it. But selling, again, is not marketing. As already pointed out, selling concerns itself with the tricks and techniques of getting people to exchange their cash for your product. It is not concerned with the values that the exchange is all about. And it does not, as marketing invariably does, view the entire business process as consisting of a tightly integrated effort to discover, create, arouse, and satisfy customer needs. The customer is somebody "out there" who, with proper cunning, can be separated from his loose change.

Actually, not even selling gets much attention in some technologically minded firms. Because there is a virtually guaranteed market for the abundant flow of their new products, they do not actually know what a real market is. It is as if they lived in a planned economy, moving their products routinely from factory to retail outlet. Their successful concentration on products tends to convince them of the soundness of what they have been doing, and they fail to see the gathering clouds over the market.

Conclusion

Less than 75 years ago American railroads enjoyed a fierce loyalty among astute Wall Streeters. European monarchs invested in them heavily. Eternal wealth was thought to be the benediction for anybody who could scrape a few thousand dollars together to put into rail stocks. No other form of transportation could compete with the railroads in speed, flexibility, durability, economy, and growth potentials.

As Jacques Barzun put it, "By the turn of the century it was an institution, an image of man, a tradition, a code of honor, a source of poetry, a nursery of boyhood desires, a sublimest of toys, and the most solemn machine—next to the funeral hearse—that marks the epochs in man's life." [6]

Even after the advent of automobiles, trucks, and airplanes, the railroad tycoons remained imperturbably self-confident. If you had told them 60 years ago that in 30 years they would be flat on their backs, broke, and pleading for government subsidies, they would have thought you totally demented. Such a future was simply not considered possible. It was not even a discussable subject, or an askable question, or a matter which any sane person would consider worth speculating about. The very thought was insane. Yet a lot of insane notions now have matter-of-fact acceptance—for example, the idea of 100-ton tubes of metal moving smoothly through the air 20,000 feet above the earth, loaded with 100 sane and solid citizens casually drinking martinis—and they have dealt cruel blows to the railroads.

What specifically must other companies do to avoid this fate? What does customer orientation involve? These questions have in part been answered by the preceding examples and analysis. It would take another article to show in detail what is required for specific industries. In any case, it should be obvious that building an effective customer-oriented company involves far more than good intentions or promotional tricks; it involves profound matters of human organization and leadership. For the present, let me merely suggest what appear to be some general requirements.

Visceral feel of greatness: Obviously the company has to do what survival demands. It has to adapt to the requirements of the market, and it has to do it sooner rather than later. But mere survival is a so-so aspiration. Anybody can survive in some way or other, even the skid-row bum. The trick is to survive gallantly, to feel

6. Jacques Barzun, "Trains and the Mind of Man," *Holiday*, February 1960, p. 20.

the surging impulse of commercial mastery; not just to experience the sweet smell of success, but to have the visceral feel of entrepreneurial greatness.

No organization can achieve greatness without a vigorous leader who is driven onward by his own pulsating *will to succeed.* He has to have a vision of grandeur, a vision that can produce eager followers in vast numbers. In business, the followers are the customers.

In order to produce these customers, the entire corporation must be viewed as a customer-creating and customer-satisfying organism. Management must think of itself not as producing products but as providing customer-creating value satisfactions. It must push this idea (and everything it means and requires) into every nook and cranny of the organization. It has to do this continuously and with the kind of flair that excites and stimulates the people in it. Otherwise, the company will be merely a series of pigeonholed parts, with no consolidating sense of purpose or direction.

In short, the organization must learn to think of itself not as producing goods or services but as *buying customers,* as doing the things that will make people *want* to do business with it. And the chief executive himself has the inescapable responsibility for creating this environment, this viewpoint, this attitude, this aspiration. He himself must set the company's style, its direction, and its goals. This means he has to know precisely where he himself wants to go, and to make sure the whole organization is enthusiastically aware of where that is. This is a first requisite of leadership, for *unless he knows where he is going, any road will take him there.*

If any road is okay, the chief executive might as well pack his attaché case and go fishing. If an organization does not know or care where it is going, it does not need to advertise that fact with a ceremonial figurehead. Everybody will notice it soon enough.

Retrospective commentary

Amazed, finally, by his literary success, Isaac Bashevis Singer reconciled an attendant problem: "I think the moment you have published a book, it's not any more your private property. . . . If it has value, everybody can find in it what he finds, and I cannot tell the man I did not intend it to be so." Over the past 15 years, "Marketing Myopia" has become a case in point. Remarkably, the article spawned a legion of loyal partisans—not to mention a host of unlikely bedfellows.

Its most common and, I believe, most influential consequence is the way certain companies for the first time gave serious thought to the question of what businesses they are really in.

The strategic consequences of this have in many cases been dramatic. The best-known case, of course, is the shift in thinking of oneself as being in the "oil business" to being in the "energy business." In some instances the payoff has been spectacular (getting into coal, for example) and in others dreadful (in terms of the time and money spent so far on fuel cell research). Another successful example is a company with a large chain of retail shoe stores that redefined itself as a retailer of moderately priced, frequently purchased, widely assorted consumer specialty products. The result was a dramatic growth in volume, earnings, and return on assets.

Some companies, again for the first time, asked themselves whether they wished to be masters of certain technologies for which they would seek markets, or be masters of markets for which they would seek customer-satisfying products and services.

Choosing the former, one company has declared, in effect, "We are experts in glass technology. We intend to improve and expand that expertise with the object of creating products that will attract customers." This decision has forced the company into a much more systematic and customer-sensitive look at possible markets and users, even though its stated strategic object has been to capitalize on glass technology.

Deciding to concentrate on markets, another company has determined that "we want to help people (primarily women) enhance their beauty and sense of youthfulness." This company has expanded its line of cosmetic products, but has also entered the fields of proprietary drugs and vitamin supplements.

All these examples illustrate the "policy" results of "Marketing Myopia." On the operating level, there has been, I think, an extraordinary heightening of sensitivity to customers and consumers. R&D departments have cultivated a greater "external" orientation toward uses, users, and markets—balancing thereby the previously one-sided "internal" focus on materials and methods; upper management has realized that marketing and sales departments should be somewhat more willingly accommodated than before; finance departments have become more receptive to the legitimacy of budgets for market research and experimentation in marketing; and salesmen have been better trained to listen to and understand customer needs and problems, rather than merely to "push" the product.

A mirror, not a window

My impression is that the article has had more impact in industrial-products companies than in consumer-products companies—perhaps because the former had lagged most in customer orientation. There are at least two reasons for this lag: (1) industrial-products companies tend to be more capital intensive, and (2) in the past, at least, they have had to rely heavily on communicating face-to-face the technical character of what they made and sold. These points are worth explaining.

Capital-intensive businesses are understandably preoccupied with magnitudes, especially where the capital, once invested, cannot be easily moved, manipulated, or modified for the production of a variety of products—e.g., chemical plants, steel mills, airlines, and railroads. Understandably, they seek big volumes and operating efficiencies to pay off the equipment and meet the carrying costs.

At least one problem results: corporate power becomes disproportionately lodged with operating or financial executives. If you read the charter of one of the nation's largest companies, you will see that the chairman of the finance committee, not the chief executive officer, is the "chief." Executives with such backgrounds have an almost trained incapacity to see that getting "volume" may require understanding and serving many discrete and sometimes small market segments, rather than going after a perhaps mythical batch of big or homogeneous customers.

These executives also often fail to appreciate the competitive changes going on around them. They observe the changes, all right, but devalue their significance or underestimate their ability to nibble away at the company's markets.

Once dramatically alerted to the concept of segments, sectors, and customers, though, managers of capital-intensive businesses have become more responsive to the necessity of balancing their inescapable preoccupation with "paying the bills" or breaking even with the fact that the best way to accomplish this may be to pay more attention to segments, sectors, and customers.

The second reason industrial products companies have probably been more influenced by the article is that, in the case of the more technical industrial products or services, the necessity of clearly communicating product and service characteristics to prospects results in a lot of face-to-face "selling" effort. But precisely because the product is so complex, the situation produces salesmen who know the product more than they know the customer, who are more adept at explaining what they have and what it can do than learning what the customer's needs and problems are. The result has been a narrow product orientation rather than a liberating customer orientation, and "service" often suffered. To be sure, sellers said, "We have to provide service," but they tended to define service by looking into the mirror rather than out the window. They *thought* they were looking out the window at the customer, but it was actually a mirror—a reflection of their own product-oriented biases rather than a reflection of their customers' situations.

A manifesto, not a prescription

Not everything has been rosy. A lot of bizarre things have happened as a result of the article:

☐
Some companies have developed what I call "marketing mania"—they've become obsessively responsive to every fleeting whim of the customer. Mass production operations have been converted to approximations of job shops, with cost and price consequences far exceeding the willingness of customers to buy the product.
☐
Management has expanded product lines and added new lines of business without first establishing adequate control systems to run more complex operations.
☐
Marketing staffs have suddenly and rapidly expanded themselves and their research budgets without either getting sufficient prior organizational support or, thereafter, producing sufficient results.
☐
Companies that are functionally organized have converted to product, brand, or market-based organizations with the expectation of instant and miraculous results. The outcome has been ambiguity, frustration, confusion, corporate infighting, losses, and finally a reversion to functional arrangements that only worsened the situation.
☐
Companies have attempted to "serve" customers by creating complex and beautifully efficient products or services that buyers are either too risk-averse to adopt or incapable of learning how to employ—in effect, there are now steam shovels for people who haven't yet learned to use spades. This problem has happened repeatedly in the so-called service industries (financial services, insurance, computer-based services) and with American companies selling in less-developed economies.

"Marketing Myopia" was not intended as analysis or even prescription; it was intended as manifesto. It did not pretend to take a balanced position. Nor was it a new idea—Peter F. Drucker, J.B. McKitterick, Wroe Alderson, John Howard, and Neil Borden had each done more original and balanced work on "the marketing concept." My scheme, however, tied marketing more closely to the inner orbit of business policy. Drucker—especially in *The Concept of the Corporation* and *The Practice of Management*—originally provided me with a great deal of insight.

My contribution, therefore, appears merely to have been a simple, brief, and useful way of communicating an existing way of thinking. I tried to do it in a very direct, but responsible, fashion, knowing that few readers (customers), especially managers and leaders, could stand much equivocation or hesitation. I also knew that the colorful and lightly documented affirmation works better than the tortuously reasoned explanation.

But why the enormous popularity of what was actually such a simple pre-existing idea? Why its appeal throughout the world to resolutely restrained scholars, implacably temperate managers, and high government officials, all accustomed to balanced and thoughtful calculation? Is it that concrete examples, joined to illustrate a simple idea and presented with some attention to literacy, communicate better than massive analytical reasoning that reads as though it were translated from the German? Is it that provocative assertions are more memorable and persuasive than restrained and balanced explanations, no matter who the audience? Is it that the character of the message is as much the message as its content? Or was mine not simply a different tune, but a new symphony? I don't know.

Of course, I'd do it again and in the same way, given my purposes, even with what more I now know—the good and the bad, the power of facts and the limits of rhetoric. If your mission is the moon, you don't use a car. Don Marquis's cockroach, Archy, provides some final consolation: "an idea is not responsible for who believes in it."

HAPPI-NESS isn't EVERY-thing
by Shelly Reese

Does customer satisfaction necessarily translate to customer loyalty and increased profits? And if it did, how would we know?

fOR THE PAST DECADE, businesses have jumped through innumerable hoops in pursuit of an elusive goal: customer satisfaction. Businesses around the globe have expended an enormous amount of effort in hopes of eliciting a smile and a well-pleased nod from car buyers, long-distance users, hospital patients, and every other conceivable consumer of goods and services.

This approbation is sought not for its own sake, but for the results it is believed to produce. In the arithmetic of modern business, a satisfied customer is a repeat customer, whose long-term patronage results in higher sales and more profit.

Or so it would seem.

Unimpeachable as the concept of customer satisfaction may appear, it has recently come under attack. As they tally results of the customer satisfaction programs instituted in the last few years, a growing number of companies are discovering—much to their surprise and dismay—that improved satisfaction scores don't necessarily translate to increased profitability.

No one would argue that customer satisfaction is unimportant. But it's become increasingly clear that measuring it in

From *Marketing Tools*, May 1996, pp. 52-58. © 1996 by American Demographics, Inc. Reprinted by permission.

Keep THEm coming BACK

by Michael W. Lowenstein

Measurements and information systems for optimizing customer loyalty and value

n 1994, the Juran Institute, a leading total quality consulting organization, presented results of a study among top managers from more than 200 of America's largest companies. While over 90 percent had an ongoing process for measuring and improving customer satisfaction scores, only 2 percent were able to show increases in sales or profit resulting from documented increases in customer satisfaction. Meanwhile, management consulting firm Bain & Company has found that between 65 percent and 85 percent of defected customers said they were "satisfied" or "very satisfied" with their previous suppliers.

Results like these indicate a tenuous correlation between customer satisfaction, perceived overall performance, and customer loyalty; or between customer satisfaction and financial performance.

That's why more and more organizations are redirecting their efforts toward optimizing customer loyalty and value. Such a move is consistent with trends in Total Quality Management. Customer-based reorganization and customer value models both derive from focusing all company processes on customers. Integrated marketing, aftermarketing, and the melding of sales, marketing, and customer service operations into "customer support" also depend on a corporate commitment to maximum customer loyalty and value. Customer satisfaction, as a concept, is benign and passive. Customer retention is proactive. Just as generating customer loyalty requires new cultural, relationship, and value-creation approaches to succeed, retention measurement and information systems must be similarly innovative.

In measuring retention, it must first be realized that there are five stages to a customer's 'life' with any supplier:

1) **Acquisition** (procuring a customer)
2) **Retention** (keeping that customer/optimizing loyalty and value)
3) **Attrition** (a breakdown in the customer's loyalty)
4) **Defection** (the effective or total loss of a customer)
5) **Reacquisition** (getting the customer back)

Perhaps the most important stage is Attrition. Once the reasons for loyalty breakdown are uncovered and understood, they often become the Rosetta Stone for getting, keeping, or reacquiring customers.

The overriding goals of customer retention measurement are:
• to identify those performance attributes and expectations that positively and

(Continued)

light of business results means considering it as part of a complex equation. A company's satisfaction score is "X," and while "X" may have improved substantially by dint of focused attention, factors "A" through "Z" affect the outcome as well. Companies that concentrate their efforts on the former to the point of neglecting the latter are likely to be disappointed.

Satisfaction Doesn't Satisfy

The evidence is that this is already happening. "I think more and more companies are questioning the satisfaction paradigm," says Jill Griffin, president of the Market Resources Center in Austin, Texas, and author of *Customer Loyalty: How to Earn It, How to Keep It.* "More and more senior executives are saying, 'Hey, where is my bottom-line, positive change?' and that has certainly created suspicion."

Business executives aren't the only ones questioning the customer satisfaction model. The sporadic success of attempts to tie customer satisfaction to bottom-line business improvements has caused a growing number of iconoclastic critics to abandon the model entirely, and has created an enormous rift in the ranks of marketing researchers.

The critics have their work cut out for them. Customer satisfaction research accounts for more than one-third of the revenues generated by the leading U.S. research companies, according to Roland T. Rust, a professor of marketing at Vanderbilt University's Owen Graduate School of Management in Nashville, Tennessee. Prestigious honors, such as the Malcolm Baldrige National Quality Award, have made customer satisfaction a major criterion for consideration. Huge amounts of time and money have been invested in customer satisfaction research by companies that assumed their investments would pay off in manifold gains in sales and profitability.

As more and more research results trickle in, however, executives and the consultants catering to them are discovering that the correlation between satisfaction and sales isn't always a direct one. Financial problems at companies noted for their high customer satisfaction scores have cast an even darker pall over the model. In 1990, for example, the General Accounting Office issued a report on 20 companies that had scored well in the 1988 and 1989 Baldrige competition. Among the key findings: While responding executives said customer satisfaction levels had increased, customer retention remained almost unchanged.

negatively impact customer loyalty; and
• to isolate problem and (unexpressed) complaint areas that may be contributing to attrition and defection among current customers.

In addition, retention research should include internal customers—the front-line sales, service, and other support staff who have the most customer contact—and former customers, those who have already defected. Incorporating the views of internal and former customers, much like seeking out unexpressed complaints, is an excellent (and often untapped) source of performance insight. Performance information on competitive suppliers should be obtained whenever possible and advisable.

When companies have asked internal, current, former (and competitive) customers for an evaluation of their performance (and performance of other suppliers), they will be able to assess the degree of leverage or vulnerability that exists. New analytical tools and aids, such as graphic depiction of "relationship" data and modeling techniques, will be required

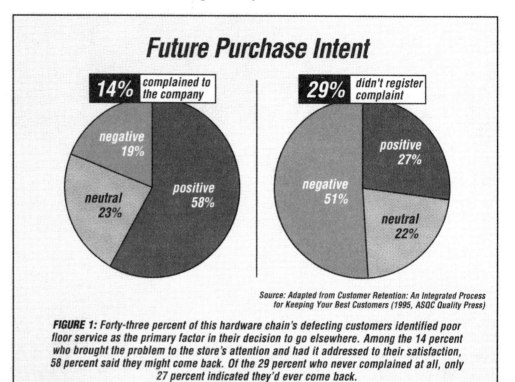

Future Purchase Intent

14% complained to the company

negative 19%
neutral 23%
positive 58%

29% didn't register complaint

positive 27%
negative 51%
neutral 22%

Source: Adapted from Customer Retention: An Integrated Process for Keeping Your Best Customers (1995, ASQC Quality Press)

FIGURE 1: Forty-three percent of this hardware chain's defecting customers identified poor floor service as the primary factor in their decision to go elsewhere. Among the 14 percent who brought the problem to the store's attention and had it addressed to their satisfaction, 58 percent said they might come back. Of the 29 percent who never complained at all, only 27 percent indicated they'd ever come back.

to better interpret the connection between performance and customer loyalty findings. These tools will provide the critical direction as to what performance areas should be prioritized for improvement (and to what degree). Strategically, this impacts allocation of scarce time, money, staff, facilities, and technology—the components of

marketing and business process—for greatest effect.

Looking at specific tools, the display of relationship data, i.e., complaints, competitive information, and customer verbatims/anecdotes, can provide insights on important, but less frequently generated, customer information.

For example, a retail discount hardware

chain relied on in-store customer service desks to identify and monitor complaints. This approach, though highly inefficient, didn't show real weakness until a more customer-driven competitor entered the marketplace. The competitor had upgraded store interiors, better product selection, and superior in-store service. Almost overnight, the chain experienced a

Some companies even reported declines in customer retention. According to Michael Lowenstein, managing director of Customer Retention Associates, companies such as Florida Power and Light, the only U.S. company ever to win Japan's Deming Prize, eventually backed away from their quality efforts because they did not show bottom-line results.

Rust observes that two of every three corporate quality improvement programs are abandoned after two years due to poor financial results. Defections like these, and the perennial problem of measuring the effect of customer satisfaction on sales, have caused widespread disillusionment, according to Christopher Fay, a principal with the Parthenon Group, a management strategy consulting firm.

"It's certainly become frustrating to executives, because businesses need a quantifiable metric that is tied to actual business results," Lowenstein remarks.

The results of customer surveys have done little to restore faith in the model. For example, a study at the University of Texas found that in most surveys of customer satisfaction, 85 percent of customers claim to be satisfied, but still demonstrate a willingness to switch suppliers.

Sensing and sharing in their clients' frustration, some researchers have modified the satisfaction model. Others have scrapped it entirely in favor of models that emphasize "customer loyalty" and "customer retention." While the difference between the approaches isn't always clear, it has sparked an acrid debate among researchers.

"The reason for the stickiness or the intransigence is there has been an investment of money, time and emotion in a technology," says Fay. That investment makes it expensive and even a little embarrassing for researchers to change their course.

Keeping 'Em Happy vs. Keeping Them

While managers may be emphatically uninterested in the schism dividing the research industry, it is their demand for measurable results that has sparked the debate. Unable to point to parallel growth in satisfaction and sales in all cases, a handful of consultants have turned to the customer loyalty model.

The difference? Customer satisfaction is an attitude. Customer loyalty is a purchase behavior, explains Griffin. In terms of sales results, therefore, customer satisfaction is relevant only to the degree at which it increases customer loyalty.

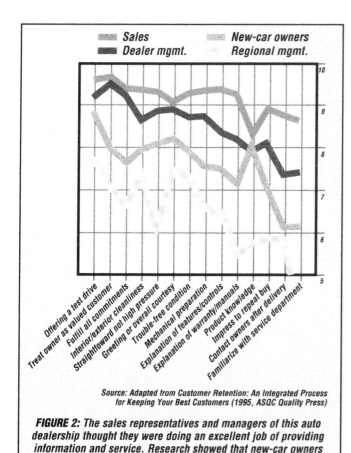

Legend: ▨ Sales ▨ New-car owners ▨ Dealer mgmt. ▨ Regional mgmt.

X-axis labels:
Offering a test drive
Treat owner as valued customer
Fulfill all commitments
Interior/exterior cleanliness
Straightforward not high pressure
Greeting or overall courtesy
Trouble-free condition
Mechanical preparation
Explanation of features/controls
Explanation of warranty/manuals
Product knowledge
Impress to repeat buy
Contact owners after delivery
Familiarize with service department

Source: Adapted from Customer Retention: An Integrated Process for Keeping Your Best Customers (1995, ASQC Quality Press)

FIGURE 2: *The sales representatives and managers of this auto dealership thought they were doing an excellent job of providing information and service. Research showed that new-car owners did not agree—and that regional company management had an even lower opinion of staff performance.*

dramatic loss of customers, and their antiquated, reactive complaint process was a key culprit. The chain was forced to immediately revamp their customer research program, a principal thrust of which became the proactive solicitation of problems and complaints.

What they found (Figure 1) was that among the customers who had defected to other stores, 43 percent identified poor floor service as the primary factor in their decision to go elsewhere. Only 14 percent brought this deficiency to the store's attention and had the problem addressed to their satisfaction. A little over half of this group (58 percent) said they might come back. But 29 percent never complained at all; they simply left, and only 27 percent of that group indicated they'd ever come back. Floor service time was a major issue among the remaining customers as well. It was clearly a complaint area requiring improvement by the chain.

Another valuable aspect of relationship data is looking at the degree of alignment or gap between the actual perceptions of customers and what staff, and others, think customers will say about performance.

The sales representatives and owners/managers of an auto dealership thought they were doing an excellent job of providing information and service to new-car owners. Research showed that dealership staff was clearly out of touch with their customers, especially in performance attributes directly related to attrition and defection (Figure 2). Regional company management's perception of dealership performance was actually more negative than the new car owners'.

When perceptual gaps are identified and understood, they can often provide the basis for staff training programs, or culture, operations, and communication improvement.

Finally, models of performance and leverage will offer the critical direction as to which performance attributes should be improved.

In the Leverage Window model, an industrial products company can isolate the potential loyalty impact of an attribute like "Proximity of Shipping Points." Most of its customers are located some distance from its plants. The Leverage Window uses simple regression, or correlation analysis (Figure 3), to show that the degree of distance could be causing attrition and defection. Competitors have plants closer to customers, causing a negative motivational effect on the perception of value.

(Continued)

"In customer satisfaction research you may end up with a 3.7 on a 5-point scale," says Fay. "What's that worth? It's unclear. But if I can say, 'this customer used to do $20 of business with us a week and now she only does $11,' then I can quantify things in a meaningful way" and measure the cost of the disloyalty.

By studying a defecting customer's behavior a company can determine what makes her act. That, according to loyalty proponents, may not necessarily be the same thing as asking her what she prefers.

"The question is not so much, 'Are my customers happy?' The real question is, 'Are my customers returning?'" Griffin asserts. "There is a world of difference between those two questions. Who cares if they're happy if they're not coming back?"

Consultants like Griffin and Lowenstein argue that by focusing on purchase behavior—such as recency, frequency, and the amount of money customers spend—they're taking the customer satisfaction model to a new level. They're not as interested in what customers say as in what customers do; and in learning to anticipate what they will do. Their model begins one step further down the line, at substantive ways that satisfaction impacts sales. And they argue that satisfaction is a meaningless ex-

ercise unless it causes customers to buy more frequently, or in larger quantities, or leads them to recommend a supplier to others. Even then, it's the purchase behaviors that produce the measurable results companies are after.

"Satisfaction is just too easy," declares Customer Retention's Lowenstein. "People have stopped caring about direct or implied warranties and money-back guarantees. They just don't care any more."

While others dismiss the difference between "customer satisfaction" and "customer loyalty" or "customer retention" as a matter of semantics, Lowenstein insists the two depend on fundamentally different mind sets. Companies can deliver top quality products and excellent service at a competitive price "and still be hemorrhaging customers," he argues, "because satisfaction does not assure you customer loyalty and lifetime value."

While customer satisfaction demonstrates management's ability to react, customer loyalty is driven by proactive behavior, Lowenstein explains. Management needs to understand its customers so well that it can anticipate changes they would like to see made. Companies must do more than meet expectations; they need to invent new ways of pleasing customers that will

In addition to new analytical tools, customer information databases are taking on far greater value and importance, supporting service, targeted marketing and promotional programs, and product/service development. At every point where the company touches the customer—even delivery and billing—input can be gathered and used to enhance loyalty.

Databases can include purchase histories of current and former customers; service records; sales call reports; inquiries and complaints (registered and proactively generated); lost customer reports; warranty and guarantee information. If the company is among the more customer-driven, the database might also have company/customer advisory council and cross-functional project team information. Of course, customer research information will be prominent in the database. There are many more examples, but these are among the most basic.

Although the development and maintenance of customer research and information databases may be the direct

(1) On-time product delivery
(2) Salesperson support/need anticipation
(3) Customer service/responsiveness
(4) Products true to specifications
(5) Price
(6) Product quality/defect rate
(7) Proximity of shipping points
(8) Product modification flexibility
(9) Product development leadership
(10) Product performance
(11) Billing/invoicing services
(12) Delivery flexibility

Source: Adapted from Customer Retention: An Integrated Process for Keeping Your Best Customers (1995, ASQC Quality Press)

FIGURE 3: Using this model, an industrial products company can isolate the potential loyalty impact of an attribute like "Proximity of Shipping Points" (7). The Leverage Window uses simple regression, or correlation analysis, to show that the degree of distance could be causing attrition and defection.

responsibility of marketing, information systems, or customer service, they should be broadly supported and utilized and made available to all. Otherwise, a customer database becomes a case study of the law of entropy: with disuse and disinterest, it soon becomes obsolete.

The bottom line for the leading-edge approaches to measurement and information systems presented here is that they reflect a company's total commitment to creating a culture and infrastructure for optimum customer loyalty and value. They are the cornerstones of customer retention.

Michael W. Lowenstein is managing director of Customer Retention Associates, a consulting organization specializing in customer retention research, corporate customer retention culture and systems evaluation, and customer loyalty action training for front-line staff and management. The address is 6920 Marshall Road, Upper Darby, PA 19082; telephone (610) 394-6450.

transform them from satisfied and fickle to delighted and loyal.

Lowenstein cites MBNA, a Newark, Delaware bank and major credit-card issuer, as an example of a company that understands the importance of customer loyalty.

"Their credo is: success is getting the right customers and keeping them," says Lowenstein, "and they don't do it by satisfaction." At MBNA, executives at the vice president level and above spend four hours or more a month making or monitoring calls to customers so they can understand what motivates their customers and better anticipate their needs.

Ikea, an East Coast furniture and housewares retailer, is another example of a company using a proactive customer loyalty program to anticipate its customer needs, he says.

"They give you a pen, a pad, and a tape measure," Lowenstein says. "They'll even lend you a car rack or let you put the kids in day care while you're in the store. It's all designed to keep you there and bring you back."

Defending the Faith

Proponents of customer satisfaction say researchers who don't find a correlation between satisfaction and sales shouldn't give

up the model. They should give up the business.

"If customer satisfaction is not reflected in your bottom line, you're doing it wrong," avers Sheila Kessler, president of Competitive Edge and author of Measuring and Managing Customer Satisfaction: Going for the Gold.

Kessler's advice: If you're going to do customer satisfaction research "do it right or don't do it at all, because you'll tick someone off. Customer satisfaction and profitability are directly linked, but if you don't focus on relating the two, your financials can slip off the cliff."

Companies that increase satisfaction scores without increasing sales and loyalty are making one of three basic errors, she says. They are concentrating on the wrong customers, asking the wrong questions, or asking the right questions in the wrong way. The most common mistake is trying to please everyone, rather than catering primarily to the handful of clients who produce the bulk of their sales, according to Kessler. "The key to customer satisfaction is not to focus on everybody," she explains. "You don't focus on the bottom feeders." Other common mistakes include using a bad sampling process and collecting so much data that it becomes impossible to synthesize, Kessler adds.

"One of the major faults that companies have is they only focus on things that are important to *them*," she argues. "They never ask the customers what's important, so they're tracking the wrong things." That's a fundamental error, says Kessler, because "there's only about a 40 percent overlap between what management says is important to customers and what customers say is important."

Finding out what's important to customers is the cornerstone of the satisfaction program at Prism Radio Partners, one of Kessler's clients. Marci Joyce, director of research for the Tucson, Arizona-based owner of 16 radio stations, concedes that the one-year-old research program is intended to improve sales for both the radio station and its advertisers. But she bristles at the term "customer loyalty."

"Loyalty to me is more of a numbers kind of word: how many people like you and how many don't, and how can we manipulate them into staying," she says. While Joyce acknowledges that she's as interested in keeping her clients and winning back lost ones as anyone, she considers loyalty a natural byproduct of the satisfaction process, not necessarily the ultimate goal.

"I look at retention as a report card," Joyce adds, because retention shows how clients receive the company's efforts. So far, Prism has been getting high marks: for the first six months of last year the company increased its revenues by $200,000 by regaining lost clients.

Although revenues increased in all Prism's markets last year, Joyce admits it would be hard to determine what percentage of that was due to satisfying customers, as compared to other market forces. "But that doesn't bother me," she said. "I'm more interested in (overall) revenue growth for the whole company."

Revolution or Evolution?

While the two sides debate the merits of customer satisfaction versus customer loyalty, the majority of marketing researchers have staked a position squarely in the middle. For them, the debate is a matter of semantics.

Of course, customer satisfaction is not an end in itself, they say. The goal of improving satisfaction has always been to improve sales by driving repeat business. Therefore, the industry has always been interested in customer loyalty. By the same token, an inability to find a correlation between satisfaction and sales is not necessarily an indication of faulty research but of failure to consider other market factors that could be affecting sales, such as inflation, regulation, and what the competition is doing.

"We're really all saying the same thing," remarks Randy Brandt, vice president and director of consulting for Burke CSA. "Nobody ever said, 'It's customer satisfaction, and all this other stuff doesn't matter.'"

In truth, loyalty and profitability will determine the marketing research industry's future direction and survival.

"More companies are demanding that the connection between satisfaction and profitability be made," says Brandt. "The years 1985 to 1995 were the decade in which the emphasis was on customer satisfaction. The next ten years will represent the decade in which the future of customer satisfaction will either be ensured, or when customer satisfaction will pass away as a fad, depending on whether or not people tie it to business results."

Even if customer satisfaction—in its original or modified form—can be consistently tied to business results, market researchers agree on one thing: it's merely a directional tool. Satisfying customers is only part of what a company must do. Failing to pay attention to every aspect of a business—from management information systems to research and development—will lead to disaster, no matter how happy the customers say they are.

"Customer loyalty is not a panacea for businesses," says Fay. "There is no silver bullet, and there never will be."

Shelly Reese is a freelance writer based in Cincinnati.

Recommended reading:

Michael W. Lowenstein, *Customer Retention: An Integrated Process for Keeping Your Best Customers*, 1995, Quality Press. For more information, call (800) 248-1946.

Jill Griffin, *Customer Loyalty: How to Earn It, How to Keep It*, 1995, Lexington Books

Sheila Kessler, *Measuring and Managing Customer Satisfaction: Going for the Gold*, 1996, Competitive Edge. For more information, call (714) 962-9921.

Contacts:

Jill Griffin
The Marketing Resource Center
Austin, TX
(512) 469-1757

Michael Lowenstein
Customer Retention Associates
Upper Darby, PA
(610) 392-6450

Sheila Kessler
Competitive Edge
Fountain Valley, CA
(714) 962-9921

D. Randall Brandt
Burke Customer Satisfaction
Associates
Cincinnati, OH
(513) 684-7505

Roland Rust
Owen Graduate School of
Management
Vanderbilt University
(615) 322-2534

Christopher Fay
The Parthenon Group
Boston, MA
(800) 927-0225

**American Society for Quality
Control**
Milwaukee, WI
(414) 272-8575

How to keep your customers

Business owners who overlook the needs of their regular clients in favor of developing prospects may soon discover a long list of inactive accounts

Ted J. Rakstis

ome business-scene observers call it "aftermarketing." Others refer to the processes involved in customer retention as "relationship marketing," "data base marketing," "one-on-one marketing," "bonding," "individualized marketing," "micromarketing," "frequency marketing," "dialogue marketing," "interactive marketing," and other variations on the same selling theme.

W hatever name you use, the objective is identical: keeping your existing customers. And there's a second goal: recovering business that your competitors now control.

Terry G. Vavra, author of *Aftermarketing*, cites a common scenario: "As an organization focuses on conquering new customers, present customers often are overlooked. Their continued patronage

or participation is assumed. Their value to the enterprise is forgotten. The organization fails to maintain them. And when current customers take their business elsewhere, their defection often is dismissed by the rationale that 'you can't please everybody.'"

Adrienne Zoble, president of a marketing and sales-promotion firm in Somerville, New Jersey, pinpoints the exact cost of failing to please current customers. In her training sessions, she mentions the "100/15 Rule."

"I begin by explaining that whatever it costs to bring in a new client or customer—whether it's $35 or $350—is called the 100 percent marketing expense," Zoble says. "Then I ask, 'What percentage of this overall 100 percent do you think it costs to sell something to an existing client?' The answer is 15 percent."

Vavra lists seven aftermarketing basics: Develop customer-information files; thank your customers for their trade; map all the points at which people in your organization come into contact with those who buy from you; provide your customers with easy access to your products or services; measure their satisfaction; stay in contact with them; and try to reclaim lost customers.

The information file should be part of a data base that tracks all customers' purchases in terms of frequency, category, and price. Instead of going for quick sales, the data is designed to build long-term relationships.

Beyond the mailing of promotional materials for upcoming sales, customer communication also is widely neglected. Vavra suggests these effective vehicles: newsletters, toll-free telephone lines, surveys, and focus groups.

As the focus-group technique originally was conceived, outside market researchers got together with a group of existing or prospective customers. They solicited their opinions, paid them, analyzed the results, and reported to their corporate client.

Today, a more company-oriented type of setting has emerged. In a Training magazine article, consultants Barry J. Farber and Joyce Wycoff elaborate: "These customer meetings are generally planned and conducted by the host company. The firm chooses customers who are willing to work with the company and able to give informed opinions. Though the customers often are given tokens of appreciation, they aren't paid to participate. In addition, the company does its own evaluation and follow-up."

The value of this focus-group style is that it directly involves front-line workers who deal with customers every day. Instead of being only names on billings, buyers suddenly have faces and voices.

When people decide to shop elsewhere, a mere handful inform companies of their decision. But Technical Assistance Research Programs in Washington, DC, calculates that 91 percent tell at least nine others about their dissatisfaction.

You no longer can rely on your instincts to determine how customers feel about your enterprise. What you need are a data base, survey findings, and other hard facts. If you can put it in writing, do so—and do it now.

Some wise entrepreneurs write down everything they think customers expect. That's a good idea, but Philip B. Crosby, founder of the "zero-defects" quality movement, has a far more unusual concept.

"I prefer to ask my clients to consider each item in terms of how to make certain that customers *did not* receive what they wanted," Crosby says. "This lets us learn how to prevent problems by seeing what's necessary to create them."

As one example, imagine that you own a hotel. How can you treat your patrons so badly that they'll vow never to return?

The process begins at the reservation level. Never send a confirmation in writing. That gives guests no assurance that a room will be waiting for them. And clutter your roadside billboards with so many slogans that the name of

the hotel is obscured. Motorists will miss the exit and be forced to turn around. In addition, always have a hotel van parked in front of the main entry doors and don't offer to help your patrons unload their luggage until they've already done so themselves.

When your visitors finally locate the unmarked registration desk, the clerk should be tied up in a long, personal telephone conversation. As the check-in at last takes place, quote a much higher price than was promised when the reservation was made. And oh yes, wave your guests in the general direction of the elevators, and give them a plastic electronic key that won't work.

"The idea of having an opportunity to establish the vital ways of making absolutely certain that customers don't receive what has been promised will bring forth your employees' creativity," Crosby says. "They'll look at the company in an entirely different way and from a very different point of view. They'll redesign the system to suit customers' needs. By using such a negative list, you can establish positive procedures that will please your customers."

The management of Marriott Corporation may have used such guidelines in 1990 when it formed a team to upgrade quality standards. Marriott long has been regarded as one of the premier customer-service hotel chains. But Les Cappetta, director of service development, points out: "Even though you've been successful, you still have to focus on the future and where the business is headed."

The hotel chain's quality-improvement team brought together people from human resources, marketing, food and beverage service, operations, and engineering. Their mission was to redefine the meaning of good customer service.

Hotel patrons were asked what they consider most essential. The survey respondents revealed that five key factors influence their return trade: cleanliness, breakfast, friendliness of personnel, value, and check-in speed.

Industry Week magazine reports: "The team measured front-desk activity and found that 75 percent of a desk clerk's time was involved in chores not related to check-in and check-out. These jobs included providing services to and answering questions from other guests, opening and closing a shift, resolving problems with reservations over the phone, and simply waiting."

The team also concluded that there

were far too many job classifications in a typical 400-employee Marriott Hotel—fifty-two for food and beverage workers, thirteen for office and administrative employees, and fifteen for housekeeping and laundry personnel.

A streamlining program was launched. By combining numerous work categories, employee skills were broadened and overhead was cut by 40 percent. The removal of telephones from front desks did away with check-in and check-out interruptions. And a single "guest-service associate" now does the work of a valet, doorman, bellman, front-desk employee, and concierge.

According to Cappetta, 98 percent of all Marriott check-ins today take less than two minutes. Guests also rate the hospitality staff's attitude as much improved.

Industry Week sums up the results: "There has been less job turnover; the newly created profile for new hires has increased the quality of job performance; and cross-training (teaching diverse work tasks) has improved understanding among workers."

candinavian Airlines System (SAS) also learned that certain employee-customer interactions are critical. In his book *Moments of Truth*, SAS president Jan Carlzon noted that the 10 million travelers served by SAS each year come into contact with an average of five SAS employees on every flight.

Because each contact lasts approximately fifteen seconds, Carlzon concluded: "SAS is 'created' 50 million times a year, fifteen seconds at a time. These 50 million 'moments of truth' are the moments that ultimately determine whether SAS will succeed or fail as a company. They are the moments when we must prove to our customers that SAS is their best alternative."

When Carlzon's book was published in 1987, SAS was in the midst of a financial turnaround. The airline had been losing about $8 million a year. By concentrating on those "moments of truth," SAS soon had annual earnings of $71 million.

Hotels and airlines win or lose because of their hospitality—or the absence of it. Home Depot, described by Fortune magazine as "a retail Disneyland for residential fixer-uppers," has become one of the most profitable chains in the United States through a store-sales adaptation of that same service-oriented approach.

Based in Atlanta, Georgia, Home Depot has more than 360 units in thirty US states and seventeen in the Canadian provinces of Alberta, Ontario, and British Columbia. They're all driven by repeat business.

Fortune reports that the average Home Depot customer spends only $38 per visit but comes to the store about thirty times a year. During the shopper's lifetime, he or she will spend some $25,000.

The magazine analyzes the Home Depot success formula: "It spends only on what directly benefits customers. The value ethic permeates the culture and is understood by customers. They shop in concrete-floored, warehouse-style outlets with the ambiance of airplane hangars, but the prices they pay are 20 to 30 percent below those of old-style hardware stores and guaranteed to be the best in town.

"(The company) encourages employees to build long-term relationships with customers. Workers are trained in home-repair techniques and can spend as much time as it takes to educate shoppers. There are no high-pressure sales tactics. Employees are on a straight salary.

"(Home Depot) pays its people as partners. To satisfy customers consistently, you must have a committed work force. Every salesperson's bright-orange apron reads, 'Hi, I'm (name), a Home Depot stockholder. Let me help you.' Instead of receiving discounts on merchandise, workers get shares in the company."

CEO Bernard Marcus asserts that Home Depot won't pay commissions to its employees until "the day that I'm laid out dead with an apple in my mouth." Retail chains that function under a commission system, he contends, are telling small customers that they have no worth.

And, Marcus adds: "I love it when shoppers tell me they were prepared to spend $150 and our people have shown them how to do the job for four or five bucks."

Marriott, SAS, and Home Depot aren't typical big businesses. They view their bottom lines not in terms of this year's payoff but in contemplation of decades-long relationships with con-

sumers. This is the most effective type of marketing, and some visionary small companies are prospering through similar practices.

David Steitz, CEO of Characters Inc., a graphics company in Houston, Texas, writes in Nation's Business magazine about his expansion from typesetting to desktop publishing. His firm has ninety-five employees and annual sales in excess of $7 million.

"We had no formal approach to seeking and analyzing customer input until recently," Steitz says. "Instead, we relied on the strong relationships between our salespeople and clients, something that is still critical. Lately, however, we also have sought to gain customer input in more direct and systematic ways."

Steitz brought in current and potential customers for focus-group meetings to learn their plans for new systems and advanced technology. In addition, he sent out twice-a-year surveys to obtain feedback on their interest in desktop publishing. This was followed by a blind survey of existing customers. The customers weren't told that Characters was the survey sponsor.

The information that was compiled prompted Steitz to invest $2 million in desktop-publishing equipment and form a sister company called Characters/Color Digital Imaging Inc. A customer provided the slogan: "Color printing on a black-and-white budget."

"Attention to customers has pointed us in other new directions," Steitz says. "At the suggestion of advertising firms that used our services, we approached their clients about services the ad firms weren't providing, such as catalogs, sales sheets, presentation graphics, newsletters, and technical manuals."

Michael J. Stineman, president of Citation Homes, a custom-home manufacturer in Spring Lake, Iowa, went beyond the focus-group concept and formed an advisory council comprised of seven builders. Each represents a different housing market and geographic location. To gain fresh insights, Stineman appoints council members to serve staggered, three-year terms.

Your Company magazine reports: "Once a year, council members are invited to Citation's headquarters for a weekend meeting. Builders arrive Friday night with their families and are treated to a dinner in their honor. On Saturday morning, they sit down to a five-hour session, which includes the

discussion of new products and how Citation is performing in the marketplace.

"Stineman says the meeting always yields information on improving the construction process and how to help builders sell more of their homes. How does he know it works? Citation retains 90 percent of its customers on an annual basis."

Jill Griffin, author of *Customer Loyalty: How to Earn It, How to Keep It*, says customer referrals and a reputation for trust and reliability are responsible for the success of Barry Steinberg. He's the president of Direct Tire, a large auto-repair shop in Watertown, Massachusetts.

Direct Tire sells service rather than price, the author explains. Repeat customers account for approximately 75 percent of Steinberg's business, and his profit margin is about double the industry average.

What's his secret? Steinberg's appreciation of the value of his customers' time is a principal factor. He schedules appointments based on their convenience and has seven loaner cars they can use while their vehicles are in the shop.

"Before I had the loaners," Steinberg says, "I was doing $50,000 to $55,000 a month in service work. Today, I'm averaging $120,000 a month, and the gross margins on service work are 30 percent higher than on tires. I'm going to add more loaners."

When customers stay with you from one generation to the next, you can be confident that you've licked the business-retention problem. The (US) National Retail Merchants Association reports, however, that the typical company loses 20 percent of its customers each year.

Can you honestly claim that you've never lost trade to a competitor? Begin recovery by writing down the names of each departed customer and the amount that he or she spent with you in an average year.

Curtis Universal Joint, a fifty-employee company in Springfield, Massachusetts, makes industrial parts and has annual sales of about $3 million. Your Company magazine relates the strategy that president Rick Hartmann used to reclaim former customers.

In 1994, Hartmann directed his staff to identify accounts that had been inac-

Rate your customer-pleasing power

How can you turn occasional customers into steady ones? Begin by evaluating what you're already doing. The following test is based on material in Richard F. Gerson's book, *Beyond Customer Service*. Answer "true" or "false":

• We have a unique service philosophy and mission statement that bolster our overall sales effort.

• We secure feedback through surveys, focus groups, and personal interviews.

• When feedback turns up new "how to keep them" ideas, we implement them as soon as possible.

• Our customer-service/retention programs are powerful marketing tools.

• We call customers to thank them and send them holiday cards.

• We use newsletters and fliers to promote new products and services.

• Our customers frequently congratulate us for consistently knowing and meeting their needs.

• We work hard to build customer loyalty.

• Our programs give us a customer base that generates steady repeat trade.

• We have a reward program that includes frequent-buyer and referral incentives.

• We've created an identity that causes people to want to buy from us.

• We're active in Kiwanis and other civic endeavors and use our involvement to further polish our image.

• If we don't have in stock what a customer wants, we immediately obtain it.

• Everyone on our sales team has been trained to deliver quality service.

Each of these practices is a vital part of a quality-centered customer-retention program. When you can turn each "false" answer into a "true" response, you'll be on your way.

tive for the previous three years. The focus was placed on those that once spent $3,000 or more a year with the company. Seventy-two firms fit that profile. Contacted by telephone, their senior managers told of numerous reasons for their departures. The most startling discovery was the fact that 45 percent left because Curtis salespeople stopped going after their business.

The company's telemarketing staff made return calls to the likeliest prospects and restored 18 percent of the defectors to active-buying status. As a result, Curtis pulled in an extra $80,000 in orders during the next six months. Hartmann looks back: "It was a real wake-up call for us. Now, we're much more diligent about keeping in touch."

Your customers represent far more than a source of direct income. By calling them occasionally for advice and resisting the temptation to tie in a sales pitch, you can tap their knowledge. They'll help you to devise preventive measures that will limit your losses.

Joan Koob Cannie, author of *Turning Lost Customers Into Gold*, offers her perspective: "If you ask them, loyal customers will tell you about problems you may not know about. And, you can act on them *before* you lose customers."

Leader of the
PACK

One way for a small company to grow in a cutthroat market is to pick one of the countless competitive strategies available and ride it for everything it's worth. Another way is to pick them all

D O N N A   F E N N

CHRIS ZANE'S COMPETITORS DON'T like him much.

Though his business is still small ($1.2 million in 1995 sales), 30-year-old Zane is already the largest independent bicycle dealer in the New Haven, Conn., market. He's confident. ("Let Wal-Mart come—I'm ready," he boasts.) He's combative. ("I'll put you out of business," he's said to other dealers.) And, most important, he'll do almost anything to attract and keep customers. ("I'll give you lifetime service, guarantee you the lowest price, fix you a cappuccino.")

He'd better. Like similar retail businesses all over America, Zane's Cycles is under siege. Superstores and chains have taken over, leaving specialty bike retailers with only one out of every four sales; in Zane's market, three independent bike shops went out of business last year alone. "The smaller guys are fading away because they won't get into the game and compete at a higher level," says Craig Seeger, a

Trek sales representative serving Zane's.

Far from fading, however, Zane has *gained* market share—growing his business 25% a year by putting into practice every customer-winning tactic he can think up, adapt, or steal. He has read the management tomes, sought out gurus, picked his suppliers' brains, conducted focus groups, and studied customer behavior in his own store and elsewhere. He aims, he says, not to sell to customers but to *own* them.

To be sure, Zane's kitchen-sink-included competitive strategy can appear scattershot. His story contains half a dozen fashionable management ideas: continual learning, the lifetime value of a customer, guerrilla marketing, bootstrapping, community-relations marketing, cost-controlled customer service. And his success begs a handful of questions: How did Zane's Cycles, an ordinary business in an extraordinarily competitive industry, create a service

standard that has become his market's price of entry? How has it become the region's most visible bike shop? How has it turned intimacy and ingenuity into competitive advantages that not even the hyper-professionalized chains can match?

But what Zane's story is really all about, what binds those ideas and questions together, is a mentality that Zane insists no business—even the smallest—can do without. Call it nonstop, no-limits, no-scheme-is-too-small competitiveness.

Even better, Chris Zane would tell you, call it fun.

ZANE LAUNCHED HIS FIRST SERIOUS assault on his competitors 10 years ago, by offering one-year service guarantees (covering parts and labor on all routine service) when everyone else was promising 30 days.

"It took them two years to realize we were taking market share away from them, and then when they started offering a year, we offered two," recalls Zane. In 1986 he learned at a Manhattan trade show that some dealers were offering five-year service guarantees. "I figured that for most people, five years is the life of the bike," says Zane. "If they've had it for longer, they're probably not riding it that much, so your liability on service would not be that great." Why not, he mulled, offer lifetime free service?

"The core of my comfort is percentages. Everyone uses the free service the first year they have the bike, but I saw only 20% to 30% come back the second year. I figured my liability for lifetime free service would be minuscule." So in 1987 Zane raised the bar to the last notch, announcing free lifetime service on all bikes and making the offer retroactive. "We wanted to make our existing customers our apostles," he says.

His competitors balked. "Free service for as long as you own the bike is ludicrous," says John Budd, general manager of Action Sports. "But we've matched Zane tooth and nail." His shop now offers lifetime free service, as do most other bike retailers in Zane's market. Many feel they have no choice, and they're resentful that Zane has forced their hands. One dealer called him last year with a proposition: "I'll drop the lifetime service guarantee if you will." Zane just laughed. He had come to regard the guarantee as the foundation of his business and had extended it to everything he sold. "A guy once came in with a six-year-old pump that had worn out," recalls Zane. "I just gave him a new one."

Why? Because of Zane's bet on what that customer's lifetime of business would be worth to his store. "The guy had spent $60 on the best pump you can buy," he says. "So he's a premium purchaser, and here I have a chance to have him fall in love with us." Because Zane had a good relationship with the manufacturer, he knew he could send the broken pump back and get credit, no questions asked—so the cost of the return was zero. The potential payoff, however, was big enough that even if Zane had been forced to absorb the cost of the pump (about $30), it still would have made economic sense for him to take it back.

Consider this: "The guy has been in twice since then," says Zane. "He's probably spent $200 on accessories [a $100 net to Zane]." And when it's time for a new bike, Zane's betting that he'll get first shot at the sale. At an average cost of $400 for a bike, with a 35% margin, he stands to make another $140. And let's not forget the intangibles. A customer who is, well, thrifty enough to have a pump repaired is likely to be so impressed with getting something for nothing that he'll spread the word. "I'll bet he's told everyone about it," surmises Zane. "Everyone" probably being other serious and heavy-spending biking enthusiasts like the pump purchaser himself. In other words, Zane's ideal prospects.

So, the total invested: $30 (assuming Zane hadn't been able to get a manufacturer's refund). Total to the bottom line: $240, *plus* the profit from referral business. The result: a minimum 700% return on investment.

CHRIS ZANE'S CONTINUAL BUSINESS EDUcation had started long before he could imagine computing the lifetime value of a customer—and it always focused on service. "If you give good service, you'll stay in business," one of his first mentors told him. "If you don't, you won't."

"Thanks, Mom," said Chris to Patricia Zane.

That was when Chris Zane was a teenager, and his company-building career was already under way. It had started in a garage when he was 12 years old and fixing bikes for his middle-class East Haven neighbors. The mechanically gifted Zane learned that a kid who delivered what he promised and made his customers his first priority could make out pretty well. "If he told someone he would fix a bike, he would do it, even if something else came up," says Patricia Zane.

Friends told their parents, and parents told their friends, and Chris Zane was soon pulling in $300 to $400 a week. "I had a Connecticut state tax ID number when I was 12," he recalls. "My dad made me get it." When he turned 16, Zane thought it was "time to get a real job" and started knocking on bike shops' doors. He landed in a downtown Branford shop but was soon told by the owner that he had better start looking elsewhere—the shop was going out of business. Zane's wheels began to turn.

"I told my parents I wanted to buy the inventory and take over his lease," he recalls. Most parents would have dismissed the idea as a childish whim, but, says Zane's mother, "we knew if he was committed to something, he would follow through. He wasn't a quitter." And Patricia and John Zane were quick to recognize a negotiating opportunity. They agreed to let their son borrow $20,000 from his grandfather on three conditions: Chris would pay back the five-year loan with 15% interest; his mother would tend the shop in the morning, but Chris would come in every day after school and do his homework at night; and, most important, his parents and grandfather would hold all the stock until he completed college. "All through high school I told my parents I wasn't going to college," says Zane. "But they told me they wouldn't give me ownership until I had a degree." He agreed.

He racked up $56,000 in sales that first year and managed to increase revenues by 25% annually over the next two years, an accomplishment that gave him self-confidence—a bit too much, perhaps. When he turned 18, Zane began to think it was time he stopped doing gear adjustment and started sitting behind a desk, leaving the hands-on business of customer service to his two employees. It didn't last for long. "I started to hear from people that the store didn't have the same feel," says Zane. "Things would slide, and we saw that business was flat. Then I woke up and put all my eggs in the service basket.

"The attitude changed from 'The customer is inconveniencing you and preventing you from doing your job' to 'The customer *is* your job,'" says Zane.

OVER THE NEXT SEVERAL YEARS, HE WENT out of his way to forge relationships with customers that would tie them to him for life. Guided by gut instinct and the ability to assimilate and apply every bit of information that might be useful to his business, Zane differentiated himself in the marketplace with a number of innovative tactics. The real kicker: like the lifetime free-service guarantee, Zane's service and marketing gambits often look expensive but usually cost him very little. Some examples:

▶ **No More Nickel-and-Diming.** "We stopped charging for anything that cost less than $1," says Zane, who started that policy 10 years ago. A customer who wanted, say, a master link—an inexpensive part that holds the chain together on a child's bike—would be given one free. "The cost to me is virtually nothing," says Zane. "We're not going to chase the pennies—we're looking at the long-term effect of giving someone a master link. You should see the look on people's faces." The annual cost: less than $150.

▶ **Community-Service Marketing I.** Zane's parents raised him with the expectation that he would give something back to the community, and he has. But he's also discovered that being a good citizen pays off. In 1989 he started the Zane Foundation, which now awards five $1,000 college scholarships to Branford High School seniors. He has financed the scholarships with revenues generated by 50 candy machines, scattered throughout the Branford area. All are labeled with Zane Foundation placards. "We're doing something our competitors aren't and that the category killers aren't. If people see that we're taking care of the community, they're more likely to come to us." After an initial investment of $2,500, Zane says, the program has paid for itself.

▶ **Community-Service Marketing II.** Zane also never misses an opportunity to work with school-age kids. He's spoken to kindergarten classes about bike safety, helped the police register bikes, and, when Connecticut passed a bike-helmet law in 1992, persuaded Trek to help him offer $40 helmets to kids at cost ($20). "Indirectly, we profited because we did something for the community," says Zane. "We also got a lot of publicity, and that boosted sales." The cost of the helmet program: $0.

▶ **Playing As If You're Bigger Than You Are.** Five years ago Zane made a strategic decision to commit 25% of his then-$36,000 advertising budget to a glossy 32-page catalog filled with his merchandise, which also offered 24 generic biking tips. Though the catalog looks original, it's actually produced by a co-op company; 16 pages are customized for Zane's Cycles, while the rest might be exactly the same for another bike dealer. Zane has exclusivity with the company for New Haven and nearby Fairfield and Litchfield Counties, so there's little chance of customers' receiving a copycat in the mail. Zane says the cost—$9,000 a year—is justified by the long shelf life the catalog earns by including the tips (advice about things like how to track your heart rate or improve your off-road riding). "People will come in with things circled in the catalog several weeks after it comes out," he says. The catalog reinforces Zane's customer-service philosophy and also gives the impression that his business is much bigger

than it really is. The same goes for his 800 number (800-551-BIKE), which works nationwide but is used mostly in Connecticut, where a town 5 to 10 miles away might be a toll call. "It costs me a $24 yearly fee, plus a maximum of $200 a month for incoming calls in the summer. It's an inexpensive way to make the business look big," says Zane.

▶ **Free Cellular Phones.** In February 1993 Zane was talking to a customer who was in the cellular-phone business and learned that while distributors charged approximately $225 for a telephone, the phone company would actually pay a $250 commission for each activation. Zane called Bell Atlantic immediately, proposing that Zane's Cycles become a phone distributor. His plan was to give away a phone to anyone who bought a bike—a value added for customers that would actually earn him a net profit of $25. Bell Atlantic was less than enthusiastic, but the rep agreed to visit Zane's shop. "I showed her the catalog, and that really set us apart from other bike shops for her," says Zane. "She began to see us an alternative channel of distribution." Bell Atlantic signed Zane up—making him the first retailer in the area to offer free phones. He activated 500 phones the first year, which earned him $12,500, plus another $25 a phone in co-op–advertising allowances. His profits are larger now, since the cost of phones fell to about $165, but commissions have remained the same.

▶ **Coffee Bar and Toy Corner.** Two years ago Zane decided he was hitting the wall in his 900-square-foot store, so he decided to move. Planning for $500 per square foot in annual revenues and striving to build Zane's Cycles to a $2-million business over the next three years, he settled on a 4,000-square-foot space just outside the main business district. Making a personal loan of $100,000 to his business, he renovated his new store meticulously, installing the most up-to-date display racks and even including a play area for children. There was just one problem. Six months after opening the new store, he began to hear from customers that the new place wasn't intimate enough. The high ceilings and white walls were uninviting, making the store feel more like a chain than the homegrown business it was.

Zane thought back to a trip he had taken to Lucerne, Switzerland, where he visited a bicycle shop that had a coffee bar. "I knew what I had to do," he re-

calls. He commissioned a cabinetmaker to build him a 14-foot mahogany coffee bar, positioning it in front of the window that separates the repair room from the retail operation. Customers could relax over a cup of gourmet coffee (the coffee suppliers provided the equipment), mull over a purchase, or just watch the mechanics. Zane would also give kids a free Snapple and sit them in front of the Lego table or a video while Mom and Dad sipped and shopped. "People fell in love with it," he says. The bar, built for him by one of his former managers, cost about $3,000.

▶ **Former Competitors as a Marketing Channel.** Call two of Zane's former competitors—now out of business—and you'll get this message: "The number you are calling is no longer in service. If you are in need of a bicycle dealer, Zane's Cycles will be happy to serve you. To be directly connected toll-free, please press zero now." By offering to pay the local yellow pages a small fraction of the defunct dealers' remaining advertising costs, Zane arranged to have their out-of-service phone numbers ring at his shop. The total cost to him is about $200 a month, which he'll continue to pay until a new book is published. Because the yellow pages helped him track the transferred calls, Zane knows he received 260 inquiries from his former competitors' customers last July alone. "The first day the line was changed, we sold a bike to a guy who asked why we closed our New Haven store," recalls Zane. "So the program paid for itself for that month." It also reinforces Zane's stronger-than-the-competitors image.

▶ **Price Guarantee.** While Zane's lifetime service guarantee was one of his best selling tools, it sometimes made customers suspicious. "They'd say, 'Sure, you're giving me lifetime free service, but what are you charging me for the bike?'" recalls Zane. He knew his prices were competitive, but customers wanted to find that out for themselves. So two years ago he started a 90-day-price-guarantee program: find it in Connecticut for less, and he'll give you the difference plus 10%. "Now we can say, 'Buy the bike, ride it, and if you find it for less, we'll take care of it.' Our pricing gained credibility." Last year, says Zane, his sales were up 54%, compared with his normal 25% growth rate; he reckons the store now handles 20% more customers. And the sales are easier. "We make money through volume because we spend less time with each customer making the hard sell—we can focus on the product," he says. Cumulatively, he's had to rebate less than $1,000. But, he says, "half the people who receive a rebate will spend it in the store that day."

"CHRIS'S MAIN OBJECTIVE IS TO TAKE market share from everyone around him," says Trek's Seeger. "I've watched his numbers go straight up while sales at the New Haven shop I used to deal with have gone down. I could see that people were going to Chris." Ray Keener, executive director of the Bicycle Industry Organization, in Boulder, Colo., says that though many bike shops are run by biking enthusiasts who do a good job of appealing to passionate cyclists, "Chris is good at going out there and grabbing people who are marginally interested and getting them into the store." Once they're there, Zane makes it difficult for them to leave without buying. And once they've bought, he blitzes them with reasons to come back—a gift certificate, a reminder that a child might be ready for a larger bike, and so on.

But there is also a downside to his devotion to customer service. His service guarantee, for example, has limited his opportunity for growth. Shortly after he initiated the guarantee, he was forced to drop a line of bicycles because the warranties "were killing us." While the manufacturer covered the cost of parts, Zane was obliged to provide free labor, and the number of repairs was cutting into his already-thin margins. With a lifetime of free service on every bike sold looming ahead of him, he decided to cut his losses and drop the brand.

A foray into the world of exercise equipment has also been problematic. In the winter of 1994, Zane began carrying a high-end line of treadmills—an attempt to diversify his business and to generate more sales in the slow winter months. He learned quickly that it wasn't a good fit. "It was very different from the bike business," he says. "Treadmills need adjustment more often than bikes do—and they're too big for the customer to load up and bring into the shop. We were going out to do in-home servicing every six weeks, and it cut deeply into our profits." Again he quickly cut his losses and discontinued the line. Still, he's committed to servicing the machines he's already sold—for life. An expensive mistake? Zane shrugs. "Those customers will see that we're honoring our commitment to them even though we're not carrying the line anymore, and they'll speak well of us."

It's a phrase Zane uses a lot when he's referring to customers—"they'll speak well of us." Indeed, every marketing gimmick, every guarantee, every freebie is designed in light of Zane's belief that the most sophisticated marketing in the world won't serve him as well as customer referrals. And that all comes down to how people are treated in the store. Zane doesn't, for example, make a point of hiring cyclists as salespeople. "I can teach anyone about a bike," he says, "but I can't teach them to be helpful or courteous. I've had people who know the product cold but who just don't have the ability to work with customers. They don't last long."

The attention to detail is an integral part of Zane's basic business philosophy, but it's also critical to his survival. Wal-Mart is coming to town, as is Ski Market, a category-killer sporting-goods store. "When a category killer comes in, you have to have all your programs in place," says Zane. "You have to work to be as strong as they are and kill them where they're weak. And customer service is where they're weakest."

He is not, in fact, comfortable with merely serving his niche, as a good specialty retailer probably ought to be. He wants to lure customers from Wal-Mart and reckons that the giant's presence will actually help him because "there will be more inexpensive bikes out there that need to be fixed." Soon he'll have a better point-of-sale computer system that will help him track customers more effectively and do more targeted marketing. Down the line, once he's hit his 1997 goal of $2 million in sales, he'll cautiously explore other markets.

And how do his competitors fit into all this? Well, they don't.

"Our 100% goal is to be *the* bike shop in New Haven County," says Zane. "And we won't stop there."

One project, however, he did stop pursuing. For seven years he had juggled college and the demands of company building, completing three years of course work toward the degree he had promised his parents he'd earn. It was a struggle. Finally, Patricia and John Zane relented. They were satisfied their son was on the road to success and were convinced of his commitment to the community. Chris, relieved to be let off the hook but uncomfortable with the prospect of unfinished business, presented an alternative scenario. "I want to be so successful that I'll be asked to give a commencement speech, and that's how I'll earn my degree," he told them. "It's not the traditional way, but there's no right path," he philosophized. He was, in fact, living proof of that. So in 1990, his parents transferred to him 80% of the stock. He'd earned it.

Relationship Marketing: Positioning for the Future

Jonathan R. Copulsky and Michael J. Wolf

Jonathan R. Copulsky and Michael J. Wolf are, respectively, principal and associate with Booz-Allen & Hamilton. They are based in New York and specialize in business and marketing strategy.

There are strategic opportunities for companies that are on the leading edge of relationship marketing techniques.

This year, almost 4 million expectant mothers will receive personalized letters about infant care from a disposable diaper manufacturer. A leading manufacturer of hair coloring products will send trial samples to regular users of competing brands. And at supermarkets across the country, shoppers will watch personalized advertisements for cookies, toothpaste, and coffee at checkout counters equipped with video screens. In these instances and countless others, advertisers are finding new ways to communicate with their customers that capitalize on and leverage the long-term relationship between the advertiser and consumer.

Advertisers are building and maintaining databases on consumers to customize and target their messages more precisely. On the other side, consumers are signaling their needs and preferences and will eventually see marketing communications and products tailored to those desires. Greater brand loyalty and sales impact are the goals of this new one-on-one association between advertiser and consumer.

Relationship marketing is changing the way advertisers use traditional media channels to build brand image and awareness. In shifting their marketing dollars from mass media to more targeted, more measurable forms of advertising, advertisers are not merely reallocating advertising budgets between existing media products; they are taking advantage of a whole new set of media choices. Utilizing these new media choices, they are building relationships—instead of just trying to make a onetime sale.

As more companies turn to relationship marketing, more advertising dollars are being funneled into proprietary media for communicating directly with consumers. The threats and opportunities facing marketing companies are clear: Those that exploit these new technologies and techniques will be able to defend their current positions and will be prepared to capture new revenue opportunities; those that don't develop effective relationship marketing strategies will risk loss of market share.

What Is Relationship Marketing?

Relationship marketing combines elements of general advertising, sales promotion, public relations, and direct marketing to create more effective and more efficient ways of reaching consumers. It centers on developing a continuous relationship with consumers across a family of related products and services.

The relationship marketing process incorporates three key elements:

- Identifying and building a database of current and potential consumers which records and cross-references a wide range of demographic, life-style, and purchase information;

• Delivering differentiated messages to these people through established and new media channels based on the consumer's characteristics and preferences; and

• Tracking each relationship to monitor the cost of acquiring the consumer and the lifetime value of his purchases.

The diaper manufacturer previously described is a good example. Huggies has spent over $10 million to set up a system that provides it with the names of over 75 percent of the expectant mothers in the United States.

The names are obtained from doctors, hospitals, and childbirth trainers.

During their pregnancies, the mothers-to-be receive personalized magazines and letters with ideas on baby care, thus building a bond between the mothers and Huggies.

When the baby arrives, a coded coupon is delivered which Huggies can track to know which mothers have tried the product. Later, as new technologies fall into place, Huggies will be able to know which mothers continue to purchase Huggies.

In this case, Huggies' parent, Kimberly Clark, is not only building diaper sales but also establishing relationships with mothers which can be leveraged across other products.

The cost of linking the consumer to the brand can be justified since the per-baby consumption of single-use diapers averages over $1,400 annually.

Other innovative programs include: Kraft's "Cheese and Macaroni Club," which sends children a packet of goodies; MTV's custom magazine which viewers get when they respond to MTV's 800 number; and Isuzu's personalized inserts in *Time*, which list nearest dealerships and are redeemable for a premium.

What's Different About Relationship Marketing?

Because relationship marketing combines elements of other communications disciplines, a natural question arises: How is it different from direct marketing, general advertising, or sales promotion? In some ways, it is all these and more. What distinguishes relationship marketing is its purpose: to build a long-term connection between company and consumer.

The objective of traditional direct marketing advertisers, such as catalog merchants or life insurers, is achieved by bypassing the retailer through alternative distribution channels.

Traditionally, the use of direct marketing by consumer durables and packaged goods companies has been low and mainly limited to couponing. Advertisers using sales promotion devices, such as cents-off coupons, sweepstakes, or "buy one, get one free" are also geared toward increasing their short-term sales by providing extra pull for their product. Both direct marketing and sales promotion seek immediate sales.

Relationship marketing does not seek a temporary increase in sales or to sell products through the mail but to create involvement and product loyalty by building a lasting bond with the customer. While it may be used to facilitate product repositioning, gain competitors' customers, or help launch new products, the ultimate goal is increased usage over time. With this clear objective, relationship marketing becomes a personalized form of communication, which crosses the previous boundaries between general advertising, sales promotion, direct marketing, and public relations.

Drivers of the Trend

Dissatisfaction with traditional approaches to building brand loyalty, coupled with advances in technology, has driven advertisers to look for new ways of connecting with consumers.

The decrease in the reach of mass media is old news: Newspaper penetration has declined to less than 70 percent of U.S. households; less than 67 percent of households watching television are tuned into network programs, down from 90 percent only ten years ago. The latest news is the flattening growth of

66UPC scanning equipment at supermarkets can track individual buying habits. 99

direct marketing and sales promotions, apparently the result of overkill.

Promotions have proved to be increasingly unsuccessful in stimulating consumers to try new brands. Manufacturers using coupons are only subsidizing purchases of current users: Nielsen surveys show that 80 percent of coupons are now used by loyal customers who would have bought the product anyway. And, as postage rates rise, many companies are reconsidering direct response.

Technological innovations make it increasingly possible for each company to have a direct relationship with the people who use its products and services. Among the major innovations are the following.

UPC scanning equipment at supermarkets can track individual buying habits. Retailers provide consumers with a card featuring a magnetic strip which permits the computer to know what products the consumer purchases. Consumers want to use the card because they receive frequent-buyer's bonus points.

Relational database technology now makes the use and analysis of databases containing large amounts of customer information more manageable.

New kinds of audience measurement, such as "people meters," can tell media planners which people are watching what.

Selective delivery and addressability allow the delivery of differentiated and personalized messages.

Telecommunication technologies, such as automatic number identification and voice response capabilities, recognize respondents to advertisements who call manufacturers' 800 and 900 numbers.

These developments come at a time when advertisers need a way to make consumers more receptive to their claims—a particularly difficult challenge when consumers are increasingly skeptical about the messages they receive from mass advertising. Messages compete in a more cluttered environment where it is often difficult to distinguish between product advantage and brand identity.

Armed with new database and communications technologies, advertisers can deal with their customers as valued

individuals and create an environment in which people want to hear the messages they receive. Relationship marketing gives advertisers the potential to build an image and connection that they just can't do with other media choices.

Three Keys to Relationship Marketing

There are strategic opportunities for companies on the leading edge of relationship marketing techniques. Successfully addressing the trend will depend on a three-pronged effort:

1. **Identify and build marketing databases of present and potential purchasers.** In the age of relationship marketing, the customer database will be as important a strategic asset for manufacturers as the brand itself. Advertisers will need the capability to use mass media and more targeted media channels as ways of prospecting for customers. Once potential customers have been identified, advertisers must capture their names and information on their life-styles in a database for future communications.

It's important to keep in mind that not all consumers are appropriate targets for relationship marketing, and not all targets are customers. Consequently, the initial database must be carefully refined and segmented. Designed and developed properly, the marketing database will allow companies to expand their internal capabilities to include relationship marketing. Marketers leading the way include Procter & Gamble, which is using 800 telephone numbers in its ads for Cheerfree detergent to target people with sensitive skin; Porsche, which has created a database of 300,000 affluent prospective purchasers of its cars; and Citicorp, which is setting up a database of customer information collected from retail outlets for its own use and for sale to third-party marketers.

2. **Deliver differentiated messages to targeted households.** Advertisers must develop the ability to communicate with a defined audience of the existing and potential users of their products. The media choices they make must therefore

offer the ability to not only broadcast the message to the entire circulation or audience, but also to target precisely defined demographic slices. For advertisers, more precise targeting means greater impact.

Mass circulation magazines are responding to advertisers' needs with "selective binding" and personalized "ink-jet printing." Applying these two technologies, an automobile manufacturer, for example, can send an ad for a high-end car to one household and an ad for a midrange car to another household. In addition, the automobile manufacturer can add a personalized message to the ad with ink-jet printing and even list the names of the nearest dealers.

Recently, MCI diverted money from its TV budget to pay for a subscriber-personalized ad in *Time*. Clearly, publishers can exploit mass reach with niche ads that provide more targeted messages.

Broadcast media are also relinquishing their positions as passive media. Telemarketing innovations will allow broadcast media to become increasingly interactive. At the same time, addressability will become an important factor in both cable and broadcast.

3. **Track the relationship to make media expenditures more effective and more measurable.** Common wisdom has it that half of all advertising dollars are wasted—the difficulty is knowing which half. The media innovations just described above will allow advertisers to pinpoint what sells and what doesn't. Consequently, relationship marketing's most important effect will be a shift in the way decisions are made about where to advertise. Traditionally, decisions have been based on various *ex ante* measures of exposure, such as cost-per-thousand, audience, or circulation. In the future, however, decisions will be made on *ex post* factors such as evidence of penetration of the required target audience or even evidence of sales results.

In this new environment, the basis of measurement changes and emphasis will shift from cost-per-thousand to the value of reaching a target market. Advertisers must evaluate the cost of gaining and maintaining a customer relationship over several years.

Positioning for the Future

Defining a relationship marketing strategy implies agreeing upon the objectives of a relationship marketing program and its role in the overall marketing strategy. Failure to define this role could lead to wasted expenditures on initiatives that detract from ongoing marketing efforts.

Once the strategy is established, implementing relationship marketing requires applying a range of skills and resources, from the initial database and product to fulfillment capabilities and feedback mechanisms. We see a number of challenges facing would-be relationship marketers:

Challenge 1: Gaining access to the appropriate systems and executional capabilities. Developing the requisite systems capability to fully pursue the opportunities offered by new technologies will necessitate a fundamental restructuring of current systems and databases. Few marketers currently possess the critical information technology skills to achieve this, while most systems personnel lack the essential marketing savvy.

Challenge 2: Developing the right organizational structure. Advertisers will need to reconfigure their reporting systems to balance the benefits of traditional brand-management structures with the customer-oriented focus of relationship marketing. Some companies will need a secondary operating structure that crosses businesses, brands, and markets. This may mean creating new divisions and redefining P&Ls, as well as defining incentives for cooperation across brands.

Challenge 3: Budgeting for lifetime customer value. The economics of the relationship marketing process require advertisers to view the value of maintaining the relationship over the lifetime of the consumer. Costs must be considered in light of their long-term value—a perspective that flies in the face of established budgeting processes.

Challenge 4: Managing an integrated communications program. Advertisers must develop integrated programs, com-

66Advertisers are definitely reallocating budgets. 99

bining traditional media vehicles with relationship marketing. The right combination can truly enhance the value of traditional media programs. The challenge is to determine which media combinations are clearly superior and then spearhead their development.

Challenge 5: Building alliances between manufacturers and retailers. Advertisers must ally themselves with retailers like Vons, Publix, and Wal-Mart, which are building their own consumer databases. Manufacturers need the information to tailor their marketing programs. For retailers, the power of relationship marketing is that brand loyalty can also mean store loyalty.

The End Game

The future? Certainly relationship marketing provides advertisers access to a richer set of tools for building brand image and awareness and spending promotional dollars more effectively.

Advertisers who fail to master the techniques of relationship marketing will find themselves outmaneuvered by more savvy competitors.

The quandary for individual advertisers lies not in determining whether to deploy relationship marketing but rather in determining how and when.

How much of a spending shift will occur? It is hard to predict. It's too soon to tell whether we will witness a paradigmatic shift in the way that advertisers allocate marketing communication budgets or simply reallocation of spending at the margin.

Presently, relationship marketing lacks the history of success to justify cessation of other types of advertising expenditures.

Technology will be a key determinant of the growth of relationship marketing. Much of the relevant technology exists today; the question is, When will it be practical and cost-effective to use on a widespread basis?

As the power of relationship marketing becomes ever more sophisticated, the information it generates will enable manufacturers not only to vary their advertising but also to alter their products to individual tastes. While privacy may become a consideration for some customers, many others will regard this attention as flattering.

Relationship marketing represents a natural, evolutionary step in the means by which advertisers communicate with their customers. It focuses on building and enhancing sustainable linkages to customers—a goal to which advertising has always aspired. Relationship marketing does not change that goal—it only provides a surer path for realizing it.

SERVICE IS EVERYBODY'S BUSINESS

On the front line of the new economy, service—bold, fast, imaginative, and customized—is the ultimate strategic imperative.

Ronald Henkoff

THE CRASH scene at the intersection of 40th Street and 26th Avenue in Tampa is chaotic and tense. The two cars are bent and battered. Their drivers and passengers are not bleeding, but they are shaken up and scared. Just minutes after the collision, a young man dressed in a polo shirt, khakis, and wingtips arrives on the scene to assume command. Bearing a clipboard, a camera, a cassette recorder, and an air of competence, Lance Edgy, 26, calms the victims and advises them on medical care, repair shops, police reports, and legal procedures. Edgy is not a cop or a lawyer or a good samaritan. He is a senior claims representative for Progressive Corp., an insurance company that specializes in high-risk drivers, high-octane profits—and exceptional service.

Edgy invites William McAllister, Progressive's policyholder, into an air-conditioned van equipped with comfortable chairs, a desk, and two cellular phones. Even before the tow trucks have cleared away the wreckage, Edgy is offering his client a settlement for the market value of his totaled 1988 Mercury Topaz. McAllister, who does not appear to have been at fault in this accident, is amazed by Progressive's alacrity: "This is great—someone coming right out here and taking charge. I didn't expect it at all."

REPORTER ASSOCIATE *Ann Sample*

Welcome to the front line of the new American economy, where service—bold, fast, unexpected, innovative, and customized—is the ultimate strategic imperative, a business challenge that has profound implications for the way we manage companies, hire employees, develop careers, and craft policies.

It matters not whether a company creates something you can touch, such as a computer, a toaster, or a machine tool, or something you can only experience, such as insurance coverage, an airplane ride, or a telephone call. What counts most is the service built into that something—the way the product is designed and delivered, billed and bundled, explained and installed, repaired and renewed.

Product quality, once a competitive advantage, is now just the ante into the game. Says Eric Mittelstadt, 58, president and CEO of Fanuc Robotics North America: "Everyone has become better at developing products. In robotics, the robot itself has become sort of a commodity. The one place you can differentiate yourself is in the service you provide."

Companies that achieve distinctive service often have to redefine their very reason for doing business. Fanuc has transmuted itself from an assembler of robots into a designer and installer of customized manufacturing systems. Progressive no

longer simply sells insurance policies; it sees itself as a mediator of human trauma. Toyota's Lexus division has invented not just a new luxury car but a whole new standard of luxury service.

Johnson Controls, a seemingly mature manufacturer of thermostats and energy systems, has discovered startup-style growth in the business of managing other companies' buildings. ServiceMaster, a company that fertilizes lawns, kills bugs, and scrubs floors, has prospered by, in effect, selling people back their own leisure time. Taco Bell has been ringing up juicy profits because it knows that its main business is not preparing food but delivering it—and not just in restaurants but in schools, hospitals, kiosks, and pushcarts.

As a result of epiphanies like these, entire companies are—literally—moving closer to their customers. At Progressive, claims adjusters who used to spend much of their time working phones and pushing papers are ambulatory. At Johnson Controls, design engineers who were once ensconced in cubicles and harnessed to their computers are out in their customers' buildings, managing the systems they helped create. Says Patrick Harker, director of the Wharton School's Fishman-Davidson Center, which studies the service sector: "Once you start thinking of service as a process instead of as a series of functions, the old distinction between the front office (the people who did the selling) and the back office (the people who pushed the paper but never saw the customer) disappears."

The changing nature of customer relationships demands a new breed of service worker, folks who are empathetic, flexible, informed, articulate, inventive, and able to work with minimal levels of supervision. "Rather than the service world being derided as having the dead-end jobs of our time, it will increasingly become an outlet for creativity, theatricality, and expressiveness," says Larry Keeley, president of Doblin Group, a Chicago management and design consulting firm. It's no coincidence that companies everywhere now profess an ardent desire to "delight" their customers.

For far longer than most of us realize—for most of this century, in fact—services have dominated the American economy. They now generate 74% of gross domestic product, account for 79% of all jobs, and produce a balance-of-trade surplus that hit $55.7 billion last year, vs. a deficit of $132.4 billion for goods.

The demand for services will remain strong. The Bureau of Labor Statistics expects service occupations to be responsible for *all* net job growth through the year 2005, spawning whole new legions of nurses, physical therapists, home health aides, and social workers to minister to the needs of an aging population, along with phalanxes of food servers, child-care providers, and cleaning ladies to cater to the wants of harried two-earner families. Also rising to the fore will be a swelling class of technical workers, including computer engineers, systems analysts, and paralegals.

THE SERVICE ECONOMY, despite its size and growth, remains extraordinarily misunderstood, mismeasured, and mismanaged. "We still have this perception that making a product is better than providing a service," says James Brian Quinn, professor of management at Dartmouth's Tuck School and author of the book *Intelligent Enterprise*. That notion, which Quinn traces back to prophets as diverse as Adam Smith and Karl Marx, is reinforced by present-day politicians, economists, trade union officials, and journalists—service workers all—who decry the demise of high-paying manufacturing jobs and rue the propagation of low-paying service positions like burger flippers, floor sweepers, and bedpan changers.

Well, it's not that simple. The service sector, whose cohorts include richly remunerated cardiac surgeons, tort lawyers, and movie stars, is as varied as the economy itself. The gap between manufacturing and service

wages is narrowing. (So, too, is the difference between productivity rates in goods and services industries. In 1992 the median goods-producing job paid only $19 per week more than the median service-producing job, according to a recently published study by the Federal Reserve Bank of Cleveland. More telling: The distribution of low-paying and high-paying jobs in each sector is virtually identical. The real problem isn't the wage gap between workers who produce goods and those who provide services. It's the wage chasm between employees with higher education and those without.

Despite the steady expansion of the service economy, American management practices, accounting conventions, business school courses, and public policies continue to suffer from an acute Industrial Age hangover. "Most people still view the world through manufacturing goggles," complains Fred Reichheld, leader of the customer-loyalty practice at Bain & Co. "We use an accounting system that was designed to serve 19th-century textile and steel mills." That system tallies returns on equipment, inventories, and other physical assets, but what really matters in a service business is the return a company reaps from its human assets—the brainpower of its employees and the loyalty of its customers. Try reporting something like "return on intellect employed" on your next P&L statement, and see how the analysts and auditors react to that.

Service executives often behave much like belly dancers trying to march to a John Philip Sousa song, subjecting their companies to management theories—both traditional and trendy—that were invented in the factory. Says Leonard Schlesinger, a Harvard business school professor who has studied service companies for two decades: "Old legends die hard. Many service firms have aped the worst aspects of manufacturing management. They oversupervise; they overcontrol."

Even new managerial precepts like total quality management, statistical process control, reengineering, and benchmarking are rooted in manufacturing. "Senior management continues to focus on incremental improvements in quality, on redesigning internal processes, on restructuring, on taking people out of the equation," says a frustrated Craig Terrill, an innovation consultant at Kuczmarski & Associates in Chicago. "That's such a defeatist approach. They should be coming up with whole new ways to serve their customers."

The good news is that an increasing number of companies are inventing new ways to reach those customers. Forcing them to change is that fabled taskmaster—the mar-

Employment

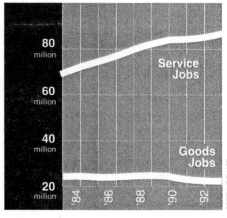

FORTUNE CHART

ketplace. Progressive Corp. used to have a winning formula for coining money in auto insurance, a business with notoriously low margins. The company, headquartered in Cleveland, wrote policies for high-risk drivers that its competitors wouldn't touch, and charged high prices to match. The ride ended in 1988, when two things happened. Allstate outflanked Progressive in the high-risk niche, and voters in California, where Progressive made 25% of its profits, passed Proposition 103, a law that sharply curtailed insurance rates.

Peter Lewis, 60, Progressive's plain-speaking chairman, CEO, and president, saw the double wake-up call as an opportunity both to revise his company's practices and to tame the public's hostility. Says he: "People get screwed seven ways from Sunday in auto insurance. They get dealt with adversarially, and they get dealt with slowly. I said, 'Why don't we just stop that? Why don't we start dealing with them nicely? It would be a revolution in the business.'"

With its round-the-clock Immediate Response program, introduced four years ago, Progressive representatives now make contact with 80% of accident victims less than nine hours after learning of the crash. Adjusters inspect 70% of damaged vehicles within one day and wrap up most collision damage claims within a week. By scurrying to the scene, adjusters obtain accurate information fast, which they feed into PACMan (Progressive automated claims management system). The streamlined process reduces costs, builds customers' good will, and keeps the liability lawyers at bay. At the crash scene in Tampa, even the driver of the other car, Xavia Culver, was impressed: "I think all insurance companies should come out and see what's going on, to help out with all the hassle and confusion."

Lance Edgy, Progressive's man on the scene in Tampa, is the very model of a modern service worker. The lead member of a six-person team of adjusters, Edgy joined

Progressive in 1990 after graduating from the University of Florida with a degree in finance. The company has invested heavily in his training, offering him courses not just in the arcana of insurance regulation but also in the art of negotiation and in grief counseling (part of his job involves dealing with the relatives of dead crash victims). Progressive's gain-sharing program, keyed to a formula based on revenues, profits, and costs, gives Edgy an opportunity to increase his base salary of $38,480 a year by as much as $5,400.

Says CEO Lewis: "To the extent that auto insurance is a commodity, our biggest differentiator is our people. We want the best people at every level of the company, and we pay at the top of the market." When a competitor recently tried to hire away three of Progressive's highly paid division claims managers by offering them large pay hikes, Lewis increased the pay scales not just for the three would-be defectors but for all 15 of their colleagues as well. Investing in people pays dividends. Progressive's net income, $267 million last year, has increased at an average annual compound rate of 20% since 1989.

For service companies, retaining good employees is essential to winning and keeping good customers. "It's impossible to build a loyal book of customers without a loyal employee base," says Fred Reichheld of Bain. "It's like trying to build a brick wall without mortar." As obvious as this connection seems, managers of service companies routinely disregard it. The annual rate of employee turnover in department stores and restaurants routinely tops 100%. Says Harvard's Schlesinger: "Most service companies operate with a cycle-of-failure mentality. They assume labor is an expendable, renewable resource, and they create a cadre of poor, unmotivated employees who couldn't care less if the customer is satisfied."

WHEN IT COMES to the link between employee turnover, customer loyalty, and profits, Lexus understands the nexus. Two-thirds of the people who buy a Lexus have bought one before, the highest repeat purchase rate in the luxury car market. That's an extraordinary statistic, considering that the first Lexus went on sale less than five years ago, and considering that the appreciation of the yen has sent the price of a top-of-the-line LS 400 sedan soaring above $54,000.

For three years running, customers surveyed by J.D. Power & Associates, the industry's leading pollster, have ranked Lexus No. 1 in product quality and dealer service among all cars sold in the U.S. "We try to

make it very hard for you to leave us," says Lexus general manager George Borst. "When you buy a Lexus, you don't buy a product. You buy a luxury package."

Wrapped in the package is a style of service crafted with the same precision Toyota put into the design of the car itself. Says Borst: "Our challenge was to get people to buy a Japanese luxury car. The quality of the product wasn't the issue. Everybody knew that Toyota could make a top-quality product. The issue was creating a sense of prestige. And where we saw the hole in the market was in the way dealers treated their customers."

When you walk into the showroom at South Bay Lexus, not far from Toyota's Torrance, California, headquarters, the most striking thing is what doesn't happen. No salesmen—sales consultants, to use the proper title—approach. They don't hover, they don't pry, they don't solicit. Even though they're paid on commission, these guys stay totally out of sight until you tell the receptionist you're ready for a consultation. Says South Bay service manager John Lane: "Customers won't stand for the hustle effect."

Like all employees at Lexus dealerships (including receptionists), Lane regularly attends national and regional training courses to learn about cars, even those made by competitors, and customers. Lane figures he received more training in his first month at Lexus than he did in his entire 18-year career at Cadillac.

But back to the showroom. If you want to buy a car—and most customers make two or three visits before they're ready—your sales consultant will usher you into a product presentation room, an alcove with no doors, no clutter, a semicircular marble-topped table, and three leather chairs that are precisely the same height. The implicit message: There are no traps and no surprises.

The first two regularly scheduled maintenances of your car are free. While you're waiting for the work to be done, you can use

Share of GDP
In billions of dollars

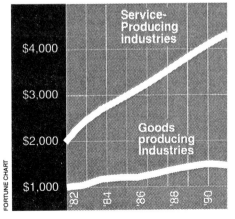

an office with a desk and a phone. Or you can stand in the customer viewing room and watch the mechanic—sorry, the service technician—attend to your car in a brightly lit garage that seems devoid of grease. If you need to be someplace, the dealer will lend you a car or give you a ride. When you pick up your vehicle, you'll find that it has been washed and vacuumed by a "valet detail specialist," whose compensation, like everyone else's at South Bay, is pegged to customer satisfaction. The annual employee turnover rate since South Bay opened its doors in 1989 is a lowly 7%.

Okay, it's one thing to provide silky service when you're selling a silk-purse-type product. But how much innovation can you possibly bring to the preparation and delivery of a $1.39 chicken taco or a 99-cent bean burrito? Plenty.

Over the past decade Taco Bell, a subsidiary of PepsiCo, has evolved from a regional quick-service restaurant chain with $700 million in system-wide sales and 1,500 outlets into a multinational food delivery company with $3.9 billion in revenues and more than 15,000 "points of access" (POAs). What, you ask, is a POA? It is any place where people can meet to munch—an airport, a supermarket, a school cafeteria, a college campus, or a street corner. Says Charlie Rogers, Taco Bell's senior vice president for human resources: "We've changed the way we think about ourselves, moving from a company that prepares food to one that feeds hungry people."

Like many business insights, this one sounds insanely simple, almost like a Peter Sellers pronouncement in the movie *Being There*. But don't be fooled. Getting from Point A to Point B necessitated a revolution in the way Taco Bell manages people, information, and machines. The first step, unveiled by President and CEO John Martin in 1989, was called K-minus. (The "K" stands for kitchen.) Martin took the heavy-duty food preparation—crushing beans, dicing cheese, and preparing beef—out of the restaurants and centralized it in commissaries run by outside contractors. The cost savings allowed Taco Bell to slash its prices. More significantly, the company was able to shrink the average size of a restaurant kitchen by 40%, freeing up more space—and more employees—to serve customers. Says Rogers: "Most of the people in our restaurants really worked in manufacturing, not service."

Once Taco Bell got the manufacturing out of its restaurants, it began to get the manufacturing out of its management. Like most fast-food chains, Taco Bell used a command-and-control system of supervision that came straight out of Detroit, circa 1960. There was one manager for each restaurant, one area manager for every six restaurants, and one repetitious, mind-numbing job for each employee. Today many Taco Bell outlets operate with no manager on the premises. Self-directed teams, known as "crews," manage inventory, schedule work, order supplies, and train new employees—make that "crew members." Team-managed restaurants have lower employee turnover and higher customer satisfaction scores than conventionally run outlets.

Regional managers, formerly factory-style supervisors who earned about $25,000 a year, are now business school graduates who oversee as many as 30 POAs. Their pay, closely linked to sales results and customer-satisfaction scores, can top $100,000. "I see myself not just as a fast-food manager but as an entrepreneur who manages a multi-million-dollar corporation with 250 employees," says Sueyoung Georgas, a fortysomething native of South Korea, whose territory in the southern suburbs of Detroit includes five restaurants, five schools, three community colleges, and a catering service that provisions banquets and festivals. With people like Georgas on board, CEO Martin is aiming to increase Taco Bell's points of access to 200,000—a more than tenfold increase—by the year 2000.

SOME OF THE MOST exciting action in services is occurring behind the scenes, deep in the bowels of the economy—down in the boiler room, to be precise. Okay, a boiler room isn't an intrinsically thrilling place. But it is for Johnson Controls, an old-line Milwaukee manufacturing company, whose founder, Warren Johnson, invented the thermostat in 1883. Sales of Johnson's traditional products—heating controls, batteries, plastic bottles, and automobile seats—continue to expand at a steady pace. But "facilities management services," which Johnson entered in 1989, is running like a racehorse, with revenues growing at a triple-digit clip.

Controls Group vice president Terry Weaver waxes euphoric when he describes the opportunity in managing the heating, lighting, security, and cleaning operations of office buildings. "It's explosive. It's almost impossible to quantify, a market worth tens of billions of dollars in the U.S. alone. It's a wave. It's a megatrend."

Yep, it's exciting. And here's why: As companies restructure, they are paring costs and focusing on what they do best (their core competencies, in B-school jargon). At the same time, they are ditching the things that they do worst, like managing their computer networks, phone systems, and boiler rooms. Through the magic of outsourcing,

INSIGHTS

- All net job creation through 2005 will come from services.

- Think of service as a process, not as a series of functions, then realign the organization.

- The changing nature of customer service demands a new breed of worker—one who is empathetic, flexible, inventive, and able to work with minimal levels of supervision.

one company's cost center becomes Johnson Controls' (or some other firm's) profit center.

Johnson Controls Chairman and Chief Executive James Keyes, 53, says service now drives his entire corporation. "Most of our growth has come from the fact that we do more for our customers." Strictly speaking, Tina Brueckner, 27, an engineer in the Controls Group's Milwaukee branch office, had always been a service worker. But she almost never met the people she was serving. Hunched in front of a computer, she designed heating, ventilation, and air-conditioning control systems to specifications drawn up by the customer or the customer's consultant.

Now, instead of basically filling orders, Brueckner finds solutions to her customers' problems. She spends at least half her time in the field as part of a four-person team that helps schools improve their energy efficiency. Says she: "Before I sat at a desk and engineered. Now I go out and talk to my customers. This makes the job a lot more satisfying."

THE OUTSOURCING phenomenon fueling growth at companies like Johnson Controls is also spreading to the consumer world. There the powerhouse is ServiceMaster, a company in Downers Grove, Illinois, that has made a mint by doing things for people that they don't want to do themselves: Dust their bookshelves, care for their lawns, and exterminate their roaches. The company, which also cleans and maintains hospitals, schools, and other buildings, reported net income of $145.9 million on revenues of $2.8 billion in 1993, its 23rd consecutive year of record top- and bottom-line results.

Chairman William Pollard, 56, admits to being miffed that his colleagues in the business community don't always treat his enterprise with the greatest respect: "They say, 'Oh, you're just the mop-and-bucket guys.' But then they look at our financial results and wonder, 'How did they do that?' " How indeed? By carefully selecting employees ("service partners" is what the company calls them), training them thoroughly, and giving them the right tools to do the job. ServiceMaster's R&D center, which is focusing this year on floor care, recently invented the Walk-Behind Scrubber, a self-propelled contraption that helped cut by 20% the amount of time it takes to clean a vinyl surface. Next year, incidentally, will be the Year of the Carpet.

ServiceMaster's real genius lies in the way it manages to instill a sense of dignity and importance in low-paid people doing menial jobs. The company's Merry Maids subsidiary rejects nine out of ten applicants for the entry-level position of "teammate." Every prospective teammate goes through a 45-question interview known as the Perceiver. Managers review the results, looking for WOO words—for Winning Others Over—such as "win," "commitment," "we," "yes," and "us."

Merry Maids' pickiness in hiring teammates stems from a new perception of why it's in business. Says President Mike Isakson: "We used to focus on the process of cleaning, making sure the home was free from dust. Now we understand that the ultimate benefits to the customer are peace of mind, security, and stress reduction." In other words, the customer wants to know not only that her home will be cleaned but that nothing will be stolen, broken, or rearranged. Says Cindy Luellen, 33, a Merry Maids office manager in Indianapolis who started out as a teammate: "This job is very rewarding emotionally, especially for a divorced, single mother with just a high school education. It's nice to have the respect of your fellow employees and your customers too."

Respect, loyalty, security, dignity—old-fashioned qualities for a new-fashioned economy. Earlier this century machines helped liberate our ancestors from the toil of the fields. In this generation, wondrous technology has freed us from the drudgery of the assembly line and enabled us to speed new products to far-off markets. As we approach a new millennium, it is people who will carry us forward. In an economy built on service, the extent to which we prosper will depend on our ability to educate, entertain, empower, and ennoble ourselves—and each other.

'My Lawyer Sent Me Flowers'

Personal touches, extra efforts and thoughtfulness can be unexpected roads to client satisfaction and loyalty

DI MARI RICKER

Di Mari Ricker, a Los Angeles attorney and legal journalist, is a former staff writer for the Los Angeles Times *and the* Boston Globe.

Last winter, Felice Andrus, a New England horse trainer and importer, was looking through an ice-laced window when she saw a curious figure making his way up her snow-packed driveway. It was someone she had never met, nor had ever expected to meet: her lawyer, who handles her business's transactional work from the West Coast.

"That just bowled me over," says Andrus, whose attorney was in the area for a convention. "Here was this person, who probably thinks it's cold when the air conditioning in California is set too low, coming to visit me when it's 20 below. He looked like an icicle, which is exactly how I look when I have to go out to the barn in the dead of winter to feed the horses. I thought, now this is a lawyer who understands my business."

And that is a lawyer to whom Andrus, owner of Arete Lippizans, says she will continue sending business. "Lawyers are not known for going out of their way," says Andrus. "When I saw this figure in the snow, I thought, any lawyer who would inconvenience himself physically just to meet a client is one who will go the extra mile for you in a business matter. That gesture spoke volumes to me."

Those little extras, say attorneys who have received feedback from clients, can be a pivotal factor in whether a client engages or stays with a firm. Some lawyers who have become attuned to such nuances say, *"Clients just love it when I . . ."*

• **Deliver large bills in person.** "If a bill is large, it makes it more palatable to sit down, look somebody in the eye and tell them why we did what we did," says Jaimie Schwartz, a commercial real estate associate with Bernstein, Shur, Sawyer & Nelson in Portland, Maine. "When you personally deliver a large bill, you take the potential for anger out of the exchange. If you send the bill by mail, the client doesn't have you to talk to when he opens the envelope. He sits there and seethes; by the time he calls you, he's irate."

Schwartz recalls once delivering an $8,000 bill, which was high for the particular client. "The client looked at the bill, dropped it on the table and said, 'Are you serious'? I said, 'Not only am I serious, but that's only the billing to date.'"

Schwartz proceeded to explain the bill in detail, re-fresh the client's memory about the extent of the work involved, and invite questions. Then, he says, "You sit there and let the dead silence flow. Eventually the client will say, 'OK, do you want to get paid now?'"

• **Plan work according to the client's schedule.** Clients are especially appreciative when their legal problems can be dealt with in the morning rather than at the end of their workday, says Tom Leanse, a commercial litigation partner with the Los Angeles office of Chicago's Katten Muchin & Zavis. For lawyers with nationwide practices, that can pose a patchwork of time-zone problems.

"If a West Coast lawyer comes into his office at 9 a.m. and returns a call from a New York client, it's lunch time there and the client is out," says Leanse. "By the time you get around to handling his problem, half of the client's day has already passed."

Instead, he makes it a point to tailor his schedule to that of his clients, even though it can be rough on a lawyer's biorhythms. "I check my voice mail every night before I go to sleep so I can deal with any East Coast problems at the beginning of the client's business day," says Leanse. "If that means staying up late to analyze an issue and getting up early so I can call the client at 9 a.m. his time [6 a.m. Leanse's time], so be it."

• **Deal with clients on a human level.** Mary May, a banking and bankruptcy partner with Fleeson, Gooing, Coulson & Kitch in Wichita, Kan., remodeled her kitchen with a loan from a bank that was also a client. When the remodeling project was completed, May gave a party at her home and invited her bank clients and the loan officers so they could see the finished product—and see her in a social, rather than a business, setting.

"We had shish kebabs, salads, rice, fresh bread. It was great fun and the clients really seemed to appreciate it. They also got to see a different aspect of me," she says.

"Part of my philosophy is that you don't do hard-core marketing. You want clients to know who you are and enjoy you on another level," says May. "By broadening the relationship, I think it solidifies it and helps clients think twice before going somewhere else."

John Frazee, vice president of the commercial real estate department of Bank IV, N.A. in Wichita, confirms this. "It was a nice gesture on Mary's part to bring us into her home," he says. "She had just finished several legal projects for us, as well as her home remodeling project, so the social gathering brought us all a nice sense of completion," says Frazee. "Being included in a realm of our lawyer's life that you don't usually get to see helped personalize the relationship and bring it to another level."

That, he says, "sets your dealing with that lawyer and her firm apart from your dealings with other firms. The others may be equally competent but you see them strictly as lawyers, with all the stereotypes and negative images that are part of the public perception, rather than as a professional who is also a multidimensional human being."

• **Give an unusual or personalized gift.** Any client can go out and spend extra money on box seats to a sports event, but not many will indulge themselves with fresh, imported flowers in the dead of winter, says Honolulu lawyer Bill S. Hunt of Alston, Hunt, Floyd & Ing. His firm sends native Hawaiian blooms to mainland clients over the Christmas holiday season. Those in frigid climes are particularly appreciative, he says, and the flowers are a distinctive touch of having Hawaiian legal representation.

Herb Rule, a commercial litigation partner with the Rose Law Firm in Little Rock, Ark., says clients love it when he makes use of his firm's locale and geographical resources to express appreciation.

Sometimes that takes the form of homespun recreational activities. At a party, Rule met a bank president and his son, both of whom enjoyed duck hunting. When he learned that the client's usual hunting spot had gone dry that season, Rule invited the father and son to accompany him on a duck-hunting trip to a spot where the water and game were plentiful. "They had a wonderful experience, and it meant a lot more to them than a dinner invitation or seats to a basketball game."

• **Help clients with nonlegal work.** While many firms stick to the four corners of the engagement letter, Rule's firm lets clients know it is happy to share its nonlegal expertise as well, at no extra charge. Often, he says, that involves helping clients with travel arrangements—not just for depositions or court appearances, but for family vacations.

"If we have friends in places where clients are going, we put them in touch with one another." Recently a client sold his business and was planning a family trip to Europe to unwind and celebrate. Rule's firm provided introductions in Ireland, London and Paris, where the client and his family were welcomed into private homes for tea. "It personalized the trip for them," says Rule. And, no doubt, subliminally made the law firm a part of the trip.

• **Participate in the client's business or industry.** Steve Noack, an agricultural business partner with Solberg, Stewart, Miller & Johnson in Fargo, N.D., says clients love to see that he makes himself knowledgeable on substantive, not just legal, developments in the client's industry.

Says Noack: "I read trade journals—*Successful Farmer* and *REC Cooperative* magazines—and attend as many agricultural conferences as I can about durum [wheat]. I keep up to date on the imports, tariffs, what's going on in foreign trade policy—the whole market for durum. Clients love it when you go beyond just being a lawyer, when you can understand what they are facing day in and day out in their line of work."

• **Ask clients' opinions of the firm's services.** When Alston, Hunt in Honolulu sent out surveys asking what clients liked and disliked about the way the firm had handled their cases, one of the responses was:

"I love this. No one ever asked me this before." Based on that encouraging note, partner Hunt knew that the firm was really on to something.

•**Act as an educational resource for clients.** Trudy Hanson Fouser, an employment law partner with Elam & Burke in Boise, Idaho, says clients love the quarterly "breakfast briefings" her firm offers on employment-related topics such as sexual harassment.

At the beginning of the year the firm sends clients an invitation that lists the dates of all the upcoming briefings and then sends updates throughout the year. "After the breakfasts, clients call us with their questions"—and their legal business.

• **Call the client without being called first.** "Clients just love it if you call them when they haven't called you," says William Graysen, a criminal defense attorney in Los Angeles. Often, he says, their initial reaction is: "You're calling me?"

Sometimes Graysen calls with an update on the client's case or simply to brainstorm the issues. "Clients are impressed when you come up with some innovative defense during the course of the conversation or ask them their opinion about the options in a case."

• **Write the client, even if there is no immediate reason.** "In 26 years of practice, I've never had a client say, 'Don't write me so much,'" says James Willcox, a litigation partner with the San Francisco firm of Adams, Duque & Hazeltine, who includes a cover letter with every document he sends to clients—even bills. "When a client opens his file, the top document should be a communication from his law firm. Clients are tired of seeing files with nothing in them but bills."

• **Make the law firm a comfortable environment for clients.** Detroit-based Dykema Gossett has found that its female clients appreciate the firm's outreach program for women. "We want women executives to feel our firm is a very comfortable place for them," says Bettye Elkins, a health care partner in the firm's Ann Arbor, Mich., office.

Toward that end, the firm has conducted women's programs on negotiating skills, downsizing, joint ventures and advertising, some of which have featured CEO-type women, she says, with whom clients enjoy being able to network.

Marilyn Lindenauer, CEO of Midwest Eye Banks and Transplant Center in Ann Arbor, is one of Elkins' clients and a seminar attendee. "I love Dykema's seminars," she says. "They project a very nice message that appeals to people like me in the most subtle way: 'We're comfortable dealing with women; you'd be comfortable dealing with us.'"

So she does. Lindenauer also deals with two other, more traditional, law firms but finds Dykema Gossett "very special in its understanding of women clients. It's not something I could get from just any law firm, no matter how competent the attorneys are."

Shortly after the firm held a program on negotiating skills for women clients, Lindenauer sent a tongue-in-cheek e-mail message to Elkins that read, "'Closing the Gender Gap: How to Be a Good Ol' Boy'—How about that for your next seminar topic?"

"There aren't many law firms you could send an e-mail like that to and know that they'd laugh," says Lindenauer. "That's part of what makes me so comfortable dealing with the firm."

And it is part of what makes her keep coming back.

The customers you lose hold the information you need to succeed.

Learning from
Customer Defections

Frederick F. Reichheld

Frederick F. Reichheld is a director of Bain & Company, where he leads the firm's loyalty practice. He is coauthor with W. Earl Sasser, Jr., of "Zero Defections: Quality Comes to Services" (HBR September-October 1990) and author of "Loyalty-Based Management" (HBR March-April 1993). This article is adapted from his book The Loyalty Effect: The Hidden Force Behind Growth, Profits, and Lasting Value, *written with Thomas Teal (Harvard Business School Press, March 1996).*

On average, the CEOs of U.S. corporations lose half their customers every five years. This fact shocks most people. It shocks the CEOs themselves, most of whom have little insight into the causes of the customer exodus, let alone the cures, because they do not measure customer defections, make little effort to prevent them, and fail to use defections as a guide to improvements. Yet customer defection is one of the most illuminating measures in business. First, it is the clearest possible sign that customers see a deteriorating stream of value from the company. Second, a climbing defection rate is a sure predictor of a diminishing flow of cash from customers to the company—even if the company replaces the lost customers—because new customers cost money to acquire and because older customers tend to produce greater cash flow and profits than newer ones. By searching for the root causes of customer departures, companies with the desire and capacity to learn can identify business practices that need fixing and, sometimes, can win the customer back and reestablish the relationship on firmer ground.

But if so much useful information can be wrung from a customer loss, why don't businesses learn or even try to learn from customer defections? In ten years of studying customer loyalty, customer defections, and their effects on corporate cash flow and profits, I have uncovered seven principal reasons:

☐ Many companies aren't really alarmed by customer defections – or they're alarmed too late – because they don't understand the intimate, causal relationship between customer loyalty on the one hand and cash flow and profits on the other.

☐ It is unpleasant to study failure too closely, and in some companies trying to analyze failure can even be hazardous to careers.

☐ Customer defection is often hard to define.

☐ Sometimes *customer* itself is a hard thing to define, at least the kind of customer it's worth taking pains to hold onto.

☐ It is extremely hard to uncover the real root causes of a customer defection and extract the appropriate lessons.

☐ Getting the right people in your organization to learn those lessons and then commit to acting on them is a challenge.

☐ It is difficult to conceptualize and set up the mechanisms that turn the analysis of customer defections into an ongoing strategic system, closely supervised by top managers and quickly responsive to changing circumstances.

Loyalty and Profits

In general, the longer a customer stays with a company, the more that customer is worth. Long-

The Satisfaction Trap

Many companies that use satisfaction surveys to learn how happy their customers are with their products or services often mislead themselves. What matters is not what customers say about their level of satisfaction but whether the value they feel they've received will keep them loyal. As tools for measuring the value a company delivers to its customers, satisfaction surveys are imperfect. As tools for predicting whether customers will purchase more of the company's products and services, they are grossly imperfect.

Satisfaction surveys have two principal problems. The first is that satisfaction *scores* have become an end in themselves at many companies but scores mean nothing unless the satisfaction they purport to measure translates into purchases and profit. The second problem is that satisfaction surveys are often poorly conceived and conducted. They measure the wrong activity or the wrong customers; they are easy to manipulate; they encourage companies and employees to invest time and money unproductively.

In many organizations, good satisfaction scores are considered a higher goal than profits and have a more immediate effect on compensation. The automobile industry pioneered the use of satisfaction surveys and probably spends more money on them than any other industry. When General Motors committed itself to reversing the inroads of foreign competition by concentrating on customers, it tied a portion of management bonuses to improvements in satisfaction scores. In the 1980s, satisfaction scores went up, as do most measures included in management bonus calculations, but market share and profits continued to go down. Nevertheless, most automakers continue to track satisfaction scores with great statistical rigor and use them in incentive and recognition programs for a wide range of employees. Today, as a result, more than 90% of industry customers report that they are satisfied or very satisfied. But repurchase rates remain mired in the 30% to 40% range. How can that be? There are several reasons, all having to do with the second problem, the way satisfaction surveys are designed and carried out.

Whenever rewards are based on satisfaction scores decoupled from repurchase loyalty and profits, the result is unproductive behavior. Employees naturally seek the easiest ways to improve scores, not necessarily the most profitable ways. One Toyota dealership offered a free auto detailing to any customer who agreed to return a survey marked "Very Satisfied" in all categories. The dealer even provided a printed copy of the survey showing how to check it off. At another dealership, a salesman pleaded with a customer to fill the form with favorable responses. "I'll lose my job here if I don't get high scores," he said. Auto companies like to advertise high marks on J.D. Power and Associates satisfaction surveys, so they've also learned how to manipulate the scores. Calling customers immediately after they've bought a car and asking about the experience is one way to keep scores high but probably won't lead to increased loyalty.

A second reason surveys don't work is that they almost never provide the information that managers need to pick the investments that will maximize customer value and, in turn, cash flow. Early successes with satisfaction programs are often a matter of picking low-hanging fruit. A car company's surveys might identify easily remedied sources of dissatisfaction – mechanics wearing dirty uniforms, customers not getting their cars on time. Once a company has made the obvious improvements, however, it's likely to find that the next level of satisfaction enhancement requires a real investment. Is it worth $10 million to retrain all the service managers? Is it worth $10 million to increase the average satisfaction score from 85% to 90%? Is it worth $100 million? These questions are basic to delivering the best value, but satisfaction surveys cannot answer them.

A third drawback is that surveys ignore critical distinctions among customer segments. Companies should pay less attention to what customers say and make a greater effort to track lifetime purchases. What makes this effort so important is that it forces a company to channel its consumer-satisfaction investments toward customers with the highest potential value, whereas satisfaction research conducted broadly across the entire customer base – the correct approach statistically–will necessarily show the influence of unprofitable customers. For example, a bank's

term customers buy more, take less of a company's time, are less sensitive to price, and bring in new customers. Best of all, they have no acquisition or start-up cost. Good long-standing customers are worth so much that in some industries, reducing customer defections by as little as five points – from, say, 15% to 10% per year–can *double* profits.

CEOs buy the idea that customer loyalty matters; they would prefer to have loyal customers. But without doing the arithmetic that shows just how much a loyal customer is worth over the whole course of the customer life cycle, and without calculating the net present value of the company's present customer base, most CEOs gauge company performance on the basis of cash flow and profit. They rarely study the one statistic that reflects how much real value the company is creating, the one statistic with predictive power: customer retention.

branch manager might hear many complaints about long teller lines, but it's perfectly possible that the branch's most profitable customers do most of their business by phone, mail, and ATM. Investing in more tellers may inflate satisfaction scores but actually deflate profits by improving service levels and increasing costs in areas that the best customers don't care about.

The Baby Bells are another example of companies using satisfaction surveys as they grope for the right management tools in an increasingly competitive environment. Most have developed surveys to help focus their organizations on customer service. But few have built systems to analyze lifetime purchases and profits from different types of customers. Those that do this analysis find that the top 10% of their customers are worth 5 to 10 times as much in potential lifetime profits as the bottom 10%. Telephone companies that try to manage through increasingly refined customer-satisfaction systems are likely to suffer the automakers' fate. While they work at raising broad satisfaction scores, competitors will lure away their best customers by delivering outstanding value to precisely these most profitable segments. Diminished cash flows will then make it more difficult to deliver good value even to average customers.

Yet another weakness of satisfaction surveys is that an increasing number of customers are tired of being surveyed. A Cadillac dealer tells this story: "One of my customers cornered me at a charity board meeting and told me, 'I got a call after I picked up my car, asking if I was satisfied with the sales experience. Then I got a call after the car was serviced, asking if I was satisfied with the service experience. Finally, someone called to check if I was happy with the ownership experience. So when am I going to get a call asking if I'm satisfied with the satisfaction-survey experience?'" One leading auto company admits that customers can get as many as six surveys in a year. Imagine how much this costs the company, to say nothing of customers' wasted time.

Companies serious about measuring the value they deliver to customers do not rely solely on satisfaction surveys. They recognize that satisfaction is an inherently unstable and temporary mental state and therefore is tricky to measure. Instead they track repurchase loyalty to determine the true value of their products and services relative to competitors'. When customers don't return for service, or when they buy another brand–these are incontestable signs that they are unhappy with the value. In business after business, 60% to 80% of lost customers reported on a survey just prior to defecting that they were satisfied or very satisfied. Some companies respond by trying to increase the sophistication of their satisfaction measures. Most automakers have chosen this approach, but they still see 90% of their customers claiming to be satisfied and 40% coming back to buy again.

The exception is Lexus, a consistent winner of auto satisfaction awards, which refuses to consider surveys the best measure of satisfaction. In the words of Dave Illingworth, the first general manager of Lexus, "The only meaningful measure of satisfaction is repurchase loyalty." Illingworth knows that the gap between satisfaction scores and repurchase loyalty can be enormous. Drive by a Lexus dealership and you'll see a satellite dish on the roof. It keeps the dealer in constant touch with Lexus headquarters and maintains a steady flow of information in both directions about customers' auto and service purchases. Lexus knows which customers are coming back for more and which are not, and it can analyze the differences between dealers who are earning superior customer loyalty and those who are not.

In depending so heavily on broad-based satisfaction surveys, companies are letting too many defectors slip through the cracks. There is a better way. To know how much companies can afford to spend to satisfy specific customers, they need to measure the return on their investment. The only way to do that is to study lifetime purchase patterns. But since they have to track purchase patterns to determine customer profitability, why not simply use this information as their satisfaction index? Customers' repeat-purchase loyalty must become the basic yardstick of success. Companies can avoid the satisfaction trap if they remember that what matters is not how satisfied you keep your customers but how many satisfied and profitable customers you keep.

What keeps customers loyal is the value they receive. One of the reasons so many businesses fail is that too much of their measurement, analysis, and learning revolves around profit and too little around value creation. Their CEOs become aware of problems only when profits start to fall, and in struggling to fix short-term profits, they concentrate on a symptom and miss the underlying breakdown in the value-creation system. They see customer issues as subsidiary to profits and delegate them to the marketing department. In the most egregious cases, years of continuing defection can mean that former customers–people convinced by personal experience that the company offers inferior value–will eventually outnumber the company's loyal advocates and dominate the collective voice of the marketplace. When that moment arrives, no amount of advertising, public relations, or ingenious marketing will prop up pricing, new-customer acquisitions, or the company's reputation.

1. MARKETING IN THE 1990s AND BEYOND: Services and Social Marketing

Although some executives do realize that profits are really a downstream benefit of delivering superior value to customers—and that customer loyalty is therefore the best indicator of strategic success or failure—they lack the tools they need to focus their organizational learning on this most basic building block of profitable growth. They make the most of standard market research, including customer-satisfaction surveys, but such tools are simply not up to the task. (See the insert "The Satisfaction Trap.") And yet the message that relative value is declining—and all the information a company needs to make sense of that bad news and design possible remedies—is available from the day trouble starts. Defecting customers have most of that information. They are always the first to know when a company's value proposition is foundering in the face of competition.

A climbing defection rate is a predictor of a diminishing flow of cash from your customers.

In Search of Failure

The lifeblood of adaptive change is employee learning, and the most useful and instructive learning grows from the recognition and analysis of failure. A first step in getting the people in your organization to focus on failure analysis—in this case, customer defections—requires overcoming their preoccupation with success. Of course, success has lessons to teach. But businesspeople today are obsessed with success—and sometimes more obsessed with other people's success than with their own. Benchmarking has become a feverish search for the nation's or the world's lowest costs, highest volumes, fastest growth. Academics, consultants, and executives scour the globe for approaches that have led to big profits in one situation so they can apply them in others. Yet this quest for best practice has created much less value than one might expect, and the people who study systems can tell us why: When a system is working well, its success rests on a long chain of subtle interactions, and it's not easy to determine which links in the chain are most important. Even if the critical links were identifiable, their relative importance would shift as the world around the system changed. So even if we could point to the critical links and more or less reproduce them, we still could not reproduce all the relationships or the external environment in which they operate.

What *can* help is the study of failure. The people

who build, fly, and regulate airplanes understand this. Airline performance in the United States, as measured by the fatality rate, actually exceeds six sigma – 3.4 defects per million opportunities – which is the demanding standard of quality many manufacturers pursue but probably don't reach. When a plane crashes, investigators retrieve the flight recorder and spend whatever it costs to find out what went wrong. The result is that in a vastly complex and extremely dangerous operating environment, accidents have become rare events.

One of the world's consummate investors, Warren Buffett, reached a similar conclusion in his very different field. In 1991, he gave a speech at the Emory Business School in Atlanta, Georgia. He told his audience, "I've often felt there might be more to be gained by studying business failures than business successes. In my business, we try to study where people go astray and why things don't work. We try to avoid mistakes. If my job was to pick a group of ten stocks in the Dow-Jones average that would outperform the average itself, I would probably not start by picking the ten best. Instead, I would try to pick the 10 or 15 worst performers and take them out of the sample and work with the residual. It's an inversion process. Albert Einstein said, 'Invert, always invert, in mathematics and physics,' and it's a very good idea in business, too. Start out with failure and then engineer its removal."

In addition to their preoccupation with success, there is another reason companies make so little use of failure analysis. Psychologically and culturally, it's difficult and sometimes threatening to look at failure too closely. Ambitious managers want to link their careers to successes; failures are usually examined for the purpose of assigning blame rather than detecting and eradicating the systemic causes of poor performance.

Defining Defection

Some customer defections are easier to spot than others. Customers who close their accounts and shift all their business to another supplier are clearly defecting. But what about customers who shift *some* of their purchases to another supplier, and what about those who actually buy more but whose purchases represent a smaller share of their total expenditures (a smaller share of wallet)?

The story of MicroScan—then a division of Baxter Diagnostics and now of Dade International, recently acquired by Bain Capital – is illustrative. In mid-1990, MicroScan was neck-and-neck with Vitek Systems in a race for market leadership in automated microbiology. Both companies made the sophisticated instruments medical laboratories use to identify the microbes in patient cultures and determine which antibiotics will be most effective. Both companies were growing rapidly, converting customers from manual testing and edging out other manufacturers of automated equipment. MicroScan had worked hard to improve quality and was thinking about applying for the Malcolm Baldridge National Quality Award.

Perhaps because diagnostics was its business, perhaps because competition had heightened its quality awareness, MicroScan was intrigued with the notion of failure analysis. To make itself an even stronger, more profitable competitor, the company decided to seek out defectors and use them to uncover and correct shortcomings. It began by asking its sales force to identify customer defectors. The sales force assumed that the company's executives meant total— that is, complete—defections and responded that there were almost none. A few customers had gone out of business, but in automated microbiology as in many other industrial businesses, total defections are relatively rare. Once companies have purchased equipment, they continue to buy consumables and service for many years.

But the sales force was ignoring the fact that defections can be partial. A customer may buy *some* equipment, *some* consumables, *some* service from other suppliers, and these fractional defections have meaning. MicroScan was not getting 100% of subsequent sales on all its accounts, and given the hotly competitive environment in which the company found itself, management chose to use this more demanding standard to measure failure. As it happened, the sales force was ignoring another fact as well: Systematic analysis of billing records revealed that, in fact, there were quite a few total defections among *small* customers.

The company interviewed every one of the lost customers and a large number of the partial defectors, searching for the root causes of each defection, especially when customers had defected to alternative microbiological testing equipment. The picture that emerged was clear, instructive, and painful. The customers interviewed were concerned about the reliability of MicroScan's instruments. They had complaints about certain features of the equipment and felt the company was insufficiently responsive to their problems.

There is always a strong temptation to rationalize these kinds of complaints: Those weren't good customers to begin with; it's not our fault that the customer's technical staff is not sophisticated enough to use our instruments; customers that use our hot line all the time aren't profitable anyway. But rationalization is just a way of failing at failure

analysis, and MicroScan's managers overcame their natural impulse to explain complaints away. Instead, they listened, learned, and took corrective action. They shifted R&D priorities to address the shortcomings customers had identified, such as test accuracy and time to result. Having learned that their line of instruments was too expensive for many small labs, they accelerated development of a low-end model and brought it to market in record time. They also redesigned their customer-service protocol to make sure that they gave immediate attention to equipment faults and delivery problems.

MicroScan's ability to learn from failure paid off. Two years later, the company pulled away from Vitek to achieve clear market leadership, and it now enjoys the bottom-line benefits that go with it. Tracking and responding to customer defections, however uncommon – and they are now less common than ever – have become central to the way MicroScan does business.

Core Customers

In the process of deciding how it wanted to define customer defections, MicroScan had to make two critical judgment calls. The first involved the size of the unit of failure. Managers tightened the definition of defection: It no longer meant the total loss of a customer but rather the loss of any portion of that customer's business. Then they defined just who the company's core customers really were, recognizing that small labs were indeed important customers. Giving core customers good reason to stay loyal was, in the long run, what made the decisive competitive difference between MicroScan and Vitek.

Unfortunately, identifying core customers is not always as easy as it looks, especially in industries where the competitive landscape is changing. But the effort is well worth it. In fact, defining core customers can be one of the most critical strategic processes a CEO ever sets in motion. Although it may uncover an unexpected well of uncertainty and inconsistency, it will lead to a deep, animated discussion of the company's basic mission and its ultimate goals.

The most practical way to get started is by answering three overlapping questions. First, which of your customers are the most profitable and loyal? Look for those who spend more money, pay their bills more promptly, require less service, and seem to prefer stable, long-term relationships. Second, which customers place the greatest value on what you offer? Some customers will have found that your products, services, and special strengths are simply the best fit for their needs. Third, which of your customers are worth more to you than to your

Rooting Out the Causes of Defections: A Case Study

Everybank, with roughly 2 million customers, was a typical superregional commercial bank. With a typical defection rate of about 20%, Everybank was losing some 400,000 customers each year; and, aware of the dire economic consequences of defection, it found ways of learning from its lost customers. (Everybank is also fictitious – a composite picture of several such banks and representative experiences.)

Everybank had administered a satisfaction – or in this case, dissatisfaction – survey to customers who closed their accounts, but the superficial information the survey yielded was not much help in pinpointing what was wrong with the business system. For example, more than half of the respondents listed price or interest rate as the primary cause of defection. But when the bank called some of them, it heard stories like this:

How long had you been a customer at Everybank?
Twelve years.
What caused you to close your account and move it?
Commonbank was right around the corner and they paid a higher CD rate.
Have Commonbank's rates long been higher?
I don't know, I just noticed recently.
What made you notice?
I was a little irritated at Everybank, and then I saw an ad in Thursday's paper.
Why were you irritated?
Because I was turned down for a credit card.
Had you ever been turned down before?
Yes, several times, but this time, the bank gave me this big come-on about being a preferred customer – and then turned me down with a form letter!

As it happened, the rates at Commonbank were almost identical to those at Everybank, except occassionally on Thursdays, because Commonbank changed rates on Thursdays and Everybank on Fridays. But of course price had little to do with the defection. The real root cause was the credit card division's failure to coordinate its marketing and qualification efforts. When interviewers pushed the questioning far enough, *most* defectors who named price on their surveys turned out not to be price defectors after all.

Everybank needed to find the real causes – or at least the 20% that produced 80% of defections – but even a good sample of the defectors is too many for in-depth, root-cause interviews that can take two hours each. The bank solved the problem with computers. Professional interviewers spoke to several hundred defectors, reviewed their interactions with the bank, created a series of questions that would permit any interviewer to uncover the real reason for a defection,

then translated that series into a computer program that enabled relatively unskilled interviewers to get to the root causes of defections in an average of 20 minutes. For example:

Why did you close your personal account at our Pine Street branch last month?
Your prices are way out of line.
Do you mean our interest rates on loans or the fees we charge for checking services?
The fees on some of my automated teller transactions and your loan pricing. That's why I refinanced my mortgage with another bank.
Have you closed any other accounts with our bank over the past few years?
Yes, I used to do all my banking with you because your branch was located next door to my dry-cleaning business, but you closed that branch three years ago.
Did you switch your business accounts to another bank when your branch closed?
Not right away. But First National offered me a package product that combined everything into one statement and gave me a better value because they considered all my balances in determining my fees. But the real key was the convenient statement.
Would you have stayed with our bank if we could have offered a comparable package?
Yes, I think so. I like long-term relationships. Anyway, I like the manager at the Pine Street branch. He goes to my church. He really wanted my business – it's over $100,000 in balances – but he told me he couldn't match First National's bundled account.
Thanks for your help. One last question. Does your current bank charge lower ATM fees?
To be honest, I'm not sure.

The computer system helped the bank question a large sample of defectors, identify core customers – in this case, the 20% of customers who created 80% of profits – and dig deep enough to find solutions. Senior managers were impressed but then grew frustrated when defection rates did not come down fast or far enough. The problem was confusion about who needed to learn. Everybank's new methods produced reliable information, but branch managers had seen customer research before and doubted that these root-cause interviews could tell them much they didn't already know about customers they had worked with for years. When branch managers were asked to look at individual names and suggest root causes, they asserted confidently that most had left to get better rates or products, or because backroom processing had made errors in their accounts – all reasons conveniently beyond the control of a branch manager.

The interviews showed, to the contrary, that roughly half of all defections resulted from branch-level problems such as customer service and complaint resolution. Some skeptical branch managers insisted on listening to the interview tapes themselves. Others accepted the root causes identified by the study but refused to believe the defectors were profitable customers until they reviewed the records. Gradually, the evidence persuaded them to open their eyes.

Then other problems arose. Many critical changes affected several departments that needed to work together. But cooperation across units was not a company habit. Worse, the failure-analysis team was itself something of a problem. The junior executive in charge couldn't get the attention of other unit heads, who were his boss's peers. The bank found that failure analysis needed the leadership of an executive with the power to assemble cross-departmental task forces, as the following example shows.

Removing the Sources of Failure

Among the most profitable defecting customers, 25% named incidental fees as a critical root cause. Large balances in multiple accounts delivered so much value to the bank, they believed, that $35 for bouncing a check was unreasonable. Top management did the arithmetic, found that 0.2% fewer defections would more than offset lower fees, and reduced them. But a new failure-analysis team, led by a senior executive, discovered that the problem had several dimensions involving several units. One was that salespeople had steered clients into products inappropriate for high-balance customers. The right products – for example, a bundled checking/money-market/savings account – had no fees. A second was that the marketing department had failed to include balances from products like mortgages and credit cards in the pricing formula. A third was that budget constraints had led the data-processing department to postpone implementation of a computer program that would link all of a customer's accounts. The final resolution of the fee problem involved many constituencies – the entire branch sales force, training, marketing, data processing, and above all a failure-analysis team with the organizational clout to do effective root-cause detective work and implement solutions.

The bank also discovered that the efficiency of learning depended on incentives. Education's first rule is that the student must want to learn. To get branch managers to stay longer with the bank and do more business with their best customers, Everybank revised its reward system to include multiyear bonuses based on each manager's success in penetrating and retaining top customer groups. The bank also found it could evaluate defection-correction teams by measuring how often root causes recurred. When people realized their bosses really cared about defections, they decided their root-cause analyses needed to be more precise. For example, credit-collection problems were high on the list of root causes, but no one knew what was wrong or how to fix it. Was it that collections officers called instead of the branch manager, whom customers knew as a friend? Were the calls too brusque? Did collections always know that a customer had $200,000 in CDs in addition to a nonperforming loan? Or was it just that customers never talked to the same person twice and had to repeat their story again and again? Each explanation would require a different solution. The root-cause survey process needed to be more precise.

Everybank found it couldn't rely on interviews alone. Not even the most sophisticated survey technology will uncover every root cause, because some customers don't *know* why they defected. For example, branch managers knew that employee turnover affected customer turnover, but few defectors mentioned it. Statistical analysis showed that personnel turnover could explain almost half the differences in customer attrition from branch to branch. Customers couldn't put their fingers on it, but they clearly perceived that employees less familiar with their own jobs and with their customers delivered lower value.

Everybank also learned that it needed to look for customer categories with distinctive attrition levels. For example, customers whose initial purchase was a particular money-market account showed loyalty well above the average, so the bank redirected new-account promotions to feature that product. Customers who opened three or more different types of accounts simultaneously had the highest retention rate, so marketing created a new product that combined checking, savings, credit card, and an overdraft line – all with one account number. Conversely, the bank found that certain promotions – CD bonus rates, for example – brought in customers with lower retention rates, so it dropped them. And upon finding that certain mergers and acquisitions brought in customers with very high attrition rates, senior managers adjusted their acquisition strategy.

In case after case, Everybank identified failure and removed its source. The combination of root-cause analysis and systematic statistical study of customer segments improved the quality of the bank's customer base. In the first year, defections in the best customer group fell by a third. But among customers who failed to cover their own costs, defections actually increased – as managers had hoped they would.

competitors? Some customers warrant extra effort and investment. Conversely, no company can be all things to all people: Customers who are worth more to a competitor will eventually defect.

The answers to these three questions will produce a list of your most obvious core customers. Identifying that group will give your management team a head start on the much more difficult task of developing the larger definition of core customer that your company will use in screening its customer base to see which defections warrant analysis. The discussion should also involve close scrutiny of some measurements and statistics that you ought to make sure you have available, among them the life-cycle profit pattern and the net present value of each customer segment, your share of customer wallet, and average customer retention by segment, age, and source.

Mass marketers such as banks and insurance companies often believe they must serve and satisfy all customers equally, and they therefore give equal attention to finding the root causes of all defections. Many companies give equal weight to first-class and third-class defectors in allocating resources to counteract defections, and some overzealous customer-recovery units spend money to save unprofitable customers or customers with negative value. Companies with high fixed costs, such as automakers, airlines, and telephone companies, fall easily into this trap. Every customer brings in revenue that helps offset fixed costs, they reason, so every customer is a good customer. But the companies that have achieved extraordinary levels of customer loyalty have discovered they

must concentrate their efforts on that subset of customers to whom they can deliver consistently superior value. State Farm Insurance, for example, which serves more than 20% of North American households, knows it must focus intently on its own kind of auto-insurance customer: the better-than-average driver who values agent service. Sir Colin Marshall, chairman of British Airways, put it this way in a recent interview (HBR November-December 1995): "Even in a mass-market business, you don't want to attract and retain everyone.... The key is first to identify and attract those who will value your service and then to retain them as customers and win the largest possible share of their lifetime business."

This is a good place to point out that all the techniques of root-cause defection analysis are important not just for customer retention but also for new-customer acquisition. After all, your new customers are some other company's defectors. By interviewing them to find out why they left and came to you and by watching to see how much of their spending you earn and retain, you can learn a great deal about them and about how to improve your company's customer-acquisition strategy. What percentage of newly acquired customers fits your definition of core customers? Are you effectively promoting your real strengths and attracting the kinds of customers your value proposition was designed to serve? How do your new customers compare with your competitors' new customers and how do they compare to your defectors? One of the secrets of sustainable growth is to find and keep the right customers – core customers. If your ad-

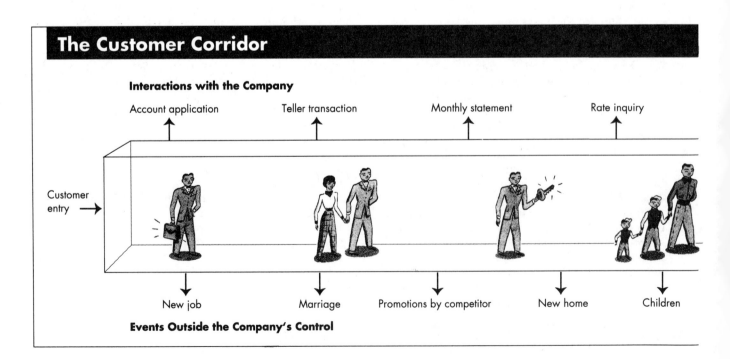

The Customer Corridor

Interactions with the Company

Account application   Teller transaction   Monthly statement   Rate inquiry

Customer entry →

New job   Marriage   Promotions by competitor   New home   Children

Events Outside the Company's Control

vertising, sales incentives, or marketing promotions draw unprofitable or marginal customers, the sooner you know it–and fix it–the better.

Root-Cause Analysis

Getting to the root causes of human behavior takes a lot of time, effort, and experience. In a factory setting, where root-cause failure analysis has been perfected over decades, the process is known as the *five why's* because you usually have to ask why something happened at least five times to get to the root of a failure. For example:

Why did the product get returned as defective?

The connector came loose.

Why did the connector come loose?

The plug was out of tolerance.

Why was the plug manufactured out of tolerance?

The intermediate stamping machine failed.

Why did the stamping machine fail?

Routine maintenance wasn't done on schedule.

Why?

There is an attendance problem in the maintenance department.

After five why's, you begin to see what needs to be fixed, though it may actually take a few more questions to figure out the best solution. Since applying this type of rigorous analysis to every single defect a plant experiences would be absurdly expensive, smart companies first perform a statistical frequency analysis, so they can concentrate their efforts on the 20% of categories that account for 80% of defects (applying Vilfredo Pareto's 80/20 rule).

Understanding weaknesses in customer value is much more difficult than understanding why a part was stamped out of tolerance in a plant. Objective fact is a big part of the five why's. The plug did not meet the precisely defined specifications for all such plugs. But the specifications for customer value are individual and tend to be subjective, so the only way to assess them is to interview customers and ex-customers and learn what they want and their views of the value they have received. The level of value a customer perceives can be defined as the time-weighted sum (more recent experiences are weighted more heavily) of all interactions with the company. So a good place to begin the search for failure is by reviewing the history of those interactions. (See the insert "Rooting Out the Causes of Defections: A Case Study.") Occasionally, a single event is so powerful it leads to defection all by itself ("your clerk swore at me"), but that is the exception. In most cases, a series of events leads slowly to a decision to seek better value elsewhere. To assess the root cause of a defection, the interviewer must typically identify three or four disappointing events and weigh them appropriately.

Sometimes it is helpful to map out the whole life

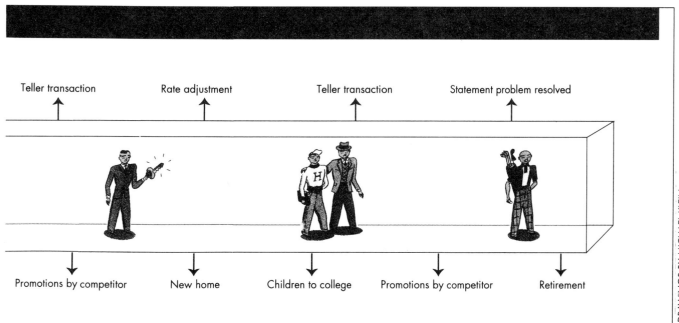

Teller transaction   Rate adjustment   Teller transaction   Statement problem resolved

Promotions by competitor   New home   Children to college   Promotions by competitor   Retirement

DRAWINGS BY MICHAEL KLEIN

cycle of a customer's interactions with the company. You can think of this life cycle as a corridor. (See the exhibit "The Customer Corridor.") Imagine that customers enter at one end and that the arrows along the top of the passage represent doorways or interactions with the company. At a bank, the corridor might start with an account application. What determines customer value is the sum of relative benefits and drawbacks, advantages and disadvantages, that consumers encounter at each doorway. The model can also show the frequency of those interactions, and frequency combined with interview material can tell a company which interactions are the 20% driving 80% of the differences in loyalty and value.

In many businesses, including banking, insurance, and other service industries, the customer corridor has a second set of doorways made up of the major changes in a customer's private life, which, along with competitors' efforts to lure the customer away, are represented by arrows below the corridor. Career moves, relocations, lifestyle changes, and almost any family watershed – a marriage, birth, divorce, or death – are often occasions for delivering additional value to the customer. In fact, if a company does not gear its products and services to such events, family upheavals will almost certainly produce defections. Banks that have analyzed defection frequencies find that changes of this kind increase the probability of defection by 100% to 300%. For obvious reasons, relocation is a prime culprit; but root-cause interviewers looking only at the arrows along the top of the corridor would miss that cause.

Once you have mapped out the customer corridor for your business, it is time to begin interviewing defectors in earnest – probing customer behavior, uncovering the root causes of each defection, and testing various solutions to see which, if any, would have saved the relationship. One secret to this process is to have the right people take part. It can't be done with focus groups. Professional focus-group leaders from outside the company cannot have the deep knowledge of the business they need to ferret out root causes, and asking groups why they made individual purchase decisions produces nothing but groupthink. (If focus groups have a role, it may be to brainstorm solutions to specific root causes once they have been determined to have a high priority

There's no substitute for having executives hear for themselves what went wrong.

for core customers.) You can't contract the interviewing to a group of market research specialists, either, because they simply cannot know enough about your organization and its competitive situation, market and pricing strategies, cost position, and capabilities. Failure analysis demands a thorough understanding of the business system and its economics and a clear sense of what scale and unit of failure to scrutinize. In other words, failure analysis requires the guidance of senior managers. And if there is any uncertainty about precisely who the company's core customers are, or if the company needs to think about altering its value proposition or modifying its distribution channels, or if the defection data is incomplete, or if competitive conditions are undergoing rapid change, or if the organization is setting about failure analysis for the very first time – and there are probably very few businesses that meet none of those conditions – then senior managers must actually perform the failure analysis themselves.

The first step is to gather the senior management group (five or ten top executives) plus a sampling of respected frontline personnel – branch managers, say, or leading salespeople. Be sure to include people whose behavior will probably need to change. You must convince them that this diagnostic process has a top priority, and you must make it clear that they will not escape without making personal phone calls to defectors. Some will be very reluctant. Most people don't relish the idea of phoning strangers, let alone strangers who've been unhappy with the value they've received, and you will have to overcome that reluctance with leadership, peer pressure, and, if necessary, coercion. There is simply no substitute for having senior executives learn directly from defectors why the company's value proposition is inadequate.

Before making the calls, the group must determine which defectors are worth calling. You need to look at market research and satisfaction surveys, consider the opinions of frontline personnel about why particular customers behaved as they did, and identify differences between your company and your competitors with regard to business processes, structure, financial incentives, quality measurement, and value proposition. If your current information system is not up to the task of identifying key defectors, it is possible to assign telephone reps to call a large sample of apparent defectors and separate the wheat from the chaff by getting answers to half a dozen questions. You need to know something about their demographics—age, income, education, and so forth. You want to know how long they've been doing business with your company and to find out enough about their actual purchase history to determine whether or not they are core customers. And you need to make sure they have actually defected to a competitor, not simply stopped buying the product altogether. (The auto-insurance customer who sells the family car and switches to public transportation is not a defector but simply a former customer.) Phone reps are often a good investment because they not only collect basic data about each customer's demographics and true purchase history, they also can set up appointments for company executives to call back for a full root-cause interview. Most ex-customers will be so delighted at the prospect of a senior executive listening to their problems and complaints that they will leap at the opportunity. Sometimes, of course, you will need to offer them an incentive. Go ahead and spend what it takes to talk with a true representative sample of your target defectors.

When you've done all this, assign each executive (yourself included) 10 to 25 defectors. When you've interviewed a quarter to a third of your defectors, you should reconvene to discuss what everyone is hearing, resolve any problems with the process, share best practices, and most important, use these early interviews to develop a preliminary list of corrective actions the company might take. Additional interviews can then focus on the most important questions and test hypotheses.

The final step is the joint development of an action plan based, of course, on the results of the defector interviews. The group will probably come up with some remedies that require little spending or preparation and can therefore be tested at once. Others may require further research or analysis because of the size of the necessary investment. The frontline managers included in the executive group will help to ensure that your interpretations of customer behavior are reasonable and that your proposed improvements can be carried out.

One word of warning: The realization that every company has some customers it's better off losing poses a special hazard to companies engaged in defection analysis. The danger is that on the basis of inadequate information, the company will mistakenly identify potentially valuable customers as dispensable, ignore the lessons they have to teach, and make no effort to retain them. Such mistakes are easy to make because some first-class defectors are disguised as third-class. They were once outstanding customers and could be again, but by the time they're ready to leave, they've already moved a substantial share of their wallet to a competitor. As partial defectors, they look like unprofitable customers. But accepting the disguise at face value means accepting undesirable defections; it can tempt the company to underinvest in the kinds of improvements that make customers want to stay. These situations call for something resembling defection archaeol-ogy—uncovering and analyzing several layers of historical and current data.

For example, one leading credit card company has built a computer system that lets its telephone reps instantly evaluate any customer who calls to cancel an account. The system is based on the potential profit from the customer's entire wallet, not merely on the company's present share, so a shift of spending to a competitor won't fool it. The phone rep can offer appropriate incentives to the best customers, and the company can watch to see whether the offers provide enough value to keep customers on board. Because of the inevitable tendency to dismiss all defectors as undesirable, knowing the true, sometimes hidden value of a defector turns out to be critically important in activating root-cause tracking systems.

In the case of a credit card company, information about a customer's entire wallet can be derived from credit-bureau reports. In banking, you can look at customers' mortgage applications to see where they keep their assets. In a few other industries, vendors make a business of collecting such data (the Nielsen ratings for television are one example). In most industries, however, the only way to determine share of wallet is to conduct a survey of your own and your competitors' customers. In other words, you have to ask.

Getting the Right People to Learn the Right Lessons

Unfortunately, useful learning is not closely related to the quantity of information available. If it were, we'd all be swimming in skills and expertise. Useful learning is instead a matter of getting the right information to the right people and giving them good reason to want to use it.

Market research with its customer questionnaires, satisfaction surveys, and focus groups was developed to give marketing departments the information they needed to set prices and design packaging, advertising, and promotions. It was not invented to help frontline employees provide better service or to give them better incentives or to solve the problems that cross departmental boundaries. Market research has the added drawback that those who learn most about customers are often the researchers, who usually are outside experts. They produce reports for managers (usually in marketing) who then interpret the findings for senior management. By the time information works its way back down the organization to frontline managers and employees in sales or service, it is too general to be at all useful.

The research we call root-cause analysis eliminates many of these weaknesses. When frontline managers and employees know the causes of customer dissatisfaction but cannot convince senior managers, the interviews that executives themselves conduct are nearly always persuasive. When frontline managers are mistaken about what is actually driving customers away, the immediacy, depth, and credibility of root-cause interviewing – they can often listen to taped interviews for themselves – overwhelms skepticism.

But although root-cause analysis enables people to learn, you still need some systematic way of getting them to want to learn. Therefore, the indispensable first step in unleashing the power of defection analysis is to make appropriate changes in measures, incentives, and career paths. In many organizations, the current incentives do little or nothing to make anyone care about fixing defections. Branch managers in a typical bank are paid bonuses on a variety of measures ranging from budgets to satisfaction surveys. Learning why customers defect takes time and energy, so unless it's clear to branch managers that their annual bonuses are tied to reducing attrition, supplying them with world-class failure-analysis technology won't improve their decision making.

Likewise, the marketing manager whose bonus is based on the volume of new deposit dollars generated through CD promotions doesn't really care if new depositors defect next year. And the credit-collections manager whose bonus is based on the balances collected from delinquent credit cards doesn't long to learn why customers defected from other bank products, such as savings and checking accounts. Often the most important barrier to learning from defections is that employees can't see how the learning relates to their own success.

Even in companies that care enough about retention to engineer effective incentives, it's sometimes necessary to remind employees how important it is to continue improving retention rates. Even though State Farm's agent-compensation structure was more heavily geared to retention than most competitors', managers at headquarters discovered that some of the company's agents had grown complacent. To shake them up a bit, the company calculated what would happen to an agent's income if he or she could achieve a one-percentage-point improvement in customer retention. The answer – a 20% increase in average annual earnings! – was just the tonic the company needed for its agents.

Lexus is another company that has cared passionately from the beginning about earning customer loyalty. The new carmaker chose dealers who had demonstrated a commitment to customer service and satisfaction. But like State Farm, Lexus has found it useful to let dealers know exactly how much their improved retention of customers is

worth to them in dollars. The company has constructed a model that can be used to calculate how much more each dealership could earn by achieving higher levels of repurchase and service loyalty. These cash-flow calculations are important reminders, even for those who already believe in the importance of customer retention, because for some reason, raising annual retention rates just a few points doesn't impress people. Perhaps we should multiply all our numbers by 100 or 1000. Every baseball fan knows there's a world of difference between a .280 hitter and a .320 hitter, but the actual difference is only four percentage points. Business needs a similar way to dramatize the enormous potential of a four-percentage-point improvement in customer retention.

Making Failure Analysis Permanent

Once you have mastered the interviewing and analysis techniques, customer defections become such a rich source of information that you will want to make the system permanent. This is both harder and easier than it might seem. To begin with, you need to build a measurement system to monitor whether and how effectively the solutions you've arrived at are reducing defection rates. Share of wallet is one such measure, and to make it really useful you need to break it down further into the percentage of customers giving your business an increasing share of wallet and the percentage giving you a decreasing share. Another essential measure is the defection rate itself, calculated separately for separate groups of customers – your best core customers, the rest of your core customers, the rest of your customers, and, perhaps, the customers you wouldn't mind losing. You also need to monitor the frequency of various root causes to make certain that problems are actually being solved and that new problems don't arise undetected.

And you need to create an ongoing mechanism that keeps senior managers permanently plugged into frontline customer feedback. Lexus asks every member of its headquarters staff to interview four customers a month. MBNA, the credit card giant, asks every executive to listen in on telephone conversations in the customer-service area or the customer-recovery units. Some of those executives make the phone calls themselves. Every company benefits when executives can combine decision-making economics with lessons learned directly from customers and defectors. The alternative is to depend on research conducted by outsiders who will never really understand your business, your competition, or your customers, and who will never really care.

Deere & Company, which makes John Deere

tractors and has a superb record of customer loyalty – nearly 98% annual customer retention in some product areas – uses retired employees to interview defectors and customers. USAA – the insurance and financial-services company based in San Antonio, Texas, that has come closer than any other U.S. company to eliminating customer defections altogether (it loses target customers at a rate of 1.5% per year, and most of that number are people who die) – treats customer defections very, very seriously and has pushed its analysis of them to a kind of pinnacle. The company recognizes that any event on the internal or external customer corridor that produces a spike in defection frequency highlights a dimension of customer value that needs improvement. USAA also tracks wallet share and retention rates separately by life-stage segment – for example, it knows when customers defect partially or entirely because their children have reached driving age and need auto insurance – so the company can spot problems and opportunities early and develop responses. In addition, focus groups of employees frequently review their customer interactions and draw up recommendations. Finally, to supplement its defector surveys, USAA has built an on-line system called Echo that enables telephone sales and service reps to input customer suggestions or complaints as they occur. Managers analyze all this data regularly to look for patterns, and they review problems and potential solutions at a monthly meeting with the CEO. The CEO then makes a formal quarterly report on customer retention to the board of directors. This careful, thorough, methodical approach to customer loyalty makes a striking contrast to the practice at most companies, where customer defection is either ignored, undervalued, or misunderstood.

The key to customer loyalty is the creation of value. The key to value creation is organizational learning. And the key to organizational learning is grasping the value of failure. As Vilfredo Pareto said more than 70 years ago, "Give me a fruitful error any time, full of seeds, bursting with its own corrections." Customer defection is a unit of error containing nearly all the information a company needs to compete, profit, and grow.

Marketing and Ethics

TYPE OF ETHICS: Business and labor ethics

DEFINITION: The process of buying or selling in a marketplace

SIGNIFICANCE: Seeks to apply ethical practices of product pricing, promotion, distribution, and marketing research strategies to the marketing of products and services

Various personal, societal and environmental factors have led to an increased awareness of ethics in business practices. Frequently, this awareness is focused on marketing activities. Continual publicity about businesses involve with unethical marketing practices such as price fixing, unsafe products, and deceptive advertising has led many people to believe that marketing is the area of business in which most ethical misconduct takes place.

Marketing and Ethics. Broadly speaking, "ethics" implies the establishment of a system of conduct that is recognized as correct moral behavior; it concerns deciphering the parameters of right and wrong to assist in making a decision to do what is morally right. "Marketing ethics" is the application of ethical evaluation to marketing strategies and tactics. It involves making judgments about what is morally right and wrong for marketing organizations and their employees in their roles as marketers.

The American Marketing Association (AMA) is the major international association of marketers. It has developed a code of ethics that provides guidelines for ethical marketing practices. Marketers who violate the tenets of the AMA code risk losing their membership in this prestigious and influential association.

Marketing is involved with a variety of ethical areas. Although promotional matters are often in the limelight, other ethical areas deserving attention relate to marketing research, product development and management, distribution, and pricing.

Promotion. The area of marketing that seems to receive most scrutiny with respect to ethical issues is promotion. Because advertising, personal selling, and other promotional activities are the primary methods for communicating product and service information, promotion has the greatest visi-

bility and generally has the reputation of being one of the most damaging areas of marketing. Misleading and deceptive advertising, false and questionable sales tactics, the bribing of purchase agents with "gifts" in return for purchase orders, and the creation of advertising messages that exploit children or other vulnerable groups are some examples of ethical abuses in promotional strategy.

Marketing Research. Marketing research can aid management in understanding customers, in competing, and in distribution and pricing activities. At times, however, it has been criticized on ethical grounds because of its questionable intelligence-gathering techniques; its alleged invasion of the personal privacy of consumers; and its use of deception, misrepresentation, and coercion in dealing with research participants and respondents.

Product Development and Management. Potential ethical problems in the product area that marketing professionals can face involve product quality, product design and safety, packaging, branding, environmental impact of product and packaging, and planned obsolescence. Some marketers have utilized misleading, deceptive, and unethical practices in their production or packaging practices by making unsubstantiated and misleading claims about their products or by packaging in a way that appeals to health-conscious or environmentally concerned shoppers. Ethical behavior involves using safe and ethical product development techniques, providing a product quality that meets customers' product specifications, using brand names that honestly communicate about the product, and using packaging that realistically portrays product sizes and contents.

Planned Obsolescence. Planned obsolescence represents an ongoing ethical question for marketers. Consumers are critical of it for contributing to material wear, style changes, and functional product changes. They believe that it increases resource shortages, waste, and environmental pollution. Marketers, on the other hand, say that planned obsolescence is responsive to consumer demand and is necessary to maintain sales and employment.

From *Ready Reference: Ethics*, May 1994, pp. 529-530. © 1994 by Salem Press, Inc. Reprinted by permission.

Distribution. Many of the potential ethical problems in distribution are covered by laws such as those contained in the Robinson-Patman Act. Nevertheless, distribution involves some ethical issues that merit scrutiny. Deciding the appropriate degree of control and exclusivity between manufacturers and franchised dealers, weighing the impact of serving unsatisfied market segments where the profit potential is slight (for example, opening retail stores in low-income areas), and establishing lower standards in export markets than are allowed in domestic markets are examples of some distribution cases that have significant ethical implications.

Pricing. Since pricing is probably the most regulated aspect of a firm's marketing strategy, virtually anything that is unethical in pricing is also illegal. Some of the primary ethical issues of pricing are price discrimination, horizontal/vertical price fixing, predatory pricing, price gouging, and various misleading price tactics such as "bait-and-switch" pricing, nonunit pricing, and inflating prices to allow for sale markdowns.

Marketing Ethics and Social Responsibility. It seems tenable to suggest that the areas of marketing ethics and social responsibility should be seen as concomitant. If marketing is authentically concerned with meeting consumer needs and concerns, it should also entail carefully evaluating how decisions impact and affect consumer expectations and quality of life.

Marketing activities can have significant societal and environmental ramifications. The rise of ecological consciousness among consumers gives social responsibility increasing stature. Consumers now are very concerned about whether the products or services they buy cause air or water pollution, landfill expansion, or depletion of natural resources. Recognizing this increased ecological concern of consumers, many companies are reevaluating the ways in which they produce and package their products and are considering the alteration of other areas of their marketing mix.

—John E. Richardson

See also Business ethics; Sales, ethics of.

BIBLIOGRAPHY

Boone, Louis E., and David L. Kurtz. *Contemporary Marketing*. 7th ed. Fort Worth, Tex.: Dryden Press, 1992.

Bovée, Courtland L., and John V. Thill. *Marketing*. New York: McGraw-Hill, 1992.

Evans, Joel R., and Barry Berman. *Marketing*. 5th ed. New York: Macmillan, 1992.

Laczniak, Gene R., and Patrick E. Murphy. *Ethical Marketing Decisions; The Higher Road*. Boston: Allyn & Bacon, 1993.

Richardson, John E., ed. *Annual Editions: Business Ethics*. 5th ed. Guilford, Conn.: Dushkin, 1993.

_____. *Annual Editions: Marketing 93/94*. 15th ed. Guilford, Conn.: Dushkin, 1993.

Smith, N. Craig, and John A. Quelch. *Ethics in Marketing*. Homewood, Ill.: Irwin, 1993.

THE NEW HUCKSTERISM

Stealth ads creep into a culture saturated with logos and pitches

Parents and teachers across the country notice a surge in teenagers sporting electronic beepers this summer. Foot soldiers in a drug cartel? Not quite. Just participants in a PepsiCo Inc. sales promotion. The cut-rate pagers beep weekly messages from sports figures and pop stars flogging soda and other teen-targeted brand-name goods.

TV viewers, used to channel-surfing past the commercials, encounter a strange phenomenon on CBS. On a winter evening, every show during a two-hour period features screen-legend-cum-perfume- vendor Elizabeth Taylor. She wanders in and out of everything from The Nanny *to* High Society, *searching for a missing string of black pearls—and shamelessly flogging her about-to-be-launched perfume of the same name. No actual commercial airs. In each case, Taylor is part of the story line.*

Smokers around the country looking for an alternative to Big Tobacco are confronted with an array of brands with funky names from Moonlight Tobacco Co. Hidden in the fine print on the sides of the distinctive packaging is the name of the real corporate parent, RJR Nabisco Inc.

What happened to the days when logos from America's biggest makers meant quality and integrity and were displayed with pride? When an ad was something that ran in 30-second slots on TV or on a page in a magazine? When commercials actually talked about the products they were trying to sell? Meet the New Hucksters: Part P. T. Barnum-style impresario, part MBA-toting tactician, they reflect the zeitgeist of a generation skeptical of any sales pitch and insatiable in its hunger for nonstop entertainment. In this postmodern advertising, sales messages, once clearly labeled, have now been woven subtly into the culture. Stealth pitches are embedded in movies, TV shows, or made into their own tiny entertainments, complete with fictional histories.

These New Age advertisers are redefining the notion of what an ad is and where it runs. Ads and even products are packaged to hide the big-bucks marketing machines that created them and to obliterate the line between advertising and enter-

tainment and—in some cases—advertising and real life. How? Some marketers aim for an ad that looks as much like an expression of the popular will, and as little like a paid sales message, as possible.

Rejecting the familiar "and now for a word from our sponsor" segue, these advertisers salt the content of a TV show, a movie, or even a video game with product mentions—or better yet, have their brands become part of the story. On the Internet, an online soap opera called *The Spot* builds its plot around the latest advertisers. Other marketers create music-and-celebrity-laced commercials that mimic popular entertainment. That's what Diet Coke did when it got the cast of *Friends* to pitch the brand—while remaining in character. Perhaps most insidious, ads have migrated from their traditional nesting grounds to invade spaces and institutions once deemed off limits.

Popular culture reflects the pervasive commercialism. TV serials, once oddly devoid of recognizable brands on the set, are now chock-full. The characters on *Seinfeld* shop at Price

A NEW GILDED AGE

The History Channel was all set to run a series of company profiles that would have been vetted—and to an extent, produced—by the sponsoring companies. But the concept created such a brouhaha that it ended up on the ash heap.

air-sickness bags on planes to toilet stalls, shopping carts, and gas pumps, few places are innocent of advertising. With total U.S. ad spending up almost 8%, to $162 billion last year, according to McCann-Erickson USA Inc., the new ad permutations aren't replacing the traditional television, magazine, and billboard messages. Rather, advertisers are adding new weapons to their arsenals because the traditional venues are packed full.

Even fresh fruit isn't immune. Quaker Oats' Snapple Beverage Div. slapped ad stickers on kiwis and mangoes this spring. It also bought ad space in bowling alleys on the arms that sweep away toppled pins. Lingerie maker Bamboo Inc. stenciled messages on Manhattan sidewalks two years ago that said: "From here, it looks like you could use some new underwear." Regina Kelley, director of strategic planning at Saatchi & Saatchi Advertising New York, warns that "any space you can take in visually, anything you hear, in the future will be branded, I believe. It's not going to be the Washington Monument. It's going to be the Washington Post Monument." That may not be such a stretch when cities across the continent have mothballed the venerable names that once graced their sports arenas in favor of the brand names of the highest-bidding advertiser, replacing Brendan Byrne Arena and Boston Garden with Continental Airlines Arena and Fleet Center.

Consumers may loathe the nonstop sellathon, but advertisers are only giving us what we want, or at least what we'll tolerate. The least-zapped commercials on TV are the fast-paced, lavishly produced soft drink spots that lean heavily on entertainment and little on product attributes. But the true postmodern advertising goes even further: It tries to morph into the very entertainment it sponsors. To that end, advertisers have taken up the role of filmmaker, gamemaker, and even novelist in a bid to create messages so entertaining, so compelling—and

Club and chew Junior Mints. Over on prime-time sitcom *Ellen*, they watch marketer *extraordinaire* Martha Stewart, in a guest-starring role, sign copies of her real-life cookbook. One of the most talked-about novels of the past season, *Infinite Jest: A Novel* by David Foster Wallace, envisions a time when years are named for their sponsors; most of the story is set in the Year of the Depend Adult Undergarment.

SNEAK ATTACKS. Advertisers, of course, have always been willing to stretch a point. And the steady volume of complaints at the Federal Trade Commission attests that there's still plenty of old-fashioned misrepresentation going on. But the new deceptions have less to do with puffery than with disguise. And while advertisers have long scouted out new territory ripe for slapping on a logo, now many are more interested in subterfuge than ubiquity.

Why are marketers going to such trouble to hide their sales pitches? It's because the buying public has

been virtually buried alive in ads. Consumers are bombarded with hundreds of ads and thousands of billboards, packages, and other logo sightings every day. Old ad venues are packed to the point of impenetrability as more and more sales messages are jammed in. Supermarkets carry 30,000 different packages, each of which acts as a minibillboard, up from 17,500 a decade ago, according to the Food Marketing Institute. Networks air 6,000 commercials a week, up 50% since 1983, according to Pretesting Co., a market research company. Prime-time TV carries more than 10 minutes of paid advertising every hour, roughly a minute more than at the start of the decade. Add in the promos, and almost 15 minutes of every prime-time hour are given over to ads. No wonder viewers zap so many commercials.

To circumvent that clutter, marketers are stamping their messages on everything that stands still. From popcorn bags in movie theaters to

MOCK 'ZINES

If sponsoring the content is good, controlling it is even better. *Guess Journal* runs upbeat stories about the jeansmaker. Benetton's *Colors* runs the same kind of controversial art that helped build the retailer's image around the world.

maybe so disguised—that rapt audiences will swallow them whole, oblivious to the sales component.

Guess? Inc. and Benetton Group both publish imitations of cutting-edge 'zines, with their jarring graphics and jumbled typefaces. Benetton's *Colors*, with a cover price of $4.50, springs from the same aesthetic—and ad budget—as the retailer's controversial high-shock ads. *Guess Journal*, which has a table of contents, masthead, and bylines, just like a real magazine, features the Guess? brand in most stories. There's either no advertising or nothing but, depending on your point of view.

BEEPER ADS. Knowing that consumers, especially young consumers, have learned to tune out conventional ads, marketers try to infiltrate their favorite entertainment. In Britain, Unilever's Van den Bergh Foods Ltd. is putting the finishing touches on a video game that will star its snack sausage, Peperami. (If you have to know, Peperami does battle with evil snack-food foes Carlos the Carrot and the Terminutter.) "This isn't a one-off cheap promotion," says Peperami Marketing Manager Paul Tidmarsh. "We are trying to produce a top-selling game. It is a new way of reaching our target audience." Van den Bergh is not the

flrst. In 1994, M&M/Mars bought a prominent role for its Snickers bar in Nintendo Co.'s *Biker Mice from Mars* video game.

Camouflaging a sales message in a teen's natural environment was what Pepsi was trying to do, too, when it came up with its beeper promotion. For $35 and a bunch of Mountain Dew box tops, kids can get a Motorola Inc. pager and six months of free service. The catch? Once a week for six months, they get beeped with an ad. By dialing the toll-free number, they'll hear messages from the likes of Lou Piniella and Ken Griffey Jr. of the Seattle Mariners alerting them to promotional offers and prizes from companies including MTV, Sony Music, and Specialized Mountain Bikes. The promotion has drawn criticism. For some adults, the combination of teens and beepers has only one association: drug dealing, which is why beepers are banned in some schools. Pepsi says the program advocates responsible beeper use. But the controversy isn't all bad for the soft-drink maker. Criticism from grownups could add to the brand's cachet with the young.

Even real life has been co-opted. To help revive Hennessy cognac two years ago, ad agency Kirshenbaum Bond & Partners hired models and actors to sit in trendy clubs and order martinis made with Hennessy. Co-chairman Jonathan Bond, whose company also dreamed up the Snapple Beverage ads, says this "word of mouth" technique was not deceptive, even though the buyers didn't identify their employer. "We were just trying to give people a chance to evaluate it," he says. "People are so cynical that you have to be more inventive just to get considered."

Meanwhile, commercials in conventional formats, such as the 15- and 30-second slots in prime time, work hard to blur the distinction between ad and program. MCI Communications Corp. had such a strong response to its Gramercy Press campaign that it extended it to additional media. The soap opera-like TV

FAKE REAL LIFE

Beware of a spontaneous product endorsement, especially for something you've never heard of from people you don't know. Hiram Walker & Sons hired cool-looking actors to hang out in bars and talk up a new drink made with an aging brand, Hennessy cognac.

commercials centered on a fictional publishing house at which all problems were solved and plots furthered with the help of MCI technology. First, a Gramercy Web site appeared. Then came a real novel purportedly written by the campaign's fictional celebrity author Marcus Belfrey and published by the fictional Gramercy Press. The real author, Barbara Cartland, and real publisher, Random House Inc., were revealed only inside the dust jacket. MCI even commissioned a two-hour pilot script for a TV series based on the story, but found no takers.

SURPRISE ENDING. The Gramercy Press commercials, though long on intrigue, did at least talk about MCI products. Other advertisers have expanded the format and toned down the pitch to produce far more subtle commercials. Guess? jeans' newest spot, which aired alongside previews in movie theaters this spring, was a 90-second black-and-white drama starring Juliette Lewis, Harry Dean Stanton, Traci Lords, and Peter Horton. It had virtually no connection to the sponsor's casual clothing, and only when the triangular Guess? logo flashed at the end did audiences find out they had been watching a commercial. "A lot of companies go for a degree of entertainment," says Guess? President Paul Marciano. "We try to be more entertaining, with a twist of intrigue, mystery." Whether audiences find it intriguing or manipulative, Marciano is committed to the minifilm format and hopes to extend his next effort to four or five minutes.

But marketers who too aggressively blur the line between ad and entertainment risk a backlash. Last month, A&E Television Networks' History Channel was forced to scrap plans for a series of one-hour specials that would profile companies. The highly regarded channel drew heavy criticism for its plan to allow subject companies to sponsor the series, help prepare the segments, cover some of the production costs, and have veto power over the final cut. A similar uproar over at CNBC

JUST LITTLE OLD US

Having a giant marketer behind a product used to be an advantage—but not when consumers are searching for something less mass-produced. Companies from Miller to GM to RJR/Nabisco have tried hiding the corporate logo behind a made-up company with a more homespun image.

hasn't quashed plans for *Scan*, a series that will examine the impact of technology on different cultures. IBM, *Scan*'s sole worldwide sponsor, will own the shows once they air and will sit on an advisory panel, though CNBC says it will retain editorial control. Making things even murkier: Two of the early segments show how priests at the Vatican use computers to digitize ancient religious texts and how commuters in traffic-clogged Bangkok use technology to work as they travel—both subjects of IBM ads in the computer giant's "Solutions for a Small Planet" ad campaign.

Other marketers spin fictions not to disguise their ads but to hide their corporate provenance. The idea is to fake an aura of colorful entrepreneurship as a way to connect with younger consumers who yearn for products that are handmade, quirky, and authentic. The seeds of the genre were planted in the 1980s when E&J Gallo Winery set up a dummy corporation to avoid using its own name in the ads or on the labels of its new Bartles & Jaymes wine coolers. A campaign revolving around a couple of faux-bumpkin entrepreneurs named Frank and Ed inspired a generation of imitators.

"A lot of people seemed to believe they were real, and we never intended that," says Hal P. Riney, head of San Francisco ad agency Hal Riney & Partners Inc., which created the ads.

INSTANT TRADITION. There is a direct line from Gallo's Bartles & Jaymes to Miller Brewing Co.'s Red Dog, which masquerades as a microbrew under the name Plank Road Brewery, and to RJR's Moonlight Tobacco Co. Moonlight markets cigarette brands with such quirky names as Politix, City, and North Star in selected markets. The cigarettes come in packages with eye-catching graphics and only the barest mention of their Big Tobacco parent. "People are looking for more personal products. They are looking for uniqueness, for things that are not the typical, average, familiar, mass-produced product that we've had around for so long," says Riney. "People are responding by creating these sort of fictional histories and fictional traditions."

Sometimes, too, companies adopt a new identity for the same reason people go into the witness protection program: The original ID has become bad news. That's what drove General Motors Corp. to dissociate itself from its innovative offspring,

NO LAUGHING MATTER

The dancing taco is part of a song-and-dance number spoofing Taco Bell, the first title sponsor on the *Dana Carvey Show*. Carvey built each week's sponsor into the gags. But the jokes were too raw for Taco's parent, PepsiCo. Despite the exposure, it bailed out of the show.

Other advertisers seek out chances for noncommercial commercials on TV and in the movies. Owning a piece of the show is one way to sneak aboard. Anheuser-Busch Co. owns a small stake in *Second Noah*, a syndicated series. The payoff? Exposure for Busch Gardens Tampa Bay, where the show is shot. Increasingly, networks are happy to cater to advertisers who want a bigger role. Witness Capital Cities/ABC Inc.'s short-lived *Dana Carvey Show*, which tried selling title sponsorships each week. The ex-*Saturday Night Live* comic lampooned sponsors' products as part of the night's entertainment. The strategy backfired in Week One, when Pepsi's Taco Bell found it didn't have the stomach for Carvey-style humor, which included calling himself a "whore" for the sponsor. Although Carvey seemed to tone down the gags after the first week, there were only three other sponsors, all Pepsi beverages, before the gimmick was abandoned. The show was canceled in April.

CAMEO HEAVEN. Sometimes, telling the show from the commercial is even harder. Elizabeth Arden Co. didn't pay for Elizabeth Taylor's appearances on four CBS sitcoms earlier this year. But the exposure for the star's new Black Pearls perfume from Arden was a marketing coup. The plot of each show was written around Taylor, playing herself, and her perfume brand. Was this market-

the Saturn. Because Detroit in general has suffered from a reputation for shoddy cars, sleazy dealers, and lousy service, GM set up a Saturn plant in Tennessee and hired Riney to package it as a small-town enterprise, run by folks not terribly unlike Frank and Ed. Whether Saturn customers are buying into better service and cars or buying into Riney's vision of small-town values, their cult-like devotion is the envy of other marketers. Two years ago, 44,000 of them trekked to Tennessee for a "reunion." Last year, Saturn was the nation's fifth-best-selling car.

Knowing that consumers are increasingly cynical about the claims in traditional ads, other advertisers have tried to ignite, appropriate, or imitate grassroots trends and fads. "When you're looking at younger consumers, you can't tell them what's cool," says Ric Militi, head of integrated communications at ad agency Lois/EJL in Los Angeles. "Generally, if it's advertised, it's immediately uncool."

That's why marketers work hard to make promotions look as unplanned as possible. Militi spotted an opportunity last fall when Spelling Entertainment Group Inc., alleging trademark infringement, forced

bar owners to stop hosting *Melrose Place* parties. The parties were springing up spontaneously at bars around the country on Monday nights when the prime-time soap opera aired. Militi quickly bought a license from Spelling on behalf of Hiram Walker & Sons' Kahlúa Royale Cream. He followed up each cease-and-desist letter the producer sent to bar owners with a marketing kit for a Spelling-sanctioned Kahlúa-sponsored party, complete with life-size cutouts of the cast, *Melrose* trivia, and plenty of Kahlúa knickknacks.

YIKES! INFOMERCIALS WITH COMMERCIALS

Infomercials aren't just the el cheapo late-night affairs of yesteryear. Now they look like regular TV—right down to the commercials. Paramount advertised its *Duckman* cartoon inside a 30-minute commercial for a music anthology. It also made its own infomercial last fall to promote the launch of a new TV series.

ing? Entertainment? Who cares? Arden got better exposure than ad-budget money could buy, and CBS's ratings for the heavily hyped evening were way up. "From a marketing standpoint, it was brilliant," says Betsy Frank, executive vice-president of Zenith Media. "It was as seamless as you can get."

While shows have started looking more like commercials, commercials have started looking more like shows. Take the new breed of infomercials, those 30-or 60-minute ads that once were the domain of the purely schlocky. Now, solid-gold marketers from Microsoft to Ford to Eastman Kodak are airing them. Gone are the tacky sets and lousy production values. These slick segments now mimic talk shows or even newscasts. Time Inc.'s infomercial for its *Rolling Stone* "Sounds of the '80s" music collection even managed to sell time to yet another advertiser. Halfway through the 30-minute pitch, a cartoon character breaks into the program. In essence, the appearance of Paramount Television Group's Duckman is a paid message inside another paid message.

Even Broadway producers are getting into the sponsorship act. When *Big, the Musical*, opened on Broadway in April, toy seller F.A.O. Schwarz got co-producer billing—and marketing mileage that extends far beyond the credits. The play's sets recreated the Fifth Avenue store

for a crucial scene. Meanwhile, the store recreated the sets. Visitors at either location could buy plenty of Schwarz-marketed *Big* merchandise. "This has not been an attempt to overtly aggrandize F.A.O. Schwarz," says John H. Eyler, president of Schwarz. At least one critic at the Detroit tryout disagreed, lambasting the show for blatantly plugging the toy store. Some of the most adulatory bits were cut before the New York opening, but the producers said the changes had nothing to do with downplaying Schwarz.

As movie screens and other venues become infested with brand-name goods, such glorified product placements may start to lose their punch. "The problem with marketing that doesn't identify itself as marketing is that consumers catch on and it loses its impact," says adman Bond. "It's not in the movie because it's such a cultural icon, but because someone paid for it."

That's why marketers work so hard to make the graft between ad and entertainment as smooth as possible. When it comes to truly smooth melding of the two, no one matches Martha Stewart, queen of the domestic arts, who combines a potent promise that housework can be glamorous with unparalleled media savvy. Her empire, which includes magazines, books, TV shows, and a nascent mail-order business, perfectly merges the Martha editorial

message with the Martha marketing message. When Martha shows us how to make puff pastry on television or how to tend lilacs in her magazine, that's information, but it's also an extended look at a living, breathing logo. Stewart so completely embodies her brand that virtually everything she does, whether it's a commercial for American Express Co. or a guest spot on *Ellen*, brings in new customers for Brand Martha.

Stewart may be the best indicator of where advertising is headed as it converges with the editorial content on our TV screens, in our magazines, and on our computers. Clearly, Stewart's fans, who are legion, want what she is selling. But what if all entertainment and information came entwined with a brand name and every human encounter were mediated by a commercial sponsor? Advertisers say they only run the commercials that bring in customers. Stop buying, and they'll rethink their campaigns. Maybe.

But in a world weary of the incessant sales pitch, you have to wonder if there's anything that's not for sale. If you find it, enjoy it while it lasts—before somebody decides to sponsor it.

By Mary Kuntz in New York and Joseph Weber in Philadelphia, with Heidi Dawley in London

Research, Markets, and Consumer Behavior

- Market Research (Articles 15 and 16)
- Markets and Demographics (Articles 17–20)
- Consumer Behavior (Articles 21 and 22)

If marketing activities were all we knew about an individual, we would know a great deal. By tracing these daily activities over only a short period of time, we could probably guess rather accurately that person's tastes, understand much of his or her system of personal values, and learn quite a bit about how he or she deals with the world.

In a sense, this is a key to successful marketing management: tracing a market's activities and understanding its behavior. However, in spite of the increasing sophistication of market research techniques, this task is not easy. Today, a new society is evolving out of the changing lifestyles of Americans, and these divergent lifestyles have put great pressure on the marketer who hopes to identify and profitably reach a target market. At the same time, however, each change in consumer behavior leads to new marketing opportunities.

The writings in this unit were selected to provide information and insight into the effect that lifestyle changes and demographic trends are having on American industry.

First, "The Frontiers of Psychographics" provides a lucid look at the resurgence of various types of qualitative research. Next, database marketing is presented as a potent new tool, used to reach customers and help secure their loyalty.

The next four articles examine the importance of demographic data, geographic settings, economic forces, and age considerations in making marketing decisions. First, a helpful background for understanding demographics is provided. Next comes a brief quiz about generations.

"Making Generational Marketing Come of Age" reveals the capability of reaching consumers—demographically, socially, and psychologically. Last in the subsection are some important recent research findings about churches.

The final subsection examines how consumer behavior, social attitudes, cues, and quality considerations impact the evaluation and purchase of various products and services for different consumers.

Looking Ahead: Challenge Questions

As marketing research techniques become more and more advanced through the use of automation and the computer, and as psychographic analysis leads to more and more sophisticated models of consumer behavior, do you believe marketing will become more capable of predicting consumer behavior? If not, why not? If so, what ethical considerations must confront the marketing profession?

Where the population lives, its age, and its ethnicity are demographic factors of importance to marketers. What other demographic factors must be taken into account in long-range market planning? What industries do you think are most concerned with these factors?

Psychographic segmentation is the process whereby consumer markets are divided up into segments based upon similarities in lifestyles, attitudes, personality type, social class, and buying behavior. In what specific ways do you envision psychographic research and findings helping marketing planning and strategy in the next decade?

THE FRONTIERS OF PSYCHOGRAPHICS

┌─ SUMMARY ─────────────────────────────────

In an effort to understand consumers' wants and needs, marketers are fueling a resurgence of qualitative research. Some fear that the focus on "soft" research is a time- and money-saving approach with potentially harmful results. Others are retooling psychologically based research for the 21st century, often with the help of computers.

Rebecca Piirto Heath

Rebecca Piirto Heath is a contributing editor of American Demographics *and author of* Beyond Mind Games: The Marketing Power of Psychographics *(American Demographics Books).*

Does red nail polish represent the pagan ritual sacrifice of small animals using teeth and nails? Sal Randazzo thinks it might. Randazzo, strategic planning director with McCann-Erickson, applies the Jungian concept of the archetype to the advertising world in *Mythmaking on Madison Avenue.*

Randazzo says that to make great ads you have to dig deep. "Great advertising finds the central truth that bonds the consumer to the product or brand," he says. Think of Betty Crocker as the Great Mother of ancient myth and the Bud Man as the hero in the Homeric tradition. "We have to be psychic archaeologists to peel back the layers to get to the dark places people don't know they have," he says.

Randazzo is one of a growing number of researchers using "psycho-qualitative" techniques to make some sense of an increasingly chaotic consumer environment. Marketers face a mission impossible trying to get intimate with consumers when those consumers behave so unpredictably. They demonstrate loyalties to brands (or not), blindly follow trends (or not), and buy according to their convictions and aspirations (or not). Individuals are innovators in some product categories, but not in others. What they say they do and what they really do are seldom the same.

To complicate things even further, trend watchers predict big changes in the American shopping public. "There's a sea change going on in consumer attitudes," says Watts Wacker, a futurist with SRI Consulting in Menlo Park, California. "We're entering an era so different from what has gone before that we need a whole new definition of what constitutes lifestyles." For example, longitudinal studies like the Yankelovich Monitor see erosion of the optimism that once defined bootstrap Americanism. "There is increasing concern from a rising proportion of people about what kind of life their children will have," says Ann Clurman of Yankelovich Partners in Norwalk, Connecticut. In 1992, 42 percent of Monitor respondents agreed that "Kids today will probably never be able to live as well as we do now." In 1995, 47 percent agreed with it.

"In the late 1980s, we saw a veritable collapse in confidence in virtually every institution we measured," Clurman says. There was an increasing feeling that life was out of control. This created a kind of "vigilante consumer" who saw the marketplace as enemy—consumers who believe if they don't watch out for number one, no one else will. The mid-1990s are showing signs of a turnaround, however, says Clurman. People are showing signs of "cautious trust," and a desire to "stop whining and get on with it."

Wacker says that old psychographic dimensions such as attitudes toward work and leisure or health and fitness don't fit today's realities. People's involvement with media, and their responses to and skills at getting information, are the most important predictors today. "There is a whole litany of new lifestyle characteristics driving the new era," he says. "We need to change the whole paradigm of doing research."

A CHANGING LANDSCAPE

Consumers' psyches aren't the only thing in flux. The advertising world faces a double-edged sword. First, there is a lot of competition out there. On the media level, people are deluged by information and overwhelmed by product choices. They are a hard sell, too, cynical over stealth advertising and dinner times ruined by telemarketers posing as surveyors. But while the need for better products and ads that cut through the din has never been greater, pressure is coming from the top for cheaper and faster research results. Overseas competitors are eating up market share. Ad agencies and advertisers are downsizing, reengineering, outsourcing, and dropping anything and anyone that doesn't obviously contribute to the bottom line.

Downsizing at ad agencies and product manufacturers started in the late 1980s. Total advertising employment fell 5 percent between 1990 and 1993, according to the Bureau of Labor Statistics, but then rose 8 percent by 1995 because of a growing number of start-up research firms, says Larry Gold, marketing research consulting director of the Advertising Research Foundation and editor of *Inside Research*, an industry newsletter.

The partial loss has been felt, however. "The advertising industry has lost a whole layer of people who used to act as methodological angels guiding the research process and making sure methods were appropriate to goals," says Frederick Elkind, a former senior vice president and director of research at Ogilvy and Mather who now heads Motivational Analysis, Inc. in Forest Hills, New York. "The industry is now adrift in competing techniques and methodologies, and experimentation is happening at every level."

Classic psychographic research, the kind that includes extensive surveying and statistical quantification, remains essential for some, but has become a luxury for others. "The trend for researchers to embrace qualititative to the detriment of quantitative is in full bloom now," says Gold. Spending on qualitative research remained stable between 1992 and 1995, while spending on quantitative research fell 4 percent, according to the 1995 Marketplace Data Survey by Prevision of Wellesley, Massachusetts.

> "We're entering an era so different from what has gone before that we need a whole new definition of what constitutes lifestyles."

"The way focus-group sessions are overrunning the research world is rather alarming to some of us," says Barbara Feigin, executive vice president, director of strategic services at Grey Advertising in New York City. "Many of the smaller and mid-sized agencies are trying to do something that brings them closer to the consumer, but they're taking the quickest, easiest, and most affordable shortcuts."

Those shortcuts are fueling a growing industry. Membership in the Qualitative Research Consultants Association (QRCA) is growing 10 percent to 20 percent a year, says Irving Merson of Merson/Greener Associates, Inc. in Tarrytown, New York, and past QRCA president. He puts the number of focus-group facilities at 1,200 and growing. Merson defends qualitative methods as viable research tools. "Qualitative research is only 50 years old, so it's a relatively young science," he says. "Like any science, it has had growing pains, but it is getting better all the time."

Current QRCA president Patricia Sabena agrees. "The old battle over whether qualitative is being used instead of quantitative is pretty much dead," she says. "We're not the bad guys anymore." These days, qualitative researchers use tighter controls and computer aids, and have better and a wider array of techniques. Sabena, who also operates Sabena Qualitative Research Services out of Westport, Connecticut, agrees with Feigin that qualitative research should not be a marketer's only resource. Jumping into a test market directly from the focus-group stage is definitely not wise, she says, but adds that qualitative research is useful for a variety of tasks, such as tweaking concepts and images for commercials, making packaging changes, and fine-tuning product development.

REVAMPING ESTABLISHED TOOLS

The information explosion, decline of hope, and new wave in research pose opportunities and challenges for established research tools like the Yankelovich MONITOR and VALS 2. Emerging industries have a greater need than established ones to get a psychographic fix on their customers.

The Yankelovich MONITOR has been tracking the ebb and flow of consumer attitudes for more than 25 years based on questionnaires administered to huge consumer panels. Doug Haley, managing partner with Yankelovich Partners, says the firm is looking for new ways to make the wealth of value and attitude information more relevant to specific product categories.

In the same way, SRI International, an academic and government think tank, reworked its VALS psychographic segmentation system several years ago and has recently undergone internal restructuring to enhance the visibility of its business and commercial programs. It has also continued to modify its psychographic research tools to better serve the business world. VALS 2, which segments the population into eight groups based on psychological attributes, has been reengineered and repositioned as a tool for understanding new product acceptance and innovation. SRI has changed the VALS algorithm and adopted a new methodology called Consumer Acceptance of Technology, says

William Guns, president and director of the Business Intelligence Center with the newly formed SRI Consulting Division.

Also on the horizon is iVALS, a project that focuses on the attitudes, preferences, and behaviors of online service and Internet users. Guns describes it as a research project in development that is not even for sale yet. SRI's Worldwide Web site (http://www.future.sri.com) allows visitors to take the VALS 2 questionnaire and get almost immediate feedback on their VALS 2 type. It also acts as a way to capture the psychographic profile of people who visit the site.

Early results of iVALS reinforce the idea of a dual-tiered society, Guns says, but one based on knowledge, not income. "It's become an issue of the knows versus the know-nots," he says. People who are out of the information highway loop are excluded more because of their limited education than because of the lower incomes less-educated people tend to have. "Education is the crucial factor in who participates in the Internet and to what degree," Gun says.

Education goes a long way toward explaining why half of Web users are Actualizers, the stereotypical upscale, technically oriented academics and professionals who cruise cyberstreets on a variety of institutional subsidies. Three in four are men, and virtually all have gone to college. Just 10 percent of the general population belongs to this psychographic segment. The other half of the Web audience represents 90 percent of the general population and is made up of four of the remaining seven VALS 2 types—Strivers, Experiencers, Fulfilleds, and Achievers. They are slightly less male-dominated than Actualizers (64 percent), and nearly as likely to have some college education (89 percent). Because they are already on the Internet but not at the same rates as Actualizers, these four groups represent the next big spurt of growth for the Net and related new media.

PSYCHO-QUALITATIVE RESURGENCE

The market research community is seeing a surge in interest in a variety of psychologically based methods. In the quest for

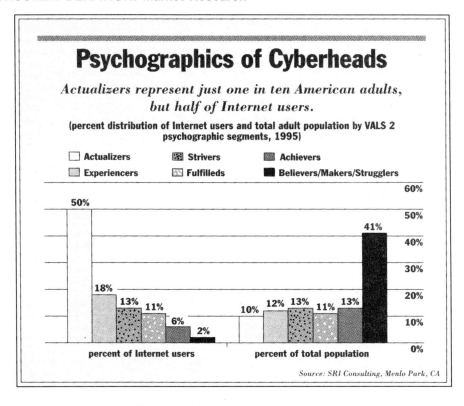

the magic microscope into consumers' minds, agencies and advertisers are using a mixture of everything qualitative and quantitative. As with iVALS, few of the techniques are brand new, but they are being retooled for the 21st century. From perceptual maps to collages and archetypal probing, the number of psychoqualitative tools keeps growing.

"We're seeing more interest in projective techniques," says Judith Langer of Langer Associates in New York City. Projective techniques probe beneath people's conscious minds to express underlying feelings. Techniques like brand personification (what Coors would look like if it walked into the room), guided imagery, and psychodrama can have consumers strutting around like cans of Arrid or acting out a confrontation with Mr. Clean.

Feigin at Grey used personification in a campaign for Sprint Business Services. When asked to imagine long-distance carriers as animals, group members described AT&T as a lion, MCI as a snake, and Sprint as a puma. Grey used the insights to position Sprint as the one that could "help you do more business" rather than taking the savings approach of the others.

Most adults probably haven't made a collage since grade school, but focus-group leaders are asking them to produce multimedia collages to bring to groups. One woman brought in a collage of pieces of shattered mirror to show how she felt when she had a migraine headache. "It was amazing," says Sharon Livingston, president of Executive Solutions in Syosset, New York. "Here was this very quiet woman who just came alive when asked to explain her masterpiece." If it hadn't been for the collage assignment, she says, the woman might never have shared her thoughts.

Some moderators give participants disposable cameras they can take home to photograph objects that represent their feelings about intangibles. In one Langer study for an apparel client, people brought in collages showing puffy beige and white things that said "comfort" to them. "It was very useful, not just in what it revealed about content," says Langer, "but for what it told us about the colors people associate with comfort." The client used the result in choosing colors for both its product line and stores.

Irving Merson of Merson/Greener As-

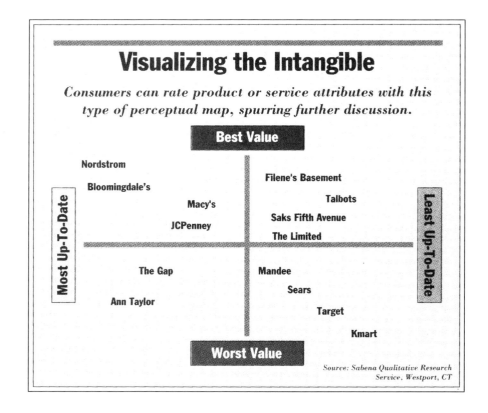

Visualizing the Intangible

Consumers can rate product or service attributes with this type of perceptual map, spurring further discussion.

Best Value

Nordstrom

Bloomingdale's

Filene's Basement

Macy's

Talbots

JCPenney

Saks Fifth Avenue

The Limited

Most Up-To-Date

Least Up-To-Date

The Gap

Mandee

Sears

Ann Taylor

Target

Kmart

Worst Value

Source: Sabena Qualitative Research Service, Westport, CT

now looking at computer quantification. Livingston has found a way to use a deck of 16 photos to predict consumers' Myers-Briggs types with a high degree of reliability.

The Myers-Briggs Type Indicator is a respected tool for measuring personality types based on respondents' tendencies toward introversion or extroversion, judging or perceiving, thinking judgment or feeling judgment, and sensing or intuitive perception styles. It is widely used by educators, mental-health professionals, human-resource specialists, and managers. "The reliability of the Myers-Briggs has been validated over 20 years," says Livingston, and now, "there's a groundswell of interest in trying to apply it to market research."

Howard Moskowitz has taken computerized psychological stimulus-response testing of consumers to a new level. His firm, Moskowitz/Jacobs, Inc. of White Plains, New York, has a network of four testing facilities in the U.S. equipped with scent labs, kitchens, and computers. Moskowitz's IdeaMap software combines psychological data with statistical modeling and uses multimedia and computerized surveys to offer clients an instant quantified breakdown of the relationships between consumer responses and product or communication concept variables.

Through self-administered questioning, groups of consumers enter responses to concepts, products, scents, or tastes into the computer. Results are based on 50 to 1,000 consumer interviews ranging from 15 minutes to 3 hours apiece. Vlasic used the technique to develop products with increasing degrees of savoriness based on a segmentation of consumers' sensory preferences. Its pickle jars now bear a series of coded labels informing shoppers about how "hot" the contents are.

Computerization has vastly accelerated the pace with which complex patterns of consumer responses can be evaluated. Moskowitz says he can get results in a day or two that previously would have taken months. "We can get quantified results almost immediately on what to

sociates uses collages along with Jung's archetype concept to identify deep feelings about brands and categories. Archetypes, or recurring patterns and underlying themes, produce images and concepts for effective selling. "It gets down to the quintessential meaning of how a consumer sees a product," he says. An allergy medicine client found that allergies represent isolation to people. "They feel alone emotionally, physically, and psychologically," says Merson. "They receive no TLC like they do when they have a cold." This gave the client ideas about the symbols and cues to which consumers would respond and how to address their concerns by showing empathy in advertising.

Patricia Sabena of Sabena Qualitative Research Services likes to visualize and quantify results for her clients with perceptual mapping. "It's not new, but it's getting more exposure," she says. She asks consumers to rate products on dimensions such as popularity and quality, and marks responses graphically in different ways—as concentric circles, grids, or hierarchically. Group members place tabs representing brands on a "map" of

the attributes under discussion and talk about why. The technique gathers a lot of information and sorts numerous brands quickly, highlights users' versus non-users' perceptions, provides feedback on packaging issues, and encourages argument and discussion. "Perceptual mapping is not an end in itself," says Sabena, "but it is a good jumping-off point."

COMPUTERIZING THE MIND'S EYE

Human beings are capable of seeing virtually millions of distinct shades and hues, but for simplicity's sake, we tend to compartmentalize the spectrum into a few primary and secondary colors. In the same way, perceptual mapping techniques are one way to make sense of the infinitely varied attitudes and behavior that qualitative research explores. Qualitative researchers are also increasingly using computers to organize their results.

Sharon Livingston specializes in "softer" projective methods like her trademarked Category Sculpting and Looking Glass techniques, but she is

call the product, how to position it, and how to create it," he says. Merging technology with psychology also provides a direct link between consumers and products. Moskowitz says that IdeaMap shows exactly how consumers' minds work regarding a specific product or category. "Chaos does not reign," he says. "There is an organizing principle to people's preferences."

Qualitative researchers are trying to understand their own customers' changing preferences, too. Last spring, QRCA held a focus group of its own members in which ten long-time researchers discussed the new realities of clients who want more for less. These professional moderators say that marketers and advertisers want more evaluatory, rather than exploratory, research. They also see a shift away from focusing on consumers' wants and needs in favor of brand equity and maximizing investment in existing products with line extensions. In other words, they want the research to tell them what to do, instead of to help them figure it out themselves.

Barbara Feigin laments the trend toward doing research not to find insights, but to confirm preconceived judgments. Grey Advertising has one of the few classic advertising research departments that remains integral to the agency despite the cuts of the early 1990s. Feigin says it is essential to understand long-term and executional strategic goals up front, then develop a blueprint based on solid research input from different sources. "Research should be the catalyst that sparks the whole strategic and creative planning process," she says. Inherent in that process is the need for insights into consumers' minds, the kind that psychographic research can help reveal.

TAKING IT FURTHER

The Quality Research Consultants Association has eight chapter groups in the U.S. and one in Canada, as well as members worldwide. It offers a membership directory, recommended standards and practices for practitioners, and other publications. For more information, call Patricia Sabena at (203) 454-1225. *Beyond Mind Games: The Marketing Power of Psychographics* provides a comprehensive overview of both quantitative and qualitative research options. *The 1996 Impulse Survey of Focus Facilities* rates and lists the features of more than 750 focus-group facilities and moderators in the U.S., Canada, and Europe. *The Focus Group: A Strategic Guide to Organizing, Conducting, and Analyzing the Focus Group Interview,* by Jane Farley Templeton, offers a framework for the appropriate use of focus-group research. All publications are available from American Demographics' Marketing Power catalog; telephone (800) 828-1133.

A Potent New Tool For Selling

Database Marketing

It may not be celebrated as a national holiday, but it's a pretty big deal around here. Happy birthday from the Claridge Casino Hotel, Atlantic City.

What time is it now in Israel? What is Mama cooking today? We at AT&T know exactly how you feel and are aware of your need to call and speak with those close to you whenever you wish.

Dear Nabisco All-Star Legends Collector: As a participant in last year's offer, you are being given a sneak preview of our 1994 All-Star Legends cards. Be the first on your block to order these special limited-edition cards. . . .

Does it seem as if a lot of companies are taking quite a friendly interest in your life these days? Helping you mark your birthday? Soothing your homesickness? Giving you an early peek at something new? If this kind of stuff is turning up in your mailbox more often, you're not alone. You're on the receiving end of a sophisticated, high-tech twist to the ancient art of persuasion. It goes by different names—database marketing, relationship marketing, one-to-one marketing. But it all adds up to the same thing: Companies are collecting mountains of information about you, crunching it to predict how likely you are to buy a product, and using that knowledge to craft a marketing message precisely calibrated to get you to do so.

It amounts to one of the biggest changes in marketing since "new and improved." First came the mass market, that vast, undifferentiated body of consumers who received identical, mass-produced products and messages—any color of car they wanted, so long as it was black. Then came market segmentation, which divided still-anonymous consumers into smaller groups with common demographic or psychographic characteristics. Now, new generations of faster, more powerful computers are enabling marketers to zero in on ever-smaller niches of the population, ultimately aiming for the smallest consumer segment of all: the individual.

A growing number of marketers are investing millions of dollars to build databases that enable them to figure out who their customers are and what it takes to secure their loyalty. Direct marketers have long been in the vanguard of database users: Catalogs, record clubs, and credit-card companies have always needed their customers' names and addresses to do business with them. But database marketing is now moving into the marketing mainstream, as everyone from packaged-goods companies to auto makers comes to believe that in the fragmented, fiercely competitive marketplace of the 1990s, nothing is more powerful than knowledge about customers' individual practices and preferences. HOG-TIED. In 1992, for example, General Motors Corp. joined with MasterCard to offer the GM Card. As a result, GM now has a database of 12 million GM cardholders, and it surveys them to learn what they're driving, when they next plan to buy a car or truck, and what kind of vehicle they would like. Then, if a cardholder expresses an interest in, say, sport-utility vehicles, the card unit mails out information on its truck line and passes the cardholder's name along to the appropriate division.

Blockbuster Entertainment Corp. is using its database of 36 million households and 2 million daily transactions to help its video-rental customers select movies and steer them to other Blockbuster subsidiaries. In Richmond, Va., the company is testing a computerized system that recommends 10 movie titles based on a customer's prior rentals. The suggestions are printed on a card that also offers targeted promotions. Customers who have rented children's films, for example, might get a discount at Discovery Zone, Blockbuster's play-center subsidiary.

Kraft General Foods Inc. has amassed a list of more than 30 million users of its products who have provided their names when sending in coupons or responding to some other KGF promotion. Based on the interests they've expressed in surveys, it regularly sends them tips on such things as nutrition and exercise—as well as recipes and coupons for specific brands. The company figures that the more information consumers have about a product, the likelier they'll be to use more of it (sample tip: Use Miracle Whip instead of butter for grilling sandwiches). KGF constantly refines its database by sending surveys to the names on its list.

Like KGF, Harley-Davidson Inc. wants to urge customers to keep using its products. That's why it mails the 256,000 members of its Harley Owners Group (HOG) a bimonthly magazine packed with listings of regional, national, and international events to encourage owners to get out on the road and use their bikes. House of Seagram uses its 10 million-name database for loyalty-building programs for existing products. It might send premiums tied to proofs of purchase—a pair of snifters, say, to someone who bought its Martell cognac. Seagram uses surveys to identify likely buyers of new products, as well as drinkers of rival brands it can send offers to. RJR Nabisco Holdings Corp. is building a database that identifies, among other things, households that have responded to past promotions.

Over on the tobacco side of RJR Nabisco's business, database marketing has long been practiced in earnest. For cigarette makers, it's a virtue born of necessity. Facing increasing restrictions on advertising, Philip Morris Cos. and RJR have assembled huge databases of smokers they can reach directly. For example, by requiring consumers who respond to offers of free shirts, sleeping bags, or other merchandise to fill out detailed questionnaires, Philip Morris has built a list of some 26 million smokers names and addresses. The companies use their lists both to market to smokers with coupons and promotions and to enlist grassroots support for their lobbying efforts.

Consumers appear to be responding to the precision marketing. But of course, this private intelligence-gathering gives some people the creeps. At best, critics say, targeted marketing efforts are intrusive and annoying. At worst, the collection, manipulation, and combination of lists of personal information amount to an ominous invasion of privacy (box, "You Can Run, But It's Tough to Hide from Marketers"). Such concerns aren't fazing the marketing types, though. According to Donnelley Marketing Inc.'s annual survey of promotional practices, 56% of manufacturers and re-

tailers are currently building a database, an additional 10% plan to do so, and 85% believe they'll need database marketing to be competitive past the year 2000. "It is one of the most important marketing developments of the 1990s," says marketing guru Stan Rapp, chairman of consultants Cross Rapp Associates.

Why all the activity? In part, it's in the name of the relentless drive to make marketing more efficient. Seagram knows that most U.S. adults aren't likely prospects for its distilled spirits: Two-thirds of them haven't had a single drink of liquor in the past 30 days. As a result, notes Richard P. Shaw, vice-president for marketing communications at Seagram, mass-market advertising has "a great deal of what we would call nonproductive reach." Of course, many conventional promotions, and much typical junk mail, are similarly wasted

HOW IT WORKS

1 THE PRODUCT

2 INTO THE DATABASE MAW

You may think you're just sending in a coupon, filling out a warranty card, or entering a sweepstakes. But to a marketer, you're also volunteering information about yourself—data that gets fed into a computer, where it's combined with more information from public records.

3 DIGESTING THE DATA

Using sophisticated statistical techniques, the computer merges different sets of data into a coherent, consolidated database. Then, with powerful software, brand managers can "drill down" into the data to any level of detail they require.

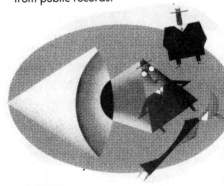

4 AN IDEAL CONSUMER

The computer identifies a model consumer of a chosen product based on the common characteristics of high-volume users. Next, clusters of consumers who share the characteristics—interests, incomes, brand loyalties, for instance—can be identified as targets for marketing eff•

because they're aimed at too broad an audience. "We're trying to kill off junk mail—junk mail defined as 'anything I didn't ask for and wouldn't be interested in,' " says Barrington I. Hill, London-based senior vice-president for product development at American Express Travel Related Services Co., which has been using its detailed database to send carefully aimed promotions to cardholders.

7 REFINING THE DATABASE

The database is continually updated with information collected from product-oriented clubs, responses to coupons, calls to 800 numbers, and sweepstakes entries, as well as with new lists from outside sources.

5 USING THE KNOWLEDGE

The data can be used in many ways: to determine the values of coupons and who should get them; to develop new products and ensure that the appropriate consumers know about them; to tailor ad messages and aim them at the right audience.

SIMULACRUM. Marketers increasingly are recognizing that past customer behavior, as recorded in actual business transactions, is by far the best indicator of future buying patterns. "It's not true that demographics is destiny," says Matt Kuckuk, senior principal at American Management Systems Inc.'s Financial Industry Group. Merely knowing Mr. Jones's Zip Code or income generally yields

6 SHARING DATA WITH RETAILERS

Cash-register scanners provide reams of information about exactly what shoppers are buying at specific stores. Merged with the manufacturer's data, this intelligence helps to plan local promotional mailings, fine-tune shelf displays, and design store layouts.

DATA: BUSINESS WEEK, COOPERS & LYBRAND CONSULTING

less insight—and opportunity—than knowing, say, that he has just applied for his first joint checking account. That probably signals a marriage, which means future openings to sell a mortgage, life insurance, long-term investments, perhaps even a college loan. It's a kind of cybernetic intimacy: In ever-expanding processing power, marketers see an opportunity to close the gap that has widened between companies and their customers with the rise of mass markets, mass media, and mass merchants. Database marketing, they believe, can create a silicon simulacrum of the old-fashioned relationship people used to have with the corner grocer, butcher, or baker. "A database is sort of a collective memory," says Richard G. Barlow, president of Frequency Marketing Inc., a Cincinnati-based consulting firm. "It deals with you in the same personalized way as a mom- and-pop grocery store, where they knew customers by name and stocked what they wanted."

Consider the dilemma of a busy casino. In the old days, the pit boss kept notebooks on frequent players. Periodically, he would pick a name from the notebook, call the high roller up, and offer a free room for the weekend. Today, with thousands of visitors trooping through on any given day, "it's virtually impossible to get to know people on a first-name basis," says Robert M. Renneisen Jr., CEO of Claridge Hotel & Casino Corp.

Now, the casino's computer keeps tabs on visitors who use its frequent-gamblers' card and sends out offers every day. Claridge's Comp-Card Gold, which offers discounts and tips on upcoming events, has 350,000 active members. They get offers ranging from $10 in coins for slot machines to monogrammed bathrobes and door-to-door limo service. "It's made us more efficient," says Renneisen. "We can target our dollars directly to customers who justify the costs."

"GREATER VALUE." In addition, by weaving relationships with its customers, a company can make it inconvenient for consumers to switch to a competitor. Don Peppers, co-author of *The One to One Future,* one of the bibles of the new marketing, cites MCI Communications Corp.'s Friends & Family long-distance discount plan. To get the discount, the customer has to form a network of friends and family members—"a substantial investment in time and energy on the consumer's part," he notes. Changing long-distance carriers means having to "reinvent my relationship," Peppers says.

All these efforts to forge ties to consumers are based on the same fundamental idea: There's no more important asset than a happy customer. Happy customers remain customers, and it's much cheaper to keep existing customers than to find new ones. Michael D. Keefe, director of Harley Davidson's HOG, is reluctant even to call the process marketing. "It's more like customer bonding," he says. If people use the motorcycle, they'll stay involved. If there's nowhere to ride, no place to go, the motorcycle stays in the garage, the battery goes dead,, and a year from now, they just sell it.

Some database marketers say their promotional offers garner response rates in double digits, considerably higher than the typical 2% to 4% for junk mail. For example, the targeted promotions that Hilton Hotels Corp. offers senior citizens in its Senior Honors frequent-traveler program, which features discounts and travel tips, have persuaded close to half of the club's members to take previously unplanned trips that included stays at Hilton hotels. And KGF says its offers to those listed on its database get significantly higher response rates than standard mass-market coupons. The database, says John T. Kuendig, vice-president for market development, is a list of steady consumers who "have a greater value to the brand."

NO CHOICE. Database marketing has its skeptics, of course. An earlier flush of enthusiasm prompted by the spread of checkout scanners in the 1980s ended in widespread disappointment: Many companies were too overwhelmed by the sheer quantity of data to do anything useful with the information. And some critics say these efforts to reach out and touch individual consumers haven't demonstrated their usefulness in many product categories. Programs that identify frequent customers and reward them may make sense for airlines, but consumers have rejected the "frequent-eater" programs offered by some fast-food chains as being not worth the bother.

Still, many companies believe they have no choice but to brave the database-marketing frontier. For one thing, most manufacturers are waging an information war with the retailers that stock their products. Large supermarket chains and giant mass merchandisers, such as Wal-Mart Stores Inc., have grown increasingly sophisticated in their use of checkout-scanner data to keep track of sales. They now base many of their choices about what to stock, what to promote, and what to charge on that information. To shape those decisions to their advantage, manufacturers need persuasive information of their own. "To the extent we have built up relationships with our consumers and know which ones will respond, we can work with retailers to help them build their businesses," says KGF's Kuendig.

BUSYBODY QUESTIONS. Databases start with information from the consumer. In transactional businesses, such as charge cards, banking, or catalogs, that's easy: The marketer simply collects information on the sale. For other marketers, the challenge is to get consumers to volunteer the data about themselves. Many packaged-goods marketers collect information that consumers divulge when they call 800 numbers or mail in coupons. In its surveys, Seagram tracks consumers' names and addresses, the brands and types of alcohol they drink, their sex, birthdate, income, and how many bottles they purchase in an average month. And GM went into the credit-card business not just to build loyalty and offer cardholders rebates on cars but also because it saw the billing process as a way to harvest reams of data about consumers. "This is a gold mine," says H. D. "Hank" Weed, general marketing manager for the GM Card.

Having assembled a list of consumers, the marketer then mixes in information from other sources. Research houses such as Donnelley, Metromail, and R. L. Polk glean vast amounts of data from public records—drivers' licenses, auto registrations, and mortgage-tax rolls. Even income, the most sensitive subject, can be estimated based on mortgages and automobile registrations. Such information isn't cheap, though. This year, for instance, Ohio sold its drivers'-license and car-registration lists to TRW Inc. for $375,000.

Wittingly or unwittingly, consumers often offer plenty of data about themselves. Think of all those busybody questions on a warranty card: What's your age, income, occupation, education, and marital status? How many children? Do you hunt, fish, or play tennis? If you think none of that has much to do with the guarantee on that radio you just bought, you're right. But National Demographics & Lifestyles Inc., based in Denver, collects those warranty cards and the precious information they reveal, then resells it to database marketers.

Increasingly, the computer itself is sifting through such data for patterns that will predict behavior. Using neural-network software, computers can plow through masses of data and determine how specified variables may depend on one another (box, "Silicon and Software That Mine for Gold"). For example, what combination of income level, investment activity, and credit-card spending is most likely to be seen among people who are in the market for mortgages? Once the network has come up with a highly specific profile of some class of customer, it's easier to find new customers matching that profile and aim at them with customized direct-marketing schemes.

SILICON AND SOFTWARE THAT MINE FOR GOLD

Marketing companies have long used computers to sift through reams of supermarket scanner data, merge and purge mailing lists, and analyze market research reports. But now, ultracheap computing power and new software are making the process much more precise.

Gathering data isn't all that difficult: Point-of-sale terminals, teller machines, and 1-800 telemarketing all contribute to the flood. The big challenge lies in making sense of what's collected, rather than throwing most of it away. The quantities of data are potentially overwhelming: Fingerhut Cos., for example, is currently expanding its collection of mail-order customer data from about 600 billion characters today to about 2 trillion characters, or two terabytes—enough to choke any traditional mainframe. Using shoppers' clubs and other incentives, supermarket chains such as Vons Cos. and Safeway Inc. are starting to keep on hand more than a year's worth of detailed data about customer purchases.

SOUPED UP. Fortunately, powerful new technologies are at hand. Neural-network software, designed after the pattern of cells in the human brain, can automatically "learn" from large sets of data on its own. By scanning thousands of data records again and again, the software can build a strong statistical model describing important relationships and patterns in the data. All that's required is a standard, high-end PC equipped with a plug-in neural-net "accelerator" board. Customer Insight Co. has tailored HNC Software Inc.'s Database Mining Workstation software, based on neural-net techniques, just for database marketing.

Once a statistical model of the ideal customer is constructed, however, con-

---

KEY DATABASE-MARKETING TECHNOLOGIES

PARALLEL COMPUTERS
Use gangs of microprocessors to scan huge volumes of data in a flash. Sold by AT&T/NCR, IBM, Tandem, Meiko, and nCube.

DATABASE SOFTWARE
Cross-indexes data records into giant matrixes, which makes finding specified records much easier. Sold by Oracle, Sybase, IBM, Informix.

NEURAL-NETWORK SOFTWARE
Can automatically build a model of customer behavior based on analysis of previous transactions. Available from HNC Software, Customer Insight.

DATA: BUSINESS WEEK

---

siderably more computing horsepower may be required to find all prospects matching the profile. So Fingerhut, Wal-Mart Stores, Delta Air Line, American Airlines, and dozens of others are turning to so-called parallel-processing systems. These devote dozens or even hundreds of micro-processors to scouring a giant database for records that meet a complex set of criteria. The more criteria specified, the longer a search can take—but the more precisely aimed the resulting marketing efforts may be. Fingerhut has chosen a parallel Sun Microsystems Inc. machine that harnesses are many as 20 high-speed microprocessors. Wal-Mart Stores Inc. leads the way in retail databases using parallel database computers supplied by the former NCR/Teradata company, now a unit of AT&T.

Rapidly analyzing zillions of past business transactions is actually key to many "reengineering" efforts these days. Businesses ranging from airlines to banks and telephone companies are striving to reorganize based on a better understanding of their customers' buying patterns. The potential gains are big: tighter inventories, more compelling product displays, fewer out-of-stock items, and higher profits. Says Thomas Blischok, a vice-president at AT&T/NCR: "If I can guarantee that every time you go to my establishment you find stuff to buy, you'll care a lot less about price."

BIG-IRON BRAWL. All of which is stirring sales in the otherwise moribund large-scale computer market. Sales of traditional mainframes have gone into long-term decline. But Gartner Group Inc., a computer market-research firm, reckons that today's $400 million commercial market for parallel computers will grow to $5 billion in 1998. IBM, the leader in mainframes, is adding parallel systems to its lineup in hopes of thwarting early advances by challengers such as AT&T, Tandem Computers, Sun, Hewlett-Packard, and even Cray Research.

What does the future hold? Lots more transaction data stored in much more powerful computers. Customers' thirst seems insatiable, says Jerre Stead, chief executive of AT&T/NCR. He was recently given a pair of hats when visiting Wal-Mart headquarters, where inspirational slogans abound. One, Stead recalls, demanded that AT&T computers be capable of storing "10 terabytes by the end of '95." The other demanded that "90% of all data [be] processed in 99 minutes." Says Stead: "We'll get there. We're working on it."

John Verity in New York

Most marketers consider the greatest benefit of the databases simply to be identifying who their current customers are and how much business the company is doing with them. First Commerce Corp., a $6.4 billion New Orleans bank holding company with five banks, has been using this technology to retain current customers and build its business. Its customers, like those at every bank, tend to bank with several institutions. But by analyzing the data available on its current checking cus-

tomers, First Commerce can try to win more of them as credit-card customers, too. The work is done with a combination of PCs and a mainframe storing hundreds of thousands of records. On a fast PC, a neural-network run can take from 30 to 60 minutes to complete.

Where there are millions of records to sift through, so-called massively parallel database computers, at typical prices of $1 million or more, may be required. These machines gang together scores or even hun-

dreds of the fastest microprocessors around, giving them the oomph to respond in minutes to complex database queries. Marketers call these complex searches "drilling down." With such speed at hand, companies can search their databases more frequently and feel freer to experiment with new strategies. "Before parallel computing, you just didn't have the juice required," says Doug Cheney, director of program development at AT&T Global Information Solutions, the former NCR Corp. and a maker of parallel database computers.

WEATHER REPORTS. Massively parallel processors from Thinking Machines Inc. are a key technology for American Express Co. Before the systems were in place, the amount of information the company could keep on each cardmember was limited to basic stuff, such as the cardmember's name and address, how long he or she had been a cardholder, and how much the cardmember had spent in the past year. With massively parallel processing, AmEx could vastly expand the profile of every customer. "We basically store every transaction," says product-development executive Hill.

Now, 70 workstations at the American Express Decision Sciences center in Phoenix race through mountains of data on millions of AmEx cardmembers—the stores they shop in, the places they travel to, the restaurants they've eaten in, and even the economic conditions and weather in the areas where they live.

Every month for a little more than a year, AmEx has been using that information to send out precisely aimed offers. They go out in millions of customized monthly bills that the company says amount to individualized newsletters sent to a growing number of customers around the world. On one British card-member's

---

YOU CAN RUN, BUT IT'S TOUGH TO HIDE FROM MARKETERS

For years, Lisa Tomaino kept her address secret. She and her husband Jim, a policeman, wanted to make it as hard as possible for the crooks he had put away to find out where they lived.

But last year, Lisa had a baby. So much for her big secret. Within six weeks, she was inundated with junk mail aimed at new mothers. The hospital had sold her name and address to a direct-marketing company, and soon she was on dozens of other lists. Efforts to get off them proved fruitless. "It was a complete violation of our right to privacy," she declares.

Private citizens, privacy watchdogs, and a handful of lawmakers have railed for years about Big Brotherism by business. But when politicians balance industry's interest in reaching markets against the customers' right to privacy, marketing usually wins. "Existing laws regulating privacy simply aren't effective," gripes Robert S. Bulmash, president of Private Citizen Inc., a public advocacy group in Naperville, Ill.

Marketers are keenly aware of the public's reaction to their unwanted attention. After all, it's their job to stay in touch with the preferences of consumers. "People worry about what we know about them and how we're going to use it, and that's legitimate," says Richard Barton, a senior vice-president for the Direct Marketing Assn. (DMA) a Washington-based trade group.

But vendors of marketing data argue that any intrusion on privacy from selling lists is offset "by the significant potential gain to consumers from the special offers and products offered by direct marketers," says Harry Gambill, president of Trans Union Corp., a Chicago-based credit bureau.

The industry has largely staved off regulation by convincing the federal government that it can police itself. The DMA, for example, runs a phone number for people who want their names removed from mailing lists. But relatively few consumers use it, and those who do contend that their names come off some, but not all, lists. "It's really meaningless," says Evan Hendricks, editor of *Privacy Times*. "It's just a public relations effort."

Lawmakers are now mulling a measure that could limit the ability of state motor vehicle departments to give out information about licensed drivers. Senator Barbara Boxer (D-Calif.) sponsored the Senate version after a deranged man used California driver records to track down a young TV actress, whom he killed.

DOLLARS FOR STATES. The proposed curbs are part of the controversial crime bill, which was resuscitated in the House and sent to the Senate in late August. But the restrictions would have limited impact. Many states objected to a ban on the re-

lease of driver information, arguing that they need the revenue from the sale of lists. The whittled-down bill now enables motorists to opt out of having their names sold. Consumer advocates complain that such provisions don't work because most are written in tiny type.

Longstanding laws, such as the 1970 Fair Credit Reporting Act, aren't much better, according to privacy experts. The statute is supposed to prevent credit agencies such as TRW, Equifax, and Trans Union from releasing financial information about a person except for "legitimate" business needs, such as a credit check.

Legitimate needs, however, have never been clearly defined. In a January, 1993, decision against Trans Union, a Federal Trade Commission administrative law judge ruled that the law bars the use of credit information to develop mailing lists. In response, TRW Inc. stopped using its credit data to develop lists, but it still sells lists based on demographic information it collects. And Trans Union has chosen to fight the ruling.

As marketing techniques become more sophisticated, the privacy of the Lisa Tomainos of the world will grow increasingly difficult to protect. And marketers will do everything they can to make sure remaining anonymous doesn't get any easier.

By Mark Lewyn in Washington

PIONEERS OF THE NEW MARKETING

A sampling of database-marketing programs:

AMERICAN EXPRESS Using massively parallel processors, it's sorting through individual cardmembers' transactions and basing promotions on what it learns.

PHILLIP MORRIS PM's Marlboro Adventure, a promotion for Marlboro smokers, distributed more than 30 million pieces of merchandise to smokers—and helped build a 26 million-name database it uses for direct marketing and lobbying.

HOUSE OF SEAGRAM Uses list of 10 million adults who drink spirits to launch new products, build brand loyalty, and take aim at drinkers of rivals' products.

GENERAL MOTORS GM regularly surveys its 12 million credit-card holders on whether they expect to be in the market for a car or truck soon, what kind of models they're interested in, and whether they would like information on vehicles. These leads are passed on to GM's marketing divisions.

BLOCKBUSTER ENTERTAINMENT Using records for 36 million households, it's testing a system that will recommend movies based on a customer's past rentals.

---

recent statement, a British Airways flight triggered an offer, printed adjacent to the transaction, of special deals on weekend getaways to New York and continental Europe. A purchase at Harrod's triggered a notice of a special sale at the store for AmEx cardholders. Since its introduction in Ireland in March, 1993, this "relationship billing" has been rolled out through Europe, Canada, and Mexico. AmEx has seen an increase of 15% to 20% in year-over-year cardmember spending in Europe and gives the new billing format much of the credit. Next year, AmEx plans to introduce relationship billing in its biggest market, the U.S.

Heavy computing firepower isn't always necessary, though. For some efforts, all it may take is a few thousand dollars' worth of hardware and software. Using a Macintosh personal computer, Yuri Radzievsky has built a database of Russian, Polish, and Israeli immigrants to the U.S. By combing lists of subscriptions to foreign-language newspapers and buyers of tickets to events such as tours by Russian entertainers, his YAR Communications has assembled lists of 50,000 Russians, 75,000 Poles, and 30,000 Israelis in the U.S. Such information is of real value to client AT&T—telephone service, after all, is one of the first things new arrivals want when they set up their households.

Using the lists, AT&T has mailed Hebrew- and Russian-language offers of discounts on calls home. Every marketer's dream is to be able to target those little slices," says Sandra K. Shellenberger, district manager of diversified marketers and multicultural marketing communications for AT&T. Response rates for such database-directed offers sometimes run as high as 20% to 30%, she says, compared with the low single digits for broader, more conventional direct mail.

Where will it all end? Few predict that database marketing will supplant mass marketing. Still, many targeted direct-mail campaigns are as glossy as any big-budget ad campaign. The mailings Seagram sends out feature lush photos and long, story-spinning blocks of copy discussing such matters as the proper way to drink single-malt scotch. Seagram also plans to rely heavily on database marketing to penetrate emerging markets, such as India and Thailand, where the proportion of affluent drinkers is so small that the use of mass media would be especially wasteful.

There's no doubt technology is shaking up traditional marketing methods. Marketers, after all, have been accustomed to thinking in broad swaths, such as adults 18 to 34 or women 25 to 49. Now, a typical AmEx segment might be business travelers who have bought jewelry abroad in the past month. Some of the offers the company has sent out in bills have gone to as few as 20 people. Says Hill: "This is a strange experience for the marketing people."

Can a faceless, distant marketer recreate the personal relationships consumers used to have with the people they did business with? More and more companies are betting that the answer is yes as they reach out to envelop customers in an automated embrace.

By Jonathan Berry, with John Verity, in New York, Kathleen Kerwin in Detroit, Gail De George in Miami, and bureau reports

A BEGINNER'S GUIDE TO
Demographics

Who are your customers?
Where do they live?
How many are there?

Answering these and similar questions can help you
sharpen your marketing strategy.

BERNA MILLER
WITH AN INTRODUCTION BY PETER FRANCESE

*Whatever you sell, customer demographics are important to
your business. Demographics can tell you who your current
and potential customers are, where they are, and how many
are likely to buy what you are selling. Demographic analysis
helps you serve your customers better by adjusting to their
changing needs. This article provides a review of the basic
concepts used in such analysis.*

*The most successful use of demographic analysis identifies
those population or household characteristics that most accurately differentiate potential customers from those not
likely to buy. The second part of using demographics is finding those geographic areas with the highest concentrations
of potential customers. Once potential customers are described and located, and their purchase behavior analyzed,
the next step is to determine their media preferences in order
to find the most efficient way to reach them with an advertising message.*

*It wasn't always this complicated. Until fairly recently, ev-
eryone practiced mass marketing, dispersing one message via
media—newspapers, radio, broadcast television—that presumably reached everyone. No special effort was made to
ensure that the message would appeal to (or even reach) the
most likely customers.*

*The result: A great deal of money was spent pitching prod-
ucts and services to sections of the audience who didn't want
or need them. In buying a prime-time spot for its television
ads, a motorcycle company would be paying to reach the
housebound elderly as well as the young adults for whom
their product was designed. A swimsuit manufacturer that ran
an ad in a national magazine would pay a premium to reach
the inhabitants of Nome, Alaska, as well as Floridians.
Gradually, it was recognized that the "shotgun" approach is
not an efficient use of marketing dollars.*

The most important marketing question a business faces
is: "Who are my customers?" And the first **demographic***
question a business must ask about its product or service
is whether it is to be sold to an individual or a **household.**
Refrigerators, for example, are household products; and most
households have only one or two refrigerators. On the other
hand, everyone within the household has their own toothbrush
and dozens of other personal-care products.

There are more than 261 million individuals in the United
States and nearly 100 million households. Those classified as
"family households" include married couples with **children** (26
percent), married couples without children (29 percent), single
parents living with their children (9 percent), and brothers and
sisters or other related family members who live together (7 percent). **"Nonfamily** households" include people who live alone
(24 percent) and cohabiting couples and other unrelated roommates (5 percent).

Different types of households are more prevalent among certain age groups. For instance, the majority of women who live
alone are over age 65, while the majority of men who live
alone are under age 45. Household types differ between **generations** as well. Younger people today are much more likely
to live in the other type of nonfamily household because they
are moving out of their parents' homes before marriage and living with friends or lovers; such living arrangements being more
acceptable today, younger people are much more likely than
earlier generations to do so.

Everyone in the United States except for the homeless lives
in either a household or **group quarters.** Many businesses ignore
group-quarter populations, reasoning that nursing-home patients
and prison inmates probably are not doing much shopping.
However, if your market is computers, beer, pizza, or any num-

For definitions for this and other terms in **bold-faced type, see the glossary
at end of article.*

From *Marketing Tools*, October 1995, pp. 54-61, 64. © 1995 by American Demographics, Inc. Reprinted by permission.

Mass marketing has since given way to target marketing, whose guiding principle is Know Thy Customers. How old are they? Where do they live? What are their interests, concerns, and aspirations? Knowing the answers to questions like these gives you insight into the marketing approaches most likely to appeal to your customers—and whether you're even shooting for the right customers in the first place! (Sometimes there is more than one set of customers: for example, research shows that low-fat frozen dinners are purchased by young women wishing to stay slim and by much older retired people who just want a light meal.)

Let's say that you find out that your customers are predominantly college graduates, and that you know in which zip codes your existing customers reside. How do you use this information?

The first step is to obtain a tabulation of the number of college graduates by zip code, which is available through an information provider (see the American Demographics Directory of Marketing Information Companies for names and numbers) or the Census Bureau. Then, for any metropolitan area that you serve, establish the percent of all college graduates in the metropolitan area who reside in each zip code. Calculate the percent of existing customers who reside in each zip code. By dividing the percent of college graduates in zip 12345 by percent of customers (and multiplying by 100), we get an index of penetration for each zip code. If the index of penetration is 100 or above, the market is being adequately served. If it is below 100, there is more potential, which can be realized through direct mail to those specific zip codes.

This analysis can be done using any group of geographic areas that sum to a total market area, such as counties within a state or metropolitan areas within a region. The object is to compare the percent of customers who should be coming from each sub-market area against the percent who are actually coming from there. The resulting indexes essentially measure marketing performance zip by zip or county by county.

Not so long ago, demographic information came printed on reams of paper or rolls of computer tape. With the tremendous advances in technology in recent years, it is now readily available on your personal computer. Demographic statistics can be obtained on CD-ROM or via the Internet, complete with software for accessing the data.

Information providers can analyze these data for you, as well as provide customized data, such as how many pairs of shoes people own and how often they shop for new ones. Census demographics can't tell you how many times a week people use floor cleaners, but it does have basic demographic characteristics that will help determine who your market is, how many of them there are, and where they live. Information providers can help you take these data and merge them with customer data to form a clearer picture of your market and its potential.

—Peter Francese

Peter Francese is founding president of American Demographics Inc., and publisher of American Demographics *and* Marketing Tools *magazines.*

ber of products that appeal to young adults or military personnel, you cannot afford to overlook these populations. This is especially important when marketing a product in a smaller area where a college or military base is present. People who live in these situations may have different wants and needs from those who live in households; in addition, the area may have a much higher rate of population turnover than other **places** do.

Refining Your Customer's Profile

Once you have determined whether you want to market to households or people, the next step is to find out which segment of households or of the population would be most likely to want your product or service. Demographics allow you to refine your conception of who your market is, who it can or should be, and how it is likely to change over time. People have different needs at different ages and lifestages, and you need to factor that into your customer profile. In addition, there are both primary and secondary markets. For instance, if you were marketing baby food, you would first target married couples with young children and single parents, and then possibly grandparents.

The U.S. can no longer be effectively treated as a mass market, because Americans and their lifestyles have changed dramatically.

This level of refinement was made necessary by the massive social, economic, and technological changes of the past three decades. The United States can no longer be effectively treated as a mass market, because the people who live here and their lifestyles have changed dramatically. Due to increasing divorce rates, increasing cohabitation, rising number of nonmarital births, and increased female participation in the labor force, married couples with one earner make up only 15 percent of all households. Dual-earner households have become much more common—the additional income is often necessary for the family to pay their bills. Thus, the stereotypical family of the 1950s has been replaced by two harried, working parents with much less time available.

At the same time, there has been an explosion in the number of products available to the American public, each of which, either by design or default, tends to appeal to the very different segments of the population.

Another important trend is the increasing diversity of that population. The United States has always been an immigrant nation. However, large numbers of immigrants from Latin America and Asia have increased the proportion of minorities in the country to one in four, up from one in five in 1980.

This increasing diversity is particularly noticeable in the children's market. Minorities are overrepresented in the younger age brackets due to the higher **fertility** and the younger population structure of these recent immigrants. The result: one in three children in the United States is black, **Hispanic**, or Asian. Nearly all of today's children grow up in a world of divorce and working mothers. Many are doing the family shopping and have tremendous influence over household purchases. In addition, they may simply know more than their elders about products involving new technology, such as computers.

The recent influx of Hispanics, who may be of any **race**, has important implications for understanding the demographic data you have on your customers. "Hispanic" is an ethnicity, not a race; a person who describes himself as Hispanic must also choose a racial designation: white, black, Asian/Pacific Islander, American Indian/Eskimo/Aleut, or "other." Confusion on this score... can result in accidentally counting Hispanics twice, in which case the numbers won't add up.

Income and education are two other important demographic factors to consider when refining your customer profile. As a general rule, income increases with age, as people get promoted and reach their peak earning years. Married couples today often have the higher incomes because they may have two earners. Married couples may also have greater need for products and services, because they are most likely to have children and be homeowners.

Income is reported in several different ways, and each method means something very different in terms of consumer behavior. Earnings, interest, dividends, royalties, social security payments, and public assistance dollars received before taxes and union dues are subtracted are defined in the **census** as money income. **Personal** income, as reported by the Bureau of Economic Analysis, is money income plus certain noncash benefits (such as food stamps and subsidized housing). **Disposable** income is the money available after taxes, while **discretionary** income is the money available after taxes and necessities (food, shelter, clothing) have been paid for.

All of these are useful measures as long as their differences are fully understood. For example, discretionary income of $30,000 has much more potential for businesses than does a personal income of $30,000. But none of these statistics measures wealth, which includes property owned. Ignoring wealth may provide a skewed picture: a 70-year-old woman with a personal income of $15,000 who must pay rent is much less able to afford additional items than a woman of the same age and income who owns a fully paid-for house, which she could sell if she needed to.

Income can be reported for people or households; household income is the most commonly used measure in business demographics since it provides the best picture of the overall situation of everyone in the household. Income is often reported as **mean income**. But mean income can be distorted by very large or small incomes, called "outliers," which are very different from most of the other values. Thus multimillionaires skew the mean income upward, overestimating the income of the population in question. Using a measure called **median income** can avoid this bias and is more widely used as a measure of income in

demographics. The mean income of all United States households is $41,000. The median income is $31,200—almost $10,000 lower than the mean.

Education is another very important and commonly used demographic characteristic—in today's increasingly technological and highly skilled economy, education makes a big difference in occupation and thus in earning power. Education is most often measured as number of years of schooling or in terms of level of education completed. Today's adults are better educated than ever before; however, only one in four adults older than age 24 has a college degree or higher. Another 23 percent have attended college. Eight in ten American adults have a high school diploma. One reason for the low percentages of college graduates is that many older people did not attend college. Therefore, we should expect to see the percentage of college graduates and attendees increase substantially in the future.

College-educated people are one of the most lucrative markets, but you may have to work extra hard to get and keep them as customers. They are more open to technology and innovation, but they are also less brand loyal, since they are more able financially to take risks. They are more likely to read and less likely to watch television than those without any college education. They like to make informed decisions about purchases; hence, they are the most likely group to request product information.

Segmenting the Market

All of these demographic data are available in easy-to-understand packages called **cluster systems** (also knows as **geodemographic segmentation systems**), which are available from information providers. Cluster systems take many demographic variables and create profiles of different individual or household characteristics, purchase behaviors, and media preferences. Most cluster systems have catchy, descriptive names, such as "Town and Gown" or "Blue Blood Estates," making it easier to identify the groups most likely to be interested in what you have to sell.

Cluster systems are especially powerful when used in conjunction with business mapping. Sophisticated mapping software programs easily link demographics to any level of geography (a process called geocoding). Some software can pinpoint specific households within neighborhoods from your customer data and then create schematic maps of neighborhoods by cluster concentrations. Geocoding can be done for **block group**, **counties**, zip codes, or any other market area. Businesses can integrate knowledge of customer addresses and purchase decisions with basic demographic data based on geography and come up with a clearer, more informative picture of customers—and where they can be found.

Cluster analysis is sometimes confused with **psychographics**, but the two are very different. Cluster systems are based on purchase decisions and demographics that cover physical characteristics like age, sex, income, and education. Psychographics measure motivations, attitudes, **lifestyles**, and feelings, such as openness to technology or reluctance to try new products. Both demographics and psychographics need to be taken into account.

Looking to the Future

It is not only important to identify who your customers are and how many of them there are today, but how many of them there will be in five or ten years, and whether their wants and needs will change.

Projections of population or households by **marital status**, age, or income can be very useful in determining the potential of a market a few years down the road. All projections start with the assumption that the projected population will equal the current population plus births minus deaths and plus net **migration**. For example, let's take projections at the household level. New household configurations occur through in-migration of residents or through the formation of a household due to the separation of an already existing household (such as when a child moves out of a parent's home or a divorce occurs). Household losses occur when existing households are combined due to marriage, when a child moves back home, etc., or when the residents in a household move away from the area (out-migration).

Projections can vary greatly, so it is important to ask about the methodology and assumptions behind them and make sure you fully understand why these assumptions were made. Accurate demographic data can be very valuable, but data that are flawed or biased can be seriously misleading.

It is important to not only identify today's customers, but to predict how their wants and needs will change tomorrow.

In general, the future population of a larger area of geography, such as the United States or a particular state, is much easier to **estimate** accurately than populations for small areas, such as neighborhoods, which often experience greater population fluctuations. In addition, the shorter the time period involved, the more accurate the projections are likely to be, because there's less time for dramatic changes to take place. There will be factors in 15 years that we cannot begin to include in our assumptions, because they do not exist yet.

You can have more confidence in your educated guesses about the future if you know a little about past population trends in the United States, especially the **baby boom** and **baby bust**

cycle. It is also important to understand the difference between a generation and a **cohort**.

The events for which generations are named occur when their members are too young to remember much about them (i.e., the Depression generation includes people born during the 1930s). That's why cohort is often the more useful classification for marketers; it provides insight into events that occurred during the entire lifetimes of the people in question.

To illustrate, let's look at the baby boomers, who were born between 1946 and 1965. In their youth, they experienced a growing economy, but they also dealt with competition and crowding in schools and jobs due to the sheer number of cohort members. Their lives were shaped by events like the civil rights movement, the Vietnam conflict, the women's movement, and Watergate. Baby boomers have seen increasing diversity and technology. They're living longer, healthier lives than the cohorts that came before them.

All these factors make baby boomers very different from 32-to-51-year-olds or 20 years ago. Traditional ideas concerning the preferences of 50-year-olds versus 30-year-olds are no longer accurate; age-old adages such as "coffee consumption increases with age, and young people drink cola" are no longer as valid as they once were—people who grew up on cola often continue to drink it. The same is true for ethnic foods and a host of other products.

The received wisdom will have to change constantly to reflect new sets of preferences and life experiences. For example, baby boomers remember when the idea of careers for women was considered pretty radical. Not so for younger Generation X women; most of them work as a matter of course, just like their own mothers. As a result, ideas about marriage, family, and jobs are changing and will continue to do so.

If you are marketing a product to a certain age range, be aware that the people who will be in that range in five or ten years will not be the same as the ones who are there now. A strategy that has worked for years may need to be rethought as one cohort leaves an age range and another takes its place.

Therein lies the challenge in contemporary marketing: the fact that it is no longer advisable to treat a market as an undifferentiated mass of people with similar fixed tastes, interest, and needs. In the age of target marketing, it is imperative to know who the customers are and how to reach them. When the customer's needs change, it's essential to know that, too, so you can adjust your marketing efforts accordingly. A working knowledge of demographics will keep you on top of the situation. It's a piece of marketing know-how that no one can afford to ignore.

Berna Miller is a contributor to American Demographics *magazine.*

(Continued)

More Info

Recommended reading

The Insider's Guide to Demographic Know-how, by Diane Crispell (1993, American Demographics Books)*

The Official Guide to the American Marketplace, by Cheryl Russell (2nd edition, 1995, New Strategist Books)*

The Official Guide to American Incomes, by Cheryl Russell and Margaret Ambry (1993, New Strategist Books)*

Targeting Families: Marketing To and Through the New Family, by Robert Boutilier (1993, American Demographics Books)*

Targeting Transitions: Marketing to Consumers During Life Changes, by Paula Mergenhagen (1994, American Demographics Books)*

Multicultural Marketing: Selling to a Diverse America, by Marlene L. Rossman (1994, AMACOM Books)*

Marketing to Generation X: Strategies for a New Era, by Karen Ritchie (1995, Lexington MacMillan Free Press)*

American Demographics magazine*

The 1995 American Demographics *Directory of Marketing Information Companies*

provides contact information for data sources.*

*Available through American Demographics, Inc.: to order, call (800) 828-1133.

Resources on the Internet

There are four different ways to reach the Census Bureau online:

1. The FTP site. At your Internet prompt, type "ftp.ftp.census.gov," then log in as "anonymous" or "ftp." Use your e-mail address as your password. Then change the /pub directory to "ftp>cd/pub."

2. The gopher server. Telnet to the server with the command "telnet gopher.censu.gov." At the login, type "gopher." By selecting "Access Our Other Information Services" at the initial menu and then selecting "Census Bureau Anonymous FTP," you can also reach the ftp site.

3. The World Wide Web site. Using a World Wide Web browser, type in the URL "http://www.census.gov" or "http:/www.census.gov/index.html." You can also reach the ftp site through World Wide Web

by connecting to URL "ftp://ftp.census.gov/pub."

4. The FTP site on the World Wide Web. The URL for the FTP site is "ftp://ftp.census.gov/." You can also send an e-mail message to "ftpmail@census.gov." Leave the subject field blank and type "help" in the message body. You will then receive instructions via e-mail.

Marketing Tools on the World Wide Web: http://www.marketingtools.com
As the Marketing Tools Web site develops, we will be creating hypertext links (which are like doorways that take you to other sites with lightning speed) to the Census Bureau and private information providers. In the meantime, the site already offers searchable, full-text versions of all past issues of *Marketing Tools* magazine, and all issues of *American Demographics* magazine and *The Numbers News* newsletter back to 1993. The 1995 *Directory of Marketing Information Companies* is also available at the Marketing Tools site.

Define Your Terms
A GLOSSARY OF DEMOGRAPHIC WORDS AND PHRASES

Demographic terms consist of fairly common words and phrases, but each one has a highly specific meaning. Study them carefully to ensure that when you discuss demographics with someone, you're both talking about the same thing.

demography: derived from two Greek words meaning "description of" and "people," coined by the French political economist Achille Guillard in 1855. Sometimes a distinction is drawn between "pure" demography (the study of vital statistics and population change) and "social" demography, which gets into socioeconomic characteristics. Business demography is also often understood to include consumer attitudes and behavior.

POPULATION COMPONENTS

The three things that add to or subtract from population are:

• **fertility:** having to do with births. There are several measures of fertility, mostly different kinds of annual rates using different base populations.

• **mortality:** otherwise known as death. There are different death rates, as there are for births.

• **migration:** the movement of people into or out of a defined region, like a state. It typically refers only to moves that cross county lines.

A related term is **mobility**, meaning change of residence. This usually refers to how many people move any distance in a given period of time, even if they just move across town.

HOUSEHOLDS/FAMILIES/MARITAL STATUS

household: one or more people who occupy a housing unit, as opposed to group quarters (dorms, hospitals, prisons, military barracks, etc.). The vast majority of Americans live in households.

householder: formerly called "head of household," the householder is the one adult per household designated as the reference person for a variety of characteristics. An important thing to check when looking at demographics of households (such as age or income) is to see whether the information pertains to the householder or to the entire household.
Household composition is determined by the relationship of the other people in the household to the householder.

family: a household consisting of two or more people in which at least one person is related to the householder by blood, marriage, or adoption. The major types of families are **married couples** (these may be male- or female-headed and with or without children), and **families without a spouse present**, which may also be headed by a man or a woman. The latter category includes single parents as well as other combinations of relatives, such as siblings living together or grandparents and grandchildren. Note that seemingly single parents may live with a partner or other adult outside of marriage.

nonfamily: households consisting of persons living alone, or multiple-person households in which no one is related to the householder, although they may be related to each other. This includes unmarried and gay couples, as well as roommates, boarders, etc.

children: The United States Census Bureau makes a distinction between the householder's own children under age 18 (including adopted and stepchildren), and other related children, such as grandchildren or children aged 18 and older. Other surveys may define children differently.

marital status: this is an individual characteristic, usually measured for people aged 15 and older. The four main categories are never married; married; divorced; and widowed. The term "single" usually refers to a person who has never married, but may include others not currently married. Likewise, the term "ever-married" also includes widowed and divorced people. "Married" includes spouse present and spouse absent. "Spouse absent" includes couples who are separated or not living together because of military service.

RACE/ETHNICITY

race: white, black, Asian and Pacific Islander, and native American (includes American Indians, Eskimos, and Aleutian Islanders). That's it. The government does not use the term African American, but many others do.

Hispanics: the only ethnic origin category in current use. NOT A RACE. Most Hispanics are actually white. Used to be called Spanish Origin. The term Latino is becoming popular, but is currently not used by the government.

It is becoming more common to separate out Hispanics from race categories and talk about non-Hispanic whites, blacks, etc. This way, the numbers add up to 100 percent.

Note: The Office of Management and Budget is considering revamping the racial categories used in federal data collection, including the addition of a mixed-race group. This may happen in time for use in the 2000 census.

GENERATIONS/COHORTS

cohort: a group of people who share an event, such as being born in the same year, and therefore share a common culture and history. The most commonly used cohorts are birth cohorts, although there are also marriage cohorts, etc.

generations: more loosely defined than cohorts, typically refers to people born during a certain period of time. These examples are not definitive:
- **GI Generation**: born in the 1910s and 1920s, served in WWII. Today's elderly.
- **Depression**: born in the 1930s. Boomers' parents. Now aged 56 to 65.
- **War Babies**: born during WWII, now aged 50 to 55. Sometimes lumped with the Depression group as the "silent generation."
- **Baby Boom**: born between 1946 and 1964, now aged 31 to 49. Further introductions are probably unnecessary.
- **Baby Bust**: born 1965 to 1976. Today's twentysomethings, although the oldest turned 30 this year. Also called **Generation X**
- **Baby Boomlet**: or Echo Boom. Born 1977 to 1994. Today's children and teens.

EDUCATION

attainment: completed education level, typically measured for adults aged 25 and older because it used to be the case that virtually everyone was finished with school by then. This is less true today, with one-third of all college students over age 25. Until 1990, attainment was measured by years completed rather than actual degrees earned. The new categories include no high school, some high school but no diploma, high school graduate, some college but no degree, associate's degree, and other types of college degrees.

INCOME

Income can be measured for households, persons, or even geographic areas. When you look at income figures, make sure you know which kind is being referred to!

disposable: after-tax (net) income. In other words, all the money people have at their disposal to spend, even if most of it goes for things we have little choice about, like food, electric bills, and kids' braces.

discretionary: income left over after necessities are covered. This is extremely tough to measure: Who's to say what's necessary for someone else? It's generally accepted that very few of the poorest households have any discretionary income at all, but also that the level of necessary expenses rises with income.

personal and **per capita**: aggregate measures for geographic areas such as states and counties. Personal income is total income for all people in an area, and per capita divides it equally by total population, regardless of age or labor force status.

mean income: the average of all income in the population being studied.

median income: the midway point, at which half of the people being studied have higher incomes and half have lower incomes.

ESTIMATES/PROJECTIONS

census: complete count of a population.

survey: the process of collecting data from a sample, hopefully representative of the general population or the population of interest.

estimate: calculation of current or historic number for which no census or survey data are available. Usually based on what's known to have happened.

projection: calculation of future population or characteristic, based on assumptions of what might happen—a "what if" scenario.

Two related terms are **prediction** and **forecast**. Both refer to a "most likely" projection—what the forecaster feels may actually happen.

MEDIA/MARKETING TERMS

The following are not defined by the government, so there are no real standards.

mature: an age segment, usually defined as those 50- or 55-plus, although some go so far as to include those in their late 40s. This is often seen as an affluent and active group, but it actually consists of several age segments with vastly diverse economic and health status. Related terms include:
- **elderly**: usually 65 and older, although sometimes narrowed down to very old (85 and older).
- **retired**: not necessarily defined by age; although most retirees are older people, not all older people are retired.

middle class: This is one of the most widely used demographic terms. It is also perhaps one of the most statistically elu-

sive: If you ask the general public, the vast majority will claim to be middle class. It might be most sensible to start with the midpoint—that is, median income ($31,200 for households in 1993)—and create a range surrounding it (e.g., within $10,000 of the median) until you come up with a group of households that says "middle class" to you.

affluent: most researchers used to consider households with annual incomes of $50,000 or more as affluent, although $60,000 and $75,000 thresholds are becoming more popular. Upper-income households are sometimes defined more broadly as those with incomes of $35,000 or more. As of the mid-1990s, this merely means they are not lower income, suggesting that there is no middle class.

lifestyles/psychographics: these terms are somewhat interchangeable, but **psychographics** usually refers to a formal classification system such as SRI's VALS (Values and Lifestyles) that categorizes people into specific types (Achievers, Belongers, etc.). **Lifestyle** is a vaguer term, and many 'lifestyle' types or segments have been defined in various market studies. Generally speaking, these systems organize people according to their attitudes or consumer behavior, such as their involvement with and spending on golf. These data may seem soft, but they often use statistical measures such as factor analysis to derive the segments.

cluster systems/geodemographic segmentation: developed by data companies to create meaningful segments based on residence, and the assumption that people will live in areas where there are a lot of other people just like them. This geographic element is one thing that distinguishes clusters from psychographic segments. Another difference is that cluster categories are virtually always based on socioeconomic and consumer data rather than attitudinal information. Each system has at least several dozen clusters. The four major cluster systems are: Claritas's PRIZM, National Decision Sys-

tems' MicroVision, CACI's ACORN, and Strategic Mapping's ClusterPlus 2000.

GEOGRAPHIC TERMS

Census geography: areas defined by the government.
- **regions**: Northeast, Midwest, South, and West.
- **divisions**: there are nine Census Statistical Areas: Pacific, Mountain, West North Central, East North Central, West South Central, East South Central, New England, Middle Atlantic, and South Atlantic.
- **states**: note: data about states often include the District of Columbia for a total of 51.
- **Congressional district**: subdivision of a state created solely for Congressional representation; not considered a governmental area by the Census Bureau.
- **enumeration district**: census area with an average of 500 inhabitants, used in nonmetropolitan areas.
- **counties**: the U.S. had over 3,000 counties as of 1990.
- **places**: these include cities, towns, villages, and other municipal areas.
- **tracts**: these are subcounty areas designed to contain a roughly homogeneous population ranging from 2,500 to 8,000.
- **blocks** and **block groups**: blocks are what they sound like: an administrative area generally equivalent to a city block and the smallest unit of geography for which census data are published. Block groups are groups of blocks with average populations of 1,000 to 1,200 people; they are approximately equal to a neighborhood.
- **metropolitan areas**: these are defined by the Office of Management and Budget, and are built at the county level. Each consists of at least one central city of the appropriate size (usually at least 50,000), its surrounding "suburban" territory within the same county, and any adjacent counties with strong economic ties to the city. Metros may have one or more central cities and/or counties. Stand-alone metros are called **MSA**s (Metropolitan

Statisical Areas). Metros that are right next to each other are called **PMSA**s (Primary MSAs), and the larger areas that they make up are called **CMSA**s (Consolidated MSAs). The U.S. currently has over 300 metros (depending on how you count PMSAs and CMSAs) that include about three-fourths of the nation's population.

•NECMAs are New England Metropolitan Areas and are similar to MSAs.

•central city: largest city in the MSA and other cities of central character to an MSA.

zip code: subdivision of an area for purposes of delivering mail; not a census area.

Two related terms are **urban** and **rural** The essential difference between "metropolitan" and "urban" is that metros are defined at the county level, while urbanized areas are more narrowly defined by density. An **urban area** has 25,000 or more inhabitants, with urbanized zones around the central city comprising 50,000 or more inhabitants. This means that the outlying portions of counties in many metropolitan areas are considered rural. Oddly enough, suburbs are commonly defined as the portions of metro areas outside of central cities and have nothing to do with the urban/rural classification system.

—*Diane Crispell*

Diane Crispell is executive editor of American Demographics *magazine, and author of* The Insider's Guide to Demographic Know-How.

The Generations Quiz

Susan Mitchell

Summary

Age is a big influence on a person's wants and needs. But it has never been the only one. A person's generational identity is a collection of attitudes and influences that can affect behavior at a given age. This quiz will help you determine how well you understand the difference between age and generation. Score ten points for each correct response, five points for each correct answer to a two-part question.

THE QUESTIONS

1. People in which age group are most likely to have moved in the last year?

  (a) 20 to 24   (c) 45 to 64
  (b) 30 to 44   (d) 65 or older

2. People in which age group are most likely to have moved out of state?

  (a) 20 to 24   (c) 45 to 64
  (b) 30 to 44   (d) 65 or older

3. Who is most likely to own a gun?

  (a) 18 to 20   (c) 30 to 49
  (b) 21 to 29   (d) 50 or older

Susan Mitchell is author of The Official Guide to the Generations *(New Strategist, 1995) and a contributing editor of* American Demographics

4. Who is most likely to believe that unions are a good influence on the nation?

  (a) 18 to 24   (c) 50 to 64
  (b) 30 to 34   (d) 65 or older

5. Households headed by people of which age are most likely to include preschoolers?

  (a) 20 to 24   (c) 35 to 39
  (b) 25 to 34   (d) 40 to 44

6. Which households are most likely to include three or more children?

  (a) 20 to 24   (c) 35 to 39
  (b) 25 to 34   (d) 40 to 44

7. People of what age are most likely to feel that the influence of religion is declining?

  (a) 18 to 29   (c) 50 to 64
  (b) 30 to 49   (d) 65 or older

8. People from which age group make up the majority of people who work at home at least eight hours a week?

  (a) 25 to 34   (c) 45 to 54
  (b) 35 to 44   (d) 55 to 64

9. Who are the best customers for TVs, radios, and sound equipment?

  (a) under age 25 (c) 35 to 44
  (b) 25 to 34   (d) 45 to 54

10. Women of which age are most likely to prefer a woman as their boss?

  (a) 18 to 29   (c) 50 to 64
  (b) 30 to 40   (d) 65 or older

11. Among full-time, year-round workers, which men (part I) and which women (part II) have the highest median incomes? (5 points each)

  (a) 25 to 34   (c) 45 to 54
  (b) 35 to 44   (d) 55 to 64

12. Men of which age (part I) and women of which age (part II) are most likely to smoke? (5 points each)

  (a) 18 to 24   (c) 35 to 44
  (b) 25 to 34   (d) 45 to 64

13. People in which age group are most likely to have at least a bachelor's degree?

  (a) 25 to 34   (c) 45 to 54
  (b) 35 to 44   (d) 55 to 64

THE ANSWERS

1. (a) The most moving experiences: The young are the restless. Thirty-five percent of people aged 20 to 24 and 30 percent of those aged 25 to 29 moved between March 1992 and March 1993. Most don't move much farther than a stone's throw, however. Over 60 percent of movers aged 20 to 64 moved to another home in the same county.
[Source: Census Bureau, 1994]

2. (d) Most likely to flee the state. The young may be the biggest movers, but when the old get going, they are more likely to keep going until they have cleared the state line. While 26 percent of movers aged 65 or older moved to another state, only 17 percent of those aged 20 to 24 got that far.
[Census Bureau, 1994]

3. (a) Most likely to be armed. The youngest adults, aged 18 to 20, are the biggest gun-toters. Nearly half (48 percent) own a firearm, up from 34 percent in 1974. In that year, the most-armed group was aged 30 to 49. [*Bureau of Justice Statistics, 1994*]

4. (a) Most likely to look for the union label. The generation least likely to belong to a union is the most likely to believe they are good for the country. Only 6 percent of Xers (aged 16 to 24) are union members, but 70 percent of 18-to-24-year-olds believe unions are a good influence. Older workers are more likely to say that unions are good for them personally, but less likely to say they are good for the nation as a whole. Nearly one-fourth (23 percent) of 45-to-54-year-olds are union members, while 46 percent believe unions are a good influence.
[*Bureau of Labor Statistics, 1995; and Times Mirror Center for the People & the Press, 1992*]

5. (b) Best place to find toddlers. The patter of little feet (children under age 6) is most likely to be heard in households headed by people aged 25 to 34. Forty-one percent of their homes include preschoolers. But if you don't care how old the kids are, check out households headed by people aged 35 to 44. Seven in ten include children of any age.
[*Census Bureau, 1994*]

6. (c) Best place to find lots of kids. They don't make families like they used to, at least when it comes to size. But some boomers are doing their part to keep up population growth. Almost one in four married-couple households headed by boomers aged 35 to 39 has three or more kids under age 18 at home, as do 20 percent of those headed by 30-to-34-year-olds. [*Census Bureau, 1994*]

7. (b) Most likely to believe God is dead. Reading all that Nietzsche in college left a lot of baby boomers believing God is at least in the infirmary. Eighty-three percent of people aged 30 to 49 believe the U.S. is losing its religion. Least likely to agree are teens aged 18 and 19, only 59 percent of whom think the influence of religion is declining. [*The Gallup Poll Monthly,* 1994]

8. (b) Most likely to be grumpy about tax laws on home offices. Perhaps older people do their best work in a bathrobe. Seven percent of workers aged 65 or older work at home for pay at least eight hours a week, a higher percentage than any other age group. But if you're marketing to home workers, boomers are a better bet. Workers aged 35 to 44 account for 31 percent of people who work at home.
[*Bureau of Labor Statistics, 1994*]

9. (d) Best customers for an awesome sound system. Bet you thought it was young people, heh-heh, heh-heh. Well, Beavis, you're wrong. It takes big bucks to fork out big dough for electronics. Households headed by 45-to-54-year-olds spend 75 percent more than average on TVs, radios, and sound equipment. Everybody else, except for those aged 35 to 44, spends less than average. [*Bureau of Labor Statistics, 1993*]

10. (a) Most likely to prefer a woman supervisor. The smart young women of Generation X are most likely to bet that a female boss will help them break the glass ceiling. Sixty-one percent of women aged 18 to 29 would prefer to work for a woman, compared with 26 percent of boomer women aged 30 to 49. Young men say it doesn't matter if the boss is a guy or a gal. Only 22 percent prefer to report to a woman, but 52 percent say it doesn't matter. Nearly half of men of all ages give this politically correct (and safe) answer.
[*Gallup Poll Monthly*, 1993]

11. part I (c); part II (b) Most likely to make the big bucks. On average, people aged 45 to 54 have the highest incomes—but a lot of people in this group don't work full time. Men aged 45 to 54 with full-time, year-round jobs earn the most of any group, with a 1994 average of $39,700. Among women with full-time jobs, 35-to-44-year-olds have the highest incomes, at $25,300. If you're after women with the biggest bucks, however, you might want to stick with this cohort as time goes on. The age at which women's incomes peak is likely to rise as more career-oriented women replace older women with fewer total years in the labor force. [*Census Bureau, 1995*]

12. part I (c); part II (b) Most likely to blow smoke. For men, the biggest percentage of smokers is found among 35-to-44-year-olds. One-third of these fellas puff. The women most likely to be snagging a cigarette are aged 25 to 34. The percentage of smokers drops off sharply after age 65, possibly a sign of the habit taking its toll.
[*National Center for Health Statistics, 1991*]

13. (b) Most likely to have a sheepskin. Thanks in part to the draft-deferment provision for college students during the Vietnam War, 35-to-44-year-old boomers are most likely to have a college degree. Twenty-seven percent have at least a bachelor's degree, compared with one in four people aged 45 to 54. Younger folks aren't far behind, however. Many Xers aren't finished with their schooling, and they may yet catch up to their elders. All this education is a big reason why consumers are so darn finicky these days.
[*Census Bureau, 1994*]

SCORING YOURSELF

110 to 130 points:
You know your customers better than you know your own family—or you are a demographer.

50 to 100 points:
You have a working knowledge of demographics, but have more important things to do than sit around playing with magazine quizzes. You really should learn more about how the generations differ. It could make all the difference.

less than 50 points:
You are generationally challenged and should take steps to remedy the situation before your customers go to someone who understands them.

MAKING GENERATIONAL MARKETING
COME OF AGE

Does the music in that ad ring a bell? Sellers are finally learning to exploit the life experiences that define each generation. What took them so long?

Faye Rice

LAST WINTER New York City radio station KISS-FM accelerated from 14th place to first in the ratings faster than a Manhattan cabbie goes through a yellow light. How? By targeting upscale black baby-boomers, tuning out raucous rap and hip-hop, and dialing up the melodious music of such honey-voiced singers as Al Green, Barry White, and Whitney Houston. "We have gotten much bigger by targeting smaller," says general manager Judy Ellis, who follows up that statement with a seemingly contradictory one. "Our target audience is 25 to 54," she says resolutely. Hmm, that's an awfully wide range for narrow casting, including as it does baby-boomers, Generation Xers, and a smattering of silents. "Well," Ellis explains, "that is how our ratings books categorize the market."

Welcome to the slightly absurd world of generational marketing, a venerable strategy

REPORTER ASSOCIATE *Kimberly Seals McDonald*

that is supposed to reach consumers right where they live, demographically, socially, and psychologically, thus rendering mass marketing passé. Instead, mass marketing is grudgingly giving way to mass confusion as marketers such as KISS stumble toward the holy grail of segment-of-one selling. Says Peter Kim, vice chairman of ad agency McCann-Erickson: "Most companies are still organized around a mass-marketing concept. Very few people in research and marketing departments even understand the concept of cohorts or generations."

A generation is defined by dates of birth, a cohort by important external events that occur during its formative years. People born between 1930 and 1939 are often labeled the Depression generation, but those born between 1912 and 1921 are the Depression cohort, since they became adults between 1930 and 1939. In reality, a plethora of names exists for some generations (see below).

That's what marketers can't quite figure out. Consider Mercedes-Benz, which is trying to woo younger buyers through the music of Janis Joplin, the raspy-voiced blues singer and boozer who died of a drug over-

dose in 1970. Dinah Shore this is not. Yet Joplin's a cappella classic, "Mercedes Benz"—you remember, "Oh, Lord, won't you buy me a Mercedes-Benz?"—which chides bourgeois materialists (herself included; Joplin owned a Porsche), is the centerpiece of the company's commercials for its C- and E-class cars, with prices starting at $31,000.

The hard-driving Joplin and the staid German company are an improbable match. But Mercedes is betting that the early-Seventies anthem will drive affluent 35- to 45-year-olds—many of whom have inhaled, to say the least—into their showrooms. "The median age of Mercedes buyers is 51. We must begin talking to a whole new generation," explains veteran adman Marvin Sloves, 61, chairman of Lowe & Partners/SMS, creator of the spot. "I don't know the generational names. Whatever everyone calls people 35 to 45 who grew up in the 1960s and 1970s is the generation we are targeting."

Markets still get defined mostly by age brackets rather than by defining experiences. Even the Mercedes ad team, which

THE DEPRESSION COHORT
(the G.I. generation)

BORN 1912–21   **AGE IN '95:** 74 to 83
% OF ADULT POPULATION: 7% (13 million)
MONEY MOTTO: Save for a rainy day.
SEX MINDSET: Intolerant
FAVORITE MUSIC: Big band
■ People who were starting out in the Depression era were scarred in ways that remain with them today—especially when it comes to financial matters like spending, saving, and debt. The Depression cohort was also the first to be truly influenced by contemporary media: radio and especially motion pictures.

THE WORLD WAR II COHORT
(the Depression generation)

BORN 1922–27   **AGE IN '95:** 68 to 73
% OF ADULT POPULATION: 6% (11 million)
MONEY MOTTO: Save a lot, spend a little.
SEX MINDSET: Ambivalent
FAVORITE MUSIC: Swing
■ People who came of age in the Forties were unified by the shared experience of a common enemy and a common goal. Consequently, this group became intensely romantic. A sense of self-denial that long outlived the war is especially strong among the 16 million veterans and their families.

THE POSTWAR COHORT
(the silent generation)

BORN 1928–45   **AGE IN '95:** 50 to 67
% OF ADULT POPULATION: 21% (41 million)
MONEY MOTTO: Save some, spend some.
SEX MINDSET: Repressive
FAVORITE MUSIC: Frank Sinatra
■ Members of this 18-year cohort, the war babies, benefited from a long period of economic growth and relative social tranquillity. But global unrest and the threat of nuclear attack sparked a need to alleviate uncertainty in everyday life. The youngest subset, called the cool generation, were the first to dig folk rock.

carefully researched its target market, gets tripped up. For instance, many 51-year-old consumers may feel as nostalgic hearing "Mercedes Benz" as those 35 to 45. (Joplin would be 52 now.)

Segmenting by age, experts keep insisting, is an ineffective way to divvy up a market. Ross E. Goldstein, a consultant at Torme & Kenney in San Francisco, explains: "It used to be that when you knew someone's age, you knew a lot about him because the population went through life stages, like marriage and having children, at fairly predictable times. Not anymore. My older brother is 52 and has a 1-year-old daughter."

Some marketers will simply toss Goldstein's brother into a vague 50-plus category and assume that his lifestyle and consumer behavior will mirror that of all 52-year-olds, or worse, 62-year-olds. Yet demographers count three and perhaps five distinct generations that are 50 and above, and first-wave boomers will join that list beginning in 1996.

The elder Goldstein's spending patterns might well mirror his age group's—until you get to the baby clothes, diapers, strollers, and such. Or his purchasing behavior could reflect a younger generation's, especially if his wife is an Xer or young boomer and her generational values prevail in the household.

If age segmentation provides so little insight into consumer behavior, why does it prevail? Because age is the universal currency in the high-stakes world of advertising and media. It is how ratings services like Nielsen and Arbitron and Starch categorize the viewers and listeners and readers they count. So when marketers throw down their dollars for TV spots, the orders go out for shows appealing to males 18 to 49, or to women 25 to 54. "It's nonsense when companies say their target market is 18 to 49. That's not a target, that is the world," says marketing consultant Carol Farmer of Boca Raton, Florida.

The renegade marketers circumvent the establishment. Listen to Steve Goldstein, head of marketing for Levi's men's jeans at Levi Strauss, talk about buying media: "Instead of looking at the typical age breaks, like 18 to 49, we want to lay a more sophisticated layer of generational information. We tell [media buyers] to find quintessential programs that resonate with the values of the generation we are targeting. The show must relate to their lifestyles and attitudes." Many advertisers stick with the 18-to-49 approach because they think, incorrectly, that it's cheaper than targeting.

Judy George, who founded the high-fashion furniture chain Domain in 1986 with $3 million, has cut promotional spending 35% since moving to generational marketing three years ago. After intensive study of her customers, George designed promotional and selling techniques for each segment.

Through research, for example, she learned that her core boomer clientele, a generation that has always valued personal growth, is as concerned about self-improvement issues as it is about decorating. So George launched two promotional series of in-store seminars. The focus of one is women's issues, and she speaks at her 18 East Coast stores on subjects like how to start a business. "Sometimes we are mobbed with customers at these seminars," she says. The topic of the other promotional forum is design, and influential decorators help Domain customers juxtapose various styles and periods of furnishings. Repeat business among Domain's upscale boomers has nearly doubled, to 35%, since the new programs began.

At the other end of the time line, George is launching a new furniture series for her retired World War II and postwar clients. The sofas are narrower, with more back support, and aren't as deep as boomer sofas—that makes getting out of them easier.

The new approach costs less. Domain has replaced newspaper advertising with direct mail, bringing ad spending at the privately held company down from 7.8% of sales to 4.8% in three years. Sales jumped nearly 40%, to over $40 million.

Lowe's, the giant home-improvement chain that has been on a tear building superstores in the South, reports similar results on a much larger scale. Consultant Farmer introduced the retailer to William Strauss and Neil Howe's book, *Generations*, and helped Lowe's develop a generational marketing program. Lowe's has since halved total advertising expenses, from 2% to 1% of sales, while revenues have doubled, to $6 billion, and profits have soared 90%, to $280 million. "With sales increasing and constant new store openings, you would normally expect advertising expenses to go up," says assistant to the chairman Thomas Smith. Like Domain's George, he and senior vice president of marketing Dale Pond attribute much of the drop to better targeting. Explains Pond: "Before, we just tried to reach as many people as possible. Now we mainly use specialty media to reach each of the consumer groups we are targeting."

To attract Generation Xers, who represent just 10% of its customers, Lowe's signed up as a sponsor for Nascar, an auto-racing organization that counts a large following of busters and late boomers. Says Chairman Robert L. Strickland: "We don't want to make the same mistake with Xers that we made with boomers. We stuck with the G.I. and silent generations too long."

The next huge generational test for marketers begins next year, when the first wave of boomers celebrate their 50th birthdays and officially enter the senior market—kicking and screaming all the way. Remember Geritol and the Lawrence Welk show? Forget it. Unlike their silent predecessors, this vast cohort will demand that companies embrace their values, such as youthfulness and invincibility, no matter what the product: food, cosmetics, tools, or corrective eye lenses. "Nothing could be further from the truth than saying boomers will be like their parents," says demographer Cheryl Russell,

---

THE BOOMERS I COHORT
(the Woodstock generation)

BORN 1946–54   **AGE IN '95:** 41 to 49
% OF ADULT POPULATION: 17% (33 million)
MONEY MOTTO: Spend, borrow, spend.
SEX MINDSET: Permissive
FAVORITE MUSIC: Rock & roll
■ Vietnam is the demarcation point between leading-edge and trailing-edge boomers. The Kennedy and King assassinations signaled an end to the status quo and galvanized this vast cohort. Still, early boomers continued to experience economic good times and want a lifestyle at least as good as their predecessors'.

THE BOOMERS II COHORT
(zoomers)

BORN 1955–65   **AGE IN '95:** 30 to 40
% OF ADULT POPULATION: 25% (49 million)
MONEY MOTTO: Spend, borrow, spend.
SEX MINDSET: Permissive
FAVORITE MUSIC: Rock & Roll
■ It all changed after Watergate. The idealistic fervor of youth disappeared. Instead, the later boomers exhibited a narcissistic preoccupation that manifested itself in things like the self-help movement. In this dawning age of downward mobility, debt as a means of maintaining a lifestyle made sense.

THE GENERATION X COHORT
(baby-busters)

BORN 1966–76   **AGE IN '95:** 19 to 29
% OF ADULT POPULATION: 21% (41 million)
MONEY MOTTO: Spend? Save? What?
SEX MINDSET: Confused
FAVORITE MUSIC: Grunge, rap, retro
■ The slacker set has nothing to hang on to. The latchkey kids of divorce and day care are searching for anchors with their seemingly contradictory "retro" behavior: the resurgence of proms, coming-out parties, and fraternities. Their political conservatism is motivated by a "What's in it for me?" cynicism.

editor-in-chief of New Strategist Publications in Ithaca, New York.

Take financial services products. Many Depression-era consumers, parents of the oldest boomers, are severely risk-averse. They prefer secure investments like Treasury bonds and CDs, even though returns are low. "They won't go into debt for any reason," says Geoffrey Meredith, president of Lifestage Matrix Marketing of Lafayette, California, who conducted a generational cohort study with his partner, University of Massachusetts marketing professor Charles Schewe. "Many boomers, by contrast, *will* go into debt for any reason," says Meredith.

He recently designed an insurance policy targeted at two generations permanently scarred by the Depression—the World War II and Depression cohorts, as he calls them. Policyholders give the issuing company, Lifetime Security Plan, the right to inherit their homes when they die. Until then, the policyholders, mostly retirees, live in their homes and receive a monthly stipend. Because people are living longer, this relieves them of many financial worries. Lifetime even provides basic upkeep of the homes. By contrast, when boomers reach age 70, Meredith predicts they may be more interested in a reverse mortgage—a loan against the equity of property—since they do not fear debt.

As generational marketers create chic new models of aging for maturing boomers, they are being forced to overhaul other franchises to capture busters. When John Sykes took the reins at Viacom's VH1 MusicFirst video network last year, he promptly conducted a study of boomers and busters. VH1, the fading sister of MTV, suffered from a murky image and ratings in Weather Channel territory. When VH1 hit the air a decade ago, the oldest boomers were just turning 40, but the network's targeted audience was, surprise, 25 to 49. First mistake. If VH1 had focused on boomers, devout music lovers that they are, it might have been a rousing hit. Instead, the initial all-music, soft rock format lapsed into a cluttered lifestyle channel of standup comedy, talk shows, and syrupy middle-of-the-road oldie clips.

ENTER THE ZOOMERS, a category that combines the youngest segment of boomers, those born between 1960 and 1965, with older busters, born between 1966 and 1970. They buy music by the ton and show no signs of stopping—behavior that VH1 ignored. Says Sykes: "There was a perception that once they passed their mid-20s they would be like their parents and stop buying music." But these consumers are still adding CDs to their collections and want a network to keep them up to date with new music.

The new format is thus chock-a-block with R&B and modern rock sensations Melissa Etheridge, Counting Crows, and R.E.M., the music that helped drive up CD sales 12% during the past two years. Sykes predicts it will do the same for his ratings.

Levi Strauss, whose jeans clad the Woodstock generation (when it was wearing clothes), is now switching generations, forsaking boomers for slackers. The wildly successful, wider-in-the middle Dockers, introduced in 1986, aimed straight at boomers and their expanding waistlines. In soothing, reality-based TV commercials for Dockers, groups of 40ish men, some graying, some balding, sat around and talked about the good old days. Sales broke $1 billion last year.

Enter the X factor. The latest commercials for Dockers are high-energy, fast-paced shockers, as irreverent as Nirvana's songs. In one, "The Red Eye," a young twentysomething—emphasis on young—insomniac rolls backward on a plane trying to get comfortable and nearly collides with a fetching female Xer holding a teddy bear.

Why change so radically? "We could see sales were close to peaking," says Robert Hanson, vice president of R&D for the Dockers brand. "We had to figure out how to make the brand emotionally relevant to younger boomers and Generation X."

Researchers focused on three cohorts—Xers and first- and second-wave boomers—using telephone interviews, in-home visits, mall intercepts, and focus groups. The research included psychographics—evaluating emotions like fear and hope that drive brand choice—lifestyle issues, and other variables. The goal was to unite the three cohorts around one concept.

Fat chance. "Our 45-year-old boomer customers said they could identify with the imagery of younger men, but that didn't work the other way around," says Dockers division president James Capon. "Many of the Xers and younger boomers referred to Dockers as their dad's pants." Ouch. Having captured boomers, Levi has decided to place its marketing chips against Xers. That's why you don't see balding fat guys in Dockers commercials anymore.

UNLIKE previous cohorts, Xers have no defining moments, so companies wooing them have little to grab at. Says Margaret Reagan, a partner at Towers Perrin, a consulting firm: "It is amusing watching marketers trying to figure out how to reach Xers."

Subaru became a textbook case of how not to market to Xers. Its grunge-scene, oh-so-hip approach fell flat with Xers, who hate to be marketed at. GM's Saturn division hit the right note in a commercial in which a young lady visits many automobile showrooms and is treated shabbily by salespeople, presumably because of her age and limited budget, until she walks into a Saturn dealership. There she is greeted warmly and the staff is attentive. "This ad is always mentioned as a favorite in the Xer focus groups I conduct," says Reagan. "They like it because they can identify with her story."

Just who are these Xers? Saatchi & Saatchi (Cordiant) conducted an extensive study of the generation, employing teams of psychologists and cultural anthropologists. The research produced four key segments: the "cynical disdainers," the most pessimistic and skeptical, and the group that has gotten all the press; the "traditional materialists," the group most like boomers, positive, optimistic, striving for the American dream; "hippies revisited," who replay the lifestyle and values of the Sixties and express themselves through music (Grateful Dead), fashion, and spirituality; and the "Fifties machos," young, Gingrich Republicans who still believe in stereotyped gender roles and are the least accepting of multiculturalism. (The more extreme can cross over to skinheads.)

The five-year-old, $100-million-plus active-wear company No Fear may be a quintessential X marketer. Cool? Its first TV commercial, on the 1995 Super Bowl, failed to mention what the company sells.

No Fear, which splashes impudent slogans like NO CURE FOR DEATH and HOODLUM on its apparel, denies any generational appeal. "We don't even allow that word [Generation X] to enter our building," says Jim Hancock, marketing director of the privately held Carlsbad, California, company. "We tend to market to people's lifestyles, those attracted to the psychological challenge of sports. They could be 14 or 50." But most sales are to Xers and zoomers.

No Fear gives the impression that it succeeds on utter hipness. Not quite, dude. This company has meticulously crafted its chic mystique through intensive research and methodical niche marketing on billboards and in enthusiast magazines for surfing, cycling, and motor and bike racing.

That is the challenge of generational marketing: It requires far more sophistication than you needed in the days of calling three networks and reaching 80% of the market. Which is, of course, why the method is shunned. Says Ann Corman of Yankelovich: "Many companies look at their competition. If none of them are doing it, they figure, why should they?"

Why? Because the payback is abundant. More important, generational marketing is the next wave, and it's here now. Companies that wait any longer may find themselves a generation behind.

Scouting for Souls

┌─ SUMMARY ─────────────────────────────────

Only one-third of Americans are religious, and fewer than 40 percent attend church. That's why churches are using demographics and other marketing information to find new souls and keep current congregations happy. "Megachurches" take the marketing approach to an extreme, while many doubting clerics refuse to touch any marketing tools. Yet those who use research are thriving.

Marc Spiegler

Marc Spiegler is a freelance writer in Chicago.

When Pastor Thomas Wolf first came to Southern California's Church on Brady in 1969, the situation seemed dire. The Southern Baptist church in East Los Angeles had seen its historically Anglo following erode to 45 people as the neighborhood became mostly Mexican. Facing fiscal problems and demographic change, church elders even considered selling off the dilapidated property. Today, after more than a quarter century of Wolf's leadership, the Church on Brady boasts services averaging 700 worshippers, drawn from an ethnic mix as diverse as East L.A. itself.

The Church on Brady posed a perfect challenge for Wolf, the first American to receive a diploma from the programs established by Donald McGavran, founder of the international "Church Growth" movement. McGavran's philosophy holds that increasing the size of a church is a legitimate theological aim, not just a natural byproduct of righteousness. To achieve that goal, pastors such as Wolf employ a well-developed array of methods rooted not only in scripture, but also in commercial marketing. Terms like "market segment," "niche," and "satisfied customer" trip easily off their tongues.

Such a bottom-line approach is not surprising when one considers Americans' lukewarm attitude toward religion. Only 35 percent of Americans could be classified as "religious" in 1995, according to surveys of religious attitudes and church attendance conducted by the Gallup Organization. In their attempts to reach the other two-thirds, many churches have turned to demographic and other information to draw new followers and keep denominations healthy.

FINDING NEW SOULS

When Wolf started rebuilding the Church on Brady in 1969, demographic informa-

> **Music plays an overpowering role in a church's success or failure.**

tion was hard to come by. He recalls how, with great difficulty, he managed to dig up a meager amount of data from the city council, county, and public schools. But he still ended up conducting lots of common-sense "windshield studies"—getting in his car and driving around neighborhoods, observing who was moving in, which businesses were going under, and other signs of change.

Today, with data available down to the census-tract level on CD-ROMs, Wolf relies much more on hard numbers. "When we plan to do a limited mailing—let's say 5,000 flyers—we'll study census-tract data to figure out where to send them, not just blanket a whole neighborhood."

Before targeting potential followers, a denomination must decide that a particular area seems ripe for a new church. The strongest indicators are expanding communities and high birth rates, says Steve Whitten of the Southern Baptists' Convention Home Mission Board, which constantly consults with local members on

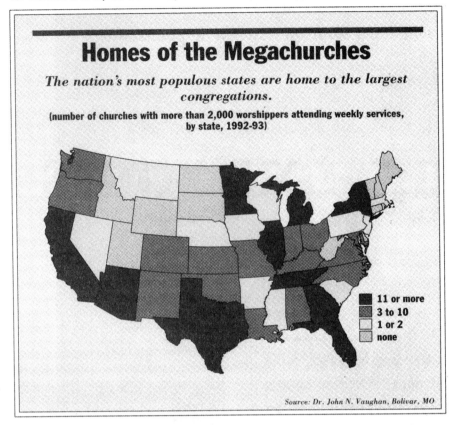

Homes of the Megachurches

The nation's most populous states are home to the largest congregations.

(number of churches with more than 2,000 worshippers attending weekly services, by state, 1992-93)

- 11 or more
- 3 to 10
- 1 or 2
- none

Source: Dr. John N. Vaughan, Bolivar, MO

the issue. From the Church of the Nazarene's central research division in Kansas City, Rich Housel echoes Whitten: "We try to identify places that seem like they have good potential, and encourage people to start the churches. Our best indicators are new homes—because churches really seem linked to the life cycle of the community—and new families. Many people who stop going to church in college come back once they have children. They're concerned about teaching their children right from wrong."

The Church of Jesus Christ of Latter-Day Saints makes intensive use of demographic data to locate new opportunities. The church conducts regular surveys worldwide, and each local unit—or "ward"—also reports member data to world headquarters in Salt Lake City, Utah. "We look at household composition and factors like fertility—age at birth of first child, number of kids—and at 'marriage markets.' In a lot of areas, we have more women than men, which has obvious implications for growth," says senior research analyst Kristen Goodman.

Methodist strategic planner Jack Heacock considers demographic research an

essential part of his success. "In the past, a lot of Methodist pastors were trying to be like the Sears Roebuck catalog, all things to all people. But in the greatest mail-order period in history, that catalog went out of business," he says. "In targeting a church's efforts, you have to get very clear on who you want to try to reach. I always start with a demographic analysis, and try to help churches target the largest market segment that other churches are not reaching."

Percept Group, a consulting firm in Costa Mesa, California, works almost exclusively with religious groups. It offers churches analyses that compare the community within a 5-mile radius of a site against national profiles. Drawing on both census data and its own research, Percept draws a detailed picture of the prospective congregation. An analysis of Colorado Springs, Colorado, for instance, reveals a slew of insights on which a new church could act, including a relatively high rate of changing religious preferences, widespread concern about neighborhood gangs, distaste for face-to-face evangelism, demand for intellectual challenge within the church context, and a

strong tendency toward "contemporary" worship styles and modern music.

"We'll look at all the demographic data," says American Society for Church Growth president Gary McIntosh. "Then we'll decide on three census tracts that seem promising and design the music, the classes, the communications, and the ads to be attractive to that group." In targeting a group he designates "Boomers and Busters," McIntosh might draw on a series of preferences such as faster-paced worships using modern-language Bibles; casual, celebratory services with practical sermons; louder sound; and more modern music. The generation raised on rock and roll, McIntosh seems to suggest, hankers for the experiential dimension of rock concerts when it wants to worship.

CURRENT CONGREGATIONS

Music plays an overpowering role in a church's success or failure, say many church-growth observers, because it can either make potential followers feel at home or alienate them. "I arrived as a pastor at First United Methodist in Austin, Texas, in 1973, and we had a fine organist who played baroque music beautifully," says Methodist planner Jack Heacock. "But I felt like we had people in the church who might be tuned to a different FM wavelength, so to speak. I suggested that we broaden the range a little, to hit a few more musical styles. We grew those two services from under 500 people in 1973 to nearly 900 people in 1988." The church's budget rose accordingly, from $160,000 to $1.5 million.

Since leaving the Austin church in 1989, Heacock has worked throughout the Methodists' Southwest Texas Conference, consulting with individual pastors to increase their flocks. "We as Methodists are ministering a program that worked well in the 1950s, but there are places where we have gotten stuck," Heacock says. "We need to learn how to surf with changes." Heacock has helped work wonders. As Methodist numbers dropped 4 percent nationwide, his conference's count rose 12 percent. Twenty-seven churches that adopted his strategies early on showed an aggregate increase of $1.6 million for ministry and mission budgets between 1990 and 1993. He does it by ensuring adequate staffing, having room to expand, and making sure churches offer subgroups to keep followers from feeling like more than passive observers.

But he also sweats the details. "Parking is crucial. The average Methodist's car brings 1.68 people to church now, whereas 20 to 30 years back, it used to bring more like 4 people," he says. Signage also plays a crucial role in attracting new members. "You need to keep a constant vigil on signs, not only on the roads and highways to help people get to the church, but also at the church," he says. "Before you even get out of your car, you should know where to park, what side the nursery is on, what side the worship is on. And it has to be just as clear inside, so people don't feel any confusion."

Finally, Heacock points out the needs created by increasingly safety-conscious

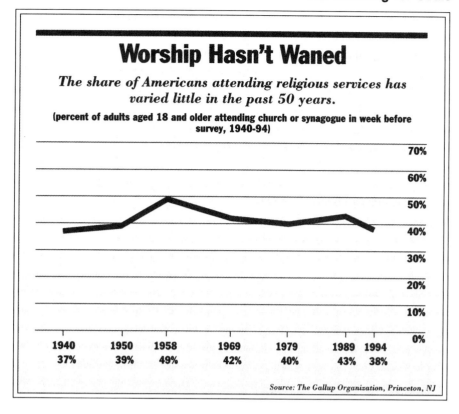

Worship Hasn't Waned

The share of Americans attending religious services has varied little in the past 50 years.

(percent of adults aged 18 and older attending church or synagogue in week before survey, 1940-94)

1940	1950	1958	1969	1979	1989	1994
37%	39%	49%	42%	40%	43%	38%

Source: The Gallup Organization, Princeton, NJ

> "The average Methodist's car brings 1.68 people to church now. Thirty years ago, it used to bring 4."

parents. "Baby boomers will not leave their infants in a room with toddlers, because they don't want to risk some kid accidentally poking their baby's eye out. With all the young families coming in, you need to have a nursery that is as classy as any room in the church."

Many churches have zeroed in on the abundant baby boomers. But second-generation church-growth expert Charles Arn, president of Church Growth in Monrovia, California, thinks that older adults are a huge untapped market. "One thing we know from experts and research is that relatively few people become Christians in their later years," says Arn. "Only half a percent or so convert to Christianity after age 55." The problem lies in the approach many evangelists take, says Arn.

Eight in ten people charged with senior

ministry in 500 large churches nationwide had received no training for the role, Arn's research found. "Seniors avoid dramatic changes in lifestyle, but many evangelists say, 'You've got to turn your life around 180 degrees,'" he says. "That's like going into a wheatfield with a cornpicker." Drawing on secular marketers' techniques, he tells churches that to attract older worshippers, they must present conversion as a process, not a single climactic event.

Arn advocates using senior members to recruit older potential converts, because market research indicates that seniors tend to trust people their own age. Arn also stresses that churches must target practical benefits to older converts, for whom Sunday School offers little appeal. Instead, he tells clients to create groups that provide companionship, focus on helping in the sphere of physical health, and help pension-dependent seniors with budgeting and financial management.

Sometimes timing is the key to capturing congregants. People approached by evangelists fall into three categories, according to a survey by Flavil Yeakley of Harding University in Searcy, Arkansas:

those who convert and stay active, those who convert then rapidly lapse, and those who resist conversion. Yeakley scored each respondent using the Holmes-Rahe stress test, which measures the cumulative stress created by transitional events such as marriage, getting fired, children leaving home, and moving.

Three-fourths of the 76 respondents exhibiting the highest stress levels converted. Within the top 30 percent stress-wise, two-thirds converted. "When people are living in their house for a long time, and they have a routine, they're unlikely to change their ways," Thomas Wolf points out. "But when they feel boxed in or unstable, those are the listening points."

MEGACHURCHES

Even in the 17th century, English statesman John Selden noted that "a glorious Church is like a magnificent feast; there is all the variety that may be, but every one chooses out a dish or two that he likes, and lets the rest alone."

"Increasingly, we see awareness of demographics as a hallmark of growing churches. Because our culture is changing so rapidly, they must go to where the har-

Church Central

Religion is most central to the lives of older, poor, and nonwhite Americans.

(percent of adults aged 18 and older who say religion is very important to them, by selected characteristics, 1994)

	percent
ALL ADULTS	60%
SEX	
Men	50%
Women	68
AGE	
18 to 29	48%
30 to 49	58
50 to 64	67
65 and older	73
REGION	
East	56%
Midwest	55
South	70
West	73
RACE	
White	56%
Nonwhite	80
INCOME	
Less than $20,000	70%
$20,000 to $29,999	58
$30,000 to $49,999	61
$50,000 or more	46

Source: The Gallup Organization, Princeton, NJ

vest is ripe," says Southwest Baptist University's John N. Vaughn, an expert on "megachurches."

Perhaps the most stunning example of a 20th-century religious cornucopia is the Second Baptist Church of Houston, Texas, which boasts more than 500 staffers and 20,000 members. Known colloquially as "Exciting Second," the church offers a health club, football field, day-care center, elementary and secondary education, and a singles group with 7,000 members.

The vigorous entertainment schedule draws in potential followers, using expertise the church gained through consulting with Walt Disney World. When church founder Dr. Ed Young decided to expand to a second location, he chose Katy, a Houston suburb that, not coincidentally,

is in one of the county's fastest-growing areas. If everything goes according to plan, the thousands of "Exciting Second"

> **"It's not that we want the preacher to just read the numbers and start preaching differently, like a politician."**

followers who live near Katy will form the core of the new church, leaving room for even more growth on the church's current 42-acre site.

Mormons also use lifestyle information to understand specific congregational needs. "One of the biggest things we look at is which groups seem most at risk, who's not participating as highly," says researcher Goodman. After studies indicated that lower education levels correlate with reduced participation among Mormons, many churches started literacy programs for followers to help them better understand the gospel. In the same manner, says Goodman, other branches have programs targeted to families or

> **Only 20 percent of America's 367,000 congregations actively pursue strategic planning.**

older people, depending on which groups seem most at risk in a particular area.

Some churches hire academic demographers to help them learn about their flocks' needs. Demographer Flavil Yeakley travels the South to help local branches of the Church of Christ. "The first step is checking how in line we are with the whole community's demographics," he says. "We'll check to see if there are large parts of the community that we're missing. If you've got a huge gap in the 25-to-45 age range, that tends to spell trouble.

"It's not that we want the preacher to just read the numbers and start preaching differently, like a politician," says Yeakley. Instead, the numbers help a

church figure out its community's needs and play to them. A large population of families with teenaged children might suggest the need for a proactive youth group, for example.

DOUBTING CLERICS

For all the entrepreneurial approaches many churches demonstrate, McIntosh of the American Society for Church Growth points out that market-savvy approaches to swelling the flocks remain more the exception than the rule. By his estimate, only 20 percent of America's 367,000 congregations actively pursue strategic planning. Kenneth Beddell looks back in frustration on the 15 years since he helped set up Religious Futurists of Dayton, Ohio, an organization formed around the theory that projections can help ministries achieve success. "We're almost out of that business altogether now, because it's really difficult to find a market for such services," he says. "Businesses the same size as these churches are taking a long hard look at the data, but you have a hard time selling them to church groups."

As a rule of thumb, the larger the church, the less sophisticated its use of data, says Clifford Grammich of the Heartland Center in Hammond, Indiana. Not surprisingly, he says, the hierarchical, stoutly traditional Roman Catholic church tends to fall particularly short. Each Catholic diocese operates independently, so the use and reliability of statistics varies widely. While New York City's diocese tracks demographics well, Grammich tells horror stories about others. "A diocese in the South had been experiencing rapid growth, so every time they reported their membership figures, they added a number that would put them on pace to hit half a million members by the year 2000," he says with an exasperated half-chuckle.

Mary Priniski of the Glenmary Research Center in Decatur, Georgia, paints a bleak picture for Catholic strategic planning. Many dioceses don't have any program in place, she says, and even if they do, the offices tend to be newly established and inexperienced. "If a diocese doesn't have a strong planning office, they don't tend to use demographics," she says.

Of course, even groups that successfully use data harbor pockets of people who decry the use of marketing, saying it drags the ways of the world into the house of the Lord. Pasadena-based religious futurist Joe B. Webb describes such types as reactionaries. Citing attacks on Pastor Bill Hybels and suburban Chicago's massive Willow Creek Community Church, Webb says, "One of the criticisms of Willow Creek is that it conducted these types of studies. But that's how it grew. Some people in the religious community don't like to think about it in these terms. They want it to be more mystical. But ultimately, the church either addresses it, or it addresses them, and people let their feet do the talking."

The crux of the problem, suggests the Church of the Nazarene's Housel, often comes down to a generation gap. "Anything that smacks of market coercion goes up against some older people's theological idea of worshipping God because it's God," he says. "But we go back to scripture, where Christ tells us to preach to all the world. We're just trying to find places to preach." Even the Church of England's Archbishop of Canterbury, George Carey, defends the practice: "People have described me as a 'management bishop,'" he told London's *Daily Telegraph* in 1991. "But I say to my critics, 'Jesus was a management expert, too.'"

George Hunter, professor of evangelism and church growth at Asbury Theological Seminary in Wilmore, Kentucky, says that churches without plans for growth invariably stagnate. In using demographic data and marketing techniques, Church Growth advocates merely use modern tools to achieve ancient ends.

"Even back in biblical times," he points out, "if you wanted to minister to lepers, you had to find out where they were."

TAKING IT FURTHER

Church Growth Today publishes a newsletter that examines issues of interest to church leaders of all denominations, including occasional statistical profiles. It also offers an extensive global database of church statistics updated on an annual basis. Contact Dr. John N. Vaughan, director of research, at telephone/fax (417) 326-3212. Percept Group provides Ministry Area Profiles for customized geographies based on census and other data. More information is available from 151 Kalmus Drive, Suite A104, Costa Mesa, CA 92626; telephone (800) 442-6277. The Gallup Organization and Roper Starch Worldwide conduct public opinion surveys regarding religious beliefs and behavior. Call Gallup at (609) 924-9600 and Roper at (212) 599-0700.

Consumer Behavior: Yesterday, Today, and Tomorrow

Judith Lynne Zaichkowsky

Judith Lynne Zaichkowsky is an associate professor of marketing at Simon Fraser University, Burnaby, British Columbia.

A s the new decade creeps in and the new century approaches, a time has come to reflect upon and predict the consumer's behavior in the marketplace. Many things have changed since the end of mass marketing and the beginning of market segmentation. Under mass marketing, Henry Ford gave the consumer the Ford in any color as long as it was black. After World War II, marketers switched from making products they wanted to making products the consumer wanted. Finding out what the con-

> *The individual-oriented consumer behavior of the past will change to a more collective style in the 1990s.*

sumer wants to purchase and why is what consumer behavior is all about.

Our theoretical models (see **Figure 1**) of how consumers make purchase decisions have

---

Figure 1
History of Approaches to Consumer Decision Making

Decade	Type of Decision Maker	Exemplar
1940s	Economic man	• Fitting of demand equations to products (statistical analyses of past data) (Telser 1962)
1950s	Irrational consumer	• Hidden meaning of goods (Haire 1950) • Use of projective techniques (Dichter 1964)
1960s	Transition from irrational consumer to problem solver	• Hierarchy of effects model (cognitions to attitudes to behavior) (Palda 1966)
1970s	Problem solver	• Prepurchase information seeking (Newman and Staelin 1972) • Labeling of products (Asam and Bucklin 1973)
1980s	Cognitive miser	• The cost of thinking (Shugan 1980) • Low involvement decisions (Hoyer 1984)
1990s	Collective decision maker	• See Figure 2

---

evolved from the economic paradigm of the 1940s, through the irrational consumer of the 1950s and 1960s, to the information processor of the 1970s, up to the 1980s cognitive miser. Tomorrow's consumers will undoubtedly have a **distinctive theoretical decision model that will grow out of the future decision making environment. It is the purpose of this article to outline that future. But first, let us take a brief look at how the study of consumer behavior has evolved since its inception.**

THE ECONOMIC PARADIGM

The 1940s view of the consumer in the marketplace was rooted in economic theory. Most scholars of economics probably still hold to the theory of Economic Man. In this paradigm, purchasing decisions are the result of largely "rational" and conscious economic calculations. The individual buyer seeks to spend his income on those goods that will deliver the most utility (satisfaction) according to his tastes and relative prices. This is a normative rather than a descriptive model of behavior, because logical norms are provided for buyers who want to be "rational."

The model suggests useful behavioral hypotheses, such as: (a) the lower the price of the product, the higher the sales; (b) the lower the price of substitute products, the lower their sales; (c) the lower the price of complementary prod-

> "The economic model ignores the fundamental question of how product and brand preferences are formed."

ucts, the higher their sales, provided they are not "inferior" goods; and (d) the higher the promotional expenditures, the higher the sales. In striving to meet these hypotheses, consumers are not only assumed to be aware of all available alternatives in the marketplace; they are also assumed to be able to rationally rank order the available alternatives by preferences. This is the case of perfect information in the marketplace and unlimited ability of the consumer.

In applying these assumptions to actual consumption, several problems became apparent. First of all, consumers do not have perfect information in the marketplace. Second, they do not

all have the same information about the existing alternatives or attributes of known alternatives. Instead, each consumer has fragmented knowledge of his or her own set of known alternatives; as a result, consumers can not always rank a set of alternatives available to them. In addition, preferences often violate utility theory, because different people prefer different styles, have different tastes, and hence make choices built on preferences rather than objective information such as price.

Problems arise with applying economic theories to gifts. Increasing the price of goods may actually make them more desirable, defying basic economic theory. Hence, inverted demand curves reflect products where increasing prices stimulate increasing sales. Perfume is a perfect example of this type of good. Most perfume or cologne is bought as a gift, and the connotations of bringing home a $2 bottle of cologne or a $50 bottle for a loved one are implicit. A relationship may not last upon receipt of the cheaper good. Hence the economic model ignores the fundamental question of how product and brand preferences are formed.

THE IRRATIONAL CONSUMER

After becoming aware that goods have "hidden meaning," scholars of consumer behavior in the 1950s took to the notion of the consumer as an irrational, impulsive decision maker. Consumers were seen as passive, open, and vulnerable to external influences. This position was an obvious reaction to the "economic man" and also represented a time when business schools were developing. Earlier, faculty trained in economics were the first to be hired, but in the 1950s psychologists were added to the payroll. Their insights from Freud to Maslow, from personality to motivation theory, seemed ever so relevant to our study of the consumer.

The two major psychological theories underlying this era were the Pavlovian learning model and the Freudian psychoanalytic model. The Pavlovian model is based on four central concepts—those of drive, cue, response, and reinforcement. Drive or motives can be primary, such as hunger and sex, or secondary, such as fear. A drive is very general and impels a particular response only in relation to a particular configuration of cues. The Pavlovian model emphasizes the desirability of repetition in advertising. Repetition fights the tendency for learned responses to weaken in the absence of practice and provides reinforcement.

The model also provides guidelines for copy strategy. To be effective as a cue, an advertisement must arouse strong drives in the person. For candy bars, it may be hunger; for safety belts, fear; for hair tonics, sex; for automobiles, status.

In the Freudian psychoanalytic model, the guilt or shame man feels toward his sexual urges causes him to repress them from his consciousness. Through rationalization and sublimation, these urges are denied or become transmuted into socially approved expressions. These urges are never eliminated or under perfect control and they emerge in dreams, in slips of the tongue, or in neurotic or obsessive behavior.

Because of these urges, the consumer's motivations for behavior are not obvious or deeply understood. As a result, Freudian psychology gave consumer behavior the tool of in-depth interviewing to get at the motives and symbols behind a purchase. If a consumer is asked why he purchased an expensive foreign sports car, he may reply that he likes its maneuverability and its looks. At a deeper level he may have purchased the car to impress others, or to feel young again. At a still deeper level, he may be purchasing the sports car to achieve substitute gratification for unsatisfied sexual strivings.

Other Freudian consumer research findings included men wanting their cigars to be odoriferous to prove they were masculine, and women being very serious when baking cakes because unconsciously they were going through the symbolic act of birth. These theories were certainly more interesting reading than the graphs and curves of economics.

One major study of this era (Haire 1950) found that when a shopping list included instant coffee rather than drip grind, the owner of the list was perceived to be a very different person. The owner of the list with instant coffee was lazy, a poor planner, a spendthrift, and a bad wife. Meanwhile, the owner of the list with drip coffee was perceived to be thrifty and a good wife. Fortunately a replication of this study was done in 1970 and housewives were no longer judged by their coffee (Wilkie 1986). However, Haire's study provided good insight to the fact that products have meaning and significance that go far beyond the physical attributes of the products themselves. Furthermore, these hidden values were thought to be a major influence on consumer decisions. To tap into the consumers' hidden motives for purchase, more indirect methods of data gathering were necessary.

Toward the end of the 1950s an empirical article started to throw doubt on the heavy reliance on psychological perspectives. A study by Evans (1959) sought to determine the personality characteristics of Ford versus Chevrolet owners. In the 1950s these were the major automobile manufacturers. Wider choice and Japanese imports did not exist. If the differences between the cars were not major, the train of thought was that the personality of the owner must be significantly different and motivate the consumer to buy one brand or the other. A carefully controlled survey of personality characteristics of 1,600 owners of

Fords and Chevrolets showed no major significant differences in personality characteristics of the car owners. The importance of this line of behavioral research to consumer products was questioned. By this time, in the early and mid-1960s, business schools were producing their own scholars and faculty. Researchers were trained by business schools rather than only economics and psychology departments. Researchers of consumer behavior gained from this marriage of economics and psychology and began to develop their own theories of the consumer.

THE PROBLEM SOLVER

In the 1960s John Kennedy became president of the United States and gave the consumer elevated status. In his message to Congress on March 15, 1962, he put forth the Consumer Bill of Rights (1963) as a social contract between business and society. Government was the ultimate guarantor of these rights, which included the right to safety, the right to be informed, the right to choose, and the right to be heard (redress). The government took Kennedy seriously and began an activist role.

The marketplace was becoming more diversified. The concept of market segmentation became even more important. Goods that the consumer wanted were now being produced, rather than just the goods the manufacturer wanted to make. Choice prevailed for the consumer, and the consumer was recognized by the highest official in the country. Consumers had the right to be informed and protected.

The government poured millions of dollars into departments whose goal was to make sure the consumer had access to information. The Federal Trade Commission flourished. Labels were put on products listing all ingredients. Advertising was regulated and measured; if it was misleading, then corrective advertising was necessary. Information was in great supply to the consumer. Ralph Nader, with his book *Unsafe At Any Speed,* emerged as the hero of the 1970s, taking on corporate giants in the name of the little man. Consumerism was everywhere.

As a result of this environment, consumer behavior researchers started to see the consumer as a "cognitive man." The irrational psychotic purchaser of the 1950s and early 1960s was left behind. The consumer was now a problem solver. He or she was receptive to products or services that consciously met his or her needs. Consumers were thought to actively search for information about the products and services they bought. *Consumer Reports* was born. Consumers were seen as striving to make the best decisions possible given their limitations.

However, consumer researchers told us that even though consumers are given information, they often fail to use it to make decisions. In an initial experiment (Jacoby, Speller, and Kohn 1974) and a follow-up (Scammon 1975), consumers were given objective product information concerning several brands available in the marketplace. The results of the first study showed that consumers felt better about their brand selections with more information, but actually made poorer choices. The study by Scammon corrected for weaknesses in the original study but still found that recall of product attributes decreased with increasing information. Consumers were still limited by the extent of their knowledge about the marketplace and their capacity to store information about the marketplace in short-term memory. Miller's (1956) rule of seven (plus or minus two) pieces of information as cognitive capacity held for the consumer.

The information in the marketplace was not organized for the ease of the consumer. Unit pricing was fine, but comparing prices across brands and sizes for products was quite a challenge. Only when unit prices were posted on one sheet in a simple linear manner by decreasing prices across all sizes and brands did the consumers shift in their decision making toward lower-priced brands. You can imagine the national brand manufacturer's enthusiasm toward presentation of this information at point of purchase.

The overriding conclusion of consumer research in the 1970s was that people can only attend to limited information at one point in time. The consumers' existing skills, habits, reflexes, values, and goals shape the way they search and use information to make their decisions. The 1970s told us that consumers' skills were limited, but at the same time the number of choices available to the consumer kept increasing. More and more choices became available in the 1980s.

THE COGNITIVE MISER

Today's consumer uses decision-making skills originally developed in the 1970s, but the 1980s consumer went farther than just recognizing man's cognitive limitations. Researchers have labelled the low-involvement decision maker (or cognitive miser) as unable or unwilling to engage in extensive decision-making activities in many cases and settle instead for "satisfactory" decisions (Olshavsky and Granbois 1979). There is too much choice and not enough discretionary time to engage in extended cognitive effort for purchases. Instead the consumer develops rules of thumb or heuristics to simplify purchase behavior. An in-store study showed that consumers go through almost no brand price comparison behavior (Hoyer 1984). Rules such as

"buy the cheapest," "buy name brands," or "buy what my friend bought" give the consumer a satisfactory choice in the marketplace that supplants an optimal choice. This is a very adaptive and rational course for the consumer to have taken in the 1980s, given the cluttered choice environment with little time for decision making and virtually no support in information handling. The cost of thinking was recognized as a limiting factor in processing choices.

The 1980s brought a focus on business and conservatism, and many came to feel that governmental regulation was more of a hindrance than a help. This was expressed in the election of Ronald Reagan. As quickly as Kennedy had made the consumer important, Reagan made him unimportant. With strokes of a pen, the FTC experienced a sharp reduction in its budget and influence. Whole departments set up by the government to service the consumer were abandoned. Consumer programs developed for the 1970s folded.

> *"Ralph Nader, with his book* Unsafe At Any Speed, *emerged as the hero of the 1970s, taking on corporate giants in the name of the little man. Consumerism was everywhere."*

The 1980s were for business. This focus was a result of several factors. First, the "baby boomer bulge" had a greater number of people for a smaller number of jobs. In the early 1970s a college graduate decided what job to take, or perhaps a trip to Europe, then work. In the early 1980s the concern was for getting any job at all. The economy was slow and competition was stiff. Business looked to the MBA to turn companies around. The student was serious and conservative due to the competitive environment. Business and engineering were in; the humanities were out. The marketplace became more competitive, more diversified. Deregulation prevailed.

Too many goods cluttered too many store shelves for the consumer. For example, the average number of products in supermarkets soared from 13,000 in 1981 to 21,000 in 1987. There are said to be 400 different brands of beer available to the American beer drinker. A new car purchaser might have 300 different types of cars and light trucks, domestic and imported, to choose from.

Along with the "over choice" and market diversity of the 1980s came decreased leisure time for the consumer, not more leisure time as predicted in the 1940s. The number of free hours a person possesses decreased from four to one since the 1970s. The reason for this is that the average time spent at work has increased seven to eight hours a week since 1978 (Stern 1987). More than 50 percent of all women are working, so household duties are done after 6 p.m. or on weekends. Single working mothers have virtually no free time and can't take care of all they want to do. This scenario has led to a demand for convenience products and convenience shopping. Home catalogs, home TV shopping, home computer shopping, and home shopping parties are part of this easier access to goods that will prevail in the 1990s. The efficiency of in-home shopping, especially through direct marketing, is exemplified by the fact that American Express sold 7 percent of all the luggage bought in the U.S. by sending mailings to affluent cardholders whose charge records showed they spent heavily on travel-related merchandise.

Thus the cognitive miser of the 1980s is a product of decreased time for shopping decisions and increased choice in the marketplace. It is an adaptive strategy to suit the decision-making environment.

THE COLLECTIVE BUYER OF THE 1990S

The focus on individual decision processes for personal purchase of products and services will be replaced by a more collective decision-making style during the 1990s. This will be caused by the changing cultural patterns of North America combined with the decrease in purchasing power of the individual consumer. The culture of North America is changing due to: (1) the rapid increase in the percent of elderly people who are neither healthy nor wealthy; (2) the aging of the baby boomers, causing a shift in values and needs; and (3) increased immigration from Asian cultures with high birth rates to offset the North American decline in population. All three categories of this cultural shift will have to rely on joint decisions for purchase of goods and services, since goods and services will be shifting to a collective consumption style rather than individual consumption in the North American marketplace.

Individuals will combine households in an increasing rate to make life more affordable. The evidence that this joint living may be a trend for the future is exemplified by the fact that 6.2 percent of all employed people are working two jobs, mainly to meet living expenses. When the economy turns down these extra jobs will not be available, and people will have to decrease their standard of living to meet day-to-day expenses.

More unmarried people will share apartments, more single-parent families will couple up, and more children will live at home longer. Thus, more people will be sharing consumer goods just due to living arrangements. Also, through the changing face of North American consumers, the marketplace will continue to change and supply more and more services for these groups (see **Figure 2**). The changing face of the consumer will alter the marketplace and the mode of decision making.

Seniors

Much has been written about the marketing opportunities for the senior segment. Right now approximately 7.3 percent of the population is over 65. By the year 2000, this group will increase by 20 percent, making it the fastest-growing segment of our population. This is one reason why marketers focus on the elderly. However, this group is not all that wealthy or all that healthy. It is estimated that 80 percent of people over 65 have chronic health problems, and 16 percent have severe physical problems. One in five Americans over the age of 85 resides in a nursing home.

The financial burden of caring for these people will be borne by extended families where possible. However, a good portion of these people will be without nearby sons and daughters to attend to them. The state will take on this responsibility in the way of retirement and nursing homes and also specially designated prisons for the elderly. A recent *Wall Street Journal* article ("Godfather of Soul . . ." 1989) reports a geriatric crime wave that appears to be sweeping the na-

---

Figure 2
The Collective Decision Maker, 1990-2000

Important Sector	*Product/Service Mix*
1. Seniors - will increase by 20%	• Bland adult food products • Smaller packaging • Nursing/retirement homes • Meal delivery services • Agencies to coordinate shared living space
2. Baby boomers - average age 45	• Recyclable packaging • Video cameras to record children • Vacations/travel experiences • Day care services • Domestic services
3. Immigrants - heavy Asian influence	• Larger packaging • Larger houses • More specialty food stores • English courses (day and night) • Acculturation courses • Asian language courses

tion. The frustrations of poverty and uselessness have contributed to a 50 percent increase during the past four years in the number of inmates over 55. More people are on waiting lists trying to get in than there are prisoners trying to get out. The elderly eat regularly in prison and are medically taken care of. At the South Carolina State Park Correctional Center, a full-time doctor writes an average of 925 prescriptions a month, and 13 nurses are on duty around the clock. The collective responsibility of the society for its poor elderly will be a major concern.

A full one-third of this market can be a delight to the sellers of goods and services, with almost all of this group's income being discretionary. But two-thirds of those over 65 will be below or near the poverty line. Right now the average annual income is $14,000 for those over 65. This is about half the national mean income in the United States. Food and shelter will be the key concern for the majority of the elderly.

The products to serve this market will focus on health and health-care needs. Since a portion of these people will be helped by families and social services, decisions about their personal consumption will be made at times by the buyer of the good rather than the user. Since costs will be shared, decisions will be shared regardless of who consumes the good.

The Baby Boomers

A full one-third of the population is bulging at middle age. In the year 2000 they will be 36 to 54 years old and at the middle of peak earnings. They are important to our view of consumer behavior because they will head 44 percent of all households and still account for a majority of purchasing power. Due to the conflicting structure of the population versus the corporate culture, there will be less moving around among this group, and they will be more stable in their jobs. Hence, their values and attitudes will change dramatically to reflect this stability. The collective decision-making style will be based on their stable environment.

The change in values from me to we. The changing values are apparent. In the near past, the conservative material ethic was necessary. In the 1960s and 1970s, the education system exploded. Wave after wave of baby boomers became educated. The early graduates got the good jobs. By the late 1970s and early 1980s we were dealing with the big group. The labor market was flooded with bachelor's degrees. Employment was a major concern. The educated focus in the early 1970s was "what job to take." In the early 1980s it was "would I get a job." No wonder the majority had a consumer conservatism, big-business outlook. They all wanted to get ahead and the environment was competitive. It was every man and woman for himself/herself.

Now a new problem is emerging that compels the baby boomers to be more stable. Organizations are typically pyramids—one president, several vice presidents, even more assistants, and so on. These pyramidal or triangular structures work extremely well when there is a triangular work force. What we have is a society in which the majority of lower to upper managers are between 34 and 44. This group can be seen as moving along without changing its structure. Those who are 34 will have to wait 20 years to get jobs in top management. Also, there are fewer younger workers around to take the jobs of those who are now 34 to 36. Structural organizations, which function on the presumption that there are a lot of people at the bottom and very few people at the top, work very well until there is nobody at the bottom. Now everyone wants to be boss and nobody exists to do the work.

In the 1990s there is little promise for baby boomers to get their promotions within companies; lateral moves and job switching are more likely to occur. Therefore, they will become more stable in their jobs, and they will look to the quality of life rather than material goods. Noncareer issues will take up the energy previously put into material pursuits of the 1980s. People will increasingly derive their personal satisfaction from activities outside the work environment.

People are also reflecting on ethics. Business ethics will be a major retraining tool integrated into every business school's curriculum. A *Wall Street Journal* article ("Tombstone Test" 1989) cites that managers want to be remembered for ethics, not sales. Eulogies such as "never cheated anyone" or "hiring employees that others have shunned" are the hope of the 1990s businessperson.

A change from needing things to wanting experiences. Besides this change of values due to the shift in focus from the job to non-work issues, the aging baby boomers also bring a shift in needs and wants. Growing up required acquisitions. However, once homes and furniture and cars are bought and the group moves over the age marker of 40, needs and wants change from possessions to experiences. A recent *Wall Street Journal* consumer survey ("Little Wishes . . ." 1989) showed three-fourths of the 2,000 consumers surveyed say they've fulfilled most if not all of their material needs. That is one reason why those who haven't married or had children are anxious to do so. It is the last chance for women in their late 30s to experience motherhood. People wishing to become respectable, ethical parents are turning from the me generation to the we generation. The BMW was nice, but that was the symbol of the 1980s. The 1990s are for children. This is the source for personal satisfaction.

Whereas the 1970s and 1980s taught independence, now it is necessary to share and be married. The number of married couples as a percentage of new households in the U.S. leaped from 35 to 60 percent in the year ending March 1987. A full 25 million American baby boomers will become first-time parents in the 1990s. This shift in focus to the home is another reason why concerns for the environment and social issues are on the rise. People want the best for their children. A socially responsible corporate image will be the advertising strategy of the 1990s.

Although the family will be back in style again, it will be a very different family. House-husbands will be as common as housewives. This is the generation of professional women—doctors, lawyers, and business people not wanting to give up a satisfactory career, with husbands who recognize the status of their wives' earning power. Two-career families will also be prevalent. Household duties such as meal preparation, shopping, and picking up the dry cleaning are just as likely to be carried out by males as females. Therefore, purchasing household goods and services will be more of a collective decision than it was in the 1960s.

The Immigrant

The third major force to change our decision-making environment is the immigrant, especially the Asian immigrant. Due to a low birth rate among North American women, immigration is a necessity for continued economic growth. Without immigration, our population would actually be decreasing. By the year 2000 there will be 10 million Asians in the United States. In 1985, Asians accounted for 41 percent of all new arrivals in Canada. With 1997 fast approaching, more and more residents of Hong Kong are expected to immigrate to the United States and Canada. The influence of the Asian culture to our marketplace will be felt far and wide. Asians are two to three times as likely to hold a college degree as the average American adult. They are also more likely to hold positions as managers, executives, or professionals. Among the Japanese, Chinese, and Filipinos, average family income already exceeds that of whites.

In San Francisco during the past 15 years, Asians have more than replaced whites. Today 41 percent of the Chinese in that city own their own homes. The cultural values and living style of the Asians contribute to this factor. Extended families living together are the norm. Grandparents, parents, and children all share the same home. The

group is cohesive and the elders most respected. Their shopping behavior reflects their living behavior, as the Chinese prefer shopping in large family groups. Buying decisions are finalized by the family elders. This collective decision making is cultural but extensive.

Hispanics, another group with emerging influence, also spend relatively more of their free time shopping with their extended families rather than alone. Choosing what to buy is another collective decision.

The influence of the Asian and Hispanic cultures will make us focus more on the opinion leader and the consensus of the group to purchase. Sales pitches will be made not to individuals but to groups. The product will now benefit the group and group relations rather than the individual person. Marketers will have to change their selling strategy to appeal to the decision style of the extended family.

The collective behavior of tomorrow's consumer will be shaped by three major forces of the population. First, the elderly will be the fastest-growing segment, and they will need help from their families and the government to provide goods and services for a comfortable existence. Financial and psychological responsibility will cause consumer decisions to be made by the care giver as well as the care receiver. Second, the aging of the baby boomer, the static corporate structure, and the shift from needs to experiences will induce the baby boomers to be more aware of how their consumption affects the environment and each other. Third, the vast numbers of Asian immigrants bring to North America a new life-style that emphasizes an extended family with great respect for the elder members. Three generations of families may live under one roof, and decisions about what to buy for the household will be collective ones with major input from the grandmothers and grandfathers.

We are on the verge of a more collective consumption style and hence a more collective style of decision making. We will acknowledge that the individual's consumption affects the total environment. Since we want that environment to be a healthy one, we will be more willing to investigate the consequences of our consumption and change our consumption habits to benefit the group. It is the recognition that only through working together collectively will individuals make a difference to better their life-style.

References

"Americans Turn to Leading Double Lives," *The Wall Street Journal*, December 1, 1989, p. A15A.

Edward H. Asam and Louis P. Bucklin, "Nutrition Labeling for Canned Goods: A Study of Consumer Response," *Journal of Marketing*, April 1973, pp. 32-37.

James R. Bettman, *An Information Processing Theory of Consumer Choice* (Reading, Mass.: Addison-Wesley, 1979).

"Demographer Challenges Belief that Golden Age Is So Golden," *Wall Street Journal*, March 29, 1989, p. B6.

Ernest Dichter, *Handbook of Consumer Motivations* (New York: McGraw-Hill, 1964).

James F. Engel, Roger D. Blackwell, and Paul W. Miniard, *Consumer Behavior*, 6th ed. (Chicago: The Dryden Press, 1990).

Franklin B. Evans, "Psychological and Objective Factors in the Prediction of Brand Choice: Ford vs. Chevrolet," *Journal of Business*, October 1959, pp. 340-369.

"Godfather of Soul Can Even Play Bingo in a Special Lockup," *Wall Street Journal*, September 19, 1989, p. A1.

Mason Haire, "Projective Techniques in Marketing Research," *Journal of Marketing*, April 1950, pp. 649-652.

Wayne D. Hoyer, "An Examination of Consumer Decision Making for a Common Repeat Purchase Product," *Journal of Consumer Research*, December 1984, pp. 822-829.

Jacob Jacoby, Donald E. Speller, and Carol A. Kohn, "Brand Choice as a Function of Information Load," *Journal of Marketing Research*, February 1974, pp. 63-69.

Christopher Knowlton, "Consumers: A Tougher Sell," *Fortune*, September 26, 1988, pp. 61, 66, 70, 74.

Joel Kotkin, "Selling to the New America," *Inc.*, July 1987, pp. 44-47.

Philip Kotler, "Behavioral Models for Analyzing Buyers," *Journal of Marketing*, October 1965, pp. 37-45.

"Little Wishes Form the Big Dream," *Wall Street Journal*, September 19, 1989, p. B1.

Ken MacQueen, "The Light Turns Green For Immigrants," *World Press Review*, December 1986, p. 48.

Susanna McBee, "Flaunting Wealth, It's Back in Style," *U.S. News and World Report*, September 1981, pp. 61-64.

Regis McKenna, "Marketing in an Age of Diversity," *Harvard Business Review*, September-October 19 pp. 88-95.

George A. Miller, "The Magical Number Seven, Plus or Minus Two: Some Limits on Our Capacity for Processing Information," *Psychological Review*, 63 (1956): 81-97.

Joseph W. Newman and Richard Staelin, "Prepurchase Information Seeking for New Cars and Major Household Appliances," *Journal of Marketing Research*, August 1972, pp. 249-257.

Richard W. Olshavsky and Donald H. Granbois, "Consumer Decision Making—Fact or Fiction?" *Journal of Consumer Research*, September 1979, pp. 93-100.

Kristian S. Palda, "The Hypothesis of a Hierarchy of Effect: A Partial Evaluation," *Journal of Marketing Research*, February 1966, pp. 13-24.

J. Edward Russo, "The Value of Unit Price Information," *Journal of Marketing Research*, May 1977, pp. 193-201.

Debra L. Scammon, "Information Load and Consumers," *Journal of Consumer Research*, December 1975, pp. 148-155.

Steven M. Shugan, "The Cost of Thinking," *Journal of Consumer Research*, September 1980, pp. 99-111.

Aimee L. Stern, "The Baby Boomers Are Richer and Older," *Business Month*, October 1987, pp. 24-28.

Lester G. Telser, "The Demand for Branded Goods as Estimated from Consumer Panel Data," *Review of Economics and Statistics*, August 1962, pp. 300-324.

"The Consumer Bill of Rights," in Consumer Advisory Council, First Report (Washington, D.C.: U.S. Government Printing Office, 1963).

"Tombstone Test," *Wall Street Journal*, July 18, 1989, p. A1.

"Why More Ads Aren't Targeting Asians," *Wall Street Journal*, July 20, 1989, p. B1.

William L. Wilkie, *Consumer Behavior* (New York: John Wiley and Sons, 1986).

rating Purchaser Personalities

Discerning customer motives helps business marketers tailor service strategies.

Richard Lancioni and Terence A. Oliva

Richard A. Lancioni is a Professor of Marketing in the School of Business and Management at Temple University, Philadelphia. His research interests include logistics, customer service, pricing, and marketing management. He has published widely in the fields of marketing and logistics with articles, and he is a member of the Council of Logistics Management, the International Customer Service Association, and the Society of Logistics Engineers. Richard is one of the leading North American scholars in business logistics and also has served as a consultant to a wide variety of Fortune 1000 *companies.*

Terence A. Oliva is a Professor of Marketing in the School of Business and Management at Temple University. He has eclectic research interests which have resulted in publications across a number of academic journals. In addition, he has coauthored one text in production management and edited another. Currently, he is on the editorial board of Organization Science. *Terry has served as a consultant to communications firms, and he has also been a consultant's consultant in the area of competitive dynamics models.*

EXECUTIVE *BRIEFING*

Traditional segmentation schemes, based on demographics alone, can't help business marketers develop effective service strategies. Managers also need know what drives their customers' behavior. A nationwide survey of industrial managers reveals that most buyers fit one of nine key personality profiles. Rather than following a one-strategy-fits-all policy, vendors should customize marketing and service strategies for each customer type they encounter. The key is to understand the underlying motivations of each personality.

Consumer marketers aren't the only ones who have to worry about service quality. Although the press tends to focus on the efforts of firms like Nordstrom's, USAA, Southwest Airlines, and Strawbridge & Clothier, service strategies are no less important in industrial markets.

In the "good old days," managers determined customer needs through market research, developed a product to fit those needs, designed a communications program, and then priced and distributed the product accordingly. Little importance was placed on customer service until after the sale was completed.

In fact, service support efforts seemed to be characterized by an Alfred E. Newman "What, Me Worry?" attitude until after the product was sold. Only then did we think about what type of service would be needed to keep the customer coming back.

In the 1990s, however, economic pressures and global competition have turned up the heat for business-to-business firms. To succeed, marketers must proactively develop service strategies to gain and retain customers. Unfortunately, as is often the case, it's easier said than done.

A starting point is determining what types of customers your firm will encounter and then customizing service strategies to meet the needs of each. Sound like target marketing? It is, with a small twist.

Profile Personalities

Traditional segmentation gives us a powerful tool for grouping customers into classes that have similar buying behaviors. Hence, we can make reasonably accurate statements about males, females, young, old, blacks, whites, Hispanics, Asians, and the like.

However, within these groupings, behavior can vary widely with respect to specific service wants

SALES MANAGEMENT

EXHIBIT 1

Distribution of sample firms

Industry	Number in sample	Firms in industry	Percent of population
Chemical	10	105	9.5
Auto parts	7	98	7.2
Insurance	15	983	1.5
Food manufacturing	12	641	1.8
Forestry	11	78	14.1
Fast foods	15	540	2.7
Plastics	17	96	17.7
Home construction	13	1,051	1.2
Banking	22	267	8.2
Consumer credit	13	759	1.7
Railroads	7	129	5.4
Totals	142	4,747	2.9

723 questionnaires were sent out, 142 useable questionnaires were returned for a response rate of 20%

and needs. Talk to people in customer complaint departments and they will give you an earful about the jerks, loud-mouths, and idiots who did not plug their products in or switch them on. From a service strategy point of view, customer personality profiles can be more important than demographic profiles in determining the proper response.

To determine the personality profiles of industrial buyers, we sent questionnaires to a stratified random sample of managers at 723 firms nationwide; 142 useable questionnaires were returned

for a response rate of 20%. (See Exhibit 1 for the basic characteristics of the sample.)

Each manager indicated which of the 14 customer types listed he or she had encountered; an open-ended "other" category was included to cover customers who did not fit any of the types. In follow-up phone conversations, we discovered that the majority of managers considered five of the 14 categories to be the same, so those cells collapsed. Exhibit 2 shows the distribution of the responses by category.

EXHIBIT 2

Customer type categories

Type of customer	Number of responses	Categories combined
Chiseler	98	
Intimidator	77	
Screamer	42	
Talker	55	
Airhead	29	
Loyal Customer	142	
Rude and Irate	41	
Abusive Nitpicker	54	
Stereotyper	30	
Complainer	9	Screamer
Grouchy	7	Rude and Irate
Empty-headed	5	Airhead
Faithful	19	Loyal Customer
Ignorant	3	Airhead
Other	—	

Exhibit 3

Industrial customer personality types

Personality type	%	Motivation	Marketing strategy	Service strategy
Chiseler	15	Low price	Discounts, volume, freebies	Demonstrate value of the deal
Intimidator	5	Control and power	Detailed specs & procedures	Be firm, follow procedures
Screamer	3	Quick problem resolution	Competitive comparisons	Fast response, empathy
Talker	4	Social interaction	Hand-holding, always available	Refocus on the issue, friendly
Airhead	2	Lazy	No effort, works out of box	Product problem diagnose
Loyal Customer	62	High degree of comfort	Provide extras	Special first class treatment
Rude & Irate	3	Poor quality product	Demonstrate product quality	Preemptive product fixes ready
Abusive Nitpicker	4	Distrust	Honest, clearly specified terms	Customer developed solutions
Stereotyper	2	Low ambiguity	Factual competitive comparisons	Have information at fingertips

In analyzing the data, nine key prototypical industrial customer personalities emerged, each having different behavioral characteristics. In short, each personality type represents a distillation of the combined experience of managers characterizing the most common customer behaviors they encounter.

Determining the personalities of the key customers—along with the appropriate marketing service strategies for dealing with them—can help managers match customer wants with what the company can supply. "Service at any cost" is noble, but costly. Matching the firm's service strategy to the customer's personality is more likely to produce mutually satisfying results.

For the firms represented in our segmentation scheme, we assume that "standard" service procedures are already in place. For example, back orders can be filled quickly, defective products can be returned for credit or replaced, order processing is quick and accurate, field service problems are handled professionally, and so forth.

Finally, no customer type is better or worse than any other. The point is that they *all* exist, and firms that learn to attract and deal successfully with them will have an edge over competitors.

Nine Personalities

Exhibit 3 presents an overview of the typology revealed in the study and includes the descriptive name, the main want or motivating desire of the customer, the marketing strategy that appeals to the customer, a suggested service strategy, and the percentage of the total customers studied that the type represents.

The percentage breakdown an individual firm encounters will vary with the markets it services. Chiselers, for example, probably make up a larger portion of the customer base for firms selling commodities than for those selling unique high-end special-order equipment.

Keep in mind that these are all paying cus-

Penetrating Purchaser Personalities

tomers, so the goal is not to avoid any of the personality types. Generally speaking, when it comes to paying customers, more is better.

The Chiseler

A customer calls to say he was shorted on an item. He tells you that the only fair compensation is a "replacement item plus a trip to Hawaii" for the inconvenience.

Chiselers make up 15% of the customer base. They are motivated by good deals and low price, but their definition of a good deal is getting something below manufacturer cost, regardless of how unrealistic that may be. Frequently, they will try to renegotiate the deal after the fact to squeeze even more out of it.

Gotta better deal?

In general, Chiselers respond to marketing strategies that stress deep discounts, volume, and freebies. Dealing with such customers can be difficult because they often want the same level of service afforded high margin products.

The Chiseler is interested in sales presentations that are filled with dollars and cents deals and cost justifications for any claim made by the salesperson. Because he or she is bottom-line oriented, all marketing promises must go in that direction. Toss out the qualitative fluff in favor of facts.

Chiselers have a narrow focus, often being driven by internal pressures to cut costs or get the best deal possible from suppliers. They have a shark-like propensity to go directly for the lowest cost without any concern for other aspects of the product or service.

Like auctioneers at a community sale trying to take prices up, the Chiseler wants to drive them down. The classic Chiseler initiates competitive bidding between suppliers to drive vendors to their lowest price points. The victor in such rivalries can win the bidding battle, but lose the profitability war.

Here are some quick tips for dealing with Chiselers:

• Never go all the way on price to get the sale. By beating the competition, you may also beat yourself.

• Cost out all business you quote to a Chiseler. Can you make profits on additional volume if you meet the Chiseler's price?

• If you get the initial order, the Chiseler will expect you to go lower on the next order.

• Be prepared to walk away. The old axiom, "Know when to hold 'em, know when to fold 'em" applies here.

• Make the relationship two-sided. The Chiseler

gets the lowest price on this deal, and you get access to his more profitable businesses.

• Leverage the Chiseler's narrow focus. Give a low price on the product, and raise price on other services that may be of limited interest.

• Try to shift the Chiseler from being price-oriented to value-oriented by focusing on the added value of your product.

The Intimidator

A fax comes in from a customer with the opening line, "My lawyer says... ." This is the trademark of an Intimidator, the type of customer who seeks tight control and power.

Representing 5% of the customers, Intimidators' definition of a good deal is one in which they dictate all the terms and the supplier simply acquiesces. Control is usually more important than price. Because they are trying to dominate the situation, they have done their homework and know what the competition is offering. They're ready to play hard ball and know their legal rights.

Intimidators react positively to marketing strategies that focus on detailed product and competitor knowledge as well as tightly developed service procedures. Hence, access to engineers and relevant technical expertise must be part of the firm's marketing strategy.

Personnel who deal with Intimidators must be smooth and confident, and unwilling to back down. These people respect power and an understanding of the rules. Hence, the service strategy must be to let the Intimidator sound-off, and then provide a carefully objective and detailed description of the firm's position. It's important to state the position firmly, yet without emotion.

Intimidators will look for the weakest person in a company to gain the maximum leverage. They are motivated to extract as much service, product, and service concessions as possible and can be especially difficult for a new salesperson or service representative to deal with. They usually play up their position by saying "I am the President" or "This is Doctor Smith."

Here is some advice for dealing with Intimidators:

• Be polite, but do not deviate from company policy or the Intimidator will raise the stakes in the next round.

• Train employees to recognize and handle Intimidators.

• Refer the Intimidator to a higher authority

because he or she is often thwarted by a counter-vailing power.

• Be patient and never show signs of weakness.

The Screamer

Your secretary buzzes to tell you some maniac is at her desk screaming and yelling. At first glance, Screamers, who constitute approximately 3% of the customer base, seem like Intimidators, but they're not.

These customers are looking for quick resolution and try to use embarrassment and the squeaky-wheel approach as a weapon. Some of this behavior may be driven by their own time constraints and responsibilities; they view any problem as just one more hassle they do not need in their life.

Screamers respond best to marketing strategies that promise quick problem resolution, for example, the "no-questions-asked money-back guarantee," free product or service replacement programs that include FedExing parts, 24-hour hotline service, and the like. Service strategies must center on listening, patience, empathy, and above all quick response. Service personnel must not become emotional and should focus on calming the individual down.

Screamers are among the most annoying customers. They will raise their voices over the smallest of issues to force concessions from the supplier. Unlike Intimidators who try to work from a power base, Screamers rely on the fact that anything will be done to quiet them. In short, the practice is a type of blackmail; interestingly, it is often the senior people who are most susceptible to Screamers.

Here are some suggestions for dealing with Screamers:

• Provide a fast solution to a problem. Speed counts because it blunts their leverage.

• Don't react negatively. Have a mechanism for passing them along to your in-house "Screamer expert."

• Have all the facts. This often mollifies a Screamer.

The Talker

An intended quick call to a customer turns into an hour and a half talkfest. Talkers, who make up 4% of the customer base, are looking for social interaction. They are motivated by the need to express themselves and their opinions to others. For the most part Talkers are benign, but they use up significant time resources and, in the process, prevent the company from adequately serving its other customers.

Marketing strategies that push the Talker's button involve personal, "we are always here" approaches. Hand-holding and customer testimonials are very successful with Talkers, who want to belong. Firms that reduce human interaction will lose these customers' business because they do not feel satisfied. Service strategy should be friendly but stress getting to the point.

Talkers are motivated by numerous factors. First, they often think they know more than the sales representative, and want to demonstrate that knowledge.

Second, some customers are culturally influenced to talk by virtue of their geographical location. Consider that, on average, Southern customers engage in more verbal discourse than do customers in the Northeast. In fact, telemarketing companies have found that they must hire sales reps who are good listeners and patient when calling Southern customers.

Third, Talkers may be motivated to communicate their ideas to others in the industry, and the sales rep provides an ideal conduit. Often, they preface statements with "This information is confidential... ," a type of "forbidden fruit" approach to prolonging the conversation.

Because the average face-to-face industrial sales call today costs $650, it is critical for companies to develop more cost-effective ways of making a sale.

Here are some tips for making Talkers (or any customers) happy within a reasonable time limit.

• Have an answer for every question raised; preparation is the key to dealing with Talkers.

• Brush up on the Talker's favorite topics—sports, restaurants, wines, etc.—to avoid a lecture and maintain the advantage.

• Be a good listener. Being atuned to what a Talker is saying, regardless of the words, often provides clues to increased sales.

• Be patient. Don't show signs of frustration or boredom, which can elicit negative reactions from a Talker.

• Maintain good eye contact, and use body language that signals you are interested in the Talker.

Penetrating Purchaser Personalities

The Airhead

You receive a letter from a customer who ordered 10,000 type C nuts when he really needed type B bolts. The explanation: "The secretary picked the number from the wrong page in the catalog." We call this type of customer, making up 2% of the customer base, an Airhead.

Airheads are motivated to expend the least effort. Typically they are lazy, unsure, or tentative in dealing with things. Hence, Airheads find it is easier to call than to read the instructions or look things up. Typically their product problems are caused by failure to plug it in, turn it on, or use improper startup procedures.

Marketing strategies to attract Airheads stress the least amount of effort on the customer's part. Programs that preempt customer effort, like calling to see if they need something, are particularly popular. Additionally, it is important to have quick-start instructions, engineering help, trouble-shooting guides, and call-back programs to ensure that everything is clear.

Service strategies should facilitate self-learning. In particular, they must help the customer diagnose the problem and offer a quick solution.

Airheads are a problem both for the purchasing company for which they work and for the vendor. Interestingly, they're easy targets for the unethical sales reps who make claims about products that may not be totally true, often taking the seller's words as gospel.

Such shortcomings present legitimate companies with an opportunity to get and retain Airheads as customers. However, you may have to seek them out because they will not have done their homework. Providing Airheads with quality products, good service and a full line of products will build brand loyalty and prevent them from "shopping the competition."

Here are some additional suggestions for dealing with Airheads:

• Smother them with service and quality to lock them in and lock out the competition.

• Offer contracts to Airheads to increase their feeling of security.

• Offer warrantees or guarantees.

• Provide the Airhead with easy-to-understand instructions.

• Offer one-stop shopping for products and services.

The Loyal Customer

An order has just been received from Susan who has purchased from you for the last 12 years. Such customers are critical to your success because their loyalty keeps the life force of the company—sales—steady. Loyal Customers make up approximately 62% of a company's customer base.

Loyal Customers' needs are being met, but they should not be taken for granted. They like the comfort and reduced risk of dealing with a known commodity. Obviously, marketing strategies should focus on keeping Loyal Customers by offering them new products first, contacting them to diagnose needs, and providing extra service and freebies.

Although this customer group sustains the company, many firms fail to appreciate this fact and take their Loyal Customers for granted, focusing marketing efforts instead on "new account" strategies. A typical example is when discounts or premiums are used as incentives to gain new accounts, but are not offered to the established customers, a slight which is often interpreted by Loyal Customers as a lack of appreciation on the part of the supplier. Keep in mind, they can get the same benefits by being your competitor's new account.

Some quick tips for keeping Loyal Customers happy are:

• Make them eligible for all new account bonus programs.

• Turn Loyal Customers into consultants. Seek their advice on re-engineering your product, service, or organization.

• Partner with Loyal Customers for just-in-time programs, new product designs, or old product redesigns.

The Rude and Irate

One of your salespeople calls and tells you that there is a customer demanding to see you, who is swearing and yelling. Unlike Screamers, who are motivated to get a quick resolution, Rude and Irate customers usually are driven by poor product or service quality. Our survey showed that Rude and Irate customers feel they have been mistreated or cheated in some way.

The best marketing strategy for these types is to install quality management procedures that ensure the company produces high-quality products. And, to mitigate problems arising out of possible misunderstandings about what the product or service is supposed to do, the sales force must know your products and those of competitors well.

The best service strategy is to be patient and understanding and to have answers for all possible complaints. This means pre-engineering answers and responses for the most common complaints to ensure a satisfactory resolution.

Even though Rude and Irate customers make up only 3% of the customer base, they can eat up as much as 40% of management's attention. Although similar to Intimidators and Screamers, the behavior of Rude and Irate customers is spurred by previous interactions with the firm. In short, this is payback time for earlier bad experiences such as problems in receiving shipments on time, incorrect billing, difficulty in getting orders processed, and delays in dealing with returns or defectives.

Having standard service procedures in place is the best solution, but here are some other tips for handling the Rude and Irate customer when the occasional problem does crop up:

• Determine if the cause of their anger is the current problem or rooted in the past.

• Be understanding. Sometimes the behavior is a manifestation of cultural or regional differences. New Yorkers generally are the most notorious for rudeness and irateness, often hanging up at the end of a phone call without saying good-bye.

• Give factual responses to all questions.

• Respond rapidly to any problem, and you may be able to convert a Rude and Irate customer to a Loyal Customer.

The Abusive Nitpicker

Many customers are cautious and require what some might consider to be excruciating detail about a seemingly unimportant issue. This kind of nitpicking is expected in a new relationship, but Abusive Nitpickers carry it to excess.

A Mistake

Driven by distrust, these customers are ready to swing into action at the slightest provocation to let you know that they will check every detail. Hence, any small problem triggers a hostile reaction. To assuage Abusive Nitpickers' inherent distrust, use marketing strategies that focus on guarantees, warranties, full and detailed disclosure relating to specifications, prices, and return procedures. Factual comparisons with the competition also help allay their fears.

Service strategy should stress knowing all the facts about complaints, offering alternative solutions, providing quick responses to remedy problems, and remaining calm and polite throughout the process.

The Abusive Nitpicker can pose other more serious problems for a company. The high level of detail demanded about a sale, product, or price can seriously compromise a firm's marketing strategy. For example, he or she may want to know how much profit a company is making on a sale. Giving this information to a customer is usually inappropriate except in bidding situations where costs must be revealed. And keep in mind that the Abusive Nitpicker might be compiling information about the specifics of your product design or marketing strategy to give to your competitor.

When dealing with Abusive Nitpickers, remember the following:

• Tell them only what is important for the sale. Evaluate all other requests before giving out any information.

• Determine what information is needed prior to the sales interaction.

• Beware of giving any information to anyone who might be a potential competitor because it could be used against you. Nitpickers turned competitors are aggressive in lowering price and will likely violate patents and royalty agreements.

The Stereotyper

Some customers categorize suppliers as being of this or that type, and then formulate a way to deal with them. To the degree that these customers correctly stereotype and deal with your firm, things can run smoothly. Problems only occur when they miscategorize you.

Stereotypers constitute 2% of the customer base and are motivated by a need for certainty. They may have a chip on their shoulder, and they want to live in a black-and-white world where everything is clear cut. Marketing strategies must focus on factual comparison charts, clear and well-organized sales presentations, unambiguous answers to questions, and identification of the customer's competitive preferences.

Because ambiguity-reduction is an important need, service strategy should stress having all the key information at one's fingertips. It's critical to empower sales and contact employees to resolve problems on the spot and issue follow-up status reports on resolution progress.

Penetrating Purchaser Personalities

Other ways to keep Stereotypers happy include:

• Act in a manner consistent with your product or brand image. Stereotypers focus on a single characteristic attributed to the firm—for example, quality—but do not need to hear all the details about why the quality is high.

• Find out what level of customer service they expect to determine if it differs from what they are receiving.

• Avoid making promises you cannot keep.

• Be careful not to box yourself in with the opening deal because it sets the Stereotyper's perceptions for future deals.

Pre-engineering Service

At this point you have found one or more of your customer's personalities. From the point of view of the service manager, some of the personalities, such as the Screamer, Rude and Irate, and Abusive Nitpicker types, may appear the same. In each case the overt reaction *is* the same: obnoxious and/or angry behavior. However, the key to

developing a successful servic standing that, as the underlyin fers, so does the service solut

A Screamer's need for quic driven by company deadlines customer may be upset about quately performing its function. And the Nitpicker may get riled if he is overcharged by 3¢ on a $10,000 order. The appropriate response for each of the above might be (1) quick resolution and turnaround for the Screamer, (2) re-engineering the product for the Rude and Irate customer, and (3) having the Abusive Nitpicking customer decide whether he or she wants a refund or credit.

Finally, keep in mind two key points when considering our estimate of the distribution of each personality type that companies encounter. First, for a given company in a given industry, that percentage might change. And, second, even though some of the personality types appear to make up a small percentage of the total, the costs of dealing with them may be significantly higher than for any other type.

The personality segmentation scheme presented here should help managers design or redesign their sales and service strategies to suit their own customer mix. In any case, pre-engineering service is better than re-engineering service.

Developing and Implementing Marketing Strategies

- **Product (Articles 25–27)**
- **Pricing (Articles 28–31)**
- **Distribution (Articles 32–34)**
- **Promotion (Articles 35–38)**

Marketing management objectives, Wroe Alderson once wrote, "are very simple in essence. The firm wants to expand its volume of sales, or it wants to handle the volume it has more efficiently." Although the essential objectives of marketing might be stated this simply, the development and implementation of strategies to accomplish them are considerably more complex. Many of these complexities are due to changes in the environment within which managers must operate. Strategies that fail to heed the social, political, and economic forces of society have little chance of success over the long run. The lead articles in this section provide helpful insight, suggesting a framework for developing a comprehensive marketing plan.

The selections in this unit provide a wide-ranging discussion of how marketing professionals and U.S. companies interpret and employ various marketing strategies today. The readings also include specific examples from industry to illustrate their points. The articles are grouped in four sections, each dealing with one of the main strategy areas: product, price, distribution (place), and promotion. Since each selection discusses more than one of these areas, it is important that you read them broadly. For example, many of the readings in the distribution section discuss important aspects of personal selling and advertising.

Product Strategy. The essence of the marketing concept is to begin with what consumers want and need. After determining a need, an enterprise must respond by providing the product or service demanded. Successful marketing managers recognize the need for continuous product improvement and/or new product introduction.

The articles in this subsection focus on various facets of product strategy. The first one, "What's in a Brand?" investigates the importance of companies' nurturing the significant link between consumers and brands. The next provides insight into understanding the differences between fad and trends. "Flops" ends this section by reflecting on some examples of infamous new-product failures.

Pricing Strategy. Few elements of the total strategy of the "marketing mix" demand so much managerial and social attention as pricing. There is a good deal of public misunderstanding about the ability of marketing managers to control prices, and even greater misunderstanding about how pricing policies are determined. New products present especially difficult problems in terms of both costs and pricing. The costs for developing a new product are usually very high, and if a product is truly new, it cannot be priced competitively, for it has no competitors.

"Ten Timeless Truths about Pricing" begins this subsection by suggesting some key principles that marketers need to be cognizant of when establishing pricing strategy. The last three articles in this subsection scrutinize the tremendous pricing pressures that companies face and suggest some ways to make better pricing decisions.

Distribution Strategy. For many enterprises, the largest marketing costs result from closing the gap in space and time between producer and consumer. In no other area of marketing is efficiency so eagerly sought after. Physical distribution seems to be the one area where significant cost savings can be achieved. The costs of physical distribution are tied closely to decisions made about the number, the size, and the diversity of marketing intermediaries between producer and consumer.

The first subsection article, "Retailers With a Future," delineates how, despite hypercompetition, some retailers are performing well. "Selling the Superstores" explores the dedication it takes to get a product on the shelves of giant retail chains. Lastly, a *Wall Street Journal* report shows why Target is a master at "micromarketing."

Promotion Strategy. The basic objectives of promotion are to inform, persuade, or remind the consumer to buy a firm's product or pay for the firm's service. Advertising is the most obvious promotional activity. However, in total dollars spent and in cost per person reached, advertising takes second place to personal selling. Sales promotion supports either personal selling or advertising, or both. Such media as point-of-purchase displays, catalogues, and direct mail place the sales promotion specialist closer to the advertising agency than to the salesperson.

The four articles in this subsection cover such topics as a critical look at personal selling, the importance of word-of-mouth endorsements, the effective use of the Internet, and a scrutiny of the best use of advertising and sales promotions.

Looking Ahead: Challenge Questions

In general, the marketing concept states that the key to business success is the satisfaction of customer needs. Some critics believe that too strict an adherence to this principle has damaged U.S. industry by leading to a dearth of true innovation, particularly in the area of product development. What emphasis do you think should be put on the product in relationship to the other elements of the marketing mix?

Most ethical questions seem to arise in regard to the promotional component of the marketing mix. Both techniques of personal selling and misuses of advertising receive substantial criticism from the general public. How fair is this criticism of some forms of personal selling and advertising? What recent examples of personal selling and advertising justify the public's criticism?

What role, if any, do you think the quality of a product plays in making a business competitive in consumer markets? What role does price play? Would you rather market a higher-priced, better-quality product or one that was the lowest priced? Why?

What do you envision as the major problems or challenges retailers will face in the next decade? How should retailers deal with them?

Given the rapidly increasing costs of personal selling, what role do you think it will play as a strategy in the marketing mix in the future? What other promotion strategies will play increased or decreased roles in the next decade?

THE VERY MODEL OF A
MODERN
MARKETING
PLAN

SUCCESSFUL COMPANIES ARE REWRITING THEIR STRATEGIES TO REFLECT CUSTOMER INPUT AND INTERNAL COORDINATION

SHELLY REESE

Shelly Reese is a freelance writer based in Cincinnati.

IT'S 1996. DO YOU KNOW WHERE YOUR MARKET-ING PLAN IS? *In a world where competitors can ob-serve and rapidly imitate each other's advancements in product development, pricing, packaging, and distri-bution, communication is more important than ever as a way of differentiating your business from those of your competitors.*

The most successful companies are the ones that understand that, and are revamping their marketing plans to emphasize two points:
1. Marketing is a dialog between customer and supplier .
2. Companies have to prove they're listening to their customers by acting on their input.

WHAT IS A MARKETING PLAN?

At its most basic level, a marketing plan defines a business's niche, summarizes its objectives, and presents its strategies for attaining and monitoring those goals. It's a road map for getting from point A to point B.

But road maps need constant updating to reflect the addition of new routes. Likewise, in a decade in which technology, international relations, and the competi-tive landscape are constantly changing, the concept of a static marketing plan has to be reassessed.

Two of the hottest buzz words for the 1990s are "interactive" and "integrated." A successful marketing plan has to be both.

"Interactive" means your marketing plan should be a conversation between your business and your customers. It's your chance to tell customers about

 From *Marketing Tools*, January/February 1996, pp. 56-65. © 1996 by American Demographics, Inc. Reprinted by permission.

GETTING STARTED

A NINE-STEP PLAN THAT WILL MAKE THE DIFFERENCE BETWEEN WRITING A USEFUL PLAN AND A DOCUMENT THAT GATHERS DUST ON A SHELF

by Carole R. Hedden and the *Marketing Tools* editorial staff

In his 1986 book, *The Goal*, Eliyahu M. Goldratt writes that most of us forget the one true goal of our business. It's not to deliver products on time. It isn't even to manufacture the best widget in the world. The goal is to make money.

In the past, making money depended on selling a product or service. Today, that's changed as customers are, at times, willing to pay for what we stand for: better service, better support, more innovation, more partnership in developing new products.

This section of this article assumes that you believe a plan is needed, and that this plan should weave together your desires with those of your customers. We've reviewed a number of marketing plans and come up with a nine-step

model. It is perhaps more than what your organization needs today, but none of the steps are unimportant.

Our model combines some of the basics of a conventional plan with some new threads that we believe will push your plan over the edge, from being satisfactory to being necessary. These include:

• Using and improving the former domain of public relations, image, as a marketing tool.

• Integrating all the business functions that touch your customers into a single, customer-focused strategic marketing plan.

• Borrowing from Total Quality theories to establish performance measures beyond the financial report to help you note customer trends.

• Making sure that the people needed to deliver your marketing objectives are part of your plan.

• "Selling" your plan to the people whose support is essential to its success.
Taking the Plan Off the Shelf First, let's look at the model itself. Remember that one of the primary criticisms of any plan is that it becomes a binder on a shelf, never to be seen again until budget time next year. Planning should be an iterative process, feeding off itself and used to guide and measure.

Whether you're asked to create a marketing plan or write the marketing section of the strategic plan for your business, your document is going to include what the business is trying to achieve, a careful analysis of your market, the products and services you offer to that market, and how you will market and sell products or services to your customer.

1. Describe the Business

You are probably in one of two situations: either you need to write a description of your business or you can rely on an existing document found in your annual report, the strategic plan, or a capabilities brochure. The description should include, at minimum:

• Your company's purpose;

• Who you deliver products or services to; and

• What you deliver to those customers.

Too often, such descriptions omit a discussion about what you want your business to stand for—your image. This is increasingly important as customers report they are looking for more than the product or service; they're in search of a partner. The only way to address image is to know who you want to be, who your customers think you are, and how you can bridge the gap between the two.

Part of defining your image is knowing where you are strong and where you are weak. For instance, if your current yield rate is 99.997 percent and customers rate you as the preferred supplier, then you might identify operations as a key to your company's image. Most companies tend to be their own worst critic, so start by listing all your strengths. Then identify weaknesses or the threats you face, either due to your own limitations or from the increased competency of a competitor.

The description also includes what your business delivers to its owners, be they shareholders, private owners, or employees. Usually this is stated in financial

your business and to listen and act on their responses.

"Integrated" means the message in your marketing is consistently reinforced by every department within your company. Marketing is as much a function of the finance and manufacturing divisions as it is the advertising and public relations departments.

Integrated also means each time a company reaches out to its customers through an advertisement, direct mailing, or promotion, it is sending the same message

and encouraging customers to learn more about the product.

WHY IS IT IMPORTANT?

The interaction between a company and its customers is a relationship. Relationships can't be reproduced. They can, however, be replaced. That's where a good marketing plan comes into play.

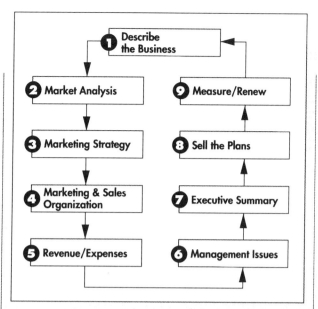

terms: revenue, return on investment or equity, economic value added, cash generated, operating margin or earnings per share. The other measures your organization uses to monitor its performance may be of interest to outsiders, but save them for the measurement section of your plan.

The result of all this describing and listing is that you should have a fairly good idea of where you are and where you want to be, which naturally leads to objectives for the coming 6, 12, or 18 months, if not longer.

2. Analyze the Market

This is the section you probably believe you own. *Marketing Tools* challenges you to look at this as a section jointly owned by most everyone working with you. In a smaller company, the lead managers may own various pieces of this section. In a larger organization, you may need to pull in the ideas and data available from other departments, such as logistics, competitor intelligence, research and development, and the function responsible for quality control or quality assurance. All have two things in common: delivering value to customers, and beating the competition.

Together, you can thoroughly cover the following areas:

• **Your target markets**. What markets do you currently compete in? What do you know about them in terms of potential, dollars available, and your share of the market? Something frequently prepared for products is a life cycle chart; you might want to do the same for your market. Is it embryonic, developing, mature or in decline? Are there new markets to exploit?

• **Customer Knowledge**. Your colleagues in Quality, Distribution, Engineering, or other organizations can be helpful in finding what you need.

The customer's objectives. What threats does your customer face? What goals does the customer have? Work with your customer to define these so you can become a partner instead of a variable component.

How is the customer addressing her or his markets? Do you know as much about your customer's position as you know about your own? If not, find out.

How big is each customer, really? You may find you're spending more time on a less important customer than on the customers who can break you. Is your customer growing or in decline? What plans does the customer have to expand or acquire growth? What innovations are in development?

What does your customer value? Price, product quality, service, innovation, delivery? The better you know what's driving your customer's purchasing decision, the better you'll be able to respond.

• **Clearly identify the alternatives your customer has**.

As one customer told employees at a major supplier, "While you've been figuring out how to get by, we've been figuring out how to get by without you." Is backward integration—a situation in which the customer develops the capability in-house— possible? Is there an abundance of other suppliers? What is your business doing to avoid having your customers looking for alternatives?

• **Know your competition.** Your competitors are the obvious alternative for your customer, and thus represent your biggest threat. You can find what you need to know about your competitors through newspaper reports, public records, at trade shows, and from your customers: the size of expansions, the strengths that competitor has, its latest innovations. Do you know how your competition approaches your customers?

• **Describe the Environment.** What changes have occurred in the last 18 months? In the past year? What could change in the near future and over a longer period of time? This should include any kinds of laws or regulations that might affect you, the entry or deletion of competitors, and shifts in technology. Also, keep in mind that internal change does affect your customers. For instance, is

Think of your business as a suitor, your customers as the object of your affection, and your competitors as rivals. A marketing plan is your strategy for wooing customers. It's based on listening and reacting to what they say.

Because customer's priorities are constantly changing, a marketing plan should change with them. For years, conventional wisdom was 'prepare a five year marketing plan and review it every year.' But change

happens a lot faster than it did 20 or even 10 years ago.

For that reason, Bob Dawson of The Business Group, a consulting firm in Freemont, California, recommends that his clients prepare a three year plan and review it every quarter. Frequent reviews enable companies to identify potential problems and opportunities before their competition, he explains.

"Preventative maintenance for your company is as

a key leader in your business planning to retire? If so, decision-making, operations or management style may change — and your customer may have obvious concerns. You can add some depth to this section, too, by portraying several different scenarios:

- What happens if we do nothing beyond last year?
- What happens if we capitalize on our strengths?
- What might happen if our image slips?
- What happens if we do less this year than last?

3. The Marketing Strategy

The marketing strategy consists of what you offer customers and the price you charge. Start by providing a complete description of each product or service and what it provides to your customers. Life cycle, again, is an important part of this. Is your technology or product developing, mature or in decline? Depending on how your company is organized, a variety of people are responsible for this information, right down to whoever is figuring out how to package the product and how it will be delivered. Find out who needs to be included and make sure their knowledge is used.

The marketing strategy is driven by everything you've done up to this point. Strategies define the approaches you will use to market the company. For instance, if you are competing on the basis of service and support rather than price, your strategy may consist of emphasizing relationships. You will then develop tactics that support that strategy: market the company vs.

① Strategies → ② Tactics → ③ Actions

the product; increase sales per client; assure customer responsiveness. Now, what action or programs will you use to make sure that happens?

Note: strategy leads. No program, regardless of how good it is, should make the cut if it doesn't link to your business strategies and your customer.

The messages you must craft to support the strategies often are overlooked. Messages are the consistent themes you want your customer to know, to remember, to feel when he or she hears, reads, or views anything about your company or products. The method by which you deliver your messages comes under the heading of actions or programs.

Finally, you need to determine how you'll measure your own success, beyond meeting the sales forecast. How will you know if your image takes a beating? How will you know whether the customer is satisfied, or has just given up complaining? If you don't know, you'll be caught reacting to events, instead of planning for them.

Remember, your customer's measure of your success may be quite different from what you may think. Your proposed measures must be defined by what your customer values, and they have to be quantifiable. You may be surprised at how willing the customer is to cooperate with you in completing surveys, participating in third-party interviews, or taking part in a full-scale analysis of your company as a supplier. Use caution in assuming that winning awards means you have a measurable indicator. Your measures should be stated in terms of strategies, not plaques or trophies.

4. The Marketing and Sales Organization

The most frequently overlooked element in business is something we usually relegate to the Personnel or Human Resources Office—people. They're what makes everything possible. Include them. Begin with a chart that shows the organization for both Marketing and Sales. You may wish to indicate any interdependent relationships that exist (for instance, with Quality).

Note which of the roles are critical, particularly in terms of customer contact. Just as important, include positions, capabilities, and numbers of people needed in the future. How will you gain these skills without impacting your cost per sale? Again, it's time to be creative and provide options.

5. Revenue and Expense

In this section, you're going to project the revenue your plan will produce. This is usually calculated by evaluating the value of your market(s) and determining the dollar value of your share of that market. You need to factor in any changes you believe will occur, and you'll need to identify the sources of revenue, by product or service. Use text to tell the story; use graphs to show the story.

After you've noted where the money is coming from, explain

important as putting oil in your car," Dawson says. "You don't wait a whole year to do it. You can't change history but you can anticipate what's going to happen."

ESSENTIAL COMPONENTS

Most marketing plans consist of three sections. The first section should identify the organization's goals. The second should section establish a method for attaining them. The third section focuses on creating a system for implementing the strategy.

Although some plans identify as many as six or eight goals, many experts suggest a company whittle its list to one or two key objectives and focus on them.

"One of the toughest things is sticking to one message," observes Mark Bilfield, account director for integrated marketing of Nissan and Infinity cars at TBWA Chiat/Day in Los Angeles, which handles national advertising, direct marketing, public rela-

what money you need to deliver the projected return. This will include staff wages and benefits for your organization, as well as the cost for specific programs you plan to implement.

During this era of budget cuts, do yourself a favor by prioritizing these programs. For instance, if one of your key strategies is to expand to a new market via new technologies, products, or services, you will need to allocate appropriate dollars. What is the payback on the investment in marketing, and when will revenues fully pay back the investment? Also, provide an explanation of programs that will be deleted should a cut in funding be required. Again, combine text and spreadsheets to tell and to show.

6. Management Issues

This section represents your chance to let management know what keeps you awake at night. What might or could go wrong? What are the problems your company faces in customer relations? Are there technology needs that are going unattended? Again, this can be a collaborative effort that identifies your concerns. In addition, you may want to identify long-term issues, as well as those that are of immediate significance.

To keep this section as

objective as possible, list the concerns and the business strategy or strategies they affect. What are the short-term and long-term risks? For instance, it is here that you might want to go into further detail about a customer's actions that look like the beginnings of backward integration.

7. Executive Summary

Since most senior leaders want a quick-look reference, it's best to include a one-page Executive Summary that covers these points:

• Your organization's objectives
• Budget requirements
• Revenue projections
• Critical management issues

When you're publishing the final plan document, you'll want the executive summary to be Page One.

8. Sell the Plan

This is one of the steps that often is overlooked. Selling your plan is as important as writing it. Otherwise, no one owns it, except you. The idea is to turn it into a rallying point that helps your company move forward. And to do that, you need to turn as many people as possible into ambassadors for your marketing efforts.

First, set up a time to present the plan to everyone who helped

you with information and data. Make sure that they feel some sense of ownership, but that they also see how their piece ties into the whole. This is one of those instances where you need to say your plan, show your plan, discuss your plan. Only after all three steps are completed will they *hear* the plan.

After you've shared the information across the organization, reserve some time on the executive calendar. Have a couple of leaders review the plan first, giving you feedback on the parts where they have particular expertise. Then, present the plan at a staff meeting.

Is It Working?

You may think your job is finished. It's not. You need to convey the key parts of this plan to coworkers throughout the business. They need to know what the business is trying to achieve. Their livelihood, not just that of the owners, is at stake. From their phone-answering technique to the way they process an order, every step has meaning to the customer.

9. Measure/Renew

Once you've presented your plan and people understand it,

you have to continuously work the plan and share information about it. The best way to help people see trends and respond appropriately is to have meaningful measures. In the language of Total Quality, these are the Key Result Indicators— the things that have importance to your customers and that are signals to your performance.

For instance, measure your ability to deliver on a customer request; the amount of time it takes to respond to a customer inquiry; your productivity per employee; cash flow; cycle time; yield rates. The idea is to identify a way to measure those things that are critical to you and to your customer.

Review those measurements. Share the information with the entire business and begin the process all over again. Seek new ideas and input to improve your performance. Go after more data and facts. And then renew your plan and share it with everyone—all over again.

It's an extensive process, but it's one that spreads the word— and spreads the ownership. It's the step that ensures that your plan will be constantly in use, and constantly at work for your business.

Carole Hedden is a writer and communications/planning consultant living in Elmira, New York.

---

tions, and promotions for the automaker. Bilfield argues that a focused, consistent message is easier to communicate to the market place and to different disciplines within the corporation than a broad, encompassing one. Therefore, he advises, "unless there is something drastically wrong with the idea, stick with it."

SECTION I: GOALS

The goals component of your plan is the most

fundamental. Consider it a kind of thinking out loud: Why are you writing this plan? What do you want to accomplish? What do you want to achieve in the next quarter? The next year? The next three years?

Like taping your New Year's resolution to the refrigerator, the goals section is a constant reminder of what you want to achieve. The key difference between a New Year's resolution and your marketing goals, however, is you can't achieve the latter alone.

To achieve your marketing goals you've got to

HELP IS ON THE WAY

THREE SOFTWARE PACKAGES THAT WILL HELP YOU GET STARTED

Writing a marketing plan may be daunting, but there is a variety of software tools out there to help you get started. Found in electronics and book stores, the tools are in many ways like a Marketing 101 textbook. The difference lies in how they help.

Software tools have a distinct advantage: They actually force you to write, and that's the toughest part of any marketing plan. Sometimes called "MBA In a Box," these systems guide you through a planning process. Some even provide wording that you can copy into your own document and edit to fit your own business. Presto! A boiler plate plan! Others provide a system of interviewing and questioning that creates a custom plan for your operation. The more complex tools demand an integrated approach to planning, one that brings together the full force of your organization, not just Sales or Advertising.

1. Crush

Crush, a modestly named new product from a modestly named new company, HOT, takes a multimedia approach. (HOT stands for Hands-On Technology; *Crush* apparently stands for *Crush*-ing the Competition)

Just introduced a few months ago, *Crush* is a multimedia application for Macintosh or Windows PCs. It features the competitive analysis methods of Regis McKenna, marketing guru to Apple, Intel and Genentech; and it features Mr. McKenna himself as your mentor, offering guidance via on-screen video. As you work through each section of a complete market analysis, McKenna provides germane comments; in addition, you can see video case studies of marketing success stories like Intuit software.

Crush provides worksheets and guidance for analyzing your products, customers, market trends and competitors, and helps you generate an action plan. The "mentor" approach makes it a useful tool for self-education; as you work through the examples and develop your company's marketing plan, you build your own expertise.

2. Marketing Plan Pro

Palo Alto's *Marketing Plan Pro* is a basic guide, useful for smaller businesses or ones in which the company leader wears a number of different hats, including marketing. It includes the standard spreadsheet capability, as well as the ability to chart numerical data. *Marketing Plan Pro* uses a pyramid process.

I liked the pyramid for a simple reason: It asks you to define messages for your business as part of your tactics. Without a message, it's easy to jump around, reacting to the marketplace instead of anticipating, leaving customers wondering what really is significant about your company or your product.

The step-by-step process is simple, and a sample plan shows how all the information works together. The customer-focus aspect of the plan seemed a little weak, demanding only sales potential and buying capacity of the customers. Targeted marketing is increasingly important, and the user may want to really expand how this section is used beyond what the software requires.

The package displays, at a glance, your strategy, the

convince your customers to behave in a certain way. If you're a soft drink manufacturer you may want them to try your company's latest wild berry flavor. If you're a new bank in town, you need to familiarize people with your name and convince them to give your institution a try. Or perhaps you're a family-owned retailer who needs to remind customers of the importance of reliability and a proven track record in the face of new competition.

The goals in each of these cases differ with the audiences. The soft drink manufacturer is asking an existing customer to try something new; the bank is trying to attract new customers; the retailer wants to retain existing customers.

Each company wants to influence its customers' behavior. The company that is most likely to succeed is the one that understands its customers the best.

There's no substitute for knowledge. You need to understand the demographic and psychographic makeup of the customers you are trying to reach, as well as the best methods for getting their attention.

Do your research. Learn as much as possible about your audience. Trade associations, trade journals and government statistics and surveys are excellent

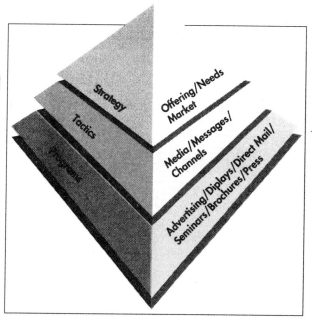

tactics you develop for each strategy, and the action plan or programs you choose to support the strategy. That could help when you're trying to prioritize creative ideas, eliminating those that really don't deliver what the strategy demands. Within each of three columns, you can click on a word and get help. Click on the heading program: a list of sample actions is displayed. They may not be what you're looking for, but if this is your first plan, they're lifesavers.

I also really liked *Marketing Plan Pro*'s user's manual. It not only explains how the software works with your computer, it helps with business terms and provides a guide to planning, walking you through step-by-step.

3. Plan Write

Plan Write, created by Business Resource Software, Inc., is exponentially more powerful than *Marketing Plan Pro*. *Plan Write* brings together the breadth of the business, integrating information as far flung as distribution systems

Pyramid Power: *Plan Write's pyramid approach asks the user to define the messages for a business as part of the tactics.*

and image. And this software places your marketing strategy within the broader context of a business plan, the approach that tends to prove most effective.

As with *Marketing Plan Pro*, *Plan Write* provides a sample plan. The approach is traditional, incorporating a look at the business environment, the competition, the product or service mix you are offering, the way you will tell customers about that mix, pricing, delivery, and support.

Among the sections that were particularly strong was one on customer alternatives and people planning. Under the heading of customer alternatives, you're required to incorporate competitive information with customer information. If you don't meet the customer's needs, where could he or she go? Most often we look only at the competition, without trying to imagine how the customer is thinking. This exercise is particularly valuable to the company who leads the market.

The people part of planning

too often is dumped on the personnel guy instead of being seen as a critical component of your organization's capabilities. *Plan Write* requires that you include how marketing is being handled, and how sales will be accomplished. In addition, it pushes you to define what skills will be needed in the future and where the gaps are between today and the future. People, in this plan, are viewed as a strategic component.

Plan Write offers a fully integrated spreadsheet that can import from or export to most of the popular spreadsheet programs you may already be using. Another neat feature allows you to enter numerical data and select from among 14 different graphing styles to display your information. You just click on the style you want to view, and the data is re-configured.

Probably the biggest danger in dealing with software packages such as *Marketing Plan Pro* and *Plan Write* is to think the software is the answer. It's merely a guide.

—Carole Hedden

resources, but chances are you have a lot of data within your own business that you haven't tapped. Look at what you know about your customer already and find ways to bolster that information. Companies should constantly be asking clients what they want and how they would use a new product.

"If you're not asking people that use your end product, then everything you're doing is an assumption," argues Dawson.

In addition, firms should ask customers how they perceive the products and services they receive. Too often, companies have an image of themselves that

they broadcast but fail to live up to. That frustrates consumers and makes them feel deceived.

Companies that claim to offer superior service often appear to renege on their promises because their definition of 'service' doesn't mesh with their customers, says Bilfield.

"Airlines and banks are prime offenders," says Bilfield. "They tout service, and when the customers goes into the airport or the bank, they have to wait in long lines."

The problem often lies in the company's assumptions about what customers really want. While an airline may feel it is living up to its claim of superior service because it distributes warm towels and mints after a meal, a business traveler will probably place a higher value on its competitor's on-time record and policy for returning lost luggage.

SECTION II: THE STRATEGY

Unfortunately, after taking the time and conducting the research to determine who their audience is and what their message should be, companies often fail by zooming ahead with a plan. An attitude of, "OK, we know who we're after and we know what we want to say, so let's go!" seems to take over.

More often than not, that gung-ho way of thinking leads to disaster because companies have skipped a critical step: they haven't established and communicated an internal strategy for attaining their goals. They want to take their message to the public without pausing to get feedback from inside the company.

For a marketing plan to work, everyone within the company must understand the company's message and work cooperatively to establish a method for taking that message to the public.

For example, if you decide the goal of your plan is to promote the superior service your company offers, you'd better make sure all aspects of your business are on board. Your manufacturing process should meet the highest standards. Your financial department should develop credit and leasing programs that make it easier for customers to use your product. Finally, your customer relations personnel should be trained to respond to problems quickly and efficiently, and to use the contact as an opportunity to find out more about what customers want.

"I'm always amazed when I go into the shipping department of some company and say, 'What is your mission? What's the message you want to give to your end user?' and they say, 'I don't know. I just know I've got to get these shipments out on time,'" says Dawson.

Because the success of integrated marketing depends on a consistent, cohesive message, employees throughout the company need to understand the firm's marketing goals and their role in helping to fulfill them.

"It's very important to bring employees in on the process," says James Lowry, chairman of the marketing department at Ball State University. "Employees today are better than any we've had before. They want to know what's going on in the organization. They don't want to be left out."

Employees are ambassadors for your company. Every time they interact with a customer or vendor, they're marketing your company. The more knowledgeable and helpful they are, the better they reflect on your firm.

At Nordstrom, a Seattle-based retailer, sales associates are empowered to use their best judgment in all situations to make a customer happy.

"We think our sales associates are the best marketing department," said spokeswoman Amy Jones. "We think word of mouth is the best advertising you can have." As a result, although Nordstrom has stores in only 15 states, it has forged a national reputation.

If companies regard marketing as the exclusive province of the marketing department, they're destined to fail.

"Accounting and sales and other departments have to work together hand in hand," says Dawson. "If they don't, you're going to have a problem in the end."

For example, in devising an integrated marketing campaign for the Nissan 200SX, Chiat/Day marketers worked in strategic business units that included a variety of disciplines such as engineers, representatives from the parts and service department, and creative people. By taking a broad view of the business and building inter-related activities to support its goals, Chiat/Day was able to create a seamless campaign for the 200SX that weaves advertising, in-store displays, and direct marketing together seamlessly.

'When everybody understands what the mission is, it's easier," asserts Bilfield. "It's easier to go upstream in the same direction than to go in different directions."

After bringing the different disciplines within your company on board, you're ready to design the external marketing program needed to support your goals. Again, the principal of integrated marketing comes into play: The message should be focused and consistent, and each step of the process should bring the consumer one step closer to buying your product.

In the case of Chiat/Day's campaign for the Nissan 200SX, the company used the same theme, graphics, type faces, and message to broadcast a consistent statement.

Introduced about the same time as the latest Batman movie, the campaign incorporates music and graphics from the television series. Magazine ads include an 800 number potential customers can call if they want to receive an information kit. Kits are personalized and include the name of a local Nissan dealer, a certificate for a test drive, and a voucher entitling test drivers to a free gift.

By linking each step of the process, Chiat/Day can chart the number of calls, test drives, and sales a particular ad elicits. Like a good one-two punch, the direct marketing picks up where the national advertising leaves off, leveraging the broad exposure and targeting it at the most likely buyers.

While the elaborate 200SX campaign may seem foolproof, a failure to integrate the process at any step along the way could result in a lost sale.

For example, if a potential client were to test drive the car and encounter a dealer who knew nothing about the free gift accompanying the test drive, the customer would feel justifiably annoyed. Conversely, a well-informed sales associate who can explain the gift will be mailed to the test driver in a few weeks will engender a positive response.

SECTION III: EXECUTION

The final component of an integrated marketing plan is the implementation phase. This is where the budget comes in.

How much you'll need to spend depends on your goals. If a company wants to expand its market share or promote its products in a new region, it will probably have to spend more than it would to maintain its position in an existing market.

Again, you'll need to create a system for keeping your employees informed. You might consider adding an element to your company newsletter that features people from different departments talking about the marketing problems they encounter and how they overcome them. Or you might schedule a regular meeting for department heads to discuss marketing ideas so they can report back to their employees with news from around the company.

Finally, you'll need to devise a system for monitoring your marketing program. A database, similar to the one created from calls to the 200SX's 800 number, can be an invaluable tool for determining if your message is being well received.

It's important to establish time frames for achieving your goals early in the process. If you want to increase your market share, for instance, you should determine the rate at which you intend to add new customers. Failing to achieve that rate could signal a flaw in your plan or its execution, or an unrealistic goal.

"Remember, integrated marketing is a long-range way of thinking," warns Dawson. "Results are not going to be immediate."

Like any investment, marketing requires patience, perseverance, and commitment if it is to bear fruit. While not all companies are forward thinking enough to understand the manifold gains of integrated marketing, the ones that don't embrace it will ultimately pay a tremendous price.

MORE INFO

Software for writing marketing plans:
Crush, Hands-On Technology; for more information, call (800) 772-2580 ext. 14 or (415) 579-7755; e-mail info@HOT.sf.ca.us; or visit the Web site at http://www.HOT.sf.ca.us.

Marketing Plan Pro, Palo Alto Software: for more information, call (800) 229-7526 or (503) 683-6162.

Plan Write for Marketing, Business Resource Software, Inc.: for more information, call (800) 423-1228 or (512) 251-7541.

Books about marketing plans:
Twelve Simple Steps to a Winning Marketing Plan, Geraldine A. Larkin (1992, Probus Publishing Co.)*

Preparing the Marketing Plan, by David Parmerlee (1993, NTC Business Books)*

Your Marketing Plan: A Workbook for Effective Business Promotion (Second Edition), by Chris Pryor (1995, Oregon Small Business Development Center Network)*

Your Business Plan: A Workbook for Owners of Small Businesses, by Dennis J. Sargent, Maynard N. Chambers, and Chris Pryor (1995, Oregon Small Business Development Center Network)*

Recommended reading:
Managing for Results, Peter Drucker

The One to One Future: Building Relationships One Customer at a Time, by Don Peppers and Martha Rogers, Ph.D. (1993, Currency/Doubleday)*

"Real World Results," by Don Schultz (*Marketing Tools* magazine, April/May 1994)*

WiN
THE
MARKET

ANSWER THESE
20 QUESTIONS AND YOU'LL HAVE A
PLAN TO DOMINATE YOUR COMPETITION

A good marketing plan can lead to success, but who has the time to make one? Unlike many of the chores of running a business, marketing is a creative process. In Grow Your Business With Desktop Marketing *(Random House), contributing editor Steve Morgenstern helps you develop an effective plan. Answer these 20 questions and you'll see a winner form right before your eyes.*

YOUR CURRENT MARKETING STATUS

The first step in creating a worthwhile marketing plan is getting a handle on the status quo.

1 How healthy is your business? Are you growing, shrinking, or at a standstill? This information is key to developing your marketing plan in three different ways:

•First, your financial direction influences your strategic marketing choices. Do you need to bring in business quickly to pump up cash flow? If so, you'll want to concentrate on making offers that generate short-term sales or fees, probably from established customers. If your business is relatively healthy, you can focus more attention on developing new prospects, a process that sacrifices short-term profitability for long-term gain.

•Second, you need to establish a set of financial benchmarks against which you can judge the success of your ongoing marketing efforts.

•Finally, marketing costs money, sometimes as obvious expense items (placing ads, sending mailings, transportation, and entertainment) or sometimes as hidden costs (your own time spent on marketing tasks). Before setting a marketing plan, you

S T E V E   M O R G E N S T E R N

must have a handle on your availability of funds to implement each strategy.

2 **What marketing channels do you currently employ?** Do you meet customers face-to-face? Do you attend trade shows, create direct-mail packages, rely on word of mouth, or make cold calls every day? List the current means you use to bring in business and figure out the cost of each.

3 **Who are your current customers?** How can you characteristically group them? What are their similarities and differences? After you identify who your loyal customers are, the next step is to analyze your customer database to look for patterns.

•Are your best customers from a particular geographical area? A local business with its customers clustered in one or two zip codes has a good idea about where to target its direct mailings and other promotional efforts.

•Are your customers from a particular kind of area? Evaluate the zip codes you serve to determine the demographics of the neighborhoods in question—a task that you can accomplish by accessing and analyzing computerized databases.

•If you're a business-to-business marketer, what are the characteristics of the companies you are serving? What business specialties do they represent? How large are your client companies? How long have they been in business? Do your clients do business in a single location, or are there several branch offices that could represent individual business prospects?

•If your business is seasonal, you'll have to identify which times of the year are hot for your company. For example, if you know there are periods when making a sale is relatively easy, you should increase your marketing efforts during those times to generate even more business, perhaps increasing capacity temporarily to gear up for the demand. If there are predictably slow periods, you might schedule special promotions or discounts to even out work flow. And if you can identify why a given period is busier than another, you may be able to re-create the demand conditions and turn a slack period into a busy one.

4 **How is your business perceived by your clients and prospects?** What kind of impression do you and your business make on your customers? Are you projecting the right image? You should make an effort to ferret out your customers' opinions of your business.

•Are you a customer's high-cost, high-quality provider or the I-guess-that's-all-we-can-afford choice?

•Are you making points by being a friendly local merchant?

AFTER YOU IDENTIFY WHO YOUR LOYAL CUSTOMERS ARE, ANALYZE YOUR DATABASE TO LOOK FOR PATTERNS IN SUCH AREAS AS DEMOGRAPHICS, BUSINESS TYPE, SIZE, AND SO FORTH.

•Are you gaining an image of reputability and solidity based on association with a large, well-known company?

•What image is conveyed by your printed materials (letterhead, business cards, promotional literature, and so on)?

•How do your strategies compare with those of your competitors'?

5 **What benefits does your business provide?** You know what products or services you offer, but can you identify their fundamental benefits? Answering this question will help you target appropriate market segments, expand your current offerings, and create persuasive promotional materials.

The key is to make the distinction between features and benefits. The computer I use features a Pentium microprocessor, a SoundBlaster audio card, a 17-inch monitor, and a 1GB hard drive. The benefits it delivers are fast performance, wonderful sound, a squint-free working environment, and plenty of storage space. Those benefits are what I was after when I went shopping for a system. As a shopper, product specifications are important insofar as they bring me closer to achieving a goal, and that goal is the ultimate benefit I'm trying to derive.

The same holds true for everything else we buy—benefits first, features second. So what's the bottom line benefit you're delivering to your customers? Pleasure derived

from more free time? A greater sense of security? Whether they're spending money to fulfill personal or business needs, it's emotional needs that drive the purchase.

6 **Who are your competitors?** You need to identify the companies that offer the same services or products as you. Where would you look if you wanted the goods or services your company provides? The yellow pages? Newspaper or magazine ads? Business directories? Would you seek recommendations from friends?

7 **What differentiates you from your competitors?** Compile a list of everyone who competes in your marketplace (a list that you should have generated from answering question 6). Get copies of their marketing materials. Then ask yourself these questions.

•How closely do your competitors' offerings match your own? Do they offer the same range of goods or services? How do their prices compare?

•What images are your competitors trying to convey? What unique features are they stressing?

•How do their marketing materials compare with your own?

8 **What changes are taking place in your industry?** "Change alone is unchanging," said the Greek philosopher Heraclitus. You can view this constant mutation as an unending assault on your comfortable status quo or as a continuing marketing opportunity. Technological innovation may offer faster, less expensive ways of producing the goods or services you provide. Regulatory changes can affect your own business directly or your customers' businesses. When their needs change, your product and marketing strategies also need to change—and quickly.

9 **What are you charging?** Pricing is another key competitive variable you need to monitor closely. On one hand, being undercut by your competitors is death in certain product and service categories and is cause for concern no matter what you're marketing. On the other hand, underpricing (a frequent mistake made by insecure small-business owners) is bad business on two counts. First, once you've covered your expenses, every additional dollar you charge is a dollar of profit for your company, so there's strong motivation to charge as much as possible. Second, the price of your product or service is often perceived as an indicator by your customers of the quality of the goods or services you're providing.

When you charge too little, potential customers won't think the low price is based on benevolence—they'll either assume that what you're selling is only worth what you're charging or that you don't know your product's true value. Clearly, there are major advantages to charging the right price for the moment and the market.

10 **What should you be charging?** To determine the right price for your product or service, research how businesses in other parts of the country or other parts of the world are doing what you're doing. Small-business innovations tend to ripple across the country—witness, for instance, the coffee bar invasion that was launched in Seattle and expanded eastward. Local trends in distant markets may reveal pretested concepts that you can apply profitably to your own business.

Tracking change requires information-gathering skills. While those skills now include knowledge of computer technology, don't overlook traditional media. Pay particular attention to the specialized newspapers and magazines covering your business and your clients' businesses. Much of this highly targeted information isn't yet available in electronic form.

11 **Are you responding quickly and accurately to the needs of current clients and prospects?** Do you offer a fast response time to inquiries, questions, complaints, and problems? Providing your clients 24-hour turnaround, for example, is a potent marketing tool.

Audit your response time by tracking when an initial communication with a customer or prospect takes place and when he or she receives the necessary response.

If there is shipping time involved in the transaction, be sure to include that in your overall turnaround figure; just because a problem is off your desk doesn't mean it's off the customer's mind.

12 **Do you have a system for following up on leads?** New business leads come from many different directions, ranging from formal lead-generating activities such as advertisements and mailings to casual conversations and newspaper clippings. Unfortunately, in the rush to get today's work done, valuable leads for future sales or assignments often get overlooked. And the shelf life of a hot lead is very short. The best lead is the one that represents an immediate intent to purchase and that's also the lead that must be followed up due to the urgency of the potential customer's requirements.

•What do you currently do to generate new business leads?

•Do you have a routine for following up on each lead in a timely manner?

•Do you follow up on an initial contact at appropriate intervals?

A SENSE OF DIRECTION

You've evaluated your marketing operations, conducted research, and reflected on the bottom-line nature of your business to determine the core benefit you provide to customers. The next step is to build on successes, confront weaknesses, and set a positive direction for the near- and long-term future of your company. The second phase of your marketing plan is a brainstorming operation, during which you can use your creativity, your observation of other marketers, input from friends and coworkers,

> RESEARCH HOW OTHER BUSINESSES DO WHAT YOU DO. LOCAL TRENDS IN DISTANT MARKETS MAY REVEAL CONCEPTS THAT YOU CAN APPLY PROFITABLY TO BUILD YOUR OWN BUSINESS.

and an arsenal of marketing tools and strategies appropriate for your business.

Timing and budget will impact your ability to implement the ideas you arrive at during this stage. But even if the good idea you have now has to be put on the back burner because of a lack of funds or time, it is still a valuable asset to be detailed in your marketing plan. In reviewing the plan at a later date, you may think of a more economical, less time-consuming way to implement the strategy. The business climate may change, making your original idea a practical solution under changed circumstances, or that good idea may spark further creative solutions as you periodically re-evaluate your marketing plan.

13 **What customer needs are not being fulfilled?** Based on your competitive analysis and keeping in mind the areas we've outlined, ask yourself:

•What are the sweet spots of opportunity in my marketplace?

•How well is my company currently prepared to target those opportunities?

•What changes would be required to effectively focus my marketing efforts on these high-potential niches?

14 **What do you want customers and prospects to know about your company?** When you think about various companies, you usually have a quick-take reaction to each one based on advertising and promotion, personal experience, its logo—the sum of all your experience with that company to date. It's a short and sweet summary. How do you want your company to be listed in your customers' mental summaries?

Many businesses create a mission statement to crystallize the answer to this question. Sometimes this statement becomes the company's advertising slogan. Even without millions of dollars to broadcast it far and wide, developing your firm's mission statement is a worthwhile exercise. Give yourself the proverbial 15 words or less to describe your business. Linger over the results for a while. Let it go and then come back and re-evaluate it. When you're satisfied, use your mission statement to test all your promotional efforts. Ask yourself, "Does this letter/mailer/brochure/ad/ speech/ whatever reflect the thoughts conveyed in the company mission statement?" If not, refocus your marketing communication materials to reflect that core message.

15 **How can you expand your offerings to current customers?** You've already run a minefield of difficulties to acquire your current customers, from getting them to notice you, trust you, buy from you, and then actually fork over what they owe you. These folks have demonstrated a willingness to buy Service A from your company. Your challenge now is to find the Service B that might also interest them.

16 How can you use your current customers to generate new business? Each of your current customers comes in contact with many potential buyers of your product or service in the course of his or her personal and/or business life. How can you encourage your loyal clients to steer new business your way?

Reminders. The first step, which is so often ignored by small businesses, is to remind your customers that you're looking for new business. Asking for referrals is often all that's required.

Incentives for leads. Some companies take the first step further by offering incentives to customers who bring in new business. This method is worth considering as long as you bear in mind a few caveats, including the possibility that an incentive program can become a bureaucratic nightmare, with elaborate point systems along the lines of airline frequent flyer plans. The bookkeeping alone is burdensome and refereeing disagreements over who's owed what can alienate a valued customer. If you do go with a referral incentive program, keep it simple.

Even if there is no direct contact between your current customers and your prospects, you can bring the opinions of satisfied clients to prospects' attention by incorporating testimonials in your promotional materials. Complimentary letters from satisfied customers can be good for much more than an ego massage—look for ways to highlight them in your brochures or product packaging.

17 Where can you find more of the kind of people who buy from you? In the first part of your marketing plan, you profiled your current customers. The question now is, Where can you find additional prospects who fit that profile? There are many avenues to explore for this answer, both within your own geographic area and expanding into new territories. Advertising is, of course, one obvious way to generate new business. It offers many possibilities.

•Check out publications that specifically address the interests of your target audience. Some may include directories of retail establishments and service providers that business and consumer shoppers refer to for purchasing.

•Regional broadcast advertising can be expensive, but local TV and especially local radio can be reasonably priced and highly effective.

•Ask your current customers where they get their purchasing information.

•The yellow pages is a cornerstone of new-business generation for many types of companies.

18 How can your customer service operations be improved? How can you go the extra yard to make service faster and more reliable? Consider these issues.

•Do you have enough personnel to handle the load? Are your recordkeeping procedures adequate for the task at hand? Can your company be reached on short notice if urgent problems arise?

•Should you consider expanding your hours of operation into the evenings and weekends so you can better fit customers' busy schedules?

•Are you making the right impression when you visit your customers' places of business?

19 Can you form alliances with mutually supportive businesses? Certain businesses naturally cluster around occasions or situations. The family that needs a caterer for a big party may also be interested in hiring a photographer or a florist, for example. Consider the situations that drive customers to call you and think about other businesses offering related goods or services.

•Investigate companies in your area, and target those that fit naturally with your company's image and purpose. Contact those business owners and propose a mutual referral arrangement.

•Share promotional opportunities. If your businesses send out bills to customers, create promotional inserts to be included with each other's statements. Or create a joint mailing, which cuts in half the postal charges that are normally associated with a mass mailing.

•Provide your marketing partner with a supply of your business cards and any literature he or she can pass along when recommending your business. And be sure to get and hand out hers as well.

•Always keep your end of the bargain and send new business to your ally whenever possible.

20 How can you increase your credibility and visibility? Personal recognition for the principals of a business is often a key selling point for a small company. The goal is to make yourself as credible and visible within your target market as possible.

•Public speaking is one popular means to achieving this end. Local businesses will often find community organizations more than willing to provide a speaking platform if your specialty is relevant to their membership.

•Attend and participate in industry conferences and conventions. Buyers and sellers of business services often come together at these events.

•Publish articles related to your field of interest. They'll have an immediate impact when they first appear in print and can then be reprinted for use in your promotional materials.

A PLAN OF ACTION
At this point, you've investigated and brainstormed. Now it's time to evaluate your options and create an action plan for the future, defining the steps you intend to take in the next six months to a year, including dates and dollar figures. You should also write down longer-range goals to guide your ongoing business development. Is Job 1 to broaden the range of services you offer, develop an 800-number ordering setup, or create a system to follow up on inquiries with personalized letters? Now is the time to establish marketing requirements, crunch budget numbers, and commit to deadlines. With your marketing plan in hand and the path to your business's future clearly outlined, you can be assured that the future of your business is literally in good hands.

Contributing editor STEVE MORGENSTERN *is president of Morningstar Communications, a marketing consultation and publication development service.*

What's in a Brand?

SUMMARY   Consumers and brands have relationships. Nurturing those relationships ensures a company's success. While juggling their many duties, brand managers must keep answering three questions: who buy the brand, what do they want from it, and why do they keep coming back. The answers are partly rational but are also based on emotional "cues" and cultural values.

Diane Crispell and Kathleen Brandenburg

Diane Crispell is executive editor of American Demographics, *and Kathleen Brandenburg is associate editor of* The Numbers News.

"He that steals my purse steals trash," says the villain Iago in Shakespeare's *Othello*. "But he that filches from me my good name . . . makes me poor indeed."

Iago didn't have much of a good name to filch, but businesses should heed his words nonetheless. A business's good name is often a brand name. Inside the customer's mind, a trusted brand is a promise of high quality and good things to come. But a tainted brand name can trigger memories of poor quality and bad service, driving customers away. That's why brand management can make or break a company's reputation.

To businesses, brands mean market share. Packaged-goods marketers know that a name can affect shelf placement in the supermarket. When customers spend an average of only four seconds examining a shelf, this can be important. And because people are willing to spend a little more to get something they trust, branded products can command premium prices.

In the 1990s, established brands face challenges that range from private-label products to deep-discount stores. Their managers must keep up with rapid changes in the way products are distributed, priced, and sold at the retail level. But brand managers' most important goal is protecting the brand's good name. To succeed, they must answer three questions: who buys the brand, what do they want from it, and why do they keep coming back.

WHO BUYS THE BRAND

Most Americans are brand-loyal to something. The annual Monitor poll conducted by Yankelovich Partners of Westport, Connecticut, reports that 74 percent of respondents "find a brand they like, then resist efforts to get them to change." Once consumers are convinced of the quality and value of a particular brand, it takes a lot of money and effort to change their minds.

Many people buy familiar brands even if they believe the product has no actual advantage. Just half of Americans think that specific brands of mayonnaise are different or better than others and worth paying more for, according to The Roper Organization. But 62 percent know what brand of mayonnaise they want when they walk in the store. Another 22 percent look around for the best price on a well-known brand. The same pattern applies to many products, including beer, coffee, and soup.

Brand behavior is complex. Not everyone is brand-conscious, and not all brand-conscious people are truly brand-driven. Depending on the product, 20 to 44 percent of Americans see no difference among brands or any reason to buy

> **Only half of Americans think brands of mayonnaise are different, but 62 percent have a favorite brand.**

higher-priced ones, according to Roper. And in a study conducted by Deloitte & Touche, only about 35 percent of consumers are willing to identify themselves as "label-seekers."

Managers, salespeople, and students are more likely than the average shopper to say that familiar labels are important to them when they shop. Clerical workers, factory workers, and homemakers are less likely to be interested in names. Asian Americans have a high interest in labels,

Mega-Brands

The first step in building loyalty to a brand is to make sure consumers are familiar with it.

(top-ten brands ranked by percent of adults who had any opinion about them, 1992)

rank	brand	percent with opinion
1	Campbell's Soup	98%
2	Hallmark Greeting Cards	97
3	United Parcel Service	97
4	Hershey's	97
5	McDonald's	97
6	Sears	97
7	Kmart	96
8	7 UP	95
9	Coca-Cola	95
10	Kodak Photographic Film	95

Source: Total Research Corporation, Princeton, New Jersey

"Pragmatists" (16 percent) are simply interested in getting value for their money.

The seven groups have different opinions about the quality of particular brands. Among luxury cars, for example, Intellects like the Lexus but give Cadillacs a mediocre rating. Sentimentals prefer Cadillacs and score the Lexus very low. The groups also shift over time in response to economic and social trends. Pragmatists, Conformists, and Actives are currently on the rise, while Popularity Seekers and Sentimentals are declining. Relief Seekers and Intellects are holding steady.

WHAT THEY WANT

Virtually everyone can identify a short list of "megabrands." The most familiar of all brands is Campbell Soup, according to To-

> When you see a can of Campbell's Tomato Soup, you react in ways that are rational, emotional, and cultural.

tal Research: 98 percent of Americans have a positive, negative, or indifferent opinion about it. Other highly visible brands include Hallmark, United Parcel Service, Hershey's, McDonald's, Sears, Kmart, 7 UP, Coca-Cola, and Kodak. These names are cultural icons, and their managers enjoy powerful advantages over the competition.

When you see a can of Campbell's Tomato Soup, you react in ways that are rational, emotional, and cultural, according to Saatchi & Saatchi Advertising. Your rational mind thinks of tangible product qualities and features, such as the price of soup. Then your emotional side summons up a memory of the warm, comfortable feeling soup gives you. Finally, cultural influences make you consider the way you will be perceived by those who see Campbell on your pantry shelf.

A brand has many features, and people tend to evaluate the benefits of these features independently, says Saatchi & Saatchi executive vice president Penelope

and blacks and Hispanics are slightly more interested than non-Hispanic whites. Label-seekers have an average amount of education, says Deloitte & Touche, but their household incomes are slightly higher than average.

In many ways, label-seekers are an elite group. They are more likely than average to own compact-disc players, microwave ovens, and home computers. They are also more likely to exercise regularly, participate in sports, and enjoy shopping. In fact, label-seekers list shopping as their fourth-favorite pastime, after TV, music, and reading.

Label-seekers say that a clothing store's selection is the most important reason to shop there, followed by quality and price. For others, selection is the most important criterion for dress clothing, but price is most important for casual clothes and shoes. Label-seekers and others agree that price is the most important thing when shopping for health-and-beauty aids.

But label-seekers rank selection second, while nonlabel-seekers mention location. In general, label-seekers see shopping as more of an exciting, emotionally fulfilling experience.

These hard-core brand shoppers are a minority of the population. But all shoppers fit into seven groups based on their definitions of brand quality, according to the Total Research Corporation of Princeton, New Jersey. "Conformists," at 12 percent of the population, choose the most popular brand because they want to belong to the crowd. "Popularity Seekers" (12 percent) go for trendy brands, while "Sentimentals" (12 percent) seek brands that emphasize comfort and good old-fashioned flavor. "Intellects" (17 percent) like upscale, cerebral, and technologically sophisticated brands, while "Relief Seekers" (17 percent) want something that offers escape from the pressures of life. "Actives" (15 percent) look for brands associated with a healthy, social lifestyle, and

Best Brands

Many well-known brands also rank high in quality.

(top-ten brands ranked by perceived quality using a 10-point scale, with 10 meaning "outstanding, extraordinary," 1992)

rank	high-quality brands	score
1	Disney World/Disneyland	8.5
2	Kodak Photographic Film	8.3
3	Hallmark Greeting Cards	8.2
4	United Parcel Service	8.2
5	Fisher-Price Toys	8.1
6	Levi's Jeans	8.0
7	Mercedes-Benz Automobiles	8.0
8	Arm & Hammer Baking Soda	8.0
9	AT&T Long-Distance Telephone	7.9
10	IBM Personal Computers	7.9

Source: Total Research Corporation, Princeton, New Jersey

Queen. To understand the rational side, the firm uses a conjoint, or trade-off, analysis technique that measures the relative value of each product attribute in the purchase decision. To understand the murkier emotional and cultural attractions of a brand, Queen conducts psychological interviews that explore societal influences and unconscious emotional needs.

Another ad agency, BBDO of New York, explores brand psychology in its own way. Its "Personal Drive Analysis" found that both Classico and Newman's Own spaghetti sauces are associated with upscale sophisticated adults. But people think of Classico in terms of "Italian" traits such as indulgence and romance, while they identify Newman's Own with the actor's individualistic and ambitious personality. BBDO uses this information to ensure that its advertising contains the appropriate emotional "cues" for each brand. Its methods can also reveal new niches by uncovering drives that current brands don't address.

Deep psychological motivations are an important part of why consumers buy, says Queen. But a brand's most powerful advantage is rooted in the human tendency to form habits and stick to routines. People's past experience with a brand is consistently the most important factor in their future brand choices, according to The Roper Organization. In the 17 years that Roper has been tracking the topic of brand choice, price and quality have almost always ranked second and third to past experience.

The reasons for choosing brands do change, albeit slowly. In 1985, quality temporarily moved into second place. In the Roper poll, price regained second place in 1986, and its lead over quality has widened considerably since then. In other words, quality is about as important to consumers as it was 17 years ago, but price is more important.

There are reasons for buying a product that go beyond experience, price, and quality. Recommendations from other people have ranked fourth in all the Roper surveys. Other considerations are how well-known the product is, how it ranks in *Consumer Reports*, and how it affects the environment.

Whether it's a box of detergent or a car, most people will buy the same thing over and over as long as it satisfies their needs. When their needs change, rival brands get a rare opportunity. Often, needs change when lives change. A woman who becomes a single parent may watch every penny and switch to the cheapest detergent she can find. A couple who has a child will replace their two-seater sports car with a four-door sedan.

Sometimes people in transition switch brands that seem to have nothing to do with the transition. Forty percent of people who move to a new address also change their brand of toothpaste, according to Yankelovich Partners in Westport, Connecticut. "A change of that magnitude opens a person's mind," says Yankelovich senior vice president Watts Wacker. "Everything comes into question."

Most emotional relationships don't last unless both partners are adaptable and accommodating, and the relationship between brands and customers isn't any different. People won't be satisfied with the same skin-care product all their lives, for example. But the brand manager of a skin-care product can keep the relationship alive. One way is by extending the line of products sold under the brand name.

Like people, brands have a life span. They are born, they grow, they mature, they reach old age, and they die. One way to delay the process is to give them a makeover. For example, since its beginning, Tide detergent has become at least four products: original powder Tide, Liquid Tide, Tide with Bleach, and Ultra Tide. Each suits a particular market with a particular need.

The danger in line extensions is going too far. Levi's succeeded when it introduced looser-fitting jeans for middle-aged baby boomers, but it failed when it introduced a line of dress suits for men in the early 1980s. Loyal blue-jean buyers thought suits made by Levi's had to be

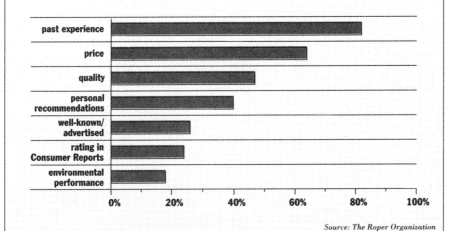

Tried It, Liked It

Knowing what to expect is the most common reason for buying a particular brand. Value and quality rank second and third.

(percent of adults who said that specified reasons were most important in deciding to buy a brand, 1992)

- past experience
- price
- quality
- personal recommendations
- well-known/advertised
- rating in Consumer Reports
- environmental performance

0% 20% 40% 60% 80% 100%

Source: The Roper Organization

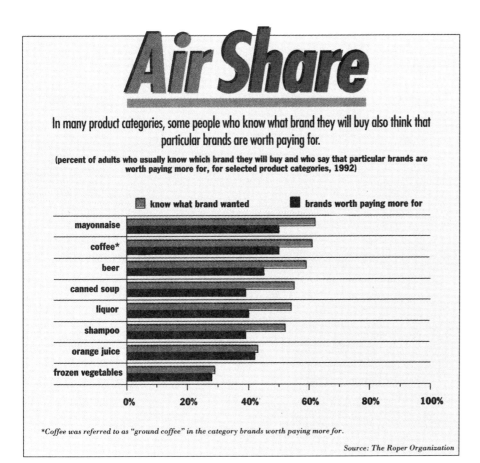

Air Share

In many product categories, some people who know what brand they will buy also think that particular brands are worth paying for.

(percent of adults who usually know which brand they will buy and who say that particular brands are worth paying more for, for selected product categories, 1992)

■ know what brand wanted   ■ brands worth paying more for

- mayonnaise
- coffee*
- beer
- canned soup
- liquor
- shampoo
- orange juice
- frozen vegetables

0% 20% 40% 60% 80% 100%

*Coffee was referred to as "ground coffee" in the category brands worth paying more for.

Source: The Roper Organization

substandard in quality and design. As that perception took hold, Levi's began to lose jeans sales as well. It recalled the upscale line and scrambled to regain its traditional market.

Sometimes an old product can be rejuvenated simply by directing its advertising at a different market. Baby boomers who were raised on sweetened cereals are now health-conscious grown-ups. Kellogg's responded to this shift by repositioning Frosted Flakes as something that is still fun to eat but also good for you. Its advertisements show adults secretly admitting that they love the cereal.

KEEP THEM COMING BACK

Remember the old slogan for Alka-Seltzer: "Try it, you'll like it"? This is the essence of brand advertising. Success depends on finding people who are receptive to change and reaching them with advertising that reflects their attitudes toward the product.

Brand advertising should reflect two broad themes, according to a two-stage model developed by Larry Percy of Lintas: USA and John R. Rossiter of the Australian Graduate School of Management. The first theme is the reasons

> **Forty percent of people who move to a new address also change their brand of toothpaste.**

people buy (brand awareness), which in this model can be positive or negative. The second is the customer's level of involvement in the purchase decision (brand attitude), which can be high or low. Purchasing aspirin is a low-involvement decision, for example. Buying a house is a high-involvement decision.

Negative motivations include solving or avoiding problems and replenishing supplies of a product. Positive motivations include sensory gratification, intellectual stimulation, and social approval. Buying aspirin springs from a negative motivation, because one buys it to stop pain.

But cosmetics and vacations are positive buys.

There are four advertising strategies that match each of the four involvement-motivation combinations, say Percy and Rossiter. For a low-involvement, negative-motivational product like aspirin, advertising should stress the product's problem-solving benefits in a simple, emphatic manner. People don't necessarily have to like aspirin ads, but they must understand the product's benefits. For low-involvement, positive-motivational products like cosmetics, "emotional authenticity" is the key element and single benefit, say the authors. For this reason, the target audience must like the ad.

An automobile is usually a high-involvement purchase, say Percy and Rossiter. As such, its advertising should provide substantial information about the brand. But people buy cars for both positive and negative reasons, and the advertising should reflect this ambiguity. If the target audience needs no-nonsense transportation, the advertising should stress but not exaggerate product benefits while creating an initial positive attitude toward the brand. If the customer is looking for style or power, "emotional authenticity is paramount and should be tailored to lifestyle groups within the target audience." Moreover, "people must personally identify with the product."

In the final analysis, many brands are nothing more or less than an image that may imprint itself in consumers' minds forever. People were still ranking General Electric second in the food-blender market 20 years after it had stopped making them. Now that's brand loyalty.

TAKING IT FURTHER
The Total Research Corporation conducts the Equitrends survey. For more information, contact John Morton; telephone (609) 520-9100. For an insightful analysis of companies that have been successful (or not) with their brands, see *Managing Brand Equity: Capitalizing on the Value of a Brand Name*, by David A. Aaker of the University of California at Berkeley (The Free Press, 1991, $24.95). The Roper Organization conducts periodic surveys about a variety of brand-related attitudes; telephone (212) 599-0700. For Larry Percy and John R. Rossiter's "Model of Brand Awareness and Brand Attitude Advertising Strategies," see the July/August 1992 issue of *Psychology & Marketing* (John Wiley & Sons, Inc.).

HOW TO
Tell Fads
from Trends

Martin G. Letscher

Martin G. Letscher is president of Martin G. Letscher & Associates in River Forest, Illinois, and a former marketing executive for Keebler, Johnson Wax, and Northwestern Mutual Life Insurance.

SUMMARY

Distinguishing between long-term trends and short-term fads early gives companies a powerful competitive edge. To separate fads from trends, ask yourself six questions: Does the new development fit with basic lifestyle changes? What consumer benefits does it provide? Can it be personalized? Is it a trend or a side effect of another trend? Is it related to other changes? And who has adopted the change?

Distinguishing between fads and trends at an early stage can make a business career. The first company to identify a trend and act on it gains a powerful competitive advantage. It happened to Starbucks coffee, which capitalized on a new consumer desire for higher quality and greater variety in coffee. It's working for Snackwell's cookies and crackers, which do the best job of combining good taste with reduced fat. And when Taco Bell first recognized the power of value pricing, it gained a powerful competitive advantage.

On the other hand, companies that miss a trend will spend their time playing catch-up to the competition. The American auto industry has spent decades paying the cost of ignoring early signs that consumers wanted cars to be smaller, higher in quality, and more fuel-efficient. IBM let Apple take a big chunk of the personal-computer market. Other examples are far too easy to find.

Correctly identifying a fad has its own benefits. Aggressive marketers can make a lot of money by reaping the short-term rewards of a fad and abandoning it just as it begins to lose its impact. More conservative companies can safely ignore a short-lived fad and concentrate on opportunities with longer-term potential. But can you really tell whether a new development will be a fad or a trend?

The following checklist can help you analyze changes while they are still in the developmental stage. Over the years, this list has been used successfully to evaluate personal-care products, home-care products, over-the-counter drugs, financial services, and cookies. But anyone in business can use these guidelines to judge the importance of a development and tell whether it is an important trend or a passing fad.

FAD

Rubik's Cube: Puzzle invented in 1974 by Hungarian architect Erno Rubik. Sales reached 30 million cubes and 10 million "solution" books by 1982, then plummeted.

Two examples with enough history for validation demonstrate this approach. In the early 1980s, when both VCRs and video games were the new rage with rapidly growing sales, this approach correctly predicted that VCRs would be a trend and video games a fad. Today, VCRs are an essential part of our everyday life and are in eight in ten U.S. households. Yet only two major video-game companies survive, and they struggle for the pocket change of our youth.

Marketers will always struggle with this million-dollar question: how do you separate long-term trends from short-term fads at the earliest possible stage? These six straightforward questions can help.

1. Does it fit with basic lifestyle changes? The recent past has been characterized by rapid and pervasive change. These basic changes in Americans' values and lifestyles have had hundreds of implications on consumer products and services.

For example, divorce and delayed childbearing have made age less important as a predictor of behavior, while life stage has become relatively more important. The entry of women into the labor force has contributed to widespread feelings of time pressure and the need for convenience. Paid employment has also created two generations of women with new attitudes toward work and family. Minority population growth has introduced new foods and other products to the general population. Adults are less likely to sacrifice their own interest for the good of their companies, families, or social institutions. These and other changes have contributed to the intense segmentation and fragmentation of consumer markets.

For these reasons, a critical question is the degree to which a new development is consistent with these important lifestyle and value changes. Which ones support the change? Which ones conflict with it? If a new development complements other important changes, it is much more likely to be a trend. If it conflicts with these basic lifestyle changes, it is almost certain to be a fad.

When a new style or product is introduced, ask yourself whether it goes with the flow of these trends. For example, we might notice fashion models sporting a new hairstyle that is attractive but requires a lot of time and effort to care for. It is unlikely that a women who is physically active—say, a frequent jogger—would adopt this new hairstyle. It just doesn't fit with her other, more important lifestyle choices.

One overriding fact about consumers is their need for time convenience. Many successful new products and services have been built on saving the consumer's precious time. But convenience has different meanings for different tasks. For household care, consumers are willing to sacrifice absolute cleanliness to save time. But they are not willing to make similar quality trade-offs when it comes to personal care. That's why hair-care products that save time but leave hair less manageable have no appeal.

The movement to shorter and more frequent vacations was clearly a long-term trend from the beginning, because it is supported by several factors. Substituting weekend trips for a single longer vacation solves several problems for people who have less free time, more intense time pressures, and a dual-earner household.

It is not unusual for some basic consumer trends to support a new product or service while others appear to be at odds with it. This is when the marketer's experience and judgment must come into play. For example, the recent success of warehouse-club outlets that sell food and a variety of other products was a surprise to many, because it conflicts with several important trends. Smaller families, smaller package sizes, and the desire for convenient shopping work against these stores. But these negatives are clearly offset by other trends, such as a new definition of the price to value relationship; the overwhelming selection of products and sizes; and desire for a shopping "experience."

A similar example is the strong interest in the new Super-Uplift and Wonder bras, which grant cleavage to women who don't otherwise have it. These products seem to go against the growth in feminism and distaste for women being viewed

TREND

Value Pricing: Taco Bell gained market share by cutting prices in the 1990s. They serve cost-conscious consumers who want fast food that is cheap, filling, and nutritious.

as sex objects. Yet the desire to meet a more traditional female ideal and the desire to be sexually appealing may be stronger forces. The lackluster performance of low-fat potato chips is yet another example. Consumers are unwilling to sacrifice taste in an indulgent snack product, despite their growing concern about health and fat consumption.

2. What are the benefits?

What benefits do consumers receive from the new product or service? How many benefits does it have, and how strong are they? Do consumers feel good about the new product, or were they reluctantly forced to change? Will making the change improve their lives in important ways? The more diverse and immediate a product's benefits, the more likely the new development will be a trend.

There has been a long-term increase in the consumption of fish and poultry, despite our long-standing love affair with beef. In fact, poultry consumption may exceed beef consumption for the first time in the mid-1990s. The reason is that fish and poultry offer many kinds of reinforcing sources of satisfaction. Compared with beef, they are healthier, lower in fat and calories, and more socially acceptable. They also taste better than we ever thought they would. Serving these foods is also a way to show concern for one's family.

So far, the sources of consumer satisfaction with chicken have not been dampened by any significant negatives. This is in contrast to other healthful sources of protein. Tofu is relatively inexpensive

FAD

Troll Doll: Created by a Danish woodcutter in 1959 as a birthday gift to his daughter. By 1964, known worldwide as a child's toy and adult's good-luck charm. Still available.

and has fewer calories than some parts of chicken. But it still tastes like library paste to most Americans.

Exercise habits have been changing faster than eating habits. One major reason is that the benefits of exercise are more evident in the short run, more varied, and more tangible. Exercise offers a wide variety of immediate benefits, but switching to low-fat food does not.

The cost-benefit question can help you sift through consumer changes in buying behavior because of tougher economic conditions. Consumers always tighten their belts when times get tough, but they usually revert to their former practices when economic conditions improve. However, sometimes changes become permanent. Permanent changes are the ones that provide benefits over and above the money saved. Private-label products, especially higher-quality "premium" ones such as President's Choice, are a good example. In the consumer's mind, higher-quality private labels are smart ways to save money. That's why they are likely to be a permanent change.

3. Can it be personalized?

The desire for greater individuality and different ways of self-expression has been one of our most important value changes in recent years, especially among baby boomers. For this reason, we should ask whether the new product or service can be modified or expressed in different ways by different people. The more adaptable it is, the greater chance it has of becoming a trend.

For example, the overarching consumer desire to promote health and well-being can be expressed by different people in different ways—through dietary changes, exercise, not smoking, and stress reduction, to name a few. That's one important reason why healthy living is a trend. In contrast, many fads in hair care, from buzz cuts to mohawks to the grunge look, have proven rigid and inflexible. Mainstream Americans will not embrace a new product or service that they see as exaggerated, extreme, or impractical.

One powerful new-product strategy is to take the benefits associated with the extreme practices of a "fringe" group and modify them so that they appeal to the average consumer. A strict diet of organically grown grains, fruits, and vegetables does not appeal to the average consumer. Yet at the same time, there is a widespread interest in healthier eating.

4. Is it a trend or a side effect?

We should distinguish between a basic trend and the specific expressions of that trend. The expressions will emerge and be replaced by other expressions of the basic theme, while the trend continues

TREND

No Fat, Rich Taste: Snackwell's scored with cookies that taste sinful but aren't. New nutrition labels that show a food's fat content should give low-fat sales a boost.

to grow. In other words, a good market researcher must separate the forest from the trees.

One example is exercise. Different kinds of exercise, such as jogging, tennis, handball, walking, in-line skating, and

Licensed Characters: Established toy category given huge boost by billion-dollar sales of "Star Wars" toys. Pee Wee Herman dolls are a classic "fad within a trend."

low-impact aerobics, can all be described as different ways to express a desire for increased physical fitness. The specific activities may be fads that can rise and fall in popularity, while the basic health/ wellness trend continues unabated.

Ethnic restaurants are another example. Different types of ethnic restaurants regularly grow and then decline in popularity. But the underlying trend is toward food that is spicier and offers a greater variety of tastes.

New types of beer are regularly introduced to create news and excitement, but deep down their marketers know they will never become a permanent part of the market. Dry beer, ice beer, and clear malt beverages such as Zima are recent examples. They cause short-term sales bumps without affecting the market on a long-term basis. Of course, there is always the hope that a market segment will become larger and more permanent than expected, such as the segment that drinks light beers.

5. What other changes have occurred?

Is the new development supported by developments in other areas? If it stands alone, it is more likely to be a fad.

How does one look for these relationships? First, look for trends that are related to each other. For example, a person's awareness of proper nutrition is likely to be related to a desire for physi-

cal fitness, no smoking, and stress reduction. If a person changes his or her eating habits *and* starts to exercise *and* gives up smoking, there is a much greater probability that he or she will make at least one long-term change. If you want to know

if a new development is likely to become permanent, look for changes in related areas.

Second, look for carryover effects. Changes in one area often have direct effects in other areas. When the miniskirt was adopted in the 1960s, it caused an immediate and major change in the hosiery market. Pantyhose and tights grew from 10 percent of the women's hosiery market to more than 80 percent of the market in less than two years. Unfortunately, sales are declining. The movement to less formal dress, including "dress-down Fridays" and growth in at-home working, is driving down pantyhose sales.

Another example is the growth of free-standing outlets that change oil in 10 or 15 minutes. This is related to the increase in self-service gas stations, the decline of corner service stations, and the tendency to keep cars longer.

6. Who has adopted the change?

It is always important to determine which consumers have changed their behavior. Two questions are particularly valuable in determining whether a new development will become a trend: support from unexpected sources and the degree of support from key market segments. If a change in consumer behavior or another development comes from an unexpected source, it has a much greater chance of being a trend.

When the number of working women started to increase in the 1950s, most of the new workers were mothers whose children were school-aged or older. The women typically worked to buy extras or to finance a college education. There was little to suggest that these "early adopters" had a permanent commitment to work. But it was a very different matter when mothers of young children started to work. This development reflected basic changes in social values and support from an unexpected source.

Another clear example comes from the political arena. It was evident that Ronald Reagan would be a powerful political force when his support first extended beyond conservative Republicans to include traditionally Democratic ethnic groups and blue-collar workers.

Two consumer groups are particularly important to the long-term potential of a new development. They are working women, especially mothers who hold professional-level jobs, and the older half of the baby-boom generation. If the new development is rejected by these two groups, it has virtually no chance of be-

Convenient Car Care: Older cars cost less, but time-pressured drivers must give them regular oil changes. Goodbye, corner service station; hello, Quick Lube.

coming a major trend. Yet acceptance by these key segments by itself does not guarantee that a new development will become a trend. They are too small in absolute numbers, too affluent, and perhaps too extreme in their values. That's why it is also important to ask whether a new development will be appealing to more mainstream consumers.

Baby boomers are now approaching the watershed age of 50. They have challenged the values and practices of previous generations at every life stage, and they will continue to do so. Two questions will help you understand the wants and needs of baby boomers. First, what life stage are they passing through? Second how will they address this life stage differently from previous generations?

Baby boomers will profoundly influence the market for investment products as they approach retirement. And a strong new-product strategy for personal-care products and over-the-counter drugs is to think about what happens to each body part as it ages. What can be done to prevent, delay, or hide these changes to each

Koosh Balls: Toy invented by former engineer Scott Stillinger and former Barbie marketer Mark Button. Peaked during 1988 Christmas season, but still available.

body part? What about anti-oxidant vitamins: could they be the next trend?

Career-oriented women have been at the center of revolutionary changes in the workplace, in most households, and certainly in the marketplace. There is every reason to believe that the far-reaching and complex changes they caused are far from over. For this reason, future changes in women's behavior cannot be extrapolated in straight-line fashion.

Separating trends from fads is an inexact science. With consumers' wants and needs changing more rapidly than ever,

the job of separating the two can only grow more difficult. That is why mature marketing judgment and intuition will always play a key role. Understanding the differences between fads and trends, and capitalizing on these differences, can result in superior marketing strategies and different approaches to new products. The potential payoffs are immense.

This Year's Alcohol: Remember the Harvey Wallbanger? Booze merchants often boost sales by introducing faddish brews. Zima is another "fad within a trend."

TAKING IT FURTHER

For more information, contact the author at 1020 North Harlem Avenue, Suite 4A, River Forest, IL 60305; telephone (708) 488-0588. Facts about some fads were taken from *Fashion and Merchandising Fads* by Frank Hoffman and William G. Bailey, published for $22.95 by Harrington Park Press of Binghamton, NY; telephone (800) 342-9678.

FLOPS

TOO MANY NEW PRODUCTS FAIL.
HERE'S WHY—AND HOW TO DO BETTER

Egg rolls for dinner: What a great idea! That was the thinking behind the decisions to launch a line of La Choy frozen egg rolls in 1988. Not measly little appetizer egg rolls, mind you: What managers for the Hunt-Wesson Inc. brand envisioned were big, meaty egg rolls that a consumer would happily eat as a main course. The egg roll offensive would complement another new idea, the Fresh and Lite line of low-fat frozen Chinese entrées. After all, La Choy was

a well-known brand name, thanks to its canned goods; ethnic cuisine was soaring in popularity; so were frozen meals. What could go wrong?

Plenty, as La Choy discovered when it rolled out its egg rolls into the East and Midwest. For starters, they couldn't be microwaved, because the shells got soggy. And it took a very long 30 minutes to heat these giant entrées in an oven. The other Fresh and Lite products didn't set the world on fire, either. For one thing, there

was the name. "It sounded more like a feminine-hygiene product," says Linda Krakowsky, an ad executive who worked on the campaign. "And it was hard to say it was fresh anyway, because it was frozen." Two years later, La Choy executives pulled the plug on both the monster egg rolls and the Fresh and Lite line: Today they say they never had the market clout to make these products succeed.

In the long and inglorious history of new-product flops, La Choy is not

GETTING SMART ABOUT NEW PRODUCTS
How a company can improve its success rate in product launches

1 ASK YOUR CUSTOMERS Don't launch a product just because the engineering department loves a new technology. Consult users at every step, from idea stage to rollout.

2 SET REALISTIC GOALS A new product might be sure to produce $20 million in sales. So don't make it a loser by aiming for $40 million.

3 BREAK DOWN WALLS Passing off a new product from one department to the next risks potentially disastrous foulups. Instead, have research, marketing, and manufacturing work together from the start.

alone. Put in the context of such historic screwups as Ford Motor Co.'s Edsel (estimated losses: $250 million), RCA's VideoDisc player ($500 million), and Time Inc.'s *TV-Cable Week* ($47 million), a few soggy egg rolls don't seem all that catastrophic. Producing flops is part of doing business in every industry, from consumer products, where relentless competition for store shelf space drives many new products to quick extinction, to electronics, where rapid technological change dooms many newcomers even after a promising start. Remember the Osborne portable computer?

IS FAILURE ESSENTIAL? And the flops and near-flops just keep coming. Among recent events: Dell Computer Corp. admits it messed up its notebook launch. Toyota Motor Corp. records disappointing initial sales for its much-heralded T100 pickup truck. Coca-Cola Co. struggles to succeed with what looked like a nifty idea—a tiny soda fountain it had designed for office use.

Overall, the new-product battleground is a scene of awful carnage. Chicago consultants Kuczmarski & Associates just studied the success rates for 11,000 new products launched by 77 manufacturing, service, and consumer-products companies. They found that only a little more than half—56%—of all products that actually get launched are still on the market five years later.

Other studies peg the long-term success rate of new products closer to 65%. But everyone agrees that most ideas never even make it into test markets. Companies had to cook up 13 new-product ideas before they came up with a winner, according to Kuczmarski. "Clearly, all is not well," says Robert G. Cooper, a professor of marketing at McMaster University in Hamilton, Ont. A specialist in new-product development, he cites a Booz Allen & Hamilton Inc. study that some 46% of all new-product development costs go to failures. That's an improvement from the 1960s. Still, he adds: "If half of a factory's output ended up as defects, you'd shut the place down."

Clearly, too, such inefficiency makes a tempting target for today's lean and hungry corporations searching for ways to cut costs and increase productivity. For U.S. companies that spent the 1980s improving efficiency and boosting quality, and that now face vicious competitive battles in slow-growth markets, raising the success rate of new products increasingly looks like one of the final frontiers. "Industry has been enormously successful at wringing operational defects out of the system," says William BonDurant, a top marketing executive at Hewlett-Packard Co. "But then you look at failure rates for new products, and they haven't changed much in 25 years. There has to be a way to drive that rate down." Adds Yoram Wind, a professor of marketing at the Wharton School: "If companies can improve their effectiveness at launching new products, they could double their bottom line. It's one of the few areas left with the greatest potential for improvement."

To be sure, there's a school of thought, ardently advocated by some executives who devote their

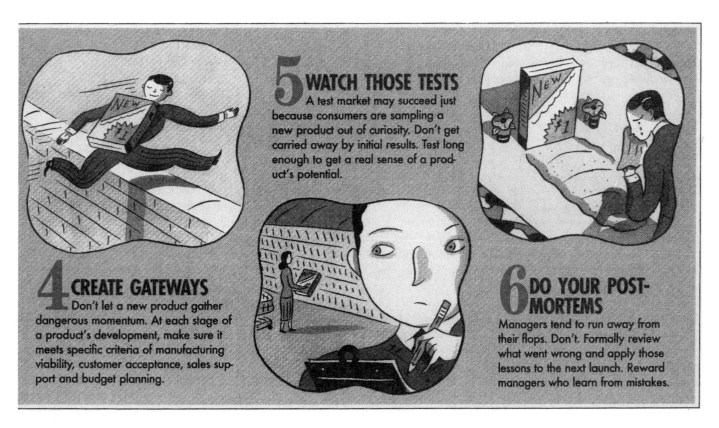

4 CREATE GATEWAYS Don't let a new product gather dangerous momentum. At each stage of a product's development, make sure it meets specific criteria of manufacturing viability, customer acceptance, sales support and budget planning.

5 WATCH THOSE TESTS A test market may succeed just because consumers are sampling a new product out of curiosity. Don't get carried away by initial results. Test long enough to get a real sense of a product's potential.

6 DO YOUR POST-MORTEMS Managers tend to run away from their flops. Don't. Formally review what went wrong and apply those lessons to the next launch. Reward managers who learn from mistakes.

lives to devising new products, that insists a certain rate of failure is essential. Says Brian Swette, general manager for new business at Pepsi-Cola Co.: "If you're batting a thousand with all your new products, you're doing something wrong." A perfect new-product record, he argues, means a company isn't taking necessary risks to develop new markets. Then, too, failure often lays the groundwork for a future success. The classic example: The not-very-sticky glue that technicians at 3M Co. turned into Post-It notes.

Yet that philosophical view isn't keeping companies from taking a much sterner attitude toward new-product development in a broad array of industries. The No. 1 priority at the Marketing Science Institute, a research group backed by such heavies as Procter & Gamble Co. and Apple Computer Inc., is the improvement of new-product development. Companies as different as Hewlett-Packard, Motorola, Colgate-Palmolive, and Chrysler have been tackling new-product issues, too. They want to figure out how invention, in-house teamwork, and customer involvement will compress development time, unleash a flood of successful new products—and keep flops at bay.

PRODUCT CHAMPIONS. It's a riddle that requires a company to understand not just its markets and customers, but itself. Sure, says Abbie Griffin, professor of marketing and production management at the University of Chicago, product development means figuring out what customers want and developing an offering to meet that need. But, she adds, it also means considering what a company is best at, how it goes about the business of devising and marketing new products, and the path those products must follow as they move through the company's infrastructure.

And the more executives, academics, and consultants delve into what it takes to make a success, the more hurdles they discover a new product must overcome. When exec-

utives at Hewlett-Packard's Medical Products Group studied 10 of their new-product failures along with 10 of their successes, they were surprised to identify a total of 14 essential tasks that determined which products worked and which didn't. The steps covered a wide range of corporate skills. Among them: figuring out which new products play to a company's core strengths, understanding how a new product should be sold, and getting an early fix on a project's costs. "We found if you missed on just 2 of the 14 factors, you failed with your product," says Mark Halloran, chief of research and development. Other studies have pinpointed the same need to master a wide range of disciplines in order to achieve success (table).

So what are the steps to new-product nirvana?

For starters, a new product must satisfy a customer's needs, not a manager's. Every new product needs a champion, of course—someone who believes in an idea and is willing to take risks to see that idea grow. But advocacy can easily turn into self-deception, dedication into wishful thinking. That's a painful lesson Steve Jobs learned. The visionary founder of Apple Computer tried to repeat his success at NeXT Inc., the start-up company that developed the sleek, black NeXT desktop computer. After burning through $200 million of investment funds, NeXT stopped shipping the $10,000 computer in February of this year. It's now concentrating on its far more promising software.

What happened? As Richard A. Page, NeXT co-founder and former hardware vice-president, put it a few months ago, when he quit: "The customers know what they want." And what they don't. For starters, they did not want Jobs's optical drive instead of the usual floppy drive. The new feature made it tough to switch work from a PC to NeXT. Even after a floppy drive was added, the machine itself remained slow, and there wasn't much software available to run on it.

True, the machine had nifty features, such as hi-fi sound. But even though Jobs tried to attract various kinds of customers, NeXT never overcame its essential, customer-hostile flaws. Students found it too expensive, even after discounts. Engineers preferred desktop workstations from Sun Microsystems Inc. Although he dropped it, Jobs insists that the NeXT computer was the right product: It was just too late to compete with the more powerful machines already out there. Yet if he had listened to customers and gone with more standard technology earlier on, analysts say, he might have had a chance.

BLIND TO THE SIGNS. Jobs was right about one thing: It's important to get to market swiftly. But it's even more important to get quality and pricing right the first time—even if that means delay. That's the painful lesson Cadillac learned with its Allanté. When General Motors Corp. launched the model with great expectations in 1987, Cadillac managers had hoped that the $54,700 coupe would bestow an aura of sexy Euro-styling on the division's whole line and expand its customer base to the younger buyers being lured away by BMW and Mercedes-Benz. It didn't exactly work out that way: The Allanté went out of production July 16, the victim of a too hasty launch and a failure to offer the right mix of price, quality, and features to finicky consumers.

For starters, the car, with its 170-horsepower engine, was underpowered compared with foreign rivals. The body, handcrafted at the Pininfarina workshop in Turin, Italy, was attractive, but not especially distinctive or well made. The roof leaked, and squeaks and wind noise marred the luxury-car hush.

These were all clear signs that the car's handlers should have waited and ironed out the bugs. But signs work only if they're heeded. One executive who worked on the Allanté later on says that Cadillac couldn't bring itself to delay the launch. "They had made a big hoopla about the introduction of this car, and when the car wasn't ready,

PEPSI A.M.

The cola giant tested a new version of Pepsi for breakfast time, but consumers preferred the taste of plain old Pepsi

they didn't want to make the hard choice and hold back," he says. The result was a car too small and expensive for core Cadillac buyers, but not really good enough to lure import buyers. No wonder Cadillac sold fewer than half the expected 4,000 Allantés in the 1987 model year. And it never sold even half its goal of 7,000 cars in subsequent years.

By the time GM decided to pull the plug, Allanté (now priced at $61,675) had finally become the ultrasmooth, high-performance luxury coupe it was originally intended to be. Cadillac had added the 295-horsepower multivalve V-8 Northstar engine and an electronically controlled transmission. But buyers were thoroughly confused. It was five years too late.

Taking a different view, Cadillac's general manager, John O. Grettenberger, says: "The car was a victim

of economics, not a failure." He says a financially strapped GM finally had to focus on its core models. Allanté's initial problems, he says, were not a result of haste. They were normal for a new venture in a market that Cadillac was just entering. And although he "would have liked to see it sell in greater numbers," Grettenberger says the Allanté taught Cadillac valuable lessons in marketing and technology that have made the Seville Touring Sedan a success.

Of course, if Allanté had gone through a more successful launch, it might have had a longer life. But even getting the new product right from the start is no guarantee of success: It must still be sold in the right way, through the right channels. A study by Cooper of McMaster shows that new-product managers double their chances of success when they successfully match a new product with the right sales force and distribution system.

"EMOTIONAL SELL." Huffy Corp, for example, the successful $700 million bike maker, did careful research before it launched a new bicycle it dubbed the Cross Sport, a combination of the sturdy mountain bike popular with teenagers and the thin-framed, nimbler racing bike. Huffy

conducted two separate series of market focus groups in shopping malls across the country, where randomly selected children and adults viewed the bikes and ranked them. The bikes met with shoppers' approval. So far, so good. In the summer of 1991, Cross Sports were shipped out to mass retailers, such as the Kmart and Toys 'R' Us chains, where Huffy already did most of its business.

That was a mistake.

As Richard L. Molen, Huffy president and chief executive, explains the company's slipup, the researchers missed one key piece of information. These special, hybrid bikes, aimed at adults and, at $159, priced 15% higher than other Huffy bikes, needed individual sales attention by the sort of knowledgeable salespeople who work only in bike specialty shops. Instead, Huffy's Cross Sports were supposed to be sold by the harried general salespeople at mass retailers such as Kmart. Result: "It was a $5 million mistake," says Molen. By 1992, the company had slashed Cross Sport production 75%, and recorded an earnings drop of 30%.

A corollary of "Know thy sales channel" is another rule: Don't sell a product just because you need some-

EDSEL AND FRIENDS: TEN WORLD-CLASS FLOPS

FORD'S EDSEL It had innovations galore—and quality problems from stuck hoods to defective power steering. Estimated loss per car—almost $1,117, or $250 million.
DUPONT'S CORFAM A synthetic leather supposed to do for shoes what nylon did for stockings. Leather was just better. Cost: $80 million–$100 million.
POLAROID'S POLAVISION Edwin Land used Polaroid's wet chemistry technology to develop an instant movie camera. But videotape technology was far better.
UNITED ARTISTS' HEAVEN'S GATE Almost $30 million over budget, this

western movie bombed so badly it almost destroyed UA.
RCA'S VIDEODISC Supposed to capture the video recorder market. A tiny problem: It couldn't tape television shows. Loss: $500 million.
TIME'S TV-CABLE WEEK A bid to outflank TV Guide. Cause of death: Ballooning costs to customize editions for each cable system. Loss: $47 million.
IBM'S PCjr The awkward Chiclet keyboard. The slow microprocessor. The unattractive price. The late launch. IBM at its worst. Marketing cost: $40 million.

NEW COKE Coca-Cola's answer to Pepsi's sweeter formula. Provoked a national uproar from old-formula loyalists. Watch for new formulation, Coke II.
R. J. REYNOLD'S PREMIER This "cigarette" didn't burn. It didn't emit smoke. It didn't taste good. Its failure persuaded CEO Ross Johnson to launch his equally disastrous buyout attempt.
NUTRASWEET'S SIMPLESSE The fat substitute that would change the way we eat. But the market is swamped with substitutes, and many consumers like fat.

DATA: BUSINESS WEEK

thing new to pump through the sales channel you have already mastered. In 1989, BIC Corp. introduced a small $5 glass flask of perfume, to be sold in the supermarkets and drugstore chains where BIC had so much distribution clout. After much hoopla, BIC sold $5.6 million worth of Parfum BIC in the U.S. before withdrawing it from stores in the first half of 1990. The cost: about $11 million.

The problem: Perfume is hardly as disposable and utilitarian as a bag of razors. Says Mark A. Laracy, president of Parfums de Coeur Ltd., in Darien, Conn., which does about $70 million a year by mass marketing knockoffs of pricey scents: "Fragrance is an emotional sell to women. But the BIC package wasn't feminine. It looked like a cigarette lighter."

TOO-SUBTLE QUAFF. Even if the product is fine and its distribution channel is right, though, it may still come to grief if consumers don't understand its benefits. Three years ago, for example, brewers fell in love with dry beer, quaffs that were supposed to have a cleaner finish. Many thought dry beer could be the boost their industry needed. Anheuser-Busch Cos., Coors Co., and a clutch of smaller foreign brewers shipped 4.6 million barrels of dry beer in 1990.

But by 1992, shipments had fallen to 3.7 million barrels—a minuscule drop of the industry's 197 million-barrel total—and brewers will be lucky to do even that much this year. Pretty sorry returns on the $40 million-plus spent in advertising for the category. Coors Vice-Chairman Peter H. Coors figures dry beer appeals to only 2% of all beer drinkers. "At the time, it seemed like an intelligent decision," he says. "Knowing what we do now, we probably wouldn't have gone with it."

What Coors knows now is that consumers, who usually only spend a few seconds in a store or bar choosing a beer—or any product—are not going to take the time needed to understand a too-subtle product like dry beer. As marketing consultant Jack Trout puts it, "Nobody can figure out what the hell dry beer is. The opposite of wet beer? It's never been explained." And it probably never can be.

Numerous as the pitfalls are, it's possible for companies to avoid them. But improving the odds in new-product development often takes some fundamental rethinking of the way a company approaches its markets and manages its own operations. Chrysler in the 1980s, for example, was a textbook case of how not to devise new products. Ignoring the need for continuing innovation, the carmaker relied throughout the decade on the K-car platform it introduced in 1981. Such models as a too-

A SMITHSONIAN FOR STINKERS

Ever wonder where new products go when they die? Some consumer-marketing giants, most notably Procter & Gamble Co., maintain archives of old products. Most companies, though, prefer to forget and move on.

But Robert McMath won't let them. For over 30 years, McMath, now 62, has been scouring trade shows and supermarkets for new consumer products. He gathers samples of winners and stinkers alike for his own collection, the New Products Showcase and Learning Center, located in Ithaca, N.Y. The entrance to the center could well bear the motto: 'Look upon these works, ye marketers, and despair.' Jammed onto steel shelving inside a concrete-floored warehouse, the more than 80,000 items contain innumerable examples of marketing's has-beens, also-rans, and never-weres.

FLOPSHOUSE. As you would expect of a man who owns over 5,500 different kinds of beverages and 3,600 shampoos and conditioners, the garrulous McMath has pondered the lessons of them all. On a shelf near the entrance sits a pack of R. J. Reynolds' Premier smokeless cigarettes, which has never made it out of test market. The problem, according to McMath: "only nonsmokers would like the product. Smokers like being wreathed in smoke." Nearby is a box of tissues bearing the curious name Avert. They were virucidal tissues that were treated to kill your cold germs when you blew your nose. A worthy goal, says McMath. But alas: "People weren't sure what a virucidal tissue was. It scared the hell out of them."

What's that box labeled Wine & Dine? It turns out to be the yupscale answer to Hamburger Helper, noodles and a sauce mix bundled with a tiny bottle of Chianti. Sad to say, the labeling didn't make it clear that the Chianti in that bottle was salty cooking wine. Consumers thought they had bought a little *vino* for dinner.

When they discovered their error, they took their wining and dining elsewhere. Ill-considered names also hurt other products. That includes the shampoos dubbed Look of Buttermilk and Touch of Yogurt, which didn't exactly promise a good hair day.

McMath's collection is good for laughs and shudders, but there's a serious side as well. A former Colgate-Palmolive Co. executive, McMath these days consults for companies that want to review past efforts in a given product category. If you want to launch a new instant coffee, for example, McMath can trot out dozens of related products, both successful and unsuccessful, from bottles of coffee syrup to newfangled coffee bags (which haven't exactly taken the market by storm). To today's brand managers, it's comforting to know there's a place where marketing's fallen can go rest in peace.

By Christopher Power in Ithaca, N.Y.

Turning more new products into hits looks like the final frontier. Companies could, says Wharton's Wind, "Double the bottom line"

narrow New Yorker sedan were launched and flopped. In addition, Chairman Lee A. Iacocca used his influence the wrong way, walking into Chrysler's styling studios and ordering up more chrome or opera windows with a wave of the hand.

As sales flagged in 1989, Chrysler President Robert A. Lutz finally convinced top executives that the company had to change its ways. So Lutz and François J. Castaing, Chrysler's engineering chief, threw out their old, compartmentalized approach to new-product development, in which a project would pass from research to engineering to manufacturing, and finally on to marketing. Instead borrowing from Japanese practices, cross-functional teams of engineers, market researchers, marketers, stylists, and manufacturing engineers began working together to design and build new models. The team approach has chopped by 40% the time it takes to develop a new car or truck. One important result: the hot LH line of sedans.

SIX STAGES. Other companies are also using team approaches to hone their new-product processes. Colgate-Palmolive Co. had a string of new-product flops in the 1980s, most notably Fab 1 Shot. The product, a slug of detergent, softener and an antistatic ingredient in a soluble bag, was sup-

posed to save consumers time and hassle, but instead it irritated users, who couldn't adjust the mix to suit their own needs. Since 1989, Colgate has overhauled its new-product process to concentrate cross-functional teams on far fewer product ideas and speed up global roll-outs of the most promising products.

Now, only about 20% of ideas make it to prototype, down from around 50%. And each idea must meet specific criteria at six different stages that lead from development to achieving a commercially viable product. While Colgate hasn't yet won a reputation as a new-products runaway winner, its latest introductions, such as Precision toothbrush and Stand-up toothpaste, have been successes.

Other companies have learned to get back to their core strengths. Campbell Soup Co. dismayed consumers and stockholders alike in the 1980s by pouring out almost 160 new products a year, with a success rate of at most 20%. "We didn't stay close to home," says former North and South American Div. President Herb Baum. The failures included such notable bobbles as Campbell's Fresh Chef line of fresh salads and soups, which had a shelf life of a week. The company was constantly misjudging which dishes would sell and which wouldn't. "We never knew what to make," says Baum. The result was spoiled food and irritated supermarket owners.

Now Campbell has cut back new products 20%, to around 120 a year. And those are mostly in areas it knows best, such as canned soups, sauces, and baked goods. When the company ventures into new areas, it

is with something such as Pepperidge Farm canned gravy, which uses technologies Campbell understands and brand names that it has already established.

INSPIRING CASES. The likes of Chrysler, Colgate, and Campbell have plenty of incentive to improve the odds for their new offerings: There appears to be a strong correlation between new-product success and a company's health. According to Thomas P. Hustad, editor of the *Journal of Product Innovation Management*, the companies that lead their industries in profitability and sales growth get 49% of their revenues from products developed in the past five years. The least successful get only 11% of sales from new products.

There are also plenty of specific cases to inspire and terrify. Gillette Co.'s stock has soared since it introduced its new Sensor razor. IBM's has floundered since it amply demonstrated its ineptitude at creating new product lines that pay. But IBM has also shown how it is possible to change: Its small ThinkPad computer is a big new-product success.

Whether it's frozen egg rolls or microchips, the message is clear: A company cannot avoid every flop. But if it learns from its mistakes, it can surely flop a lot less often. And understanding failure is clearly a key to success in this ferociously competitive decade.

By Christopher Power in New York, with Kathleen Kerwin in Detroit, Ronald Grover in Los Angeles, Keith Alexander in Pittsburgh, Robert D. Hof in San Francisco, and bureau reports

TEN TIMELESS TRUTHS ABOUT PRICING

Allan J. Magrath

Allan J. Magrath is Director of Marketing Services of 3M Canada, Inc., and author of two books and over 30 journal articles on marketing. One of his books is Market Smarts *from John Wiley & Sons, New York, New York 1988.*

There are several principles in the area of pricing that marketers need to be cognizant of and for which they need to develop skills. We will discuss individually each of these "Timeless Truths About Pricing."

TRUTH NUMBER 1: Pricing Is Just One Part of the Overall Revenue-Generating Strategy

Marketers first and foremost need to learn to be as independent of price as possible and still generate good profits. This is accomplished through a variety of "revenue diversifiers."

One revenue diversifier is new distribution. Marketers should always be looking for new channels to leverage revenue up. For example, a bank in Pittsburgh is dispensing postage stamps alongside its automated teller machines—a new form of distribution for a very old product. Coca-Cola has developed a new way of dispensing its syrup in small offices through what it calls "Break-mate," a product that allows it to get into small offices without a huge vending machine. Hollywood movies today are distributed and made for pay TV, network TV, and video cassettes, so movie companies no longer are dependent solely on distribution to the movie houses. Kirsch, the leading drapery hardware manufacturer in the United States, has traditionally had a strong market hold through department stores. It is now heavily concentrating on getting into specialty chain stores, which are getting more and more consumer business. IBM is now looking at department stores to distribute some of its personal computers.

Another way to diversify revenue is to get into services. Heinz, for example, has bought Weight Watchers and has diversified its revenue by getting into the service business. Echo Labs, which started out making chemicals to clean buildings, has now become a turnkey building maintenance company. It owns ChemLawn, so it takes care not only of buildings but of lawns and gardens as well. Combustion Engineering started out building power generating plants and now also runs them. Delta Airlines fixes other airline's planes. Caterpillar Tractor today handles the parts distribution for the Rover Group in the United Kingdom and for Navistar.

Another revenue diversifier is different marketing of the same products. For example, CBS records was just bought by Sony. CBS is now introducing classical music for baby boomers who don't know much about classical music and think they should know more. The company has taken some "easy listening" classical pieces and repackaged them into a series of "CBS Master Works," aimed at customers who know little about classical music. Another example of new marketing for old products is the revival of the fountain pen; some fountain pens are now selling for $3,500 each.

From *Journal of Consumer Marketing*, Winter 1991, pp. 5-13. © 1991 by MCB University Press. Reprinted by permission.

Another market diversifier is to go global, to diversify geographically. Disney is now opening theme parks in Japan and Europe. Armorall Inc., recognizing that 57 percent of all car owners live outside North America, is taking its automotive cleaners and protectants outside the United States.

A final idea for diversifying revenues is to market new products. New products are a sure fire way to boost margins and diversify revenues so that marketers don't need to depend solely on price increases. Rubbermaid is an example. In the last few years, new products have come to be 30 percent of its total company sales. Rubbermaid has grown dramatically and became one of the Fortune 500 most admired corporations in the United States.

TRUTH NUMBER 2: Pricing Strategy Must Be Closely Tied to Market Share Strategy

You cannot have a market share strategy that is separate from a pricing strategy. The two just go together. The case of Caterpillar Tractor will serve as an example.

Caterpillar had 50 years of sales growth and profits. It had a 27 percent return on equity, excellent products, a superb parts delivery system, probably the best dealers in the world in the heavy construction machinery business, and a reputation for quality. Then the Japanese company Komatsu cut prices 40 percent below Caterpillar's. As a result, between 1981 and 1986, 11 percent of the U.S. market went to buying Komatsu instead of Caterpillar machinery. Caterpillar lost $953 million between 1982 and 1985.

Caterpillar now faced a choice: It could either lose money or lose market. It chose to lose money, recognizing that if it didn't hold on to its share, it would not be able to fight back. Komatsu's, which targeted 15 percent, reached only 12 percent by 1986; today it is down to 9 percent. Caterpillar is back to profitable pre-1981 levels. Its significant emphasis on new products, emphasis on improvements in quality (even beyond what it already had), and aggressive automation of its

factories have helped the company regroup and back its rival down.

Caterpillar had to select a strategy which encompassed survival, profitability, and market share goals. Once a company decides to maintain its share, it usually has to tough it out and often loses money until it can fight back to improve its margins and get its customers back.

TRUTH NUMBER 3: Pricing Strategy Always Involves Cost Strategy

If you are in a price fight, you have to make sure you have a *cost strategy*. A cost strategy is the defining of *unit cost targets* for your core products (in other words, 80 percent of the volume that you sell). Unit cost targets are those unit costs you must hit in order to hold onto your share.

Setting these targets allows the rest of your operation to try to find unit cost savings. These savings might be found through productivity gains, through out-sourcing, through material substitution (substituting less expensive materials and materials that result in less waste), through reformulation of the product itself, or through a process change, such as automation, cellular manufacturing or other factory improvements.

Timex offers one example of cost strategies that tie directly into pricing strategies. The watch market today centers on inexpensive watches that are trendy in fashion with short lifecycles. Timex used to make most of its watch parts itself, but it recognized that by being vertically integrated it tended to be very slow in making model changes in a market that was speeding up. The company went to out-sourcing to get some control over model timing and parts acquisition. At the same time, it leveraged its buying power with suppliers to keep its costs competitive in order to get a faster payback on shorter lifecycle products.

Another example is Ford Motor Company. Like all North American car companies, Ford has recognized that its cars cost more to build than the Japanese cars, and it is looking for ways to engineer costs out of the car while keeping the quality high. It is now testing palladium, a cheaper alternative to expensive platinum, for the inside of the catalytic converters. Caterpillar is another illustration of how cost strategy is tied to pricing. Caterpillar has put together a program for automating, computerizing, and consolidating manu-facturing in all its factories. It used to take about 20 days to assemble the clutches for some caterpillar machines—it now takes four hours. Revitalizing the factories in this way has reduced costs, giving the company room to reduce prices in line more with Komatsu, and helping to retain customers.

One reason cost strategy is such a key part of pricing strategy is that it allows the firm to focus unit saving efforts on the different departments within the company. For example, out-sourcing involves the purchasing department. Product reformulation or raw material substitution involves laboratories. Process change involves the engineering and manufacturing departments. By specifying what the unit cost targets are, you can identify what the component parts of the cost strategy are and then identify what department must be involved in implementing strategy.

Another reason cost strategy is a key part of pricing is that the firm has to decide how much of the cost improvement is going to lower prices to the customer versus flowing directly to the bottom line. In the case of automotive manufacturers, where the intention is to price competitively with the Japanese, only a portion of the cost-saving will likely accrue to the bottom line. In other instances, such as with Timex, watch prices may remain up and some of the saving may flow down to the bottom line.

TRUTH NUMBER 4: Pricing Strategy Must Be a Derivative Of Your Price-Performance Equation Versus That of the Competition

If you are offering excellent performance or quality, you should expect to command some premium in the price. Rather than always asking "How price sensitive are customers?" you should try asking, "How benefit sensitive are customers to our extra performance?" With this attitude, you sell up to the built-in performance rather than down to the price of someone whose product may not have the same built-in price-performance.

Lone Star Industries has come out with a breakthrough concrete called Pyrament, a super strong, very fast-drying cement. Regular cement cures from seven to fourteen days, and normally a 10-inch thick bed of concrete is needed to provide the strength required for highways and airport runways. Pyrament sets in four *hours,* and only 7 inches of Pyrament offers the same strength as 10 inches of concrete. When considering pricing, the company should ask who benefits from this extra performance? Airport runway repairs is one market that it is targeting. Another potential market is the Interstate Expressway, where firms do night-time repairs. The fast-drying product allows such operations to reopen within four hours instead of shutting down for several days. Since shutdown time is expensive, Lone Star can focus on the purchasers' benefit sensitivity relative to the price charged. Regular concrete costs from $60 to $80 per ton; Lone Star's Pyrament will be between $120 and $180 per ton. The question to Lone Star then is: "Is the cost of time delay involved with regular concrete worth twice the cost to substitute Pyrament?" By focusing on benefit sensitivity instead of price sensitivity, a firm can get a good idea of the upper price premium to charge for the performance in its products. The firm also can focus only on those customers who will appreciate the extra performance.

Yokohama Tire, a Japanese firm, has just designed an all-season radial that is asymetrical. It gives the driver better steering response, more stability when turning corners, and better road contact in the rain. The company has recognized that although this tire gives superior performance, the majority of drivers will not pay a premium for it, given the already high cost and long life of all-season radial tires. Since the ordinary driver, whose tires often outlast ownership, simply does not appreciate that extra performance, Yokohama has targeted the product to Corvette owners across North America. By taking a benefit sensitivity mindset to market, the firm has become sensitized to both the price/value relationship and the target market.

TRUTH NUMBER 5: Pricing Must Always Consider the Segment You're After

Firms that "average price" their products across market segments are losing sales by not exploiting to their advantage the fragmented nature of most markets. Let's consider discount airfares. In a December 1988 survey, business travelers were asked, "What are the most important things you care about when you choose an airline?" The things that mattered most to these business travelers were (1) large number of schedules from which to choose, (2) fast check-in, (3) physical comfort, (4) on-time flights, (5) safety, and (6) friendly service. Price is number 14 on the list; and yet much of the airline pricing is across the board. Many discounts and deals often don't differentiate between the tourist, who is often a price shopper, and the business traveler, who is required by his or her job to fly all over the country. With their undifferentiated pricing, airlines have turned business travelers into price shoppers, and their often slim profit margins don't allow them to provide those things the business traveler *really wants.*

As part of the segmented approach to pricing, marketers have to learn to identify the *buying center* of the segment. Within each organization, there is a buying center with multiple players who all care and think about price differently. Therefore, not only should a firm price between market segments differently, but often it should present the price *differently* within the same organization.

For example, suppose a company is going to sell some forklifts to a large supermarket that has a large central warehouse. Within that warehouse is a purchasing manager, who may be concerned with the actual price per forklift. There is also a maintenance manager, whose concern is the unit repair cost of the forklifts. The manager of Receiving and Shipping may be concerned with downtime costs, a different kind of a price derivative. Finally, the warehouse manager, who may be the one making the final choice, may view price in terms of the total lifecycle of the forklifts, taking into account the initial purchase price (the focus of the purchasing agent), repair costs

(the concern of the maintenance manager), and such things as fuel costs, other costs of running the machines, downtime costs (the Receiving and Shipping manager's concern), and safety/environmental issues as well. Thus every player has a different concern. A marketer needs to focus on knowing all the players in the buying center, their roles, and their resultant view of price. Roles may include specifier, orderer, user, influencer, and approver. The marketer must also find out which of these players is the "quarterback" and what are his or her concerns.

TRUTH NUMBER 6: Upward Price Leverage Requires Continuous Investment in Brand Equity

According to the Marketing Science Institute, high brand equity can command the highest prices in the market. High brand equity goes naturally with high price, for several reasons:

1. *Customer loyalty.* Customers continue to buy favorite even if prices rise.

2. *More shelf space.* Distributors like suppliers whose brands are proven best sellers.

3. *Trade term preferences.* High brand equity suppliers may pay less to "rent" shelf space from resellers.

4. *Brand extension launching.* Brand equity can be used for launching variations. Examples are Coleman, which moved from tents and lanterns into everything from canoes to sleeping bags, and Nabisco, which extended Ritz Crackers and Oreo cookies into many other flanker brands.

How then does a marketer keep brand equity up to ensure that pricing is as high as possible? Four keys are involved in doing this:

1. *Position consistently.* The consumers have to know exactly what to expect when they buy the product or service.

2. *Stay top-of-mind.* When somebody asks, "which brands do you prefer," you have to be one of the first brands they think of.

3. *Reinforce familiar associations.* Brand

associations tend to build brand equity, so you have to build the kinds of associations that people are comfortable with and then constantly reinforce them. Prudential Insurance does this with the "rock" which connotes safety and security and similar associations in relation to insurance and financial services.

4. *Deliver on the product's promise.* The product must look like, feel like, and work the way the consumer expects it to. Dial soap, after 40 years, is still the category leader in its soap market. Chips Ahoy, a 25-year-old brand, is still the leading chocolate chip cookie. Both of these brands have kept their brand equity high and, as a result, still obtain excellent margins. Honda auto buyers are very loyal in repeat purchasing Hondas because a Honda car "delivers" on the buyers broad performance expectation.

Failing to sustain brand equity can be very costly, because regaining one lost share point usually costs much more than holding onto it. There is a multiplier effect. Once you have lost brand vitality, you have to spend disproportionately against competitors to buy back that share.

Brand sales momentum and price premiums cannot be sustained without reinvestment. This means either advertising, a form of mass communication, or personal communication, that is, making sales calls and investing in more representatives to sustain your leading position. These are the investments that will keep brand equity high.

The brand may also be changed over time as it is refined and improved. Continuous product improvement is one of the big mainstays of Japanese marketing strategy. The classic case in North America is Procter & Gamble. Its disposable diapers sold today have many enhancements that the original ones did not have. Tide has been changed for a number of reasons over the years, in response to changes in washing machines, fabrics, environmental issues, and family lifestyles. Some companies can even keep consistent positioning while changing the product on the run. At McDonalds, for example, you can now get breakfast, salads, and various new entrees.

Today's McDonald's experience is not at all like the McDonald's of the 1950s. Being able to execute continuous brand equity change while preserving the essence of what the brand represents is the mark of a supremely excellent marketer.

TRUTH NUMBER 7: Astute Pricing Requires Design of a Sound Price Discount Schedule

Dealers and distributors perform marketing, selling and logistics functions for the marketer. Marketers, in designing a discount structure, should consider what functions these dealers perform and what percentage of the sales dollar flowing to the dealers is actually rewarding them for these functions. Much of the margin is helping the dealer and distributor defray the cost of shipping, inventorying, financing receivables, paying a sales force, covering branch overheads such as computers and representatives' cars, and similar expenses. Such expenses must be deducted from any gross margins that they earn.

An example will illustrate what can happen when a marketer doesn't take this into consideration. It was reported in *Forbes* magazine that QMS Inc., which produces high-quality, moderately priced laser jet printers, offered its retail dealers markups that were really not consistent with the costs the dealers were incurring to stock, sell, and display the printers. As a result, the dealers simply didn't order that product from QMS as QMS believed they would. Seventy-one million dollars worth of inventory piled up, and QMS had to go to the bank to cover the cost of carrying this unsold inventory. After making $9 million profit in 1987, QMS lost $5 million in 1988, in large part because it didn't pay enough attention to the design of an appropriate structure of discounts for dealers.

There are four issues that a marketer needs to consider when designing price discount structures for dealers:

1. How many volume breaks are they going

to have in the discount schedule, and what is the minimum order size?

2. What is the percentage size of each break? That is, how much extra discount do they give for each of the volume breaks on the schedule?

3. What is the shape of the discount schedule? What is the slope of the line? Are the percentages at each break equal, or do they rise proportionately less, or more, as the volume rises? The linearity of the discount slope is important.

4. What is the maximum discount, in terms of the dealers' order size?

If there are too many breaks in the discount schedule, ordering can become very chaotic, because people are constantly moving up and down the discount schedule just through normal sales fluctuation. The reverse schedule, one with too few breaks, also causes problems. For instance, if a discount schedule had only two breaks, one at the bottom and one that depended on buying a large amount of product, very few dealers would qualify for the extra discounts and thus they would not be very motivated to grow, since the next break is so far from their reach. Marketers must therefore determine the ideal number of breaks to prevent chaotic ordering while giving dealers incentive to grow.

It is also important to have the right amount of discount at each step on the schedule. If very steep discounts are offered, there may be enough extra margin so that the dealer, when moving up to the next level, can profitably redistribute the product to a smaller dealer. You thus have wholesalers wholesaling the product to other wholesalers or dealers. On the other hand, if there are very shallow percentages at each break, then the schedule is not providing much incentive. With such low motivation, perhaps 80 percent of the orders may be coming from 20 percent of the dealers.

The case of a Canadian publisher will illustrate how a poor discount design can lead to a major retail fiasco. The publisher came out with a four-volume set of encyclopedias which was predicted to be a very good seller. There was every indication from the majority of the

independent bookstores that they are happy to sell the books at the publisher's suggested retail price of $175 per set. However, there was a very steep step in the discount schedule which allowed for huge volume discounts. Two chain stores, which control a great deal of the Canadian retail book buying market, purchased in large volumes, recognizing that the books would be good sellers. Because they could purchase them from the publisher for $75 or $80, they decided that they could retail the books at only $99 a set and still make a little money. All the independent bookstores had already paid $125 a set, the best discount they could get at the quantities at which they were ordering. After the public began comparison shopping, the independents were stuck with all the encyclopedias that they ordered. The ultimate result was that the independents shipped back all their inventory to the publisher, wrote hundreds of nasty letters, and subsequently boycotted several of that publisher's later books.

TRUTH NUMBER 8: Pricing Plans Should Not Be Overly Complex or Out of Sync With Efficient Shipping Units

A complex pricing schedule allows for errors in both the communication and calculation of pricing. It also works against a quality emphasis in marketing, which is the notion of "getting it right the first time." The *Wall Street Journal* stated that Chrysler's Omni had 8 million pricing combinations possible for the car buyer, because of the many options available and all their combinations. Chrysler did two things to simplify the situation. First, it made three of the options standard. Second, it bundled a number of the options into two bundled packages, the optional choice was cut from 8 million to 42, a much more manageable number.

Marketing should always try to make sure that the pricing unit that will be ordered by the distributor is in sync with the shipping unit from the warehouse. Marketing may discover when they analyze their pricing that they have prices for 100 or 50 or 25 cartons when in fact it may make more sense to have a pallet price or a full truckload price, which might be, say, 37 or 72 cartons. When the price is in sync with the way the warehouse and shipping operate, orders can be shipped more quickly and efficiently. Many old pricing conventions were set up prior to computers and used round numbers to simplify manual order preparation, but these selling units are not etched in stone. They are much better tied to warehousing and shipping units.

TRUTH NUMBER 9: Measuring Pricing Performance Requires Tracking Systems

Pricing is one of the least measured of the measurable marketing activities. Most companies have detailed statistics on new product sales, the effects of promotions on volume of distribution, company share of different distribution channels, and how much business goes through specific distributors. When it comes to pricing performance, however, tracking systems usually are incomplete, haphazard, or nonexistent. A marketer who wants to improve pricing performance should probably have a tracking system to measure it.

What are the characteristics of a good tracking system in pricing? First, the files that document tender bids should be centralized. Centralized bidding files allows for more analysis and more proactive strategy setting on bids. If bids can be loaded and categorized in a personal computer, a marketer can see what bids are upcoming and how the previous several years' bidding practice has gone relative to competitor's price positioning.

Second, it is good practice to graph information on pricing performance. Looking at competitor's prices on a line graph gives some kind of time history, some longitudinal performance that shows various competitors in relation to each other. Charts can reveal whether there is a specific pricing strategy that one of the competitors seems to be pursuing vis-á-vis everyone else.

A third aspect of monitoring price performance when tracking bids is analyze the win-lose ratios. Marketers should look at

tender histories to see what kind of record they have on different tenders. Are they getting better, staying the same, or doing worse? Win-lose ratios help in sales forecasting by giving the marketing department a good feel for potential volumes in key bid markets such as government business. They are like batting averages in baseball.

Finally, there should be systematic measuring of slippage from list prices. Slippage against list prices can occur because of giving customers special quotes or giving discounts that relate to payment terms, sales promotions, or other buying allowances. These are really just price cuts in another form.

The place to communicate and discuss price tracking information is in operating committee meetings with the division or business team. By looking at graphs, won-loss averages, slippage from list prices, and the like, they can gain insight into pricing realities and can then consider specific ways to remedy any problems. With data showcased in such a setting, everyone involved can start making some plans to improve decision making in the area of price performance.

TRUTH NUMBER 10: Implementation of Pricing Plans Calls for High Negotiation Skills

Negotiations about price takes place, face to face between the field sales force and buyers, whether buyers are purchasing agents, end users, or distributors. What makes a good negotiator on price, and what type of training is needed to turn a sales force into a good negotiator?

Good price negotiators have certain common traits. First, they know all the key players in the game and they know what their particular piece of the price negotiation is. They also know what the "best offer" range is, that is, what the ceiling and the floor price are. Good price negotiators also need to have a keen sense of how to "sell around" price objections. They have integrity, are fair and friendly in a professional way, and they negotiate for the best mutual win-win arrangement.

However, a management with a great price strategy can run into problems if its reps don't know how to negotiate at the customer level. Even in firm's where reps are given little latitude to move off published prices, they still indirectly negotiate price by influencing the product mix purchased by the customer. Fortunately, negotiating is a skill that can be learned. There are many good courses available. Also reps who are good at negotiating can teach other reps how to improve.

As a result of many studies, a great deal is known about what purchasing agents like and don't like about salespeople. They don't want the sales rep to focus on the product in a self-serving way. They don't like peddlers. The purchasing agent is looking for solutions, not necessarily specific products. Therefore the rep has to figure out how to sell *solutions.* Purchasing agents also respect a very professional, dependable, and friendly sales representative. They desire integrity, helpfulness, and follow-up in reps.

The following are characteristics of a successful price negotiation:

1. Both parties feel they got as much as they can expect.

2. Both feel that the negotiation was fair.

3. They would negotiate with each other again.

4. Both feel a sense of having preserved face.

5. Both parties will work toward the fulfillment of the agreement following the negotiations.

Summary

Following is a recap of the "Ten Timeless Truths About Pricing."

1. Pricing is just one part of an overall revenue-generating strategy. Marketers should think of it that way and try to become less price-dependent by diversifying revenue streams. There are many ways to boost revenue without raising price.

2. Pricing strategy is absolutely tied to market share strategy.

3. Pricing strategy always involves cost strategy, because if you're going to fight on price, eventually you're going to have to get down to costs.

4. Pricing strategy is derivative of the price-performance equation relative to one's competitor. Pricing is not an absolute science but rather a relative science. The customer obviously has multiple choices.

5. Pricing must always be considered relative to the segment or the group of customers being pursued; otherwise it's just average pricing and money is being left *on the table.*

6. Upward price leverage is clearly a function of brand equity. The more equity you have in the brand, usually the higher price premiums you can command. Obviously, it is important to contemporize brands, and doing so requires continuous investment in brand awareness and product improvement.

7. Astute pricing requires careful engineering of a discount schedule design. Marketers have to consider the number and steepness of price breaks, where minimum orders cut-in and where maximum discounts cut out.

8. Pricing plans should not be too complex or too far out of sync with efficient shipping units. Complicated systems usually cause errors and compromise a total quality effort in marketing.

9. Marketers need to track price performance by centralizing bidding files, using graphs, studying win-lose bid ratios, and systematizing the measurement of price performance against list prices.

10. The results of a pricing plan ultimately depend on good one-on-one negotiating skills with customers. This calls for a search for win-win pricing scenarios and the maintenance of a very professional but friendly sales force. Price negotiating is just a small part of customer relationship building. The emphasis must be on gaining customers, not just orders.

STUCK!

HOW COMPANIES COPE WHEN THEY CAN'T RAISE PRICES

Grandparents love them. So do parents. And kids do look awfully cute running around in their Oshkosh B'Gosh Inc. bib overalls. But in the past few years, the Wisconsin-based maker of high-quality children's clothing has faced increasing price resistance from consumers. To strengthen its ties to retailers, the company is working closely with department stores, helping to pay for new store fixtures and fancier displays. To lower costs, it's overhauling production processes and investing in worker training to become a highly flexible manufacturer. And in an unprecedented action to jump-start sales, Oshkosh will slash prices by 6% to 8% on its entire 1994 spring line of clothes.

It's not just Oshkosh, by gosh. All across the marketplace, companies are snipping away at their price tags. Mercedes-Benz is lowering prices on some luxury cars by almost 15%. Compaq Computer Corp. is slashing prices on its top-of-the-line personal computers by 23%. Borland International Inc. has chopped the list price on its latest Quatro Pro spreadsheet from $495 to $99. Boeing Co. is effectively freezing the prices of its commercial airplanes for the next five years. Says Ron Woodard, executive vice-president of Boeing Commercial Airplane Group: "Our airplanes cost too much."

RETHINK EVERYTHING. It's the Age of Disinflation—and it's creating a business landscape that few of the managers of these companies have seen in their professional lifetimes. The savvier among them aren't just whipping

out the markdown pen, though. Like Oshkosh, a growing number of corporations are recognizing that ferocious pricing pressure means that they have to rethink virtually every aspect of how they do business. In this unfamiliar and treacherous terrain, they're having to abandon many of their old, inflation-inspired business habits. To preserve profits and eke out growth, companies are being forced to come up with radically different corporate strategies, manufacturing techniques, marketing tactics, compensation structures, and approaches to financing.

Battered by worldwide overcapacity, brutal global competition, slow growth, and high unemployment, corporate pricing power has clearly been crumbling. Since 1990, consumer price inflation has fallen from a 5.4% annual rate to its current 2.7% yearly pace. At the same time, producer price inflation is down from 4.9% to 0.5%. It adds up to "a paradigm shift as profound in its significance for disinflation as the oil crisis of 1973 was for inflation," says Peter L. Bernstein, an economic consultant in New York City.

EXPOSED. In the new world of disinflation, cost-cutting is, of course, essential. But by freeing prices of the distortion of inflation, this challenging environment is also restoring prices to their traditional role as economic arbiter: They are the signals that tell companies and individuals how the marketplace truly values the goods they make and the services they sell. The price a company charges is, in turn, the culmination of every decision

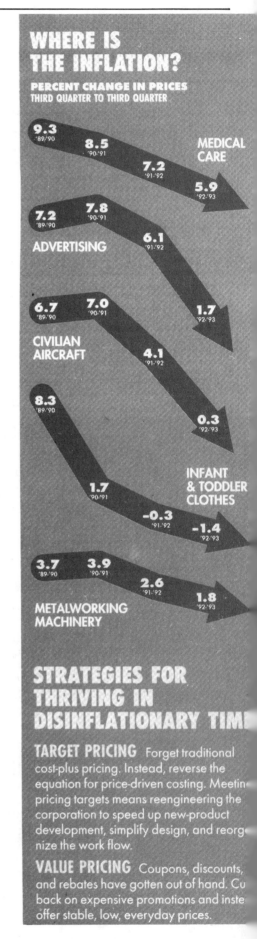

WHERE IS THE INFLATION?

PERCENT CHANGE IN PRICES
THIRD QUARTER TO THIRD QUARTER

MEDICAL CARE
9.3 '89-'90
8.5 '90-'91
7.2 '91-'92
5.9 '92-'93

ADVERTISING
7.2 '89-'90
7.8 '90-'91
6.1 '91-'92
1.7 '92-'93

CIVILIAN AIRCRAFT
6.7 '89-'90
7.0 '90-'91
4.1 '91-'92
0.3 '92-'93

INFANT & TODDLER CLOTHES
8.3 '89-'90
1.7 '90-'91
-0.3 '91-'92
-1.4 '92-'93

METALWORKING MACHINERY
3.7 '89-'90
3.9 '90-'91
2.6 '91-'92
1.8 '92-'93

STRATEGIES FOR THRIVING IN DISINFLATIONARY TIM

TARGET PRICING Forget traditional cost-plus pricing. Instead, reverse the equation for price-driven costing. Meetin pricing targets means reengineering the corporation to speed up new-product development, simplify design, and reorg nize the work flow.

VALUE PRICING Coupons, discounts, and rebates have gotten out of hand. Cu back on expensive promotions and inste offer stable, low, everyday prices.

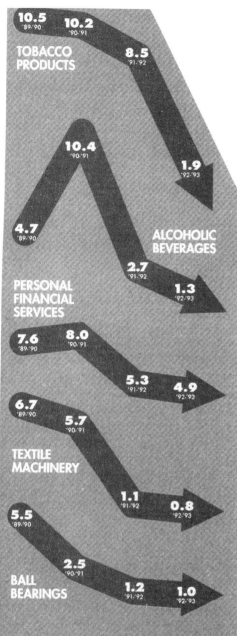

10.5 '89-'90   **10.2** '90-'91

TOBACCO PRODUCTS   **8.5** '91-'92

10.4 '90-'91   **1.9** '92-'93

4.7 '89-'90   ALCOHOLIC BEVERAGES

2.7 '91-'92   **1.3** '92-'93

PERSONAL FINANCIAL SERVICES

7.6 '89-'90   **8.0** '90-'91

5.3 '91-'92   **4.9** '92-'93

6.7 '89-'90   **5.7** '90-'91

TEXTILE MACHINERY

1.1 '91-'92   **0.8** '92-'93

5.5 '89-'90

2.5 '90-'91

BALL BEARINGS   **1.2** '91-'92   **1.0** '92-'93

STRIPPING DOWN Offer cost-conscious customers quality products with fewer bells and whistles at a cheaper price.

ADDING VALUE Introduce innovative products sold at a modest premium. Back them with strong merchandising and advertising campaigns.

GETTING CLOSE TO CUSTOMERS Find out what customers really want and give it to them. Use the new information technologies to closely track their needs and your costs.

GOING GLOBAL The future is now. It's a way to increase unit volume, and less mature markets offer more pricing flexibility.

DATA: BUREAU OF LABOR STATISTICS, BUSINESS WEEK

it has made along the line. Without the cloak of inflation, all those decisions are directly exposed to the ruthless pressures of the marketplace.

A number of companies are beginning to chart some imaginative paths across the new landscape of disinflation. They're redesigning products for ease and speed of manufacture or stripping away costly features that their customers don't value. Many are paring back expensive rebates and discounts in favor of stable, low, everyday prices. They're seeking to gain a bit of shelter from relentless pricing pressure by forging closer links with their customers or accelerating new-product development. They're working to improve productivity not just with layoffs but by tearing down bureaucratic barriers between departments and investing in high-tech hardware. Over the past 18 months, real equipment spending has increased by 24%, with about two-thirds of the increase concentrated in information technologies. "The management challenge of the 1990s is to reduce costs—and increase the perceived value of the product," observes Arthur L. Kelly, a private investor and director of Deere, BMW, and Nalco Chemical.

Above all, the relentless pressure of disinflation means that companies must constantly review all aspects of their business to make sure they're doing whatever it takes to offer customers high-quality goods at low prices. "We are in a period of low to no inflation that we may live with till the year 2000," says Southwood J. "Woody" Morcott, chairman and chief executive of Toledo-based Dana Corp., a $4.9 billion producer of automotive parts and other industrial products. "That means you have to get productivity improvements forever."

Of course, it may be too early to say that disinflation is here to stay. Inflationary pressures usually ease during slack times, and both the Federal Reserve and bond traders are convinced that inflation will roar back to life as the economy picks up. Many executives see rising prices on the horizon, too, arguing that business costs are being propelled upward by higher taxes,

government mandates, and President Clinton's health-care-reform package. No doubt, inflation scares will periodically roil the markets, and there will always be some companies or industries that are able to raise prices. Even now, the 14% decline in the value of the dollar against the Japanese yen is forcing Japanese companies to hike prices in the U.S. on everything from memory chips to cars, which could give domestic rivals in those markets some pricing room.

Still, certain industries, such as tires and energy, lived with lower prices through much of the 1980s. By the turn of the decade, gale winds of international competition and deregulation propelled disinflation into a broad array of manufacturing and consumer-goods businesses. What is most striking now is the spread of disinflation to previously immune sectors of the economy, such as legal services and health care. Even in the pharmaceutical industry, which enjoyed the luxury of raising prices at twice the rate of inflation through the 1980s, price-cutting is becoming rampant.

PLENTY OF GOODIES. To be sure, disinflation's spread is far from bad news. It means that consumers won't have to worry about sticker shock every time they pick up a box of detergent. And corporations can count on stable or falling prices for a host of raw materials, parts, services, and labor—not to mention capital costs, which are at their lowest levels in 25 years.

But inflation was the devil we knew—and the devil that companies had learned to live with. When prices were soaring, hiking revenues and reported profits was as simple as changing a price tag. Pay raises were easy, too. "When you have inflation, it covers up a lot of sins," says Eugene P. Beard, chief financial officer at Interpublic Group of Companies Inc., the advertising-agency holding company.

Disinflation, by contrast, is a much sterner taskmaster. A 1% drop in price will slash operating profits by 12.3% for the average Standard & Poor's 1000 company, assuming that costs and volume remain the same, figures Michael V. Marn, a consultant at

FOR JAPANESE COMPANIES, A DOUBLE WHAMMY

In the 1960s, Japanese imports were synonymous with cheap. Then, in the 1970s and 1980s, they became known for quality. Now they're getting a new label: expensive.

Even as most American companies struggle to hold down prices, Japanese companies are going the other way and dramatically hiking their U.S. prices. From cars to memory chips, the wholesale price of Japanese-made goods has jumped 7.3ᶜ since last year (chart). That's far faster than the 0.5ᶜ rise in average U.S. wholesale prices.

But executives at Japanese manufacturers have little reason to crow. Forced to raise prices by a deadly combination of a strong yen and a weak economy at home, they are losing market share to U.S. rivals. That's why many Japanese exporters are increasingly adopting a strategy of moving factories—and jobs—out of Japan.

In the short run, Japanese companies are raising export prices to keep profits from crashing. A year ago, a dollar in U.S. sales bought 125 yen. Now it only brings 108 yen, a 14ᶜ drop in revenues.

In some markets where there are few U.S. competitors, Japanese companies have been able to raise wholesale prices with relative impunity. In consumer electronics, price hikes by such companies as Sony Corp have been largely absorbed

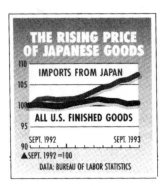

THE RISING PRICE OF JAPANESE GOODS

IMPORTS FROM JAPAN

ALL U.S. FINISHED GOODS

SEPT. 1992   SEPT. 1993
▲ SEPT. 1992 = 100
DATA: BUREAU OF LABOR STATISTICS

by U.S. retailers. "We were certainly not able to raise our prices to maintain our margins," says Kurt Larsen, senior buyer at Best Buy Co., a Minneapolis-based consumer-electronics chain, "and I didn't see anyone else doing it."

But most Japanese exporters are finding that big price increases can hurt them. Take Toyota Motor Corp., which in September announced price rises averaging 3.9ᶜ on comparable 1994 models. Ford, by contrast, only raised its average list price by a minuscule 0.2ᶜ. That's a key reason Ford's sales in recent months are up by some 9ᶜ over the previous year, about twice Toyota's increase.

And ironically, when Japanese companies try to hold the line on prices, they're open to antidumping suits. Eastman Kodak Co. recently accused Fuji Photo Film of selling imported photography supplies below cost, in part because

Fuji didn't boost U.S. prices when the yen rose. Kodak's complaint will be investigated by the Commerce Department, which could levy heavy tariffs on Fuji.

STATESIDE RUSH. With the yen stuck at current levels, moving production out of Japan is looking more and more like the right strategy. Over the last year, Nissan, for example, cut its exports from Japan by 26ᶜ, while increasing production in the U.S. and elsewhere by 22ᶜ. And Honda Motor Co. recently announced that by next spring all Honda Civics sold in the U.S. will be made in Ohio.

Even Japanese makers of consumer electronics products such as VCRs and camcorders are feeling pressure to shift production out of Japan. Already that's been happening in the color-TV industry: As Japanese companies have invested heavily in U.S. and Mexican production facilities, few color TVs are now being exported from Japan to the U.S.

Japanese companies have adapted to currency shocks before. But in disinflationary times, they are being pressed harder than ever. If their prices keep going up, the tag "Made in Japan" may become a euphemism for "Too expensive to buy."

By Michael J. Mandel in New York, with Neil Gross in Tokyo, Lois Therrien in Chicago, and bureau reports

---

McKinsey & Co. To avoid that kind of devastation, a growing number of companies know that they can no longer let their internal processes determine price. Rather, it's price that must determine process.

In the traditional approach to pricing, a company comes up with a selling price by adding up its costs, factoring in overruns, and putting an acceptable profit margin on top. These days, such cost-driven pricing is a recipe for too-high prices and a nice wide opening for lower-cost rivals.

That's why some companies are reversing the price equation. At General

Motors Corp.'s Cadillac division, for example, marketers begin by setting a target price for a new model. "Then, you say your profit is so much, and you back down into the cost. We never used to do it that way," says Janet Eckhoff, Cadillac's director of marketing and product strategy. "We're backing into the [price] from the customer's perspective now." Her boss, GM Chief Executive Jack Smith, is a big believer in the target-pricing technique.

This seemingly simple shift in pricing philosophy has profound implications for product development,

sourcing, manufacturing, and management. For example, target pricing won't work if it takes five to six years to develop and produce a car: Costs, competition, and consumer demand will have shifted too much in half a decade. To set a realistic sales price, the development cycle must be three years or less, as it was with the Neon, Chrysler Corp.'s new $9,000 subcompact. In turn, speeding up the development cycle requires stitching together teams from engineering, design, finance, marketing, and production. It means empowering workers and using lean manufacturing techniques. It means working with suppliers to deliver quality parts. Many of these efforts were already under way as companies strove to improve productivity, quality, and customer responsiveness. But disinflation has made them vastly more urgent.

TEAM EFFORT. Compaq is a case in point. After being battered for several years by low-cost personal-computer rivals, Compaq struck back in 1992. It now builds computers that cost up to 60% less through what it calls "design to price."

Here's how it works: A design team comes up with specifications for a new computer. It sits down with marketing, manufacturing, customer service, purchasing, and other departments. Based on a price target set by marketing and a profit-margin goal from management, the team determines what the costs will have to be. To achieve cost targets, engineers design products with fewer parts, and reuse parts from existing designs. Compaq's factories have been overhauled to crank out products more cheaply. And supplier contracts have been renegotiated, cutting material costs by $212 million in 1992 and $425 million this year.

The first products manufactured under the new pricing system, the Prolinea personal computer and the Contura notebook computer, came out in less than eight months. Since the third quarter of last year, Compaq's sales volume has skyrocketed 64%, and profits have nearly doubled.

Cincinnati Milacron Inc. is another manufacturer that is paying renewed attention to manufacturing during the design process. It now builds machine tools with 30% to 40% fewer parts. On the new Maxim 500, a machining center it introduced last year to replace its T-10, design streamlining reduced the number of fasteners from 2,542 to 709 and cut assembly time from 1,800 hours to 700 hours. Altogether, the approach cut production costs by 36%—and the selling price for the Maxim 500 is the same as it was for the machine it replaced. Plus, the Maxim takes up 60% less floor space, can be installed and started up in two days instead of two weeks, and makes much

more rapid changeovers, which sharply increases productivity.

Similar tactics paid off in lower production costs for Milacron's plastic injection-molding machines, which now typically sell at 7% to 9% below list price. "Five years ago, we couldn't be profitable with that [discount]," says Milacron CEO Daniel J. Meyer. "Now, we can not only be profitable, we're gaining market share."

Other companies are seeking to escape pricing pressure by embracing a "value-added" strategy—introducing a new or improved product that can still be sold at a premium price. Intel Corp. has its Pentium microchip, Gillette Co. has its Sensor razor system, and Goodyear Tire & Rubber Co. has its Aquatred, an all-season radial designed to provide better traction on wet roads. The Aquatred costs an average of $90, about 10% more than Goodyear's previous top-of-the-line mass-market tire. Yet the company has sold more than 2 million Aquatreds since its introduction two years ago. Goodyear concentrates on speeding new products to market and backing them with strong merchandising and advertising campaigns once they get there. "If you can have a richer mix, that's as good as a price increase on the lower end," says Chief Executive Stanley C. Gault.

QUALITY GENERICS. But selling value may be the toughest marketing job around these days. For one thing, the quality of many generic products, from diapers to cigarettes to drugs, has dramatically improved in recent years. The inroads of generics forced Philip Morris Cos., for example, to slash

prices on its flagship Marlboro brand by 40¢ a pack. With brand loyalty on the wane, it's a challenge for marketers to find the right price gap between a name brand and a low-cost rival. "A brand will carry a premium, but the question is how much of a premium?" says George J. Bull, Grand Metropolitan PLC's CEO for food operations.

Moreover, consumers now expect low prices even on many value-added products. Emerson Electric Co., an $8.2 billion instruments-and-electronics maker, finds it increasingly difficult to raise prices even on innovative products. "In general," says Emerson CEO Charles F. Knight, "customers see little reason for price increases." Emerson and most other manufacturers, he adds, are sharing whatever cost reductions they get with their customers, putting even more downward pressure on prices.

That has some companies taking virtually the opposite tack from premium pricing: They're stripping down, selling a product at a cheaper price by offering less. It's a tactic Southwest Airlines Co. has exploited to become the most profitable carrier in its industry, and United Airlines Inc. may emulate it by setting up a new low-cost subsidiary to compete against short-haul rivals. Says Robert L. Crandall, chief executive of AMR Corp., parent of American Airlines Inc.: "The market is telling all the traditional airlines that they must compete in a low-cost, low-price world."

Even such a flashy brand marketer as Reebok International Ltd. is stripping down. Its best-known sneaker is

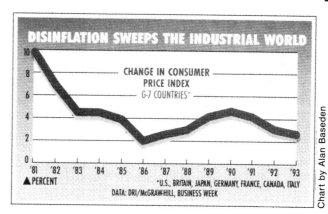

DISINFLATION SWEEPS THE INDUSTRIAL WORLD

CHANGE IN CONSUMER PRICE INDEX G-7 COUNTRIES*

▲ PERCENT

*U.S., BRITAIN, JAPAN, GERMANY, FRANCE, CANADA, ITALY
DATA: DRI/McGRAW-HILL, BUSINESS WEEK

Chart by Alan Baseden

the $135 Shaq Attaq, named after Shaquille O'Neal, the popular center for the Orlando Magic basketball team. But sales of such top-of-the-line sport shoes, after surging for much of the 1980s, have been slowing sharply industrywide. So Reebok plans to launch four different versions of the Shaq Attaq next year, with prices ranging from $60 for a stripped-down sneaker to $130 for a gadget-laden one. It expects to sell most of its shoes in the $50 to $80 range in 1994—about $10 to $15 less than last year's best-selling range.

Another costly tactic that some companies are stripping away is the frenzied rebate and discount strategy they once relied on to lure customers. They're using the savings from eliminating such costly promotional gimmicks to pay for everyday low prices. Consumer giant Procter & Gamble Co., for example, has slashed its promotional spending to help pay for 10% to 25% price cuts on several of its products, including Pampers and Luvs diapers, Liquid Tide detergent, and Folger's coffee.

LEAN TAB, FAT MARGINS. And on Oct. 4, Burger King Corp. abandoned coupons, discounts, and direct mail as key weapons in the fast-food wars. Instead, it's using everyday low "value pricing" and "combo meal" bargains, much like McDonald's Corp. and Taco Bell before it.

In most markets, Burger King is cutting the price of its croissant-sandwich breakfast combo to $1.99 from $2.47, and its Whopper hamburger with french fries and a drink is down to $2.99 from $3.72. The savings from getting rid of promotions means that the new strategy won't have much of an impact on profit margins in the near term, and higher volumes will eventually show up in better margins, says Sidney J. Feltenstein, Burger King's senior vice-president for marketing.

New information technologies are also helping some companies price better. Data bases and computer networks allow managements to move away from traditional average-pricing techniques. Instead, the new information technologies let companies closely track customer preferences and finely target prices, says McKinsey's Marn. Similarly, new accounting systems, such as activity-based cost accounting, allow managers at Hewlett-Packard, General Electric, and Dana to quantify in depth the costs of production inefficiencies. And having a better handle on production costs encourages smarter pricing.

In industries such as health care, the pressure of disinflation is also driving companies into mergers and alliances that would once have been unthinkable. Consider Merck & Co.'s $6 billion purchase of Medco Containment Services Inc., the country's largest drug discounter. Then there's Columbia Healthcare Corp.'s $5.7 billion acquisition of HCA-Hospital Corp. of America, which will create the nation's largest hospital chain. The purchase fits with Columbia's push to add volume and cut costs in response to price pressures. "Our strategy is focused on believing that prices will come down," says Columbia CEO Richard L. Scott.

Is the U.S. 'the most price-competitive market in the world'?

Nevertheless, considering the inflation experience of the past three decades or so, does it make sense for companies to go through the turmoil of adapting to a disinflationary world? It certainly seems so, especially as price wars rack industry after industry, from airlines to cigarettes. "We've found the U.S. to be the most price-competitive market in the world," says David de Pury, co-chairman of the board at ABB Asea Brown Boveri Inc., the Swiss-Swedish maker of capital equipment.

The pricing pressures are global, though. Japan is flirting with deflation, as is most of Europe. Worldwide, overcapacity plagues machine tools, chemicals, consumer electronics, and computers. Zenith Electronics Corp. figures its prices for VCRS and TVS have dropped more than 3% a year since 1984. Its lost revenue from falling prices tops $2 billion over the past 10 years, says CEO Jerry K. Pearlman.

Continued corporate bloodletting also means that disinflation is likely to be a fact of life for some time. In just the past few weeks alone, Woolworth Corp. said it plans to eliminate 13,000 jobs, four major drug companies reported a total of 11,000 layoffs, and Anheuser-Busch Cos. announced a 1,200 person cut. Overall, employment is about 3.5 million workers below what the job count would be if the U.S. were in a typical post–World War II recovery, according to Stephen S. Roach, economist at Morgan Stanley & Co.

Disinflation, like inflation before it, is taking on a momentum of its own. Pricing pressure leads to more restructurings, and restructurings lead to more disinflation. Every twist in pricing strategies for a low-inflation world ends up reinforcing the disinflation trend.

Today, prices are signaling companies to move beyond the slash-and-burn strategies of cost-cutting and reinvent their organizations to thrive in a world of low inflation. Low everyday prices—with vast everyday implications—are here to stay.

By Christopher Farrell in New York and Zachary Schiller in Cleveland, with Richard A. Melcher in Chicago, Geoffrey Smith in Boston, Peter Burrows in Dallas, Kathleen Kerwin in Detroit, and bureau reports.

MORE TO OFFER THAN PRICE

STRATEGY: Many small businesses find they can't compete with larger firms when it comes to discounting services. But there are many other ways to keep customers coming.

JAN NORMAN

Jan Norman is The Register's *small business columnist. Her column, It's Your Business, appears on Monday. Write her at* The Orange County Register, *P.O. Box 11626, Santa Ana 92711 or E-mail to* jnorman@link. freedom.com

Paul Pancher has been renting cranes to construction and manufacturing companies for 32 years. The '90s one-two punch of fewer jobs and more competition has brought the price cutters out of the woodwork, luring customers away from Pancher's company, Hydrocranes Inc. of Yorba Linda.

Pancher is certainly not alone. Video stores, contractors, dry cleaners, repair shops, retailers and hair salons all feel the effect of rivals offering the same product or service for a lower price.

Promising the lowest price in town is a game few small businesses can win. So, It's Your Business asked in Problem 310, how is a small firm supposed to survive against lower-priced competitors?

If customers bought only on price, there would be no Rolls-Royces, Dom Perignon or Nordstrom, many entrepreneurs replied. Small companies can excel with nonmonetary competitive strategies that work better in the long run.

PERSONAL TOUCH

"I've lost some customers (to lower-priced competitors), then four or five months later they're back," Pancher says.

The competitor usually offers a lower hourly rate but manages to drag the job out so the total bill is higher.

Often the price cutter is a large company, whose workers have no incentive to be cost-effective partners with the customer's firm, Pancher says.

"Either my son or I are on the job site personally, always looking for the fastest and safest way to do a job," Pancher says. "We make the customer aware that we're doing all we can to make his or her project profitable."

That strategy has kept Hydrocranes going more than three decades.

Friendly service can be a way to compete against lower-priced rivals, says Lewis Wong, general manager at Pepper Spray Protection, a Laguna Hills retailer of personal protection products.

QUALITY AND SELECTION

Wong always explains to his customers the difference in pepper sprays. For example, some sprays are more effective or spray farther than others. And that usually adds to their price.

"We carry products from reputable manufacturers who have been in the business 20 years or more."

Wong also has competition from carwashes and locksmiths that stock one size of pepper spray. He carries several brands, sizes, carriers (such as pepper spray in holsters or on key chains) and styles (sprays and foam).

"If you have good-quality products and friendly service, your customers will come back to your store and tell their friends," Wong says.

Mike Macres agrees.

Macres Florist has been under the same family ownership and located on the same corner in downtown Santa Ana since 1936.

Quality has made that possible, he says.

A common tactic in the floral industry is to offer some flowers below cost to lure customers into a shop. One chain sold two dozen roses for $9.95, Macres recalls, but the roses were small, on short stems, uncleaned and sold in an untidy bundle.

"Customers see the poor quality of the special and buy something else in the shop," he says. "There's an old saying that people become more disappointed in a product they received than the price they paid. They remember where they got that product and don't go back."

INFORMATION

Small businesses also can compete with low-balling competitors by selling more than the basic product.

"In our business, customers want to know more about what pepper spray can and can't do, for example, how effective is it, how does it differ from Mace, whether it works on animals," Wong says.

Pepper Spray Protection taught classes for state certification until a new law eliminated that requirement as of Jan. 1. Wong still has films on pepper spray use for customers to view and allows them to test the various products before buying.

Prestige Quality Collision Repair in Westminster also supplies information with every auto-repair estimate it makes, says partner Olga Shrewsbury.

Most auto-body repair shops charge the same labor rates, but some give a low estimate to get the job,

then tell the customer that additional repairs are needed, she says.

"When comparing an estimate that is lower than ours, I go over the estimate line by line to show customers exactly what is needed and how the work will be performed," she says. "I also explain that we have the necessary equipment and training to perform the repair properly and cost effectively."

APPLES TO APPLES

Omitting necessary work from bids is common in the construction industry, says Marlene Andrews of Andrews Construction and Maintenance of Orange.

"We ask people who are soliciting bids to compare apples to apples and make sure every bid covers the same things," she says.

Andrews works with many homeowners associations that need property repairs. Sometimes competitors have a lower bid by promising to do a job in fewer hours, then end up with the job half done.

"We've also done repairs where it was clear that shoddy materials and inexperienced labor were used previously, so you know the previous company cut corners to lower their price," she says.

INTEGRITY

In the construction industry much of the lower-priced competition comes from contractors who don't have the required state license. Such firms should be reported to the state, but many people who hire contractors don't even check the license or reference, Andrews says.

Another common problem in construction, she says, is the customer who says "Your competitor says he will do the job for X amount of money. Can you beat that price?"

"We don't think that's ethical, so we always say 'go with that guy, and

WHAT TO DO IF YOUR PRICES AREN'T LOWEST

Some tips for distinguishing your company when you don't have the lowest prices:

- Service.
- Selection.
- Value and extras included at no charge.
- Quality work or product.
- Convenience.
- Unusual or hard-to-find products or services.
- Staying Power (no fly-by-night operator).
- Continuing communication with customers.
- Knowledge and training.
- Integrity.
- Personal attention to customer.
- Availability and quick response.
- Guarantees.
- Cleanliness of place of business.

Source: The Register

next time don't tell us the other bids,'" Andrews says. "We don't know if they're telling us the truth. And if a person soliciting bids will play games like that, we're not sure we want to work for them in the first place."

Karen Herb, owner of Orange County Secretarial Services in Lake Forest, experienced firsthand the potential problems when a client persuaded her to lower her price on a large word-processing contract.

"The procurement officer kept asking me for a better price because the other services they were subcontracting to had agreed to prices more than 25 percent lower than my standard hourly rate," Herb says. "Because the work was a high volume of straight production typing and easy to perform, I finally reduced my price to a little higher than the other services."

However, the project that was supposed to be simple quickly became chaotic, and required so much management time from Herb that it wiped out all her profit.

"I was shortsighted about all the pieces that are built into fair-market value," Herb says. "I remind clients that I won't reduce the quality, and I ask them not to expect me to reduce the price.

"I wish I had recalled my own philosophy before I took a project that . . . left me with an unhappy client and cost me money and a lot of aggravation."

REASONABLE PRICES

In the competitive environment of the '90s, small businesses can't overprice their products or services and survive.

"But you can't do a job for free," Andrews says. "We bid a job what it will cost us plus profit. If someone low-balls us, we say 'take it.' We know what it costs to do the job."

The dry-cleaning industry is notorious for cut-throat pricing competition, says Ken Nhieu, partner of Queen Cleaners in Anaheim.

"Many new stores charge low prices to build up their clientele," he says. "Or they underprice us on shirts but charge much more than we do for pants."

FIX IT

Finally, small business owners can turn a competitor's low-price tactics to their advantage, Shrewsbury says.

She tells of a hair salon that charged fair prices and worked hard to earn a good reputation. Then a new salon opened across the street and hung out a banner "Haircuts $6."

Instead of trying to match the price, the owner of the first salon hung out a banner of his own: "WE FIX $6 HAIRCUTS!"

Your Secret Weapon

Discover Your Unique Advantage and You Can Charge Top Dollar

Thomas J. Winninger

Consultant Thomas J. Winninger coaches more than 60 corporate clients per year. He is president of the Winninger Institute for Economic Strategy in Minneapolis, specializing in marketing.

FIRST RULE: TALK "VALUE" Recently I walked up to the meat department of a grocery store. After a couple of minutes, someone emerged from behind the mirrored glass and asked, "May I help you?"

I answered, "I notice that your meat prices are a little higher than in other places that I shop."

The man lashed back with, "Don't complain to me about meat prices. I don't set the price. The manager does."

"Where is he?" I asked.

"He's out playing golf."

Let's analyze this situation. When I indicated that prices here were somewhat higher, I didn't say I wasn't going to buy. I was giving the employee a chance to explain "value."

But unfortunately, he chose to defend price.

Imagine the opposite scenario. He could have come out and said, "Good morning. My name is Mike Wilson, and I'm the assistant manager. How may I help you?"

And when I delivered my comment about prices, he could have said:

"We appreciate your sharing that with us. We spent years building a meat department that serves customers who want the highest value for their grocery dollar. The cuts you see here are the finest available. What type of meat are you interested in?"

He seemed to be ignorant of something crucial—both when you face low-price competitors and in practically any business negotiation. It is a basic rule of the market that all reasonable people understand price dynamics. They know they should be ready to pay a *premium price* for *premium value.*

Because premium value is often the real issue, we must educate customers on buying decisions. They are often confused, simply because we fail to inform them.

A typical customer looks at paint and says, "Gee, this one's $12 a gallon, and this one's $15. That price is too high." A typical merchant hasn't been doing his job.

Recently I did a job for an upscale regional paint manufacturer in the Northwest whose price for its product tends to be a little higher. This is because it sells premium paints. It adds more bonding and pigment to the paint than its competitors do. *Tell the customer about it.*

A smart buying decision should be based upon cost over time, not price. If I buy $300 worth of paint, and that paint is guaranteed to stay on my house for 5 years, why not spend $100 more and get a paint guaranteed to stay on for 10 years? The cost of 5-year paint is $60 per year. The cost of 10-year paint is only $40 per year. You will get 5 extra years for only $100, or $20 a year. The cost of labor will be the same. Why not use the best for less?

The price merchant can be deadly, but only to those who compete on price. Another niche in any market is selling value.

When customers understand this price versus value decision, 73 percent of them lean toward value, away from price. But the value organization must explain this to them, or they will be confused. In judging prices alone, they will think they are comparing apples with apples—when they are really comparing bananas with apricots.

Now, picture this small-town scene. It *could* be the setting for a disastrous price war. But one local businessman —call him Michael Brody—decides to help merchants compete:

Brody walks alone on the sunbathed sidewalk toward Brody Hardware Inc. As he walks, he glances into storefronts and waves whenever a local businessperson looks his way.

He yanks open the door with the gold-leaf "Brody Hardware Inc." on the glass. Harold, the store manager, is the first employee he sees.

"Well, Sam's coming to town," says Michael.

"You mean Wal-Mart?" asks Harold.

"Yes, and Sam's Club, too. We just got the word at the Chamber's Development Committee meeting. They figure both stores will open next spring out on the edge of town by the fairgrounds. That means we've got work to do."

From *Success*, January/February 1995, pp. 48A-48H. Adapted from *Price Wars: How to Win the Battle for Your Customer* by Thomas J. Winninger. © 1995 by Thomas J. Winninger. Reprinted by permission of Winninger Press/St. Thomas Press.

"You mean we've got to cut our prices and save money every way we can."

"No, Harold, that's *not* what I mean. I mean we've got to reposition ourselves.

"There's no way we can fight Sam's Club by lowering our prices. They'd win every time. We're going to segment the business—differentiate this place from Sam's hardware and hand-tool department. We've got to reengineer our approach to our market."

On Thursday and Friday, Michael talks to several business owners. It is clear that all of them were alarmed about Sam's scheduled arrival. But Michael knows that people buy from a merchant for various reasons, only one of which is low price.

On Saturday morning, his friends see that his latest column in the *Merchant Today* newsletter is headlined, "Fight, or Cut Bait?" The column reads:

Wal-Mart is coming to town. What does that mean to you? Competition is not disastrous. It is advantageous. Fish stay healthier when there is a predator in the pond.

Remember: 73 percent of consumers buy for reasons other than price.

Your challenge is to convince customers that they are getting value that is greater than the price they are paying.

Many reasons exist for people to buy from you. Give them enough reasons and they gladly pay a little more. Give them value and service, and they come back.

We've got to fight low price with high value and with service that's so good that people tell others about it.

By Monday, his words have been cut out and posted on many company bulletin boards. Michael gets a call from a banker who has a number of the local businesses among his customers.

"You were right trying to prevent panic," his caller says. "WalMart and Sam's Club won't drive all the local businesses into bankruptcy unless they take the bait and compete on Sam's playing field.

"If a business does a good job, the effect of a Sam's Club probably will be no more than to bring more people to town. And some of them can be attracted to buy at local specialized businesses."

At the banker's suggestion, they form a merchants' group to plot a common strategy. Most of the members are people who provide services for business—bankers, insurance agents, builder-contractors, accountants, advertising, and PR professionals. They call it the Value Merchant Task Force.

When a business signs up, the group gets background from the owner and then brainstorms to discover ways for him to provide his customer with more values and services. Alarm soon gives way to confidence within the group—and enthusiasm for battle.

Soon a new consensus emerges among the Value Merchant Task Force. "We're going to fight this warehouse store. We're not giving in to price-only competition.

"Not only would we lose if we do, but our customers, those who want service and value, those who want us to be specialists, would also lose. We pledge not to let that happen."

When you differentiate with value, you can give the super-store price-merchant types a run for their money. Super-stores

---

Find Your Strength

The following questions may help identify profitable niches.

1.

What makes me different from my competitors?

2.

If I ceased to exist, why would my customers miss me?

3.

What do customers ask for that I don't have?

4.

What need do I fill that no one else in the market fills?

5.

What need could I fill for my customers if I wanted to?

6.

Have I segmented my market precisely enough?

7.

Who are my best customers? Why? What needs of theirs do fill?

8.

Do customers buy my whole line of products and services? What part of the line is most popular? Most profitable?

9.

Where are the customers I want to capture?

---

have less value. Selection is limited to what comes from factories at a good buy each week. Shoppers usually have just one choice, so they'd better like it. They quickly learn that if they see something they like, they'd better grab it, because it probably won't be around next shopping trip.

For the upscale customer, a good independent merchant always beats a price merchant. So the real battle is for those confused customers who waver between upscale value and service on the one hand and "a low price" on the other.

You cannot prevent the price merchant from reeling in some of these customers. He will get his share. But you can maintain your competitive position by working hard to sharply differentiate yourself from price merchants, especially by:

1) Supplying value to offset price differences.
2) Making fewer errors in billing, shipping, and delivery.

3) Targeting items that the competitor doesn't carry—different brands and different sizes, for instance.

4) Upscaling the shopping environment and improving your relationships with customers.

Differentiation is the secret weapon in competing.

Long ago, manufacturers had to learn how to differentiate in marketing. A good example is their classic ploy of developing unique second brands, to be distributed within distinctly different price positions.

Hallmark markets its Hallmark cards in department stores, and its Ambassadors cards in other locations. Burlington House rugs are marketed through upscale boutiques. Its second brand, American Lifestyle rugs, is sold to mass-market channels. Coors sells Keystone beer in retail outlets, where its low price makes for a better fit and does not dilute Coors's image as a premium beer.

A variation is to market different labels, with some reference to the mother brand on the product label. Dutch Boy paint sells its flagship brand in home improvement stores, while its Fresh Look and Performer brands are sold by Kmart. This differentiation in merchandising was an early form of seeking the right niche in the market to guarantee sales to a special and important group of customers.

A niche is a segment of the market that has significantly different needs from the broader market—an unserved, or underserved, segment.

MICROMARKETING

Select niches that you can dominate. Choose them from your current business environment—the niches you understand better than others. Many people seem to think they have to change their entire operation to start serving a niche. If you take a better look at your business and learn to think like your customers, you will find pockets where you can stand out. You don't have to reinvent the wheel. It is more realistic for independents to look for profitable niches in their present markets than to step into new ones.

By specializing, a company can match the unique needs of a specific group of customers with a package of products or services that can't be found elsewhere.

Some people call this *target marketing*. Others call it *market segmentation, micromarketing* or *focused marketing* No matter what you call it, it is a sweeping trend.

Advertising to a large, homogeneous market is increasingly ineffective. The mass market has splintered. Independent business is confronted not with one big picture window but with thousands of shards of glass.

The great opportunity in niche marketing is for independent business. Price marketers cannot efficiently or profitably service narrow submarkets. An estimated 40 percent to 60 percent of advertising dollars are wasted through the mass-media, price-shopper focus. On the contrary, current trends *favor* independent specialty businesses and *hamper* mass merchandising.

If you have dreams of becoming a champion niche marketer, expunge from your mind any concept of "average customer."

To a niche marketer, there is no such thing—only customers with special needs that are definitely *not* average.

When you think about it, the concept of *average customer* is bizarre.

If 50 percent of your customers are crazy about your product or service, and 50 percent feel so-so about it, what does that mean—that your *average customer* thinks it is pretty good?

If 20 percent of your customers buy every week, and 80 percent about every three months, does the *average customer* buy once every three weeks? No.

Advances in technology now make it possible to carve out niches and target them with a precision that was once inconceivable. Consumer goods companies (such as Nintendo, Kool-Aid, and Waldenbooks) have demonstrated that interactive relationships with individual customers can be more effective than traditional hit-and-miss, one-for-all advertising campaigns. Niche marketing and one-to-one interaction can be combined in a powerful strategy called "relationship marketing."

Instead of trying to corral a large market share of all available consumers, the idea is to win a large share of each consumer's budget The loyal customer making repeat purchases brings you

---

Service Strategy

In one of my seminars, entitled "How to Play the Price War Game," after I greet everyone seated around the platform, I offer an injection of courage:

"If the price merchants scare you, relax. Fight back with high value. Practice value-added tactics, like Culligan Soft Water—which delivers bottled water as well as servicing soft-water units."

Value is defined as "quality relative to price." Quality includes all *non price* attributes involved—both attributes of the product and associated customer service.

The first step is to develop a program for solidifying position in the market by increasing "perceived value."

You can keep price merchants at bay by differentiating your store with:

- Personal service, which includes friendly, helpful, and knowledgeable employees who know clients by name.
- Merchandise in-stock.
- Variety of brands and guarantees.
- Signs indicating location of merchandise.
- Quantity supplies for businesses that need them.
- Delivery included.
- No-questions-asked return policy.

Shop the competition. Take good notes on what they don't do. See what they offer and compare it with what you offer. Look for gaps that they have that you can fill.

You want battle tactics that are relatively easy to implement—so you can counterattack immediately.

Hit the price merchant where his defenses are weakest. Product service is one good place to start.

a substantial profit that justifies building relationships through micromarketing.

The relationship with a customer doesn't end with the purchase. It begins with the purchase. The purchase of an item should be the beginning of a long-term relationship, cemented by the quality of your service and delivery.

The technology of micromarketing also allows you to identify trends. The company that first identifies and takes advantage of a new trend leaves competitors in the dust—and keeps moving forward.

THE CUSTOMER'S THE THING

The most effective way to differentiate your company is to give service that's better than customers expect.

It is effective because the majority of businesses pay only lip service to serving customers. Many seem to think that printing a story on "customer service" in the employee newsletter constitutes a customer service program.

I was very impressed a while ago when I stopped at a Chevron station. I didn't expect to see an attendant at a service station who *insisted* on pumping the gas, at no extra charge, instead of letting me do it. I noticed that the rest room looked extremely fresh.

I did not realize that Chevron had positioned itself as a *service* station rather than a *gas* station. It deliberately intends to differentiate itself in this way within the service-scarce gasoline market. The field is wide open.

Chevron's target customers, says a company spokesman, are those people whose cars are important and who are looking for more than gasoline. Chevron's print advertising campaign underlines the company's commitment with a picture of a squeegee, a dipstick, a restroom key, and a tire valve.

Its customer service philosophy is: "If customers believe they are really going to get better service, they won't go elsewhere to save a few pennies."

Meanwhile, competing department stores are selling the same goods at the same locations. All of them are becoming generic, with a proliferation of products and services. Competing airlines fly the same aircraft over the same routes. They offer the same frequent-flier programs.

Most banks offer nearly identical rates and services. Office machine dealers offer equipment that looks the same and appears to do the same thing. Competing resort hotels put the same pictures of the same beach in their brochures. In one mall, I found six places carrying the same brands of shoes.

Knowledge is power. If you study your own industry for one hour each day, you'll be more knowledgeable than most experts.

In this look-alike landscape, total customer service is a sure way to differentiate.

An upscale car manufacturer improved his service and increased sales by including in the sticker price free maintenance service for 24 months. And the customer also gets regular maintenance service at 2,500-mile intervals. The car is picked up at the customer's house in the evening after work, serviced, and put back in his garage the next morning before he leaves for work.

PREPARE FOR BATTLE

Knowledge is power. The more you know about what others need, the more valuable you are.

Study your industry at least an hour a day. Plan that hour of study during your high-energy period of the day—for most people, that's midmorning. Study your marketplace, customer, product, and service.

That hour will place you among the more knowledgeable people in your field. But commit yourself to becoming *the most* knowledgeable person in the field.

Stay informed about changes in the needs and wants of customers. Each day, listen to and record your customers' reactions. And always *listen* and *make notes* on their requests. In fact, regular attention to this task should be part of *every* employee's job. Ask *open-ended questions* to gain information. Maintain *ongoing* interaction and *two-way* communication with customers.

The manager of a large retail store discovered four main considerations influencing parents who bought children's clothing. Value pricing, item popularity, brand selection—and *their concern that their kids would either wear out or grow out of their clothes.*

To counter that fourth consideration, the company introduced the KidVantage children's apparel program.

It offered both a wearout warranty and discounts for frequent purchases. A garment is replaced at no cost with an identical item, or a similar one of equal value, if it wears out while the child is still wearing the same size in clothing bought elsewhere. A warranty on the back of all cash register receipts guarantees the replacment.

Under the frequent-purchase program, customers receive a KidVantage card that records purchase amounts in the clothing departments. After they buy $50 in children's clothing, parents get a 10 percent discount on their next clothing purchase. A $100 purchase entitles a shopper to a 15 per-cent discount.

And the bottom line is: The company found that when customers redeemed their cards to receive their discounts, they were spending more money in the children's clothing department than they did prior to the KidVantage program.

Stanley Marcus, former chairman of Neiman Marcus specialty stores and a businessman for 50 years, says one of his pet peeves is "managing by the numbers."

"Most store managers," he says, seem to rely on the computer for all management information.

"They avoid customers. They think customer contact is a waste of time. I've walked into department stores and found buyers in their offices wearing sweat suits.

"That tells me that they have no intention of spending time on the selling floor. They spend their work hours tied to the computer screen."

Picture a room full of people typing away at computer keyboards, taking time now and again to discuss their creative ideas. They produce impressive-looking reports that include plans for new products. The trouble is that no one ever leaves the room while they are developing the product. Inevitably, these people don't know what customers *want*.
They will calculate that the wonderfulness of their new product, together with the persuasiveness of their marketing, will be all that's needed to sell it—when they don't even know if anybody wants or needs the thing.

Says Marcus: "I haven't seen a computer that can plug into a customer, ask questions about whether he's satisfied, whether merchandise and service met his expectations, and then respond to his answers. Supervisors and management-level people don't spend enough time on the selling floor to find this out. You learn by meeting customers, understanding merchandise, and observing salespeople."

A futurist once said, "If you listen to what your customer is asking for today, you will be able to track the demands of your customers in the future. Out of today's *requests* come the *demands* of tomorrow."

Let me tell you something that McDonald's did that I admire. It looked at its demographics and found that children were always coming into the drive-throughs but got confused when asked what they wanted. Of course, it is difficult for a child to think when a voice on the speaker says, "May I help you, please?"

So McDonald's put together a children's meal in a box that it called a "Happy Meal." It is only a burger, which kids usually order anyway, with an inexpensive toy, an order of fries, and a small drink. But it was a powerful idea.

The kids liked it because all they had to say was, "I want a Happy Meal." McDonald's liked it, because it made sales increase.

PAY YOUR PERFORMERS

It's critical to create a system that does more than reward the top producers for outstanding results. It is almost as important to reward average people for outstanding effort. You want to sustain people as they perform the process that leads to achievement. In a sales environment, it often pays to give weekly awards to someone who handled the toughest customer or received the most heartfelt customer compliment. Or to the employee who had the largest single transaction of the week—or the lowest transaction that required the most effort. You need to breed heroes.

KNOWLEDGE IS POWER

Whether you sell stocks and bonds or fast food, you need to define the primary market segment that is tuned most closely to the value that you offer. To determine your market segment you must (1) analyze each transaction, (2) develop a simple system

of tracking transactions, (3) compile them by definable market segment, and (4) notice which list is longest and determine how many such people actually exist who can become part of your market.

Not every person you talk to or who walks through the front door of your store is part of your market segment. The better you are at defining your most important customer and his highest need, the more successful you will be.

Know thy customer. With every fact and insight gleaned about your own buyers, you sharpen your power to profit.

Identify a Central Demographic Model (CDM) of your good customers. These are the customers who have the *greatest need* for your product and service. Who are they exactly—male, female? And what age group?

Don't Copy the Enemy . . .

When competing with low-price superstores, it is a mistake to stick signs on everything with only the price listed. You are only identifying with price-driven organizations.

Anything that suggests that you are horizontally competing with a price operation is counterproductive. If your carpet is the same color—if your uniforms have the same design and color—if your logo is similar—if your buying line indicates that you concentrate on price and not on value—then you will be competing with the price merchants. And customers will think that the *only difference* is that your prices are a little higher.

What does each type of customer buy? How *much* does he buy? How often? When? *How* does he buy—fax, catalog, mail order, walk-in? Cash, check, credit card?

Why do my customers buy from me and not somebody else? Is it quality? Price? Packaging? Variety? Location?

In today's environment it's imperative to monitor the buying frequency of your customers and calculate the average purchase. You must know how much they are spending on a typical transaction.

Not all customer demands are equal. Sales reps have what they call "A" accounts, "B" accounts, "C" accounts, and "D" accounts. You have different types of customers, and classifying them in categories is essential. It is imperative that your "A" customers receive the highest service and response. None of us is going to stay in business very long if we give marginal clients "A" attention.

In these changing times, we must serve the *best* customers, not just all customers, and realize that if a customer is not part

Exploit His Weakness!

The price merchant lowers his price to buy market share, but he can't buy loyalty. He doesn't offer credit, free delivery, unconditional guarantees, and a pleasing shopping environment. But you can.

Compete on value, keeping in stock the items your customers need, offering expert knowledge of your products, unconditional guarantees, and so on. These things are important to the customer. You set the terms: exceptional value and service. And you will thrive as long as you follow a strategy of everyday fair prices and big value.

Price merchants usually offer limited technical service for the products they sell. You, however, must offer superior service—and really brag about it. Tell the world that you carry a large inventory of parts, that your people get state-of-the-art training, and that you provide on-site servicing of products within hours of any malfunction.

of the grocery industry come from perishable departments—produce, deli, bakery, meat. Yet the items in these departments represented less than 25 percent of most stores' gross sales. That means they were virtually giving away the grocery items and the health and beauty aids.

If only one out of four customers buys from the deli and if that department makes a high profit, why spend so much time and space on grocery products? Why not reformat the store and direct the customer to spend more time with profitable perishable items? I worked with a business that had more than 3,700 customers in its database. When we analyzed buying frequency and type of buying, we found that only 600 of these customers really contributed to profit.

The implication is that we could have eliminated 50 percent of the customers without affecting the bottom line.

Local shoppers in Mike Brody's town soon realized that they had to make real sacrifices to shop at Sam's Club. The superstores are sometimes out of stock. They're in out-of-the-way locations. If you shop there, you are apt to lose money by buying the large superstore sizes and not using all their contents and by buying impulse items because they are at lower prices.

of our Central Demographic Model and doesn't buy from us, it will not hurt our feelings or our bottom line to lose him.

Many value merchants are going out of business because they spend 80 percent of their time and resources to satisfy customers who buy infrequently and spend little.

Unfortunately, they are spending only 20 percent of their time and resources on the "A" customers who want to spend more and are capable of doing so.

A major advertising agency spent so much time looking for new business that it lost its largest account. When that account left, it took with it almost a third of the agency's business. Can you imagine how much business the agency would need to get from those small accounts to equal what it lost?

Refine your sense of priorities.

Devote an hour a week to making your staff members the most knowledgeable people in your field. But this has to mean a lot more than just knowing how to locate an item. The staff should actually be able to tell customers what and why they should consider buying.

Know your product better than anybody else, because typically a premium customer will seek out the specialist for his help in making buying decisions. The jeweler gives seminars on how to select the right stone for the upcoming wedding. The bridal store acts as a consulting specialist and, while consulting with people about their weddings, sells bridal gowns. A do-it-yourself hardware store gives plumbing seminars, lawn-care seminars, woodworking seminars.

Next essential step: Focus your efforts and resources on departments that generate profit.

Understand *where* you make your profit. I was surprised some years ago to learn that more than 50 percent of the profits

It was amazing. Three years later, they were still standing—and making more money. They'd discovered their true value.

Three years after Sam came to town, the merchants are a little surprised that they're still standing up. They're like Clint Eastwood, who, after a gun battle, carefully examines himself for bullet holes and is surprised to find no wounds.

The businesses that survive in Michael Brody's town did things that Sam didn't.

A restaurant began accepting take-out orders by fax.

Superstores don't do that.

Store employees went to the offices and homes of good customers to conduct business.

Superstores don't have the time.

A pharmacy specialized in 24-hour phone service, not merely so customers could order prescriptions and sundry items, but so they could ask questions. The questions are answered by a retired physician.

Superstores can't be bothered.

The Task Force published red-and-white, pocket-size directories entitled *Value, Quality, Service: Where to Find It.* The directories itemized every service imaginable that Sam did not provide.

A few businesses have closed, but they were the ones that chose to go head-to-head with Sam's. Their closed storefronts still display signs with lower prices to show they were competing with the Club.

Retailers With a Future

Five benefits distinguish companies that compete on value.

Leonard L. Berry

America is "overstored," with too many retailers competing for too few customers. From 1968 to 1993, square footage for U.S. shopping centers increased 216%— four times the growth in retail sales during this period. Many retailers operating in America today are casualties waiting to happen, poised to be among the thousands of retail failures that occur annually in the United States (12,952 in 1995).

But it's the mediocre retailers that need to fear hypercompetition the most. High-performance retailers—retailers with a future—just keep growing while mediocre competitors, with no special competence or flair, struggle to survive. Retailers with a future know they must compete on value, not price. The single biggest mistake many of America's retailers are making today is assuming that value and price mean the same thing to consumers. They do not. Price is only a part of value.

To consumers, value is the benefits received for the burdens endured. Potential benefits include quality merchandise, caring personal service, pleasant store atmosphere, convenience, and peace-of-mind. Burdens include both monetary costs (price) and non-monetary costs, such as store employees who know little about the merchandise and don't care, slow checkout, inadequate parking facilities, and sloppy, unattractive, or poorly merchandised stores.

Retailers become, and stay, successful with a strong benefits-to-burdens offer. They maximize the most important benefits to targeted customers and minimize the most critical burdens. They compete on value, not solely on price—or not on price at all.

Gasoline is the classic commodity product, yet a minority of these customers buy strictly on price. In 1994, Copernicus, a marketing research and consulting company, did a national study of the purchase decision criteria gasoline customers use and found that only 20% simply wanted the lowest price. The other 80% wanted a reasonable price plus other benefits, such as personal service when needed, clean rest rooms, pay-at-the-pump convenience, good lighting after dark, and a convenience store on the premises.

Competing on Value

Price is price; value is the total experience. If customer service is generally poor and merchandise looks the same from one store to another, then most consumers will indeed want the lowest price because they have no reason to pay more. But offer them a fulfilling shopping experience, and you build a company with a future. That's what Home Depot does. And Victoria's Secret. And Starbucks Coffee. And Pier 1 imports. And Sears, resurrected at the 11th hour by new leadership.

> Price is price; value is the total experience.

None of these companies competes strictly on price. Home Depot gives customers the confidence to be do-it-yourselfers. Victoria's Secret turns an awkward product category once called "foundations" into a romantic, sexy category called "intimate apparel." And while Victoria's

---

EXECUTIVE *BRIEFING*

Retail failure rates are high with no relief expected. Yet, despite hypercompetition in many markets, some retailers are performing well. What they have in common is compelling value for customers created through a bundle of benefits that outweighs shopping burdens. Retailers who offer a dominant merchandise assortment, fair prices, respect for customers, time and energy savings, and fun can engender the type of loyalty that secures their future.

 Reprinted with permission from *Marketing Management*, Spring 1996, pp. 39-46. © 1996 by the American Marketing Association.

Secret was reinventing lingerie as a fashion category, Starbucks was transforming coffee into a fashion beverage. With exciting products from all over the world, Pier 1 turns each store visit into an adventure. And Sears didn't jump-start its comeback with a price message; it invited consumers to try the "softer side of Sears."

Retailers with a future are led by executives who have a good answer to the question: "What do we want to be famous for with customers?" Great retailers are famous with customers for delivering a valuable bundle of benefits, a bundle that customers depend on receiving. Competitors might match the prices, but they won't be able to duplicate the entire bundle.

To compete on value, retailers need to include at least five types of benefits in their bundles: (1) a dominant merchandise assortment, (2) fair prices, (3) respect for customers, (4) time and energy savings, and (5) fun (see Exhibit 1).

Dominant Assortments

One of the most powerful forces for change in retailing is the emergence of category killers—retailers that stock a complete merchandise assortment for the category in which they compete. Category killers like CompUSA, Office Depot, and Bed Bath and Beyond offer consumers a one-stop shopping alternative to limited-assortment competitors. In effect, the influence of category killers has raised customers' expectations of retail merchandising practices.

The used-car lot with 50 or 75 vehicles for sale is acceptable until the customer experiences CarMax, which offers over 500 used cars. The mall bookstore with 15,000-20,000 titles is just fine until a book lover experiences a Barnes & Noble superstore with more than 100,000 titles. The department store appears to have an adequate lingerie selection until Victoria's Secret opens in the same mall and presents new possibilities. The traditional pet store with a few thousand stockkeeping units looks and feels like a pet store is supposed to look and feel until a Petsmart store arrives in the market with 25,000 square feet of bright, airy shopping space, 12,000 SKUs, an in-store kiosk offering an additional 80,000 SKUs, and a full complement of in-store services, including pet grooming, a veterinarian clinic, and a pet adoption center.

Retailers with a future invest in category dominance with maximum merchandise breadth and depth for their chosen business. They don't just dominate with vast assortments but dramatize their dominance with sensory merchandising, interactive technology, unique departments, and special services. When consumers enter Victoria's Secret, they experience an impressive visual display of merchandise, sensuous aroma, and the sounds of the London Philharmonic Orchestra. At CarMax, customers sit down at a computer with a salesperson to identify the cars on the lot that meet their specifications. Not only does CompUSA sell more

than 200 children's software titles, it also designed a special Compkids section where children play with computers and sample the software.

Retailers with a future use assortment dominance to generate in-store excitement, offer so much merchandise that customers can comparison shop without going to another store, and commit to the best in-stock performance of all competitors. And, by carrying goods and services complementary to the core line, they sell a total solution to the customer's problem. Home Depot, for example, sells material for building a deck, the know-how to build it, and the plants and fertilizer to landscape it.

Becoming an assortment dominator is more about attitude than store size or format. A 3,000-square-foot bookstore can reinvent itself as a seller of children's books, videos, and educational toys and become an assortment dominator. The attitude is that no competitor will have a better selection—or present it in a more compelling manner. Sears currently is expanding separate specialty store chains to sell furniture and hardware, a strategy that frees up more of the existing department store space for apparel and housewares—the "softer side of Sears." The specialty store strategy is enabling Sears to achieve more assortment dominance in both soft goods and hard goods.

Assortment dominators are top-of-the mind, first-choice outlets for one or more categories of merchandise. Although specialists in every category they feature, they are not necessarily specialty stores in the traditional sense. They are killers—big-store killers, medium-store killers, small-store killers, catalog killers—no matter what the case.

Pricing Fairness

Many retailers today engage in unfair and confusing pricing practices that erode their credibility and drain profits. The three-level "strawman" pricing scheme is typical of such practices: A phony "regular price" to be quickly lowered, the "sale price" at which most of the merchandise is expected to be sold, and deeper markdowns to clear slow-selling merchandise. In one survey, 75% of respondents said department stores purposely priced merchandise high only to mark it down for an advertised sale. Retailers with a future reject trickery and price products at an everyday level that represents good value for customers. Their prices earn the customer's trust, not destroy it.

Pricing fairness does not necessarily mean the *lowest* price. Even though some successful retailers promise everyday lowest prices in their promotions, very few companies can actually employ this strategy because it requires a cost structure significantly lower than that of competitors. And most executives know they can't back up this kind of promise because a competitor with a lower price always lurks around the corner. In his book, *Customers for Life*, automobile retailer Carl

Sewell claims that someone can always charge a dollar less—because they are smarter than you and control their costs better, or dumber than you and don't know what their costs are.

Instead, most retailers with a future follow the principles of everyday *fair* pricing:

• Most of the merchandise is sold at regular (non-sale) prices that represent a good value for customers. The retailer strips waste from operations and gives customers their money's worth.

• Sales promotion events are legitimate, meaning that the merchandise on sale is marked down from its regular price, rather than being marked down from an inflated, phony price.

• Prices are easy for customers to understand. They are communicated in a simple, straightforward manner without any hidden charges.

Taco Bell, which brought value pricing to the fast-food sector, is an everyday fair-pricer. Taco Bell's strategy is to offer the best value fast meal whenever and wherever customers are hungry. To implement this strategy, Taco Bell discarded traditional business approaches that gave the consumer only 27¢ worth of food for each dollar. Through machine-made tacos, off-site production, more training, more empowerment, and less employee supervision, Taco Bell now gives its customers more than 40¢ worth of food per dollar.

In a recent speech, Taco Bell chairman John Martin explained: "Imagine a dollar bill. If consumers give you 100 pennies, what do they get back? They get 27¢ worth of food, 8¢ worth of advertising, 13¢ worth of overhead, 11¢-12¢ worth of occupancy costs, and so on. We say, instead of giving them 27¢ worth of food, let's give them 40¢ worth of food. If you're going to do that, then you've got to get this other stuff down. Of this other stuff, what is important to customers and what is not?"

EXHIBIT 1

Retailers with a future

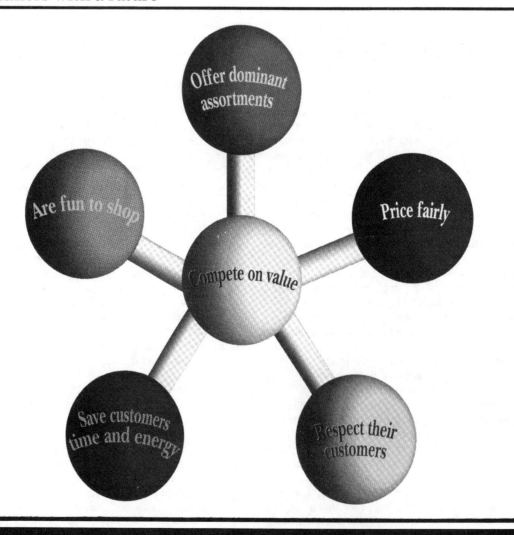

As recently as 1990, Taco Bell assigned one supervising manager for every five restaurants. Multiple field management layers have since been eliminated and today supervising managers are responsible for 30 or more points of distribution. Store construction and operating costs have been significantly reduced by centralizing food preparation and reconfiguring restaurants from 70% kitchen/30% seating to 70% seating/30% kitchen.

Everyday fair pricing works best in conjunction with other strong benefits. Barnes & Noble superstores have a dominant book assortment, architecturally innovative store designs, spacious and comfortable interiors, responsive customer service, front-of-store parking convenience, coffee bars, and fair pricing. The pricing is straightforward, typically 10% off the publisher's list price on all hardback books, 20% off paperbacks on the *New York Times* bestseller list, and 30% off hardbacks on the *Times* list.

Respect for Customers

Having formally studied quality of service in America for more than 12 years, I am convinced that a *customer-respect deficit* exists in U.S. service businesses, including retailing. Customers are the lifeblood of every retail company, yet all too often they are treated badly. Something as basic as respect can influence a company's competitiveness because it sends a clear message to customers: Respectful service signals customers that a company is worthy of their loyalty; disrespectful service signals that they should take their business elsewhere.

The sidebar on the next page presents 10 of the most common complaints customers express about service firms. Each of these is linked to disrespect—from cheating customers ("True Lies") to ignoring them ("Misplaced Priorities"). Disrespectful service is so common that customers notice, and remember, when a company treats them well. Retailers with a future respect their customers' time, desire for a courteous, professional service experience, and demand for fair treatment.

Some retailers treat customers as if they were houseguests. They prepare for their guests' arrival, plan special surprises to delight their guests, and make their guests feel welcome and comfortable. By investing in respectful service and making it a priority, retailers with a future turn a business basic into a customer draw.

Tattered Cover. One of America's most successful independent book retailers, Tattered Cover operates two stores in Denver. The main store is in a four-story, 40,000-square-foot building. Customers love this store because it feels like home, with wooden bookshelves, antique furniture and desks, and "151 comfy chairs and couches," as one employee puts it. Customers are encouraged to touch the books and may sit and read all day if they wish. They can sit in a church pew in the religion section and relax on a psychiatrist's couch in the psychology section.

Tattered Cover's culture is to put customer and book together. On a slow day, Tattered Cover will handle 300 special orders; on a fast day, up to 650. "Diligence and doggedness are what we do best," says owner Joyce Meskis. "We search for the elusive title wanted by the customer." General manager Linda Millemann adds: "We have always been willing to special order. Managers from other stores say, 'Well, you are big enough to do that,' but that is how we got big."

The company's employees are trained to be nonjudgmental about customers' purchases. "People buy sensitive books. It's the customer's right to read what he or she wants," floor manager Sidney Jackson explains. This nonjudgmental attitude is reinforced by the wide variety of publications in stock—about 220,000 different books and approximately 1,300 newspapers and magazines.

Tattered Cover's competitive advantage is the atmosphere of trust and community that pervades the stores. Check-writing customers are not asked to furnish identification and all employees get a key to the store on their first day of work. Meskis started this practice in 1974 when she bought the store and continues it to this day, even though the company now has more than 400 employees. The key symbolizes to employees that Tattered Cover is their store. Employees also are allowed to borrow any of the books in inventory, a policy that creates more informed floor personnel and symbolizes complete trust.

The respect shown employees encourages the respect they provide to customers, which fosters intense loyalty to the store. Indeed, it is the way human beings are treated at Tattered Cover that sets this retail company apart.

Royers' Round Top Cafe. Round Top, Texas, a town with 88 residents, is not exactly a prime setting for a retail success story. Yet, Royers', a 38-seat restaurant, attracts 300–400 customers on a typical Saturday, many of whom travel from Houston, 80 miles away. The draw is wonderful food, world-class pies (it's a nickel extra if you don't have ice cream with the pie), and respectful service.

Customers wait for their tables on the front porch, where they help themselves to beer and wine on the honor system. Once seated, customers are never rushed through the meal. "Eating is an event that should be enjoyable and relaxing," says owner Bud Royer. "I absolutely will not let the floors be swept until the customers at the last table walk out the door. I don't want that last table to feel like we are rushing them because we want to go home."

The restaurant accepts no credit cards but does not turn away customers without cash.

The customer eats, takes the bill home, and mails in a check. No one has failed to pay the bill yet. The customer-respect deficit in retailing creates an opening for retail companies that are prepared to treat customers well. Size-of-company is not important; size-of-commitment is. To assess your company's commitment, consider the "Customer Respect Checklist."

Save Customers Time and Energy

Studies consistently report that consumers perceive their free time is dwindling. In a series of studies by the Americans' Use of Time Project, national samples of adults were asked whether they "always," "sometimes," or "almost never" felt rushed to do the things they have to do. In the 1992 survey, 38% of the sample indicated they "always" felt rushed, up from 32% in 1985 and 22% in 1971. The perception of time poverty is greatest for consumers who combine work, marriage, and parenthood. In the latest study, nearly two out of three working mothers (64%) reported always feeling rushed.

Perceived time scarcity contributes to stress. In a 1991 survey by Hilton Hotels, 43% of the sample agreed that they often feel under stress when they do not have enough time. In the 1993 National Study of the Changing Workforce, 80% of respondents said their jobs require them to work very hard, 65% said they must work very fast, and 42% said they feel "used up" by the end of the day. From a 1994 study reported in *American Demographics* comes the finding that 60% of Americans feel under great stress at least once a week, and 19% feel this way almost every day.

Too little time and too much stress have a negative impact on personal energy levels, which is not conducive to a leisurely visit to the shopping mall. Consumers now visit malls less frequently and visit fewer stores in less time when they do go. A 1994 national poll conducted by Maritz Marketing Research found that one-third of adult shoppers reported shopping at malls less frequently than just a year earlier, citing limited money and time as the main reasons.

Yankelovich Partners asked consumers in a survey what they would do on a free Saturday or Sunday. Sixty-nine percent said they would watch television and 46% said they would take a nap. A hidden competitor for stores is the increasingly appealing idea of staying home. In Yankelovich's annual *Monitor* study, consumers are asked what is important in deciding where to shop. "Makes it easy to shop" was rated important by 55% of the respondents in 1988 and by 67% in 1993.

Retailers with a future save customers time and energy. They invest in making their stores easy to get to and easy to get through and/or making shopping possible without going to a store at all. They compete on convenience, offering maximum access, one-stop or no-stop shopping, logical store design, quick transactions, and no-hassle returns.

Common Customer Service Complaints

True Lies: Blatant dishonesty or unfairness, such as service providers selling unneeded services or purposely quoting fake, "low-ball" cost estimates.

Red Alert: Providers who assume customers are stupid or dishonest and treat them harshly or disrespectfully.

Broken Promises: Service providers who do not show up as promised. Careless, mistake-prone service.

I Just Work Here: Powerless employees who lack the authority—or the desire—to solve basic customer problems.

The Big Wait: Waiting in a line made long because some of the checkout lanes or service counters are closed.

Automatic Pilot: Impersonal, emotionless, no-eye-contact, going-through-the-motions non-service.

Suffering in Silence: Employees who don't bother to communicate with customers who are anxious to hear how a service problem will be resolved.

Don't Ask: Employees unwilling to make any extra effort to help customers, or who seem put-out by requests for assistance.

Lights On, No One Home: Clueless employees who do not know (i.e., will not take the time to learn) the answers to customers' common questions.

Misplaced Priorities: Employees who visit with each other or conduct personal business while the customer waits. Those who refuse to assist a customer because they're off duty or on a break.

—Len Berry

Walgreen. With nearly $500 in sales per square foot (compared to the drugstore industry average of $300), the country's largest drugstore chain focuses on making its stores easy to get to and get through. Walgreen's targeted customer is the high-frequency shopper who visits a drugstore more than five times a month. Although these shoppers represent just 10% of the population, they account for 50% of Walgreen's sales.

High-frequency customers buy general merchandise as well as pharmaceuticals in drugstores, and the key to attracting them is convenience. Walgreen's strategy is to blanket markets with freestanding stores that are easily accessible—stores on the "corner of Main and Main"—and

Customer Respect Checklist

✔ Do we trust our customers? Do we operate our business to effectively serve the vast majority of customers who are honest, or to protect ourselves from the small minority who are not?

✔ Do we stand behind what we sell? Are we easy to do business with if a customer experiences a problem with our offerings? Do we have a sense of urgency to make the customer whole? Are front-line employees empowered to respond appropriately to a problem? Do we guarantee the goods we sell? Do we guarantee our service?

✔ Do we stress promise-keeping in our company? Is keeping commitments to customers—from being in-stock on advertised goods to being on time for appointments—deemed important in our company?

✔ Do we value our customers' time? Do we anticipate periods of maximum demand for our offerings and staff accordingly to minimize customer waiting? Are our facilities and service systems convenient and efficient for customers to use? Do we prepare new employees to provide efficient, effective service before putting them in front of customers? Do we teach employees that serving customers supersedes all other priorities, such as paperwork or stocking shelves?

✔ Do we communicate with customers respectfully? Are our signs informative and helpful? Are our statements clear and understandable? Is our advertising above reproach in its truthfulness and taste? Are our contact personnel professional in appearance and manner? Does our language convey respect, such as "I will be happy to do this" and "It will be my pleasure?" Do we answer and return telephone calls promptly—and with a smile in our voice? Is our voice-mail system caller-friendly?

✔ Do we respect all customers? Do we treat all customers with respect, regardless of their appearance, age, race, status, or size of purchase or account? Have we taken any special precautions to minimize discriminatory treatment of certain customers?

✔ Do we thank customers for their business? Do we say "thank you" at times other than after a purchase? Do our customers feel appreciated?

✔ Do we respect our employees? Do our human resources policies and practices pass the employee-respect test? Do our employees, who are expected to respect customers, experience respectful treatment themselves? Would employees want their children to work in our company when they grow up?

—Len Berry

---

provide ample parking, drive-through pharmacy windows, wide aisles, low shelves, excellent in-store signage, and scanner-based checkouts.

Intercom, a satellite-based computer system linking all Walgreen stores, maintains customers prescription records for timely use in emergencies. Where state law allows, customers can obtain a refill at any Walgreen's store. A customer living in Texas who forgets her medicine on a trip to Arizona need only visit an Arizona store for a refill. Walgreen's customers can reach a pharmacist 24 hours a day via a toll-free 800 number, and the company will send the prescription via overnight mail. Through Intercom, Walgreen can provide a patient's prescription records to hospital emergency rooms 24 hours a day, seven days a week.

Once the customer's name, address, and prescription information are put into the Intercom system, a label and receipt are printed automatically. Refills require no new information, and Intercom can supply customers a printout of prescription purchases for their tax and insurance records. Walgreen is currently rolling out Intercom Plus, its "next generation" pharmacy system that will improve customer service and productivity further and enable pharmacists to provide more counseling to patients.

Fun to Shop

Consumers who are selective in their shopping choices are unlikely to spend time in undifferentiated and lackluster stores. Retail dullness—merchandise sameness, boring displays, worn and tired stores, and/or an absence of in-store events—is a losing strategy in today's and tomorrow's marketplace.

The pace of sensory stimulation is so great today that many consumers are easily bored. Their reality is global travel, 50-plus television channels in the home, multimedia computers, on-line access to virtually any kind of material on the Internet, innovative marketing campaigns from companies such as Nike, and innovative retailing from companies such as Warner Brothers Studio Stores. Consumers today are used to being entertained and they expect it in exchange for their time, effort, and money. As the worlds of retailing and entertainment continue to merge, dull retailers will fade into oblivion.

Whether selling computers or cars, food or footwear, books or bracelets, retailers with a future make shopping fresh, stimulating, and exciting. They keep new merchandise flowing into the store so regular shoppers can always discover something new. They directly appeal to the customers' appetite for sensory adventure, entertain customers while they educate them, and dazzle them with the dramatic.

West Point Market. An outstanding specialty food store in Akron, Ohio, that has been in business nearly 60 years, West Point Market is the quintessential sensory retailer. Flowers are everywhere: in front of the store, in the parking lot, at the store entrance, in the aisles. The property has more than 80 trees, the delivery truck is painted with dancing vegetables, merchandise signs are hand-drawn in soft colors by an artist, exits are marked by hand-carved wooden signs, and colorful balloons decorate the entire store. And there's more:

• Information and recipe tags on West Point's shelves educate shoppers on how to use the products: "This creamy mild cheese with caraway seeds slices well for ham sandwiches on hearty rye."

• The market's "Customers of Tomorrow" program includes kiddie shopping carts and cookie credit cards (good for a free cookie on each store visit).

• Rest rooms feature classical music, almond soap, indirect lighting, and, of course, fresh flowers.

• Product tasting and in-store demonstrations are common. As many as four events—one chef cooking pasta, another preparing salsa recipes, and another preparing a cold pasta with a new avocado dressing, plus a bread sampling table—might occur simultaneously on a Saturday.

Everyone in this store is smiling—customers and employees alike—because West Point Market makes food shopping fun.

The Container Store. A highly successful chain based in Dallas, The Container Store sells merchandise designed to help people organize their homes and their lives. Every conceivable product to bring efficiency to a kitchen, organize a closet, or tidy an office is available at The Container Store. There is no "back of the store" here; every corner is beautifully merchandised. Employees sit in the store aisles assembling components into finished products while customers gather around to watch, chat, and learn more about the product. Unique merchandise, a bright and airy decor, live product demonstrations, and happy, helpful employees all make The Container Store fun for shoppers.

Barnes & Noble. Customers frequently take their time strolling through this bookseller's superstores, perusing the well-stocked magazine section, sitting in a chair to read or people-watch, enjoying a coffee at the in-store Starbucks, perhaps meeting a friend, and then finally purchasing some books. At Barnes & Noble, customers can have a literary and social experience in one store visit.

In a 1995 speech, Leonard Riggio, Barnes & Noble chief executive said "The store is the principal message. Too many retailers devote too much attention to advertising, instead of creating great stores.... Bookstores never again will be considered sleepy places." Poverty of time and energy is not an issue for Barnes & Noble because shopping these stores is not a chore; the company sells a product—books—that offers busy consumers a sense of stability and relaxation in stores that are entertaining.

Value Compels

Surviving hypercompetition in American retailing requires an unprecedented level of strategic and operating excellence. Only the fittest of America's retailers can feel any security whatsoever about the future. Retail fitness is defined by the value delivered to customers. Value is not price, nor is it one of anything else; value is a compelling bundle of benefits well worth the customers' money, time, and effort.

America's consumers, increasingly selective and expectant, can find many sources of compelling retail value. They have no reason to patronize mediocre retailers that offer nothing special. Every retailer needs to ask and honestly answer this question: If our company were to disappear from the landscape overnight, would customers really miss us? For retailers with a future, the answer is a resounding "yes." Like salt, they have no satisfying substitute.

About the Author

Leonard L. Berry holds the JCPenney Chair of Retailing Studies, is Professor of Marketing and Director of the Center for Retailing Studies in the College of Business Administration at Texas A&M University, College Station. He is also editor of the "Arthur Andersen Retailing Issues Letter" and was AMA President for 1986-87. His books include: *On Great Service: A Framework for Action* (New York: The Free Press, 1995); *Delivering Quality Service: Balancing Customer Perceptions and Expectations* (New York: The Free Press, 1990); *Marketing Services: Competing Through Quality* (New York: The Free Press, 1991); and *Service Quality-A Profit Strategy for Financial Institutions* (Homewood, IL: Business One Irwin, 1989). Len has twice won the highest honor Texas A&M bestows on a faculty member: the Distinguished Achievement Award in Teaching (in 1990) and the Distinguished Achievement Award in Research (in 1996). He is a member of the board of directors of CompUSA and Hastings Books, Music, and Video Inc. In 1995, he was elected as a public member of the board of directors for the Council of Better Business Bureaus.

M A R K E T I N G The giant chains are
the hottest channel in retail, and they can
take even tiny consumer-product makers
national overnight. But getting onto their
shelves isn't easy, and staying there is harder
still. How do you do it? Here's an inside look
at one company's 15-week campaign

Selling the Superstores

Susan Greco

Las Vegas, January 7—*It's Saturday, the second day of the Consumer Electronics Show. In the wake of an unpredictable holiday season, John Koss Jr., sales vice-president of Koss Corp., is receiving mixed signals from the major retail buyers here. Home entertainment has been white-hot for the big stores, but lately sales of some Koss audio products have turned cold.*

Koss is anxious as he enters a cramped exhibit room for a 5:15 meeting with Target, a $13-billion chain of more than 600 stores. This is one of his biggest mass-merchant accounts, carrying 10 stock-keeping units (SKUs), or models, worth $2 million.

The tension is palpable. Teri Kohler is an influential buyer who has championed Koss headphones back at Target's Minneapolis headquarters, but you'd never know that at this meeting. She smiles rarely and squelches small talk. Koss, for his part, keeps his arms crossed. He'll admit afterward, "I'm still not as comfortable with her as I'd like."

Koss knows that Koss Corp.'s revenues and margins are down, owing in part to disappointing sales to some large retailers. So Kohler's receptiveness is crucial. Will she go for the new products displayed in the Koss booth? Will she at least keep the current Koss mix? Will she continue to force Koss's prices down?

Koss listens closely for clues. If the Koss line fared well over the holidays, he'll survive the downturn and come back strong in 1995. And if not, well, he's in trouble.

Koss Corp.'s five largest customers, including Target, kick in about 40% of annual sales. A powerful group of mega-retailers—comprising electronics superstores, discount department stores, and catalog showrooms—accounts for well over 75% of Koss Corp.'s revenues.

Koss will meet with many of those accounts at the Consumer Electronics Show (known as CES), the inauguration of the year's whirlwind sales campaign. By April the buyers will have locked in their choices and completed their storewide "planagrams," the master merchandising diagrams that top retailers use to maintain chainwide consistency.

Koss's success at CES will affect Koss Corp.'s sales, brand visibility, and efficiencies on the factory floor—not to mention the company's ability to retain quality sales reps, fund product development, and keep its bankers happy.

Koss Corp., a second-generation family business, had for many years concentrated its sales efforts on independent hi-fi stores. But when, eight years ago, the company emerged from Chapter 11, it set off with a distribution blueprint that focused on the biggest mass merchants.

The move was a calculated gamble. The Koss brothers, sales vice-president John, 38, and chief executive Michael, 41, mapped out the strategy together. Oh, they had to deal with objections from Dad (John Koss Sr., inventor of

stereo headphones) and with the exacting demands of the so-called power retailers, but the brothers have not regretted their decision. "It puts our 'phones on more people's heads," says Michael.

Koss Corp. is profitable, has plenty of cash, and recently surpassed $35 million in annual sales, up from $26 million two years ago. Thanks in part to accounts like Wal-Mart and Target, each worth an easy million or two, "The Chapter"—as employees refer to that period in bankruptcy court—is ancient history.

"I cannot imagine starting fresh without these accounts," says John Koss. "If you don't get a Wal-Mart or a Kmart, you have to go regional."

Valley of the Giants

They don't call 'em power retailers for nothing.

Today mass merchandisers book about 40% of all U.S. retail sales, and none of them cast a longer shadow than the discount retailers. By popular estimates, the top discounters—chains with 50 stores or more—book 11% to 13% of all retail sales (second only to supermarkets) even though they account for less than 3% of all retail establishments. Discount-store sales have grown two to three times faster than the retail industry as a whole.

Discount retailers define themselves by just one rule: Bigger is better. The average store covers more than 86,000 square feet. And Wal-Mart, with some of the biggest stores, is in every state but Vermont, has more than 2,100 stores, and rang up $83 billion in 1994 sales. Having conquered many of America's small towns, Sam Walton's creation is now moving into the big cities—along with Target, Kmart, and such specialty stores, or "category killers," as Office Depot, Toys 'R' Us, and Home Depot. Winning shelf space from any of those giants is cause for celebration. Business with the chains, easily worth hundreds of thousands of dollars to several million dollars in sales, can take you national overnight.

But it's not the potentially huge sales alone that make the power retailers so attractive. As Koss points out, their numerous outlets "are the best product advertising. People can see your product and try it." Koss Corp. is betting that customers who have its low-end headphones will trade up during a visit to, say, Tower Records, where music lovers check out Koss headphones at the listening stations. Couple that experience with Koss's guarantee, and chances are, Koss wins customers for life. And it all begins at…Wal-Mart or Sears or Target.

Or Kmart. John Koss lost that account several years ago. Should he recover it, in one fell swoop Koss headphones would ship out to at least 1,700 stores.

But how do you win the hearts of the superstore buyers? To start, you need a great product priced to move rapidly. The Koss product line, once reserved for audio aficionados, has expanded to cover a wide range of price points and products, including PC accessories. You must have catchy packaging. John Koss is always trying to improve the company's point-of-sale displays. Don't neglect your office systems: Wal-Mart, Target, and other large chains don't write paper orders these days; electronic data interchange (EDI) is a must that Koss has had in place only since 1993. And you'd best deliver. It's not unusual for power retailers to expect turnaround in three to five days. And, Koss says, "you can't ship Wal-Mart short, or they cancel the order."

To get your foot in most doors, you'll need well-heeled sales reps hitting the pavement. But as important as reps are to certain chains, some chains, like Wal-Mart, all but ban reps. Those chains want to talk directly with company owners. *You.*

Working the Crowd

LAS VEGAS, JANUARY 6— *"Please stay at the booth,"* John Koss implores his older brother as the doors open at the Consumer Electronics Show. *"I have three appointments all coming at 2."* Mike is dying to walk the floor, but John calls the shots here.

A half dozen independent reps work the booth at all times. Some wait anxiously for buyers to show up for appointments; others wait anxiously because they have no appointments scheduled. The best reps are wanted for booth duty at several vendors' exhibits. That's why you don't see all that much of Koss Corp.'s top three rep firms: House of Representatives, based in Sudbury, Mass.; Consumer Sales, in Chicago; and Triad, out of Eden Prairie, Minn. With vendors competing for the reps' time, it was hard work getting 50 of those reps to the sales meeting the night before at Anthony's restaurant, in Las Vegas. Koss Corp.'s marketing team mailed no fewer than four clever, timed-release invitations to each rep. A $70 Lands' End jacket was the prize for attending. The theme: "Take the chill out of cold calling."

The convergence of audio, video, and

How to Court the Power Retailers

The power retailers are all the same—and all different. In the absence of a rule book, we offer commonsense approaches:

Take names. Ask around to identify absolutely the right contact at corporate headquarters. State your case on your own or with the aid of independent reps. And *don't* go above the buyer's head. Marty Burks, a buyer for Sears, is blunt: "If they don't know whom to get the information to, they're not going to get any consideration from me."

Leave your name. "You'll make six phone calls before you get a call back," Best Buy merchandising manager Bob Griffin warns. But "if a sales rep is a pest," he cautions, "that can definitely hurt."

Get help. Don't underestimate the value of a few good rep firms—they eat rejection for breakfast. When you reach buyers, ask them for reps' names, but don't put them on the spot. Your company should be "rep friendly," but distributors and rack jobbers can also open stores' doors.

You oughta be in show biz. Trade shows are excellent places to be "discovered" or to meet the buyers with whom you've been playing phone tag. "I like to see people we'd otherwise never be exposed to," says Target buyer Teri Kohler.

Make your pitch. Be opportunistic. "A lot of it is the pitch," agrees Best Buy's Griffin. What impresses? Knowledge of the competition and the consumer. "If you're not customer driven, nothing else matters."

Watch the details. Follow-up is everything. Send out what you've promised. Pronto. After a trade show "there are a hundred people you have to see," asserts Jeff Martin, a onetime sales manager at Koss who now heads his own rep firm, House of Representatives. Be ready—with promotional ideas and an advertising allowance—for that next call from Wal-Mart.

Get the first order. This is a test and only a test. How you handle the initial order defines your product's nationwide rollout. One power retailer gave Lisa Frank, CEO of a Tucson arts-and-crafts business, a huge first order and requested immediate turnaround. "We scrambled," Frank recalls. The retailer did delay the ship date, but only after Frank met the deadline.

Get the next order. "Initial orders don't mean anything," states Jeff Martin. John Stone, president of Opus, agrees. Product innovation and snazzy packaging "got us in the door," says the Bellingham, Mass., manufacturer of bird feeders. "What you do beyond that is what keeps you in." Stone has invested close to $100,000 in technology to meet retailers' inventory needs.

computer technology generates a hopeful (and loud) buzz on the floor of the cavernous Las Vegas Convention Center. Koss has aptly chosen to play up its noise-cancellation headphones. The brothers want their booth to state clearly that even in a mature market, Koss is still innovating. "Welcome to the Quiet Zone," says the banner, promising a needed respite from the relentless techno beat.

"CES is the most grandiose version of all the meetings" between buyer and seller, says Bob Griffin, a merchandising manager at Best Buy. Everyone at CES is jockeying for position. "Lots of our VPs and regional managers go to CES," continues Griffin, "and they can see what we go through as merchants." John Koss is truly a resource to the overloaded buyers. That's why one sales rep, Lynn Biter, is so upset when one of his accounts doesn't appear for a morning appointment. "Johnny can tell them what's good, what to order," says Biter. "He could teach them the business."

The Kmart and Wal-Mart buyers won't make appointments; Koss can only hope they'll make a pit stop at his booth. Anyway, buyers who do set times often fail to show. Everyone is routinely late. It's an expensive waiting game.

The show serves also as a forum for unfinished business. Dan Lemon, the buyer for the 205-outlet Army and Airforce Exchange Services, chides Koss about a late shipment, though he concedes, "Koss does a good job."

Koss takes criticism in stride. "It's almost better if you've made a mistake," he says. "Because then they get to see how you react." Bob Norris, the buyer from Ames, a New England chain, remarks that getting an extra Koss speaker "messed up my planogram." The planogram is the buyer's bible. In this case, Koss Corp. was lucky and gained an SKU from its error. While a small chain or an independent store might decide overnight to stock a product, power retailers have little such flexibility. They make decisions by March and April for the rest of the year. If your product's not on the planogram, you're generally out of luck until next year.

Inventory turnover outweighs most other measures of success in these circles, and CES presents an opportunity for Koss to probe his products' sales performance. "Christmas was good," says Kyle Turner as Koss and two sales reps take their places in the meeting room. Turner buys video and audio accessories for Blockbuster Music, a chain of more than 100 super-

stores. But he brings a mixed message: he wants cheaper models, at $20 or so, from Koss. "Forty dollars is too much for an advertised item," the buyer says.

Koss taps quietly into his Hewlett-Packard pocket computer. "Will Blockbuster Music pick up any new brands?" he inquires.

"No," says Turner. "We don't need to have the world's selection."

Koss pushes. "Are you eliminating any Sony SKUs?"

Actually, Turner shares with Koss, he may add some low-end Sony models in the $10-to-$20 range.

That's the kind of tip Koss has been waiting for. Sony already controls about half the headphone market and threatens to gobble up more. To retain his shelf space, Koss must be more competitive on the low end. In recent years mass merchants have consolidated product selection and reduced the number of suppliers they feature. Koss Corp. has found itself odd man out on several occasions. That's how Koss lost Kmart and, last year, Circuit City. Since then, the company has worked furiously to expand its line and price points. Headphones priced higher than $19 seem pricey to buyers whose stores carry stripped-down versions for $3.

One afternoon, as both brothers head for closed-door meetings, three buyers from Wal-Mart Canada arrive—unannounced, with no appointment. Other buyers, less important to Koss's future, are kept waiting. When that happens, the marketing team squirms. "These buyers are used to seeing the top guy," explains a staffer.

At times John Koss, the middle child who's everybody's pal, doesn't always know when to stop talking. That's evident when he and Michael meet Nancy Prasek, the buyer from Lowe's, a $6.1-billion home-building chain in the Southeast, a region where Koss Corp. is weak. "We've been trying to get in there for years," Michael whispers.

Prasek says she has time to look at only a few models, but John Koss walks her through the entire line of some 40 products. She glares at her watch. The rep assures her, "We really want your business!"

"You do?" she responds with mock amazement.

Some buyers are not bowled over at meeting CEOs and sales managers. Target's Teri Kohler is another who seems to care little for titles.

When Michael breezes into the Target meeting, the buyer is unimpressed. "My wife loves Target," the CEO says,

pronouncing it in mock French, *Tarzhay*. She smiles, barely, as in "So?"

The meeting includes the Triad sales rep and Koss manager Lenore Lillie, who was assigned to the account after striking a rapport with Kohler.

Kohler notes that sales of Koss products are down at Target but declines to specify models. She complains that Koss still owes her 1994 product-rebate dollars. And, oh yes, did she mention that Target ran out of stock on a popular headphone? It's almost an aside, but Lillie nearly chokes on the news.

Still, Kohler is not all cold water. She likes the new SportClip model—which does away with the headband—but not its $35 price tag. She invites Koss to submit a quote. Kohler must wrap up her planogram by mid-February, so the group agrees to reconvene in three weeks at Target's Minneapolis headquarters.

Koss types into his computer. The deadline doesn't leave much time to work on pricing and packaging.

MILWAUKEE, JANUARY 20— *"I have never been so walking dead,"* says John Koss, finally back in his office. *"It felt like everyone who came through the booth wanted to talk business. Unlike past years."*

He's putting CES into perspective. "My goal was to gain a feeling for the attitude

Superpower Summit: A Lexicon

The power retailers. Wal-Mart, Kmart, and Target combined operate more than 5,000 stores and account for 80% of sales among 42 discount-department-store chains.

Category killers. Specialty retailers like Home Depot, Office Depot, Toys 'R' Us, and Best Buy have seen their influence expand faster than you can say Newt Gingrich. In 1993 the category killers' sales were up 19.9%.

Regional discount department stores. After years of consolidation and brushes with bankruptcy, regional chains have revived. The strongest—Caldor, Ames, Bradlees, Venture, Hills, and ShopKo—kicked in nearly $12 billion in 1993 sales.

Warehouse clubs. Their popularity waxes and wanes. PriceCostco and Sam's Warehouse Club lead the pack.

Supercenters. Wal-Mart, Kmart, Target, and others operate warehouselike stores combining food and general merchandise; they stretch out to 100,000 or 200,000 square feet.

of the buyers. If they're optimistic about Koss and Christmas, we can expect business to grow."

He's in a quandary over the pricing conundrum with Target. "She wants a higher average retail price," he notes. Yet she's wary of taking a chance on the untested SportClip. "I'll put it on a string for her if she likes." Huh? "I'll take it right back if it doesn't sell."

Koss takes his relationships with buyers seriously. "I used to get depressed when he didn't come to the booth," he says, talking about Kmart buyer Tom Hooks, who won't acknowledge having been at CES. Still, at Hooks's request, Koss promptly mails new-product information—and waits. "Your chances are better than 50-50," the buyer tells him.

But Koss has no time to dwell on disappointment. In the month after CES, the sales chief crisscrosses the country, appealing to buyers on their own turf: from San Francisco to Minneapolis, and from Delray Beach, Fla., to Dallas, to Richmond, Va., to Nashville. Valentine's Day finds him in Chicago. He calls on the Good Guys! (a rising San Francisco-based electronics chain), Software Etc., Target, Office Depot, Circuit City, the Army and Airforce Exchange, Brendle's, and Sears. Wal-Mart Canada requests a quote, and Koss puts a note in his computer to plan a trek to Ontario.

Koss's reps are also working the phones and hitting the road. Within weeks of CES, Triad has landed Koss Corp. a new account. An ambitious young rep, Steve "Slammer" Stamy, placed seven SKUs at Minneapolis-based Media Play, a hot new superstore for books, music, electronics, and sports apparel.

John Koss can't say enough about Triad's contacts. "They know who's who in the zoo when buyers change," he says. "They're located in a retail mecca. Software Etc., Best Buy, Musicland, and Target are all in their territory. They know five or six buyers at Target."

You Can't Just Do It Yourself

"Reps are a conduit," suggests Best Buy's Bob Griffin. "They don't make anything, so they get a bad reputation. But a good rep, he asserts, "can definitely make a line." He mentions Jeff Arundel, Triad's cofounder. "Jeff knows how I work. If I didn't see Jeff, I wouldn't do as much business with any of his vendors."

"There are good sales reps and bad ones," Target's Kohler allows. "Even though the reps are paid by the manu-

facturer, they have to represent us as well. A rep should be very open with all issues." She won't rate individual rep firms.

Koss, nevertheless, wouldn't dream of going to the Target follow-up meeting without Triad by his side.

MINNEAPOLIS, JANUARY 27—*Koss enters the Target meeting with purchasing manager Lillie and a Triad rep. Kohler shares the year-end numbers that show how Koss Corp. stacks up on margin, sell-through, inventory turnover, and product returns. Her opinion hasn't changed on the SportClip. "It's still too expensive," she says. Koss disagrees, but both sides concur that the standard "clam pack" packaging isn't going to tell the SportClip story. Koss knows he ought to have seen that before the show.*

Such meetings make up the bulk of "program selling." "You get the stuff placed, and then you have to plan the advertising," Koss explains. Even after the product has hit the store, Koss likes to say, "you still don't know if the dogs will eat the meat." If one model doesn't play with consumers, you must have a substitute.

Out of Stock Blues

MILWAUKEE, JANUARY 31—*During a lull in sales calls, Koss takes a visitor shopping.*

First stop: Wal-Mart. Apparently outranked by Sony, Koss headphones have been relegated to a bottom rung on the slat wall. "We have plans to change that," Koss says, tidying up the display.

The nearby Target store is brighter than Wal-Mart. Target aims for a department-store look. But Koss's best-selling, $20 headphones, the TD-60 model, are out of stock. Worse, three pegs are wasted on a model that sells poorly.

At Best Buy, Koss's demo, a pair of $39 computer speakers, doesn't work. The Sony speakers operate just fine. John Koss fiddles with wires to no avail. "If something's not working, we want to know right away so we can replace it," he says, walking off to find a manager.

"You can get depressed when you go to a bunch of stores and everything is wrong," says Koss.

That is the gap between *sell-in* to the buyer and *sell-through* to the consumer. Sometimes it feels as if your product has fallen into a black hole.

To remedy such problems, Koss has appealed to at least one superstore "re-buyer" (the buyer's assistant). Some vendors rely on the folks who actually stock shelves, the rack jobbers, to make things right. Few sales reps will play housekeeper, but the best make spot checks.

"The buyer might say that product's not selling," says Lee Adams, a Koss rep in Bedford, Tex. "And I can say, 'That's because it's in the back room.' I gain credibility, and the buyer fixes the problem."

DELRAY BEACH, FLA., FEBRUARY 1—*Thanks to the connections of a Florida rep firm, Koss is finally talking with the buyers at Office Depot headquarters. The office-supply chain is bullish on Koss products. "Interested in 'phones, speakers, microphones," John Koss enters into his pocket PC. This could be a $500,000 account. But it's unclear when he'll get an answer.*

It Can Take a While

HOFFMAN ESTATES, ILL., FEBRUARY 14—*Sears buyer Marty Burks confides he wants to give more business to a select few vendors like Koss. Burks had the numbers on the headphone market laid out—the market size, the best-selling price points, where Sears fits in. Koss is impressed. "He's got the market data down better than anyone else."*

Recently, Koss discovered that he and his reps have been chasing the wrong buyers at PriceCostco and Brookstone. Or that's what he's been told. And it was only after penning a letter to Kmart's buyer Hooks, several years ago, that he went "direct." The buyer replied, "It's good that you wrote me." The sales vice-president took that as a sign he should handle the account himself, and he says, "I will live and die by that."

MILWAUKEE, FEBRUARY 23—*Hooks phones Koss to check sales projections. The Kmart buyer is planning a detailed presentation to his own boss. Koss grows hopeful. "I'd been told no by now in prior years."*

It's easy to become agitated by the long selling cycle. It's said that even buyers grow weary. To alleviate the tension, Koss has taken up an aggressive form of gardening he calls "yardening." He has no patience with seeds; he plants large trees.

Sometimes the faxes, the phone calls, the Fed Ex packages, the trade shows, and the endless discussions about pricing, positioning, and turnover ratios add up.

MILWAUKEE, FEBRUARY 24—*Kmart calls. It will take two Koss units. After four years of pitches, Koss will get 1,700 new outlets.*

A few weeks later Koss is at work on a special Kmart promotion. He imagines a huge bin of earbud 'phones selling for $2.99. "It's great exposure," he says.

But $2.99? "The more traditional thinking is, 'Oh, man, that's dragging the name down into the dirt,'" he concedes. But from his perspective, he's buying tens of thousands of billboards for $2.99 each. "We've been talking about this a lot, our mission," he continues. "We had a very complicated mission statement. Finally, we all just looked at each other and said, 'You know what it is? We want a Koss stereophone on every head.' That's really what we want. Just like Taco Bell wants a taco in everybody's hand."

MILWAUKEE, APRIL 26—*John Koss is gratified to have added Kmart, Wal-Mart Canada, and Media Play as customers in 1995. He continues to improve relations with Target (which will test the SportClip at Koss's price), Wal-Mart, Sears, Best Buy, Service Merchandise, Bradlees, Ames, Lech-mere, the Army and Airforce Exchange, the Good Guys!, Software Etc., and CVS. Circuit City, Office Depot, and OfficeMax still have him on the edge of his chair. And he's already admitting he'll probably wait until next year for Lowe's, Brookstone, and Caldor. As for CompUSA, the computer superstore, Koss says, "we're not even on square one."*

Who's Who in the Zoo

The megaretailers might seem a challenging bunch to tame, but their central buying and distribution make it easier for small companies to launch products nationally *if* they can get through to the buyers who count. As he interviews potential sales reps John Koss keeps one question foremost in mind: "Do they know who's who in the zoo?"

Here is a rundown of the top 15 discount retailers:

NAME	LOCATION	DESCRIPTION	SALES	NO. OF STORES	NO. OF SKU'S	STORE-MANAGER BUYING POWER?	PROGRAMS FOR SMALL VENDORS?
Wal-Mart Stores	Bentonville, Ark.	Discount department store	$82.5 billion	2,142	50,000	Yes	Yes
Kmart Corp.	Troy, Mich.	Discount department store	$34 billion	2,364	65,000	No	Yes
Sears Merchandise Group	Hoffman Estates, Ill.	Specialty mass retailer	$32 billion	801	220,000	Yes	Yes
Sam's Warehouse Club	Bentonville, Ark.	Membership warehouse club	$19 billion	430	3,500	Yes	Yes
PriceCostco	Kirkland, Wash.	Membership warehouse club	$16.2 billion	187 in U.S., 45 elsewhere	3,500	No	Yes
Target Stores	Minneapolis	General-merchandise discount retailer	$13 billion	623	Not available	Yes	No
Home Depot	Atlanta	Home-improvement retailer	$12.5 billion	359	45,000	Yes	Yes
Toys 'R' Us	Paramus, N.J.	Toy specialty chain	$8.7 billion	618	10,000	No	Yes
Montgomery Ward	Chicago	Specialty mass retailer	$7 billion	409	2,500	No	No
Circuit City Stores	Richmond, Va.	Consumer-electronics chain	$5.1 billion	352	3,600	No	No
Best Buy	Eden Prairie, Minn.	Consumer-electronics chain	$5.1 billion	204	200,000	No	No
Meijer	Grand Rapids	Supercenter	$4.4 billion	92	100,000	Yes	Yes
Office Depot	Delray Beach, Fla.	Office-supply megastore	$4.3 billion	440	5,600	No	No
Service Merchandise	Brentwood, Tenn.	Jewelry/hard-goods retailer	$4 billion	408	23,000	No	No
Wal-Mart Supercenter	Bentonville, Ark.	Supercenter	$3.5 billion*	158	80,000	Yes	Yes

*1993 figure   Sources: Retailers and Chain Store Guide Information Services, Tampa, Fla.

—*Researched by Robina A. Gangemi*

Target 'Micromarkets' Its Way to Success; No 2 Stores Are Alike

New Reality of Retailing: What Sells in Phoenix May Not in Scottsdale

Catering to Ethnic Customers

Gregory A. Patterson

Staff Reporter of The Wall Street Journal

Phoenix—Shoppers searching for such diverse goods as religious candles, bicycle trailers and portable heaters need only visit a local Target store.

But there's a hitch: The Target store on Phoenix's eastern edge sells prayer candles, but no child-toting bicycle trailers. The Target 15 minutes away in affluent Scottsdale, Ariz., sells the trailers but no portable heaters; those can be found 20 minutes south in Mesa.

Confusing? Perhaps, but it makes perfect sense to Target, the 623-store discount chain owned by Minneapolis-based Dayton Hudson Corp. Target is a master at what retailers call "micromarketing"— a consumer-driven, technology-packed strategy to tailor merchandise in each store to the preferences of its patrons. It is a big reason that Target is growing rapidly even as things slow for its top competitors.

America has more racial, ethnic and lifestyle diversity than ever, and micromarketing aims to satisfy the resulting panoply of consumer preferences. It used [to] be that U.S. consumers, no matter their origins, gravitated toward a mid-American monolith, says John Costello, senior executive vice president of Sears, Roebuck & Co. Not anymore. These days, he says, "Consumers are interested in preserving their culture."

'POWERFUL ADVANTAGE'

What's more, micromarketing allows retailers to stand out in an increasingly crowded marketplace. After crushing smaller competitors with lower prices, big retailers like Target and Wal-Mart Stores Inc. now are using micromarketing to battle each other.

"I can't think of a more powerful advantage," Target President Ken Woodrow says of the company's micromarketing.

Under Mr. Woodrow, Target has spent millions of dollars on the sophisticated computer system needed to stock thousands of different items in each store. It has weaned its buyers off the notion that the best purchases are big purchases. And it has strong-armed sometimes reluctant vendors into providing Target with specialized merchandise to make its new strategy work.

Target's push into micromarketing seems to be working. Target last year recorded an impressive 7% same-store sales gain and an 11% boost in operating profit. And the 65 new stores Target plans to open this year far exceed any other chain, including rivals Kmart Corp. and Wal-Mart.

LEADING A PACK

Though micromarketing isn't the sole source of Target's success—its sunny decor and smart clothing assortments also contribute—it is the one area where Target really stands out from its competitors. "Hardly

any retailer is as far along with micromarketing as Target," says Chicago retail consultant Sid Doolittle.

Though ahead of the pack, Target isn't alone on the micromarketing path. Wal-Mart sells silky, first communion dresses in stores that serve Hispanic communities. Many Nordstrom Inc. department-store buyers also work the selling floor to ferret out local tastes. Sears carries Essence brand hosiery, made in colors and sizes that are more appealing to African-American women, in stores with a large black clientele.

"Everybody is trying to crack the [micromarketing] code, particularly national retailers," says Robert Giampietro, the Target vice president who leads the effort. "It comes down to having the right merchandise in the right store at the right time."

SOME RELUCTANCE

That is easier to say than to do. Kmart and Venture Stores Inc. have struggled with their respective micromarketing programs. Part of the problem is that Kmart, which still is wrestling with getting its basic marketing programs into shape, is reluctant to plunge whole-hearted into the more complicated world of micromarketing. "We try not to get caught in too many one-store projects," says Richard Pellino, Kmart's divisional vice president for women's wear.

Target's own micromarketing initiative was born out of embarrassment. In September 1989, Target opened its first Florida stores while conducting a nationwide marketing effort with Wil Steger, the first person to cross Antarctica on dog sled.

That fall, Target's Florida stores brimmed with parkas, gloves and sweaters. They didn't sell. And Target told Mr. Giampietro to start the micromarketing program.

Early efforts focused mainly on obvious climatic differences, things like keeping heavy coats out of Southern California and laying on the rain gear in Seattle.

After initial experiments succeeded, Target in 1992 began investing heavily in new computer equipment. And it began working with its buyers to get the new type of merchandise it needed. Some vendors resisted. Hallmark Cards Inc. and American Greetings Corp., Mr. Giampietro says, were slow to present Target with the black and Hispanic greeting cards and wrapping paper it sought. So, Target hooked up with another card supplier that could provide the merchandise. Some 18 months later, the two big card companies brought out their own ethnic lines—and got back some of the Target business.

Target's micromarketing also faced internal hurdles. Buyers resisted micromarketing because they figured their success lay in making big, profitable deals yielding brisk sales through all the stores, and they eschewed buying smaller lots.

But the watershed event came from Target's success at selling team-logo athletic apparel in the same markets where their fans lived. That business grew from almost nothing in 1991 to $100 million last year, according to insiders. Now, the buying staff, "clearly understands why there is a need to do business this way," says Target spokeswoman Susan Eich.

CHECK OUT THE COMPETITION

Target requires its 150 Minneapolis-based buyers to visit the stores for which they buy as well as their competitors. Moreover, Target gives its stores the ability to add merchandise without gaining approval from buyers.

The other key to Target's success is a complex computer-driven combination of

buying, planning and store operations that works like a cafeteria. Buyers create merchandise assortments that fit the racial, ethnic and age features of different clumps of customers. Then planners, treating each store the way a diner fills a lunch tray, match the merchandise to the community profile. Managers at the store level refine the model from what they know about local tastes and practices.

Target uses its flexible system to do things it couldn't before, such as display children's dolls in 96 variations—all depending on demand in 96 variations—all depending on demand at individual stores.

The industry adage that "retail is detail" is ever more true in micromarketing. In practice, attending to details for Target means carrying local favorite Jays potato chips in Chicago but stocking Saguaro brand chips in Phoenix. It also means sending more one-piece bathing suits to its stores on Florida's western coast, where the crowd is older, while packing off extra bikinis to the younger patrons of that state's eastern stores.

The sum of different products carried in any of its stores is only 15% to 20%, but the mix is different in almost every store. Target's goal is to increase the proportion of goods contoured to local tastes to 30%, according to Bart Butzer, a regional manager. "Then we will truly be micromarketed," he says.

BATTLE FOR SPACE

On top of all this, Target continually feeds actual sales data into its computers. The result: sales and profit tallies for each square foot of space. Target uses the results in the battle among products for space on its shelves, a process called "space wars." Successful performance by hunting gear one month likely will lead to more space, and perhaps less for fishing equipment, if it lags.

Two Phoenix-area stores illuminate Target's approach. The Arcadia Crossing store in east Phoenix and the store five miles away in Scottsdale opened in the past eight months. They are the same size and have identical layouts. Health

and beauty products, housewares, sporting goods and electronics line the outside walls, while apparel assortments take up the middle. Every worker wears a red shirt or blouse and khaki pants or skirt.

But a walk thought the Scottsdale store with manager Ellie Bernards shows how differences among the two stores' patrons yields differences in their merchandise. Ms. Bernards makes one of her first stops in the sporting-goods department where both sides of a 24-foot aisle are stacked nearly 10 feet high with in-line skates and accessories. The merchandise sells briskly to Scottsdale's young, affluent families who have 50 miles of paved pedestrian paths nearby. The store in Phoenix—whose buyers have an average household income 42% below those of the Scottsdale store—carries only half as much skating merchandise.

The bicycle trailers just a few paces away also are a big item for Scottsdale yuppies. "We couldn't give those away in Phoenix," Ms. Bernards says.

Tooling through the home accessories department, Ms. Bernards breezes past half a shelf of religious candles, stopping only to note that they aren't selling in Scottsdale. But the Phoenix store, with is substantial clientele of Hispanic Catholics, makes a brisk business of them. "I don't know why we have these here," Mr. Bernards says.

The Phoenix store also appeals to Hispanics by stocking Spanish-language compact disks and five Spanish-language Disney movies. But country-and-western sells in Scottsdale. The store carries at least six racks of country CDs, while the Phoenix store carries only a few. Similarly, the Scottsdale store is preparing its own western-wear boutique, while a few racks of that apparel can be found in Phoenix.

Such differences among stores of the same chain will only multiply in the future, says Al Meyers, a retail consultant in Price Waterhouse's Management Horizons division. "The high performance retailers of the future will be those who carry products specifically selected for their own customers," he says. "The days of retailers being all things to all people are over."

The DEATH *and* REBIRTH *of the* SALESMAN

Today's customers want solutions, and companies are remaking their sales forces to satisfy them. But total quality goals and sales quotas still clash.

Jaclyn Fierman

I sold systems that people didn't want, didn't need, and couldn't afford.
—Bill Gardner, 23-year IBM veteran, now retired.

NOT SO long ago, many salespeople might have regarded Gardner's admission as the mark of a colleague at the top of his game, one so skilled he could persuade people to act against their own interests. Today, his dubious achievement is more likely to be seen as embarrassing, unenlightened, counterproductive, and even, under some new compensation systems, a shortcut to a smaller bonus. Merely pushing metal, as IBM insiders say, or slamming boxes, as Xerox salesmen daintily describe the act of closing a copier deal, won't carry a sales force in the Nineties. Companies now measure success not just by units sold but also by the far more rigorous yardstick of customer satisfaction. As vendors ranging from Hallmark Cards to Marshall Industries—and even IBM—have discovered, if

REPORTER ASSOCIATE *Ani Hadjian*

THE NEW SALESMAN

■ **Today's best salespeople see themselves as problem solvers, not vendors.**

■ **They gauge success not just by sales volume but also by customer satisfaction.**

■ **To reinforce that view, companies are increasingly making customer satisfaction an element in salespeople's pay.**

■ **Despite the new attitudes, selling requires the same mix of grit and persistence that it always has.**

you anticipate what your customers need and then deliver it beyond their expectations, order flow takes care of itself.

As more managers awake to the challenge, old stereotypes are fading faster than Willy Loman's smile and shoeshine. Forget the mythic lone-wolf sales ace; today's trend-setting salespeople tend to work in teams. The traditional sample case? It's more likely to hold spreadsheets than widgets, and the person hauling it around probably regards herself as a problem solver, not a vendor. These days you don't "sell to" people, you "partner with" them. At the rhetorical frontier of the new sales force, even the word "salesman" is frowned upon; the preferred title is "relationship manager."

Let's admit that the rebirth of the salesman in corporate America remains a work in progress. Not all companies or all salespeople will adapt equally well to the extra training and teamwork that today's more cerebral sales approach requires. Moreover, as long as salespeople work on commission—as they do in virtually every major company today—the rhetoric of total customer satisfaction will inevitably clash with the reality of sales targets. "Come quota time, you still reach for the low-hanging fruit," says Robert Rodin, CEO of electronics distributor Marshall Industries in El Monte, California, one of the few companies to have eliminated commissions.

That said, companies that dismiss the new, more collaborative sales methods as a fad are likely to slip behind. Today's demanding buyers are running out of patience with mere product pushers, whether at the new-car showroom, on the floor of a department store, or in the corporate conference room. Jon Gorney, head of information services and operations at Cleveland's National City Corp., captures the mood in speaking of one of his chief vendors: "I don't want IBM coming in here anymore and telling me they have some whiz-bang technology unless they can tell me exactly how it will help my business."

As it happens, IBM knows better than most the dollars-and-cents argument for a more customer-conscious sales approach. Robert LaBant, senior vice president in charge of Big Blue's North American sales and marketing, says every percentage-point variation in customer satisfaction scores translates into a gain or loss of $500 million in sales over five years. What's more, he says, developing new business costs Big Blue three to five times as much as maintaining the old. Says LaBant: "We used to be focused on moving products and were paid on the basis of which ones we sold— $500 for this, $1,000 for that. It was critical that we turn that around."

I F EVER there was a business that cried out for a new way of selling it's that of moving cars from the showroom floor to the driveways of America. The familiar but widely despised old approach is known among automotive historians as the Hull-Dobbs method, after Memphis dealers Horace Hull and James Dobbs, who reputedly created it following World War II. In the old Hull-Dobbs drill, customers exist to be manipulated—first by the salesman, who negotiates the ostensibly final price, then by the sales manager and finance manager, who each in succession try to bump you to a higher price.

Car buyers are fed up. A survey by J.D. Power & Associates found that only 35% felt well treated by their dealers last year, down from 40% a decade ago. Just 26% of buyers rated the integrity of their dealers excellent or very good in 1983; by last year, that figure had dropped to 21%. "People feel beaten up by the process," says Jack Pohanka, owner of 13 import and domestic franchises in the suburbs of Washington, D.C. "You think you got a good deal until you walk out the door. The salesmen are

inside doing high fives, and the customer is lying out on the street."

Enter Saturn and its original, no-dicker sticker system. As everyone knows by now, the price you pay for a Saturn is the one on the sticker (between $9,995 and $18,675, depending on model and features). But that's only part of the package. Buy a Saturn and you buy the company's commitment to your satisfaction. A ritual reinforces the promise. When you pick up your new car, an entire team gathers around you, including a representative from service, sales, parts, and reception. They let out a cheer, snap your picture, and hand you the keys. Corny? Maybe, but last year Saturn scored third in a J.D. Power customer satisfaction study, just behind Lexus and Infiniti, which cost up to five times as much.

A fervent convert to the Saturn gospel is Jack Pohanka. One of 180 Saturn dealers in the U.S., Pohanka has seen firsthand the method's effect on customer loyalty and salesmen's morale, and he has extended Saturn-like practices to all his other franchises. "You have to let people walk out the door and not harass them," he says. "That way they may come back or refer a friend to you." Take your car in for body work to any Pohanka dealership and you will get it back vacuumed, washed, and even polished. "Our goal," says Pohanka, "is to exceed customer expectations."

Transforming combative salesmen to customer servants required what Pohanka calls "Saturnization." Every one of his 465 employees, including mechanics and receptionists, went off-site for three days of classroom exercises and physical challenges, similar to the training that Saturn requires of all its dealers. The high point of the cultural remake was the familiar "trust fall"— a backward leap off a 12-foot stepladder into the arms of fellow workers.

Pohanka contends that postfall salesmen no longer compete with each other and so don't hesitate to refer customers to one another if a different Pohanka franchise would better meet a buyer's needs. He points to a 25% jump in sales at the company in the first five months of the year, twice the national rate for cars and small trucks. For his sales staff, the new system translates not only to higher commissions but also to a better frame of mind. Says his Saturn general sales manager Brian Jamison: "I was planning to get out of this business. I couldn't stand all the games we played with customers. This way feels a lot better."

Saturn and Saturn disciples like Pohanka reformed their sales methods to exploit a screamingly obvious market opportunity; for IBM a sales force remake was simply a matter of survival. The company has cut its cost of selling by close to $1.5 billion in the

past two years. Its worldwide sales and marketing team, now 70,000 strong, is close to half the size it was in 1990.

Those who survived are part of a new operation that is a cross between a consulting business and a conventional sales operation. Big Blue now encourages buyers to shop for salesmen before they shop for products. Gorney of National City Corp., a superregional bank (assets: $30 billion), handpicked Don Parker as his sales representative after interviewing a half dozen IBM candidates. Says Gorney: "I wanted this person to be a member of my team." An engineer by training, Parker maintains an office at National City, and Gorney has sought his help to drive down the bank's costs of delivering services within the bank and to retail customers in the branches.

Consultants obviously need a more sophisticated set of skills than metal pushers, and IBM has not stinted on their training. For the 300 people like Parker who head client teams, the company has developed a voluntary yearlong certification program. The classroom component consists of a three-week stint at Harvard: one week devoted to general business knowledge, one to consulting, and one to the industry they specialize in serving. For the rest of the year, enrollees work on case studies and then write a thesis on their particular customer. Harvard professors grade the papers. So far, 28 IBM employees have received the certification, along with a raise. (Parker is in the midst of writing his thesis on National City.) Those who fail can keep trying.

In their new role as purveyors of solutions rather than products, IBM's sales teams don't always recommend Big Blue's merchandise. About a third of the equipment IBM installs is made by DEC and other competitors. Says senior vice president LaBant: "In the Eighties we never would have recommended another company's product because all we were paid to do was install Blue boxes."

L IKE IBM, Fletcher Music Centers in Clearwater, Florida, understands that the key to winning and keeping customers is to figure out what they need, sometimes before they figure it out themselves. A few years ago Fletcher was struggling along with other dealers in the moribund business of selling organs. "There is no natural market for organs," says Fletcher president John Riley, 42. "No one goes to a mall to shop for one." But after conducting focus groups with its main clientele, senior citizens who retire to Florida, Fletcher realized that what these people wanted wasn't so much a musical instrument as companionship.

Today Fletcher drums up business by positioning a "meet 'em and greet 'em" salesman at the keyboard within earshot of elderly mall patrons. "What's your favorite song?" he'll ask. And to the peels of *Chattanooga Choo Choo,* he'll begin his line of patter: "Where ya from? You just moved here? Do you play the organ at all? Ever seen one like this? It's specially designed for someone just like you with no musical background. Come on inside and try it out."

Once inside, the prospect is treated to a pitch heavy with subtext: Buy from us because we can help enliven your retirement years. Whether the customer springs for the $500 used model or the $47,000 top of the line, free weekly group lessons—good for a lifetime—come with the package. Says Riley: "We've seen a fair share of romances develop at these lessons."

Then there are the small details that show elderly customers how much Fletcher cares about their needs: large type on the keys and outsize knobs that arthritic fingers can easily manipulate. Says Sherman Wantz, 75, who just bought his fourth Fletcher organ: "They know how to treat elderly people without making them feel like children. They appeal to a desire in older people to continue accomplishing things in their lives." Such satisfaction is music to Fletcher's ears. Pretax profits reached $3.5 million last year on sales of $24 million.

Building durable customer relationships is one thing when you're hawking mainframes, cars, or organs; it's a rather different story when you're pushing a product as short-lived as a greeting card. That's why the sales force at Hallmark Cards, the world's largest greeting card company, concentrates on pleasing retailers. Says Al Summy, a vice president of sales and service for cards sold through large merchandisers like Target, Kmart, and A&P: "We're not selling *to* the retailer, we're selling *through* the retailer. We look at the retailer as a pipeline to the hands of consumers." Anything his salespeople can do to make Hallmark products more profitable for retailers, he figures, will ultimately benefit Hallmark.

As a result, Hallmark is reorganizing its entire sales and marketing operation into specialized teams designed to work effectively with product managers at major retailers. In the old days—less than 24 months ago—Hallmark sold pretty much the same mix of cards to every store. Now, using data derived from bar codes at the checkout counter and laptops that supply merchandising information from Hallmark headquarters, salespeople can tailor displays and promotions to a retailer's demographics.

James River Corp., which sells toilet tissue, napkins, Dixie cups, and the like, also understands that when it puts its head together with its retailers', both sides benefit. Specifically, James River shares proprietary marketing information with its customers that enables them to sell more paper products. For instance, it told its West Coast client, Lucky Stores, how often shoppers generally buy paper goods and which items they tend to buy together. Lucky has since reshelved all its paper products and managed to win market share in the category from competing stores.

James River has reorganized the way it calls on customers. Previously, three or more salespeople would approach a company like Lucky Stores: one with plates, one with cups, and one with toilet paper. If all three secured orders, Lucky was obliged to buy three full truckloads, one for each product, to get the lowest price from James River. Today, a unified team from James River will sell Lucky Stores one truckload with a mix of paper products at the lowest price.

At James River, as at Hallmark and IBM, building a sales force for the Nineties has meant a thorough rethinking of a salesperson's job. But an important aspect of managing a sales team hasn't changed much: how you motivate flesh-and-blood salespeople. It remains the same idiosyncratic blend of financial incentive, inspiration, and cajolery it always was. After all, sales is a tough job. Says Larry Chonko, marketing professor at Baylor University in Waco, Texas: "You still need fire in your belly, you still get rejected four out of five times, and you still need energy to get up in the morning and say, 'I can do it,' even if you sold nothing yesterday."

One of the more visible motivators in the game today is Frank Pacetta, 40, who is something of a folk hero at Xerox for having turned around the company's flagging Cleveland and Columbus, Ohio, sales teams. Pacetta has also become a minor media presence of late, thanks to a profile in the *Wall Street Journal;* a major role in *The Force,* a new book about Xerox salesmen by David Dorsey; and the publication of his own manual for sales managers, *Don't Fire Them, Fire Them Up* (reviewed in Books & Ideas).

Pacetta uses a hyperbolic mix of praise and shame to inspire his team of 70 reps in Columbus. For his winners, Pacetta holds testimonial dinners, dispenses effusive hugs, and has them ring a ship captain's bell at the completion of a deal. Weak performers can expect a month-long visit on their desk from an ugly troll doll Pacetta swiped from his son. Salespeople who aren't sufficiently fired up after three consecutive visits from the troll are fired—the title of Pacetta's book notwithstanding.

Sales, Pacetta style, boils down to three simple steps: Identify the customer, make sure your product fits the customer's requirements, and ask for the sale. To minimize resistance on step three, Pacetta recommends the "presell," which he likens to a conversation he might have had when convincing his wife, Julie, to marry him:

"Julie: 'I don't like the way you dress, I don't think you make enough money, and you drive like a maniac.'

Frank: 'If I let you pick out my suits, if I double my income, and if I promise never to exceed the posted speed limits—will you marry me then?' "

In marked contrast to Pacetta's freneticism stands another master of sales motivation, 140-year-old Southwestern Co., America's oldest extant door-to-door sales company. It peddles Bibles and Bible study guides to millions of families, and its Nashville boot camp turns its young sales trainees, mostly college kids on summer vacation, into some of the most dogged salespeople in the country. How's this for a drill? After a week of classroom training, the graduates fan out to assigned territories across the country and settle down to work—up to six days a week, 13 hours a day. Southwestern salesmen ring as many as 65 doorbells a day to make 30 demonstrations, each lasting 20 minutes. Sticking to that schedule, they can expect to close one to three sales a day, enough to earn over $5,500 their first summer. The company, which is privately held, rings up over $100 million a year in revenues.

Don't discount Southwestern as an anachronism. The company's working alumni, well over 100,000 of them, have carried their skills to places like IBM, Xerox, Procter & Gamble, and Wall Street and in many cases are leading the sales revolution going on today. Says alum Marty Fridson, 41, who runs high-yield securities research at Merrill Lynch: "There's nothing magical about sales. You want to be truthful and present a credible story so people will want to do business with you in the future. To sell effectively, you need to present the facts, list your supporting arguments, and learn all the nonverbal cues your customer gives while you're making your presentation."

With one element of sales motivation—how they pay their salespeople—many companies believe they can improve on tradition. IBM, for example, is following a budding trend to base compensation partly on customer satisfaction. Salesman Don Parker says that 45% of the variable component of his paycheck depends on how Jon Gorney at National City Corp. rates him. If Gorney is pleased with the way Parker has helped him meet the bank's business objectives, Parker says that he stands to make "a lot more this year than ever before."

At Hallmark, too, customers get a say in how well some salesmen are paid. In a pilot project, about 100 employees have taken a 15% cut in base pay and made that portion of their income variable, based on retail sales of Hallmark products. If results are good, those salesmen stand to make more than 15%. The point, of course, is to encourage these workers to focus on helping retailers do their job better.

Electronics distributor Marshall Industries has taken this thinking to the next logical step and eliminated commissions altogether. Marshall's 600 salespeople earn a straight salary, with a bonus opportunity of up to 20% more based on pretax corporate profits. In the latest fiscal year, with sales over $800 million, the bonus was 10%.

Marshall CEO Robert Rodin overhauled the compensation system when he realized the distortions that quotas and commissions were creating in the system. "How can you say you're pursuing excellence if you give away TV sets to your top salespeople? Customers got their parts ahead of time so the salesmen could get their prizes. But guess what? Those customers wanted on-time delivery, not early delivery."

Rodin says his people hoarded inventory in their cars in case they needed it. And in the mad rush to meet monthly quotas, salesmen shipped "anything that wasn't nailed down, to any customer on our list, regardless of their credit standing." The mania strained the shipping department's ability to complete orders accurately: "You can imagine what bleary-eyed warehouse people do at two in the morning."

Rega Plaster, 32, a top Marshall saleswoman, worried at first when Rodin took away commissions: "I wondered where my motivation would come from." She says she was pleasantly surprised at her response: "Within a month, it was like being able to breathe again. This takes the sliminess out of selling. Now I can spend time with smaller accounts and nurture them, and I can do it with a clear mind and conscience." Sales at her Milwaukee branch have risen from a monthly average of $850,000 last year to over $2 million.

FOR ALL the hype and half measures, salespeople in the Nineties can make the world a better marketplace. Any inefficiencies wholesalers and retailers squeeze out of the supply chain will benefit consumers by keeping a lid on prices. And smart solutions from any corner have a far-reaching payoff. At the very least, the new ethos may herald the decline of in-your-face salesmen who sell things people don't want, don't need, and can't afford.

Talk of the Town

Turning loyal customers into advocates for your products or services

Jill Griffin

Jill Griffin is president of The Marketing Resource Center in Austin, Texas. She conducts seminars on loyalty marketing nationwide, and works with clients that range from Fortune 500 companies to small businesses.

If there's any doubt about the awesome power of word of mouth, consider that an enthusiastic response to that oft-asked question, "Seen any good movies lately?" can turn a low-budget movie with little or no advertising support into a multimillion-dollar hit. For example, *Home Alone* seemed to sneak into theaters one Thanksgiving as just another children's movie. Word of mouth made it a wild success. Conversely, bad word of mouth can move the needle in the opposite direction.

Referral is the most powerful pathway for any business to recruit new customers. When a new prospect comes to you through a second-party endorsement, you have three distinct selling advantages:

1. *Less Selling Time Is Required.* That's because much of the selling has already been accomplished by your referral source. Trust and believability are key factors in making the first sale. And winning trust and believability takes time. These important factors become almost non-issues when people get a referral from someone they know and respect.

2. *These Prospects Have Greater Loyalty Potential.* Workshop facilitator Laura Peck used to advertise, but due to financial problems she discontinued the ads and began cultivating her own network of friends and acquaintances for clients. Now, two years later, her business is thriving. "When I advertised, I seemed to attract people who came because of the discount I offered," she says. "These clients would cancel sessions and generally were not repeaters. The people who were most enthusiastic and continued with their sessions were almost always clients who had been personally referred."

3. *People Come Ready to Buy.* Why does a customer who comes back to Direct Tire in Watertown, Massachusetts, spend $173 during an average visit and new customers who have been referred by someone else spend $224? According to Direct Tire President Barry Steinberg, the answer is quite simple: The big spenders have usually been putting off a major repair or purchase until they can find a repair shop they can trust. Once they hear about Direct Tire's service, they come in and spend.

Earning Word of Mouth: Four Proven Strategies

1. Give 'em Something to Talk About

Windham Hill's William Ackerman literally learned the record business from the ground up. In the late 1970s, as a contractor and carpenter, Ackerman was hired to build warehouses for two small, folk-oriented record companies in the San Francisco area. In between his sawing and hammering, he got to ask a lot of questions.

In his spare time, Ackerman played guitar on campus at Stanford University. People were constantly asking to record his music into their cassettes. With $5 each from 60 people and a small loan from his friend and eventual partner, Anne Robinson, Ackerman recorded *In Search of the Turtle's Navel*, an album of guitar solos.

"The sum total of my ambitions consisted of selling 300 records, which was the minimum order the record pressing plant demanded," said Ackerman. "I fully envisioned a closet of my house laden with at least 100 extra records for the rest of my life."

After selling approximately 60 copies to friends, Ackerman gave some extra records to ten FM radio stations. Listeners began calling the stations to inquire about his music. Soon a few record stores contacted him, and orders began to slowly flow in.

Today the company sells about $30 million worth of records a year wholesale. Robinson and Ackerman attribute word of mouth in the early years as fundamental to their success. Robinson explained, "We found there were a lot of people who said that they went to their friend's house for dinner and heard our music. Then they had to have it because it spoke to them, so they went out and bought it and then played it for their friends."

2. Continually Search for New Ways to Earn the Talk Factor

A computer check-writing program called Quicken has become the most successful personal finance program ever written, holding an impressive 60 percent market share. The company generates annual sales of more than $33 million and sells close to 1 million units annually.

The company's sales force comprises exactly two people. But Scott Cook, CEO of Intuit, the maker of Quicken, sees it differently: "Really, we have hundreds of thousands of salespeople. They're our customers." Scott speaks of his customers as "apostles" and states that Intuit's mission is to "make customers feel so good about the product they'll go and tell five friends to buy it."

To create this phenomenal word of

mouth with such potential mass-market appeal, the Quicken program had to be fast, cheap, hassle free, and, above all, easy to use. And Intuit is on a constant crusade to meet these objectives. One such example is the Follow-Me-Home program, in which Quicken buyers from local stores are asked to let an Intuit representative observe them when they first use Quicken. This way, Intuit gets continual feedback on how the product might be made just a tiny bit easier for first-time users. "If people don't use the product," says Tom LeFevre, chief programmer, "they won't tell their friends to use it, either."

3. Get Your Product in the Hands of Influencers

Conventional wisdom says that in order to get a group of "opinion leaders" to earnestly spread the word about a new product, its maker must first give the product away.

Not so with Approach Software, a start-up in Redwood City, California. Approach found a way to earn initial sales from opinion leaders and then triple the number of people who purchased its product on the advice of friends or associates in the six months following the product's launch. How did the company do it? By offering a low introductory price and a 90-day, money-back guarantee. Carefully selected, influential users were asked to try the company's first product, a database software program designed for non-"techies." Approach's limited-time offer of $149 (competing products costs as much as $799), plus free technical support, quickly got the innovative software into the hands of thousands of small-company CEOs and other targeted customers.

4. Turn Centers of Influence into Full-Time Advocates

Fifteen years ago, Jay Stein decided to expand his Greenville, Mississippi department store. As a stroke of luck, several well-to-do women from Greenville volunteered to help out during the store's liquidation sales of some designer clothing. Commenting for the Wall Street Journal, Stein said, "They had firsthand knowledge of this better merchandise, because they had worn it for years." The experi-

ence convinced him that the concept was worth replicating. When Stein Mart opened its second store, this time in Memphis, he created a designer boutique department in the store, and he and his wife recruited socialite friends to operate it.

Today, "the boutique ladies are our secret weapon" says Jay Stein. Because the job has become a local status symbol, there is a waiting list of women anxious to become a boutique lady. Their activities are focused on "spreading the word" about designer merchandise. For example, when a shipment of $39 designer silk separates arrived at the Jacksonville Stein Mart, boutique lady Joy Abney called fellow board members at Wolfson Children's Hospital and "told them to get over here." Joy's friends obliged by spending $2,000 in her department that same day.

Getting the Word Out About You

Let's examine the tools you need to maximize your talk factor.

• The quid pro quo

Advocacy is not a totally selfless move on the part of your endorser. The advocate wants to keep you going so you'll be able to continue doing business with him or her. Moreover, when you perform well for the new customer and he or she is satisfied, you make the endorser look good. In some ways, the new customer now "owes one" to the endorser. So the next time you are shy about asking for an endorsement, remember that there is something in it for the advocate as well.

• The Satisfied Customer File

Make a point of adding a satisfied customer story to your file every week. Write up the stories, including the names, addresses, and phone numbers of the satisfied customers. Ask each one, in advance, for permission to use his or her name as a reference. When you're trying to win over a tough prospect, scan your file, identify a success story that nearly matches the prospect's situation, and invite the prospect to contact the customer directly for a reference. Among sales professionals, this technique is known as reference selling.

Lynn Green, a sales engineer at Dat

I/O Corporation in New Hampshire, was selling a product for $15,000, against a competitor who was offering something similar for only $2,000. When the prospect objected to the higher price, Lynn asked him to seek the advice of her own customers who had used the competitor's products in the past but had switched back to hers. "Once again, my existing customers made the sale for me," she says.

The lesson Green preaches is to develop good rapport with your existing customer base. And she discovered that her customers enjoy helping her out. "If you and your company have a customer's loyalty, it can pay off in more ways than one," she says.

• The testimonial letter

Prospective customers like to see testimonials from companies in their industries and from their regions of the country. Ask your satisfied customers and clients to write you a letter on their company letterhead outlining how your products or services helped their organizations. Make sure the writers answer questions such as:

- How long did he or she use your product?
- How does yours compare with others he or she has used?
- What was the scope of the project or sale?
- What were the tangible results?

A statement of specific results can be very powerful in building credibility. Excerpts from testimonial letters in my files that refer to specific results include one from a hotel client: "Jill created a marketing and sales system for each of our five AmeriSuites hotel properties. The result has been a 19 percent increase in corporate business this past year."

Make the testimonial letter development process as easy as possible for the client. I've had several clients who have suggested that I write the letter for them. I love it when this happens. They review it and may make some changes. From the draft, they finalize the letter.

• The preheat letter

Juanell Teague, who operates a successful consulting business for established and aspiring speakers, suggests an approach called the "preheat letter" to turn satisfied clients into advocates. Ask your satisfied clients to write a letter to be sent to between 5 and 40 of their personal contacts. You get your clients to provide you with names, addresses, and phone numbers, along with their letterhead and envelopes. You prepare the mailing, including postage, and return the letters to them for signatures and mailing. About a week later, you make follow-up calls.

Juanell advises that the most successful preheat letters accomplish four objectives:

- Explain the client's requirements that you filled
- Describe how he or she found you
- Outline the work you accomplished
- Recommend you

Perhaps the simplest way to use the endorsement for selling is by asking your client for referrals and then promptly following up. Asking for referrals should be a natural part of your interaction with your client. As we discussed earlier, satisfied clients benefit by giving you referrals. Don't be shy. Just ask.

There is a right way and wrong way to ask for referrals:

Wrong: You don't know anyone else who might be interested in my product, do you?

Reason: Based on a negative supposition. Leads the client to say no.

Wrong: Do you know someone who might need my product?

Reason: Provides the client with the opportunity to just say no.

Right: Who do you know that might appreciate knowing about my services?

Reason: Takes a more positive, proactive approach that implies "I'm a problem solver."

Once you have been given the first name, ask, "Who else do you know?" and repeat the process until your client runs out of referrals.

• **Recommend-a-Friend rewards**
Customers who send friends to the $3.6 million Indy Lube quick-lube chain get a $10 certificate toward their next oil

change. It's a way to thank customers who take the time to fill out an Indy Lube referral card and give it to a friend. The new customer uses the card to get $5 off his or her first oil change. The Indianapolis company won 35 new customers that way in one month alone. When Indy runs a contest among its 15 locations for most customer referrals in a month, CEO Jim Sapp says, he redeems as many as 50 referral cards per store.

Experience has shown that you can expect a larger number of friends' names if your customers are guaranteed that their name will not be used in soliciting their friends. Response from friends will be higher, however, if you are allowed to reference the name of the friend who provided the name. Therefore, you may want to give the customer a choice of whether his or her name will be used in solicitation.

• **Say "Thank you!"**
Any action on anyone's part in referring a prospect to you deserves a thank-you. The rule is simple: Thank the person in writing. Thank the person right away. Whether or not you convert the referral into a customer or client, the source for the referral deserves recognition. A thank-you message from a realtor might read, "Thank you for suggesting that Paul and Brenda Logan call me regarding their real estate needs. I met with Paul and Brenda on Tuesday and enjoyed talking with them. The Logans mentioned how enthusiastic and complimentary you were in giving them my name. I truly appreciate your confidence in my abilities." Notice that the note does not say, "I got the Logans' listing. Thank you." If the realtor did receive the listing, then that piece of information could be incorporated into the thank-you note. But the most important thing about the communication is that the client is properly thanked for the referral. Period.

• **Keeping the word out about you**
Have you had the experience of being out of touch with a colleague or client and then running into him or her unexpectedly and learning something to the effect that "My neighbor was just asking

about…I completely forgot that you provide that service"?

The key is to keep yourself top of mind with those people by creating a simple yet effective system for staying in touch. Consider this blueprint for maintaining a network of clients and market influences who are likely to provide you with contacts and leads for future business:

- *Write notes.* Two to three sentences is all it takes to say to someone "I was thinking of you." Note cards are great for this purpose. If you write five notes a day and you are in business 250 days a year, that's more than 1,200 extra contacts.

The key to this tool is to maintain a good mailing list of clients and addresses; doing so is crucial to your ability to stay in touch.

- *Use the telephone.* Make a minimum of five brief calls a week. Take the opportunity to ask the person you call for their opinion on something you are undertaking. William James once said, "The greatest need of every human being is the need for appreciation." Let them know you respect their opinion.

- *Meet face-to-face.* Make five personal contacts a month. Practice the "out to lunch" method by calling and inviting three clients to lunch. Pick a popular lunch spot. Mix new clients with long-term clients. Make it a social affair that can pay you business dividends.

Be Ready for More Customers

Think twice before you launch a plan to encourage personal recommendation referrals. Properly executed, it can produce dynamic results. But when a business is not ready for expansion, having a lot of new customers can threaten quality by reducing standards in order to meet demand. The result can be disastrous: disillusioned prospects, dissatisfied customers, low employee morale, and general frustration at not being able to provide good service. When this happens, unhappy prospects and customers will tell their friends, and a downward business spiral begins—just the opposite of the happy ending you'd envisioned at the start!

The 'Net Effect

Does Internet marketing really work?
We found four companies that say yes

Tom Dellecave Jr.

If you think the future of Internet marketing is being mapped out in the advertising hotbeds along Madison Avenue, Don Jones has some news for you. It's not. It's happening in Pittsburgh.

Hundreds of miles from the young visionaries and glass towers of New York, 58-year-old Jones is delivering on the Internet's marketing promise to change the way companies conduct business. From two buildings in a nondescript office park deep in the heart of the rust belt, Jones's firm, Industry.Net, is bringing together companies that have something to sell with companies that have something to buy. And he's doing it online. "We bring sellers to a place where hundreds of thousands of buyers come every day," he says.

Jones's success has been unprecedented on the Internet. Even software-industry heavyweight Jim Manzi, who grew Lotus Development into a multibillion dollar company before selling it to IBM, saw Industry.Net's potential. He joined the company as President and CEO in late January.

What Manzi and others see is the viability of Jones's vision of a future electronic marketplace.

His 4-year-old company makes use of the World Wide Web, the most popular part of the Internet. The approach is simple: make it easy for buyers by giving them a single place to shop. Through Industry.Net, more than 200,000 companies are reaching the more than 150,000 buyers that Jones attracts to his site each day. For manufacturers, Industry.Net has become a new and effective marketing vehicle with which to peddle their wares—an electronic business-to-business shopping mall.

Industry.Net is not alone. A handful of other companies have also managed to do what others in the business community have struggled at: Turn Internet marketing into good business. Federal Express is attracting thousands to its site by providing customer service online; Holiday Inn is using the Web to sell directly to customers; and Air Products & Chemicals has posted complex product information on its site.

As different as their takes are on Internet marketing, there are some striking similarities among these companies. They all agree that: The Internet initiative must bring into the fold information systems, marketing, and customer support among other departments; Web sites must be interactive, allowing the user to take control of the experience; and the strategy must be part of the overall marketing program, not its forgotten stepchild. Through an understanding of what this medium offers, these companies have found exciting new ways to deliver their messages and set the standards that other Internet marketers are emulating.

FedEx

Delivering online customer service

Nearly half of all companies on the Web are there with the intention of building brand awareness, according to a recent study by Forrester Research Inc., a Cambridge, Massachusetts-based technology research firm. If that's the goal, Federal Express Corporation is one of the few companies realizing it. The Memphis, Tennessee-based company is attracting as many as 18,000 people to its site each day by giving them the ability to track their packages on the Internet. Once on the site, the customer sees the FedEx logo hanging under a globe with a FedEx package whizzing by.

At first, marketing was an afterthought. The primary reason for the FedEx site was to give customers

Adding a Human Touch To Home Pages

In the race to turn the Internet into an effective sales and marketing tool, Web pioneers have faced some major road blocks. At the top of the list are concerns over security and the lack of personality on the virtual sales call. Officials at Rockwell Telecommunications in Downers Grove, Illinois, think they have found a way to eliminate those shortcomings.

Rockwell developed a technology that initiates a customer-service call from the company to the Web surfer each time the person clicks a specific icon on that company's home page. The technology, called Internet ACD, is currently being tested by Cooperative Marketing Concepts (CMC), a Memphis, Tennessee-based customer service call center with such clients as MCI, Federal Express, and Williams Sonoma. "It makes a lot of sense," says Traci Sampson, executive vice president for business development at CMC. "There's still that human element."

Internet ACD (short for automatic call distributor) allows companies to bypass the Internet's security shortcomings, because no transactions are actually taking place electronically. At the same time, Web surfers get the opportunity to interact with a real person.

CMC has been piloting the program with client Sharper Image. A person on the Sharper Image home page who wants assistance simply clicks on a clearly marked icon. A message is then forwarded to a black box at the call center where the call requests are queued. When a customer service rep is available, the message is sent to the rep's computer monitor and a call to the customer is initiated. Depending on the information the customer volunteered, the rep could know the person's name and the nature of her problem before the call goes through. If the Web surfer is using a dial up access provider and only has one phone line, the call request can be delayed until the person logs off.

"It's a different sales dynamic," Sampson says. "You now have the ability to turn marketing into an opportunity to close a sale." Sampson adds that the technology allows companies to maintain closer relationships with their customers. Customers will like it, she says, because they still are the one's in control.   —T.D.

some value-added benefits, says Robert Hamilton, manager of electronic commerce at Federal Express. "We weren't thinking of this as an ad tool. It was less about eye candy and more about changing people's behavior." Now, instead of calling a customer service center, Web surfers just type their package ID number onto a special section of the FedEx Web site to get an update on the location of their package.

The results have been a tremendous marketing success for Federal Express. After tracking packages, customers on FedEx's Web site stay to get the latest information on FedEx news, special offers, and new services. "It has laid a nice foundation for where we want to go over the next year," Hamilton says. "You'll see more information and really useful transaction-type applications."

But FedEx's success at building its brand online is in fact a rarity. While better marketing may be the goal, most companies have fallen short of achieving it. "For a lot of companies that go on the Web, the typical experience is that nothing happens," says Mary Cronin, author of three books on doing business on the Internet. "These companies have to start thinking through how they plan to get noticed."

FedEx has done that by incorporating its online efforts with other marketing department programs. On every brochure, television ad, or print ad that carries a FedEx phone number, its universal resource locator (URL), or online address, appears as well. Eventually, Hamilton hopes to see television ads specifically designed to tout the Web site.

And the company's Internet efforts have extended beyond the marketing department, too. FedEx sales reps have found success using the Web site's tracking capabilities to lure customers. "[Our customers' salespeople] aren't tracking just to see that the package is there," says Rob Shirley, vice president of sales for FedEx logistics services. "They're tracking so they can tell their customers where the package is. Before this, the people responsible for buying and selling products never got close to shipping."

But it's FedEx's future plans that really have the sales department excited. The company is already testing an online order-entry process that it plans to offer customers. Under the system, customers with home pages will link to FedEx's computers where product catalogs for those companies will be maintained.

When a person wants to buy a product from a company with a catalog, he'll click an icon and type in the purchasing information. FedEx's computers will assign a tracking number and notify the company's shipping department. FedEx is still deciding whether the order-entry sites will also be accessible from the FedEx home page. "It's a much more integrated approach," Shirley says. "FedEx has already marched right up to the order-entry process. This moves us one step farther into a company's business to help them get closer to their customers. We think of it as a trading network."

Because much of the technology infrastructure was already in place, Hamilton says that FedEx was able to control its costs. The company spent under

$100,000 on its site, mostly on some additional hardware, design, and support.

Adding functionality through the Internet was not a big leap for FedEx. More than 65 percent of the company's orders are taken electronically. Larger customers can send and track package through Federal Express's own network, called Power Ship. And smaller customers, using FedEx diskettes, can dial up shipping and tracking information using a modem. "We've been doing electronic commerce privately for eight years," Hamilton says. "The Internet is not a first step for us. It's a next step."

While FedEx doesn't have hard numbers, Hamilton is convinced that there's been a cost-savings associated with the Web site, too. Each of the tracking inquiries that FedEx now receives online previously had been taken by the company's call center. As the company's business has grown from 2.1 million packages shipped in 1994 to 2.4 million in 1995, it has been able to handle more inquiries without increasing the size of its call-center support staff.

Holiday Inn
Closing the sales loop
Holiday Inn first went on the Internet last June, and Ann Glover, manager of reservation training and marketing coordination, admits she didn't know exactly

what to expect. "Initially we just wanted a presence," she says.

But it didn't take long for the Atlanta hotel giant to see the potential of its new venture. Nearly 17 percent of all adults in the U.S. and Canada have access to the Internet, according to a recent survey by Nielsen Media Research and CommerceNet, a Menlo Park, California-based consortium of companies exploring the Internet's business potential. At least half of the people on the Web hold either professional or managerial positions, and one quarter earn more than $80,000, according to the same study. These are the types of people that Holiday Inn wanted to reach when it set its Internet course.

As the company's vision of online marketing evolved, it began to see three opportunities: an inexpensive advertising medium, an information source, and, perhaps most important, a new distribution channel. By the end of August, Holiday Inn had added the ability for guests to check availability and price, and book rooms at any of its 2,100 hotels.

While Holiday Inn won't disclose the number of reservations that it has taken online, Glover says that it has already exceeded expectations—although online still accounts for a small fraction of the 25 million room nights that are booked each year. But sales executives at Holiday Inn see greater value in using the Internet as another selling tool than as a new distribution channel. "As we work with customers who have Internet access, it's another resource for them," says Bob Huffman, vice president of travel industry sales for Holiday Inn. Customers are able to use the Web site both to view rooms and as an information resource on the company.

Huffman says that there will be a point when the Internet will become a vital selling tool for the hotel chain. "From a sales perspective, it's not that effective at this point," he says. "I don't see this being a huge distribution channel in the short term, but there's no doubt that it will be in the long term."

Holiday Inn's site includes news, statistics, and even an interactive travel trivia game with the occasional Holiday Inn-focused question. When bringing up the Holiday Inn site, Web surfers first see an illustration of a desktop with a series of icons that the person can use to access other Holiday Inn pages.

This type of interactivity is what sets successful Web sites apart, author Cronin says. "One thing companies must realize is that this isn't broadcast. You

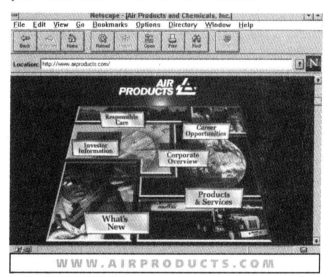

have to get people to come in and look around."

In October 1995, Holiday Inn added a separate Web site for its luxury Crowne Plaza hotels that incorporates sound and video, and in January it began adding a separate home page for each of its hotels. Eventually Web cruisers will be able to view hotels and rooms from their PCs before making the decision to make a reservation. The company also plans to leverage some of its alliances to fill out its service offering. For instance, a person making a reservation in Florida might be able to click on a Delta Airlines button to go directly to Delta's Web site for flight information.

Among the biggest challenges for Holiday Inn has been tracking activity on its site and developing a solid profile of who is accessing it. The company has moved away from measuring hits, the number of accesses to each page, and is currently trying to develop a system that tracks people and what they do on the site.

Kim Bayne, president of wolfBayne Communications, a Colorado Springs, Colorado, Internet marketing consultancy, says that these tracking problems will begin to disappear as third-party auditors get involved with measuring traffic. The Audit Bureau of Circulations recently announced that it would begin testing different Web auditing methods, and Nielsen is working with another research company to develop a better method for measuring click patterns.

Air Products
Mixing the right information formula
Air Products & Chemicals Inc. went on the Web because investors demanded financial information and customers wanted faster access to product information. The company's old methods of disseminating information weren't cutting it in the digital age, explains Steve Cameron, supervisor of communications at the Allentown, Pennsylvania, chemicals and gas manufacturer.

So when Air Products initially staked its claim to the Web in January, it simply took existing information and transferred it to the electronic medium. But that was just phase one of the project. Phase two will be taking advantage of the Internet's interactive features. That's what the company has in store for the rest of this year. "The easier we make it for customers

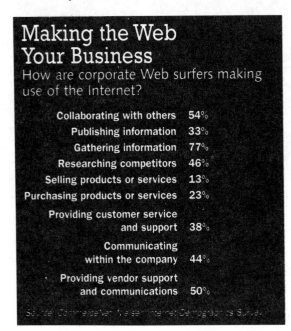

Making the Web Your Business
How are corporate Web surfers making use of the Internet?

Collaborating with others	54%
Publishing information	33%
Gathering information	77%
Researching competitors	46%
Selling products or services	13%
Purchasing products or services	23%
Providing customer service and support	38%
Communicating within the company	44%
Providing vendor support and communications	50%

to get information on our products and services, the better it will be for us and them," Cameron says. "Interactivity is the key to that."

Analysts agree that that type of foresight is important for a company to reach its online potential. "A lot more companies are getting a grasp on how the Web fits into their overall marketing programs," Bayne says. "A year ago I may have dissuaded people from going on the Internet. But there's been this snowball effect. Now I recommend getting up and running. I figure at least they're experimenting with it.".

The challenge for Air Products has been determining what should go online and what shouldn't. The company's products are accompanied by volumes of product literature, and Air Products also maintains large catalogs that are broken down by individual industry.

The company is working to put these catalogs online in an interactive format that will allow customers to conduct searches for Air Products offerings by typing in what they're looking for. Product information and specifications will also be kept online so that potential and existing customers can easily view them without having to maintain large bound volumes on their office desks. "We're only touching the surface as far as what we can provide," Cameron says.

Air Products' URL now appears on all brochures and sales literature, and it's being advertised in the industry trade magazine *Chemical Week*.

Industry.Net
The electronic shopping mall
When Don Jones began thinking about how to bring his vision of an automated buying and selling process to the Internet, he didn't look to the marketing gurus on the East Coast. Instead he thought shopping malls: If you make it easier for buyers by giving them a single place to go, they'll set a path to your door. "It's a secret that the retail industry learned a long time ago," he says.

Like Federal Express, Industry.Net was using diskettes to distribute information. But in 1994, when Jones received his first demonstration of the World Wide Web, he realized that technology had finally caught up with his vision. Since bringing its service to the Internet, Industry.Net has grown from 65 employees to more than 160.

What does Industry.Net offer? More than $185 billion in purchasing dollars to which Industry.Net's more than 165,000 buyers hold the purse strings. They're lured through the attraction of one-stop shopping. Except they're shopping for manufacturing equipment instead of pants and socks. Instead of posting their own Web sites, companies spend $3,500 (for a small, regional company) to as much as $40,000 (for a large multinational) to have Industry.Net do it for them.

Large companies like Honeywell, IBM, and Siemens are finding marketing successes on Industry.Net, but smaller companies may find its cost too high. Canary Labs Inc., a 10-person software developer in Altoona, Pennsylvania, spent $20,000 to be on Industry.Net for two years. It decided not to renew the service for 1996. The sales leads it was generating didn't warrant the cost. "We didn't have

the immediate sales to point to that would have justified that kind of expense," says Ed Stern, Canary's vice president. In fact, the company was only closing about one lead per month that was generated from Industry.Net. He adds: "We finally made a decision to put our own home page on the Net."

But Jones's model has proven successful. So much so that in late January, software pioneer Jim Manzi jumped on board. Industry.Net also has its imitators. One example of this is Boston.com, a Web site devoted to the greater Boston area. Visitors can browse *The Boston Globe*, download real estate information, or get ticket information for the Celtics.

Jones goes to great lengths to make sure that people know about Industry.Net. The company exhibits at 85 trade shows a year and sends a newsletter to 130,000 manufacturers every three weeks.

His reasoning is sound. "We focus more on pleasing the buyer community than we do our clients," Jones says. "If we have buyers, the clients will come." That logic works on Madison Avenue; it works in Pittsburgh; and as Don Jones is making clear, it works in cyberspace too.

FIRST, GREEN STAMPS. NOW, COUPONS?

P&G wants to end these sales boosters—and rivals may follow

Last year, makers of everything from Kitty Litter to ketchup barraged the average American household with about 3,000 discount coupons. For Procter & Gamble Co., that was 3,000 too many. The consumer-goods giant has already cut its use of coupons in half. And in an upstate New York test watched closely by marketers nationwide, P&G has eliminated coupons completely.

As P&G sees it, those coupons cost too much to print, to distribute, and to process, and they don't benefit enough consumers. "We decided that coupons have to go," P&G President Durk I. Jager said at a trade meeting, according to *Supermarket News.* Some packaged-goods rivals are joining in with their own coupon cutbacks in this P&G test area. The cutbacks aren't likely to spell the end of coupons—a century-old promotional tactic. But as big marketers and retailers alike struggle to reduce waste, coupons are likely to become a lot less abundant.

NARCOTIC. Coupon promotions—which cost marketers roughly $8 billion last year—have always been inefficient. Of the 292 billion coupons issued in 1995, the overwhelm-

ing majority missed their mark. Redemptions dropped for the third year in a row, to 5.8 billion (chart). That's just 2% of the total, half of the rate in 1980, according to coupon processor NCH Promotional Services in Lincolnshire, Ill. The decline came partly because manufacturers, eager to limit their exposure, have cut the average time before expiration from 7.6 months in 1988 to 3.5, according to coupon processor CMS Inc.

Love them or hate them, coupons have become a narcotic that marketers can't easily kick. Although most coupons never get used, shoppers have come to expect them. Some

83% of consumers use coupons some of the time, and 27% say they use them every time they shop. Any marketer that attempts to kick the habit does so at its peril, as Procter found out a few years ago, when it tried to cut couponing in its diaper business. Rivals stepped up their own cents-off promotions, and P&G was forced to abandon the experiment.

This time, however, P&G could find some allies. "We may as an industry have begun to rely too heavily on [coupons]," says Robert H. Bolte, vice-president for corporate marketing services at Clorox Co.

A SLOWER CLIP FOR COUPONS

NUMBER OF COUPONS DISTRIBUTED

325
300
275
250
0
'90 '91 '92 '93 '94 '95
▲BILLIONS

NUMBER OF COUPONS REDEEMED

8
7
6
5
0
'90 '91 '92 '93 '94 '95
▲BILLIONS

DATA: NCH PROMOTIONAL SERVICES

CHARTS BY RAY VELLA/BW

which is planning its own test in up-state New York. Procter's archrival in diapers, Kimberly-Clark Corp., the maker of Huggies, says it's also experimenting with a coupon cutback in the region. Lever Brothers Co. is said to be doing the same. The company declined to comment.

P&G's test is in keeping with its recent cost-cutting binge. It has closed dozens of plants, chopped thousands of jobs, and slashed discounts to trade customers, which have helped it to lower prices. Will prices fall more if P&G bails out of coupons? One food executive in P&G's test market says supermarkets are running better specials, as they pass along savings from handling fewer coupons. Generally, though, marketers are likely to do more in-store promotions, such as free samples. And instead of blitzing the market, they'll aim promotions at the likeliest customers. They also may use more "clipless coupons," where the cents off are deducted at the cash register as a part of frequent-shopper programs.

BACKLASH. But diehard coupon clippers won't give up without a fight. In Buffalo, Erie County Legislator Raymond K. Dusza has organized a petition drive he says has already garnered 20,000 signatures calling on P&G to rescind its decision. "I'd let my teeth fall out before I would buy another tube of Crest," wrote one angry shopper to a Syracuse newspaper. Wegmans Food Markets Inc., a regional chain, says the backlash hasn't affected sales.

With so many consumers eager for coupons, there will always be marketers to accommodate them. And sometimes for good reason: A coupon is still one of the best ways to get shoppers to try a new product. Cereal makers have stopped the buy-one-get-one-free coupon wars of recent years, but are not likely to dump coupons altogether. Nor are some smaller brands, which have a better chance of attracting new users—rather than helping existing customers—with a coupon offer. Still, coupons are likely to cease being a second form of currency at the cash register. Instead, they'll do what they do best: give an occasional boost to a new or revamped product.

Zachary Schiller in Cleveland

Global Marketing

It is certain that marketing with a global perspective will continue to be a strategic element of U.S. business well beyond the 1990s. The United States is both the world's largest exporter and importer. In 1987, U.S. exports totaled just over $250 billion—about 10 percent of total world exports. During the same period, U.S. imports were nearly $450 billion—just under 10 percent of total world imports. By 1995 exports had risen to $513 billion, and imports to $664 billion—roughly the same percentage of total world trade.

Whether or not they wish to be, all marketers are now part of the international marketing system. For some, the end of the era of domestic markets may have come too soon, but that era is over. Today it is necessary to recognize the strengths and weaknesses of our own marketing practices as compared to those abroad. The multinational corporations have long recognized this need, but now all marketers must acknowledge it.

International marketing differs from domestic marketing in that the parties to its transactions live in different political units. It is the "international" element of international marketing that distinguishes it from domestic marketing—not differences in managerial techniques. The growth of global business among multinational corporations has raised new questions about the role of their headquarters. It has even caused some to speculate whether marketing operations should be performed abroad rather than in the United States.

The key to applying the marketing concept is understanding the consumer. Increasing levels of consumer sophistication are evident in all of the world's most profitable markets. Managers are required to adopt new points of view in order to accommodate increasingly complex consumer wants and needs. The markets of the late 1990s will show further integration on a worldwide scale. In these emerging markets, though, conventional textbook approaches can cause numerous problems. The new marketing perspective called for by the circumstances of the late 1990s requires a long-range view that looks at the basics of exchange and their applications in new settings.

The selections presented here were chosen to provide an overview of world economic factors, competitive positioning, and increasing globalization of markets—issues to which every marketer must become sensitive. "Beware the Pitfalls of Global Marketing" warns of how shortcomings in marketing strategy can fell a good product. The next article advises that many American businesses have not yet truly embraced the global marketplace. "Hot Markets Overseas" reveals how small companies are successfully marketing their products and services in emerging economies abroad. The last article conveys some important suggestions for using the Internet as a means of extending a market outside the United States.

Looking Ahead: Challenge Questions

What economic, cultural, and political obstacles must an organization seeking to become global in its markets consider?

Do you believe that adherence to the "marketing concept" is the right way to approach international markets? Why, or why not?

With reference to "Beware the Pitfalls of Global Marketing," describe situations you are familiar with where shortcomings in marketing strategy have felled a good product.

In what ways can the Internet be used to extend a market outside the United States?

UNIT 4

Beware the Pitfalls of Global Marketing

Shortcomings in a campaign,
like inadequate research and poor follow-up,
can fell a good product.

Kamran Kashani

Before Kamran Kashani became professor of marketing at the International Management Development Institute (IMEDE) in Lausanne, Switzerland, he worked for Coca-Cola, General Tire, and Continental Can International. He is the author of Managing Global Marketing, *published by PWS-Kent.*

It's fashionable today to enthuse over globalized markets and cite glowing examples of standardized marketing winners around the world. True, some markets *are* globalizing, and more companies are taking advantage of them with signal success. But the rosy reports of these triumphs usually neglect to mention the complexities and risks involved; for every victory in globalization there are probably several failures that aren't broadcast. It's not fashionable to talk about failure.

To get an idea of the complexity and the risks in global marketing, examine the case of Henkel, West Germany's leading industrial and consumer adhesives producer. In 1982, Henkel decided to pump new life into its internationally accepted but stagnating consumer contact-adhesive brand, Pattex. The strategy called for expanding the Pattex brand to include newly introduced products in fast-growing segments of the market. The idea of using Pattex as an um-

brella faced heavy opposition, however, from among Henkel's country subsidiaries worldwide. "People were shaking their heads and saying it can't be done and shouldn't be done," recalls the product manager responsible for the decision.

The subsidiaries' doubts led to a consumer test of the umbrella branding concept in West Germany, Austria, and Benelux. According to the test results, Pattex could be repositioned without hurting sales, and it could enhance the prospects of a broader product range. The highly positive survey responses helped soften local managements' opposition. The

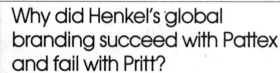

Why did Henkel's global branding succeed with Pattex and fail with Pritt?

global branding of Pattex as "strong universal bonding" took effect soon after.

Almost from the beginning, the relaunched brand showed good results. Today Pattex is Henkel's top brand in consumer adhesives in Europe and in 20 other countries. Surpassing all management expectations, the new products account for close to one-half of the brand's total sales of approximately 100 million deutsche marks.

Thus encouraged, Henkel's management took a similar step a few months after the relaunch of Pattex. This time the subject of umbrella treatment was Pritt, the company's number one brand around the world in glue sticks. Previously, Henkel had repositioned Pritt from "stick gluing" to "simple all-purpose gluing," but with little success. Nevertheless, the experience with Pattex gave top management reason to hope that a coordinated, standardized package design and communication strategy might do the trick this time.

Besides, the major subsidiaries had changed their tune: they endorsed an internationally harmonized Pritt line. In fact, the champion of the concept was the Benelux unit, one of Henkel's largest. Many executives in headquarters in Düsseldorf also viewed the Pritt decision as the next logical step after Pattex.

What more could central product management possibly ask for?

There was one potential problem, however, with the Pritt plan. A quickly arranged consumer survey in West Germany and Benelux had shown that the harmonized line might still be insufficient to turn the broader Pritt umbrella brand around. While comparative test results indicated some improvement over the current package design, they still put UHU, Pritt's global archrival, ahead along many consumer-perceived dimensions. But Pattex's encouraging performance and the unusually strong support from the leading subsidiaries persuaded the head office to proceed with the harmonized line anyway.

In the months that followed, while Pattex maintained its sales climb, the new strategy failed to im-

> ## The "Learn to Speak Polaroid" campaign made all the right moves.

prove Pritt's ho-hum performance, to everybody's surprise. The brand did not lend support to the lesser products under its umbrella, and their sales continued to stall. Today worldwide sales still hover far below expectations, and Pritt remains a one-product brand standing for stick gluing and not much more.

What explains the success of one program in the face of heavy subsidiary opposition and the failure of the other in spite of warm local support? Henkel management has discovered two reasons. Headquarters let forceful subsidiary officers drown out early warnings based on research about Pritt, and they hastened the decision. It was a case of enthusiasm substituting for hard data. Moreover, when the early results disappointed hopes, the subsidiaries diverted

Pritt's promotion funds to other products in a search for immediate payoff. With no central follow-up, the local units did nothing to make up the lost promotion support.

Accordingly, the Pritt plan got neither the initial scrutiny nor the later subsidiary backup that Pattex had enjoyed. Combined, the two handicaps proved fatal to Pritt's global branding.

Winners and Losers

To ascertain why certain global marketing decisions succeed while others fail, I recently studied 17 cases of marketing standardization at 9 American and European multinationals. Nine of the ventures were successes, but in eight, the companies failed to meet their objectives. This article reports on the findings of the study.

A systematic comparison of the "winners" and "losers" reveals that the differences in outcome often depend on the processes underlying the decision making. In other words, my study shows that the ways global decisions are conceptualized, refined, internally communicated, and, finally, implemented in the company's international network have a great deal to do with their performance.

I have identified five pitfalls that handicap global marketing programs and contribute to their suboptimal performance or even demise. The pitfalls include insufficient use of formal research, tendency to overstandardize, poor follow-up, narrow vision in program coordination, and inflexibility in implementation. I'll take these up in turn.

Insufficient Research. Formal research is of course not alien to marketing decision making, yet many a global program has been kicked off without the benefit of a reality test. Nearly half of the programs examined included no formal research before startup. And most of the companies paid for this omission afterwards.

A case in point was Lego A/S, the Danish toy marketer, which undertook American-style consumer promotions in Japan a few years ago. Earlier, the company had measurably improved its penetration of U.S. households by employing "bonus" packs and gift promotions. Encouraged by that success, it decided to transfer these tactics unaltered to other markets, including Japan, where penetration had stalled. But these lures left Japanese consumers unmoved. Subsequent investigation showed that consumers considered the promotions to be wasteful, expensive, and not very appealing. Similar reactions were recorded in several other countries. Lego's marketers thus got their first lesson on the limitations of the global transferability of sales promotions.

Lego management examined consumer perceptions of promotions only *after* the program had failed. In the words of one headquarters executive close to the decision concerning Japan, "People at the head office in Billund and locally believed so much in the U.S. experience and its transferability that they didn't see any need to test the promotions."

This case typifies managerial complacency toward use of market information. At the extreme, it exhibits itself as "we know what we need to know," an attitude that discounts the necessity of research in the early phases of a program. This blinkered outlook often accompanies an assumption that one market's experience is transferable to others—as though the world has finally converged and market idiosyncracies have disappeared. Even managers' enthusiasm can get in the way of research. Henkel learned this point in its almost casual dismissal of Pritt's consumer survey results.

Shortcutting the early step of research in a decision process is likely to be costly. Of the cases in the sample, nearly two-thirds of the global programs that did not benefit from formal research before launch failed in their mission, while the same proportion of those that relied on research succeeded.

Overstandardization. Paradoxically, without some diversity of practice in the organization, marketing standardization will not work. When a program is burdened with too many standards, local inventiveness and experimentation close to the markets dry up. Local innovation is exactly what a global program needs to keep itself updated and responsive to evolving market conditions.

In the mid-1970s, when Polaroid introduced its pathbreaking SX-70 camera in Europe, the company employed the same advertising strategy—including TV commercials and print ads—it had used in the triumphant launch of the product in the United States. To headquarters in Cambridge, Massachusetts, the camera was a universal product with a universal consumer benefit: the pleasure of instant photography. Therefore, the communication approach should be standard around the world. Well, the product was surely universal, but the television commercials, featuring testimonials from personalities well-known in the United States, like Sir Laurence Olivier, were not necessarily transferable to Europe. At least, that's what Polaroid's executives there thought.

Unperturbed by subsidiaries' concerns, Cambridge set strict guidelines to discourage deviation from the global plan. Even local translations of the English spoken in the commercials had to get approval from the head office. As one senior European executive recalls, "We were treated like kids who have to be controlled every step along the way."

The Europeans were proved to be right. The testimonials by "unknown" personalities left consumers cold. The commercials never achieved much impact in either raising awareness of Polaroid for instant photography or pulling consumers into the stores for a closer look at the camera. Even though the SX-70 later became a winner in Europe, local management believes that the misguided introductory campaign in no way helped its performance.

Fortunately, the lesson was not forgotten a decade later, when Polaroid's European management launched a program of pan-European advertising to reposition Polaroid's instant photography from a "party camera" platform, which had eroded the brand's image and undermined camera prices, to a serious, utilitarian platform. But this time, headquarters didn't assume it had the answer. Instead, it looked for inspiration in the various advertising

Would local managers buy DEC's Europe-wide sales program?

practices of the European subsidiaries. And it found the answer in the strategy of one of the smallest subsidiaries, Switzerland's. With considerable profit, the Swiss unit had promoted the functional uses of instant photography as a way to communicate with family and friends. A pan-European task force charged with setting the advertising strategy tested the concept in major markets. These tests proved that the Swiss strategy was transferable and indeed produced the desired impact.

Thus was born the "Learn to Speak Polaroid" campaign. The two-year European project is considered one of the company's most successful advertising efforts. Subsidiaries outside Europe, including those in Australia and Japan, liked the strategy so much that they adopted it too. The experience is a source of pride for European management and a reaffirmation that "Europe can take care of itself."

What made the SX-70 and "Learn to Speak Polaroid" campaigns decidedly different was the decision-making processes involved. Promoting the SX-70 was a top-down process. But in "Learn to Speak Polaroid," the subsidiaries were offered the opportunity to influence the outcome, and they took it. Furthermore, "Learn..." was a product of the diversity found in the subsidiaries' communication strategies. The task force had the luxury of choosing among several solutions to the problem. It also had the wisdom to test the chosen strategy for confirmation of its impact around Europe.

Finally, and perhaps most important, even after adopting the pan-European program, local management retained the freedom to adapt the campaign to domestic tastes and needs. For example, where tests showed that the "Learn..." tag didn't convey the intended meaning in the local language, the subsidiary was free to change it. The message was more important than the words. Moreover, while the copy and layout for print ads remained fixed throughout Europe, local units could choose their preferred illustrations from a large set of alternatives prepared by the ad agency.

The contrasting outcomes of these two campaigns underscore a point clear to experienced marketers that, for a global program to achieve its aims, the scope of standardization need not be total. Any such program usually can attain its objectives through standardization of a few elements in the marketing mix of a product or service. Never too many elements, however, these are the leverage points around which the rationale for standardization is built.

With Pattex, for instance, the global branding strategy depended on the use of a successful brand for new products, uniform positioning of the entire range, and harmonized package designs. Local units, on the other hand, had authority over a set of decisions including communication strategy, pricing, and distribution channels. They could even decide on the package illustrations pertaining to the uses of adhesives. These matters, though important to the marketing success of Pattex in each country, did not impinge on the rationale or the crucial elements of standardization.

Nor did the flexibility allowed in the execution of "Learn to Speak Polaroid" advertising weaken the campaign. Deviations in execution didn't distract from the common mission; rather, they helped strengthen the effort by bringing local expertise to bear on the details. Overstandardization would have destroyed the incentive for local contribution, a price no global marketing program can afford to pay.

Poor Follow-up. Impressive kickoff meetings, splashy presentations to country heads, and the like are important attention-getters at the start of a campaign. But the momentum will be lost, as in the case of Pritt's promotional support, if these are not followed by lower key yet concrete steps to monitor progress and solve problems as they come along. These post-launch activities can determine whether a program survives the domestic organization's other priorities.

The differing experiences of Digital Equipment Corporation and another U.S.-based computer company, which I will call Business Electronic Systems (BES), are instructive. Not long ago, DEC's European operation installed a standardized sales management program in its 17 regional subsidiaries. Aimed to improve sales force productivity and customer service, the program touched on many aspects of overseeing

the region's 2,500-strong sales force. But as sales operations were traditionally considered a local matter, sales managers were at first predictably unenthusiastic about using the system. It was considered an infringement on their authority.

What gradually sold them on it was the continuity of attention the program got in the two years after its highly visible launch. Through watchful monitoring of progress toward full implementation, coordinating sessions among local sales managers, and periodic messages of reinforcement from top management, sponsors at regional headquarters made sure that the program received priority from subsidiary officials. The coordinating sessions for subsidiary sales managers were particularly helpful, highlighting the payoffs from use of the system and furnishing a forum for dealing with common problems. These sessions proved to be invaluable for taking a creative solution produced in one market and spreading it to the other 16.

At BES, which installed a standardized software-house cooperation program in Europe, the picture was much different. Regional headquarters conceived the program to help penetrate a market segment where BES was weak – small and medium-sized accounts. The program required a big change in sales force operation: no longer in control of the hardware and software package, the sales force had to determine its content jointly with a software house that had access to the smaller accounts. The success of the standardized program depended on how well the sales force carried out its new assignments in BES's eight country and subregional European operations.

Like DEC, BES gave the project a highly visible launch. Top management left no doubt that the software-house cooperation strategy enjoyed its

> It took nonconforming managers to make Unilever's household cleaner a success.

wholehearted support. But the program never got the follow-up attention it needed. The responsibility for overseeing the project kept changing hands in the head office. Partly as a result of these switches in management, efforts to monitor progress in the subsidiaries dwindled.

The main problem, however, was the absence of a communication channel for sharing and building on subsidiary experiences. Each unit was obliged to find its own solutions to problems common to many. Hence the wheel was reinvented every time. Moreover, many country sales managers resented having to implement an unpopular program. Some gave up; others reluctantly carried on to the end, which came in three years. The reason: poor performance.

The quality of follow-up is of paramount importance when a global program introduces abrupt changes in local practice. As DEC's example shows, timely follow-up measures can go a long way to ensure subsidiary involvement and compliance. Without such measures, as BES learned, the program can easily succumb to local management's lukewarm interest.

Narrow Vision. A coordinating organization is needed to look after the health of a global marketing program because, as we have seen, a program's success depends so much on what happens after its launch—whether problems in implementation are resolved, and how the program's content is adapted to evolving internal and market conditions.

Two common mechanisms employed to manage a global program through its launch and beyond are those based, respectively, in the headquarters and a "lead market." Under a headquarters mechanism, the formal authority for a program rests with a central line or staff function like worldwide product management, regional management, or international marketing coordination. Under a lead market mechanism, a subsidiary is assigned the responsibility to define and manage a given program for all the participating "follower" countries. The choice of a lead market is usually a function of its expertise or experience with a particular product or service.

Though popular, both approaches have serious weaknesses. Headquarters, by definition removed from the firing line, nevertheless makes decisions that are supposed to keep the program fine-tuned to changing subsidiary market conditions. Similarly, the lead-market structure lacks the global perspective and information sources to coordinate international activities well. That is especially true when the lead market is also the home base for successful products that are globalization candidates. In these cases, management isn't always willing to adopt its "tried and proven" marketing ideas to different conditions prevailing elsewhere in the international organization.

But the main problem with both mechanisms is narrow vision; in each, only a single perspective is represented. As such they are not open to a continuous stream of inputs from local markets. Nor do they provide a forum for debating alternatives or sharing solutions to common problems. As a result, local management often justifiably regards headquarters or lead-market decisions as narrow, insular, top-down, and even dictatorial.

Unilever's experience with its household cleaner Domestos shows how a decision-making structure representing a single view can hamper global market-

ing. In the 1970s, the Anglo-Dutch company targeted Domestos for international expansion and assigned development of a global "reference mix" to the brand's lead market in the United Kingdom, where Domestos had been well established for a long time. But years and several market entries later, top management was still waiting for a repeat elsewhere of the UK's success story. Later analysis identified a key contributor to the problem: the lead market's insistence on a home-brewed recipe of positioning Domestos as a "lavatory germ killer" in markets already crowded with specialized and lower priced competition.

Where the product had won penetration, it had done so largely by deviating from the lead market's guidelines and staking out a whole new product category. In West Germany, Domestos was positioned as an all-purpose sanitary cleaner, and in Australia as a "bathroom plaque remover"—an innovative platform with potential for universal application, as consumers in many markets now show a growing concern with the appearance of their bathrooms.

To avoid the problems inherent in center-based or lead-market mechanisms, Unilever's detergent unit recently opted for a multisubsidiary structure to coordinate brands in Europe. The European Brand Group (EBG) is a decision-making body that includes executives from headquarters and a number of large subsidiaries.

So far, the company's experience with this mixed organization has been encouraging. As an example, EBG was instrumental in developing and launching a lemon-scented version of Vif, Unilever's successful abrasive liquid cleaner, across Europe in record time of a few months. Most important, the introduction outfoxed Procter & Gamble, which was known to be planning a similar move with its Mr. Clean; Vif Lemon won the race to market in every single country. Unilever management hopes that such gains in coordination will reinforce EBG's mandate to "view Europe as one business" and help speed up harmonization of marketing practices around the continent.

Rigid Implementation. Standardized marketing is a means of reaching an end, never an end in itself. When global marketers forget that obvious truth, standardization risks becoming rigid and ultimately self-defeating. Two common manifestations of rigidity are forced adoption and automatic piloting.

Forced adoption is the outcome of a tendency to ignore local units' reservations about implementing a standardized marketing program. Higher level management's typical reaction is to close the exit door on this ground: "After all, what's left of global marketing if the implementation isn't universal?" Theoretically, this is right. And ardent globalizers would argue that local resistance can be expected in any standardized effort and that without some central direction, a program would never get off the ground. But forced compliance rarely delivers the anticipated rewards. Among the programs I studied, every case of forced adoption had eventually flopped.

It is true that a subsidiary's objection may stem from resistance to ideas originating from outside. But local management's reservations may also be based on a sound understanding of its domestic market. When Nestlé launched its innovative cakelike Yes chocolate bar in Europe, the UK organization refused to take the product because a soft bar assertedly

Lego's packaging was just fine for kids, but parents buy toys.

would not appeal to British tastes. Subsequent market tests validated this local opinion. Forced adoption would have led to failure on a large scale.

Whatever the reasons for local opposition, forced compliance destroys any commitment to program implementation. And no global program, no matter how sound, can survive such absence of commitment.

Automatic piloting is symptomatic of inflexible program management in the face of changing market conditions. Lego's costly difficulties in the United States illustrate this problem. The company, whose motto has been "kids are kids and alike around the world," pioneered standardized marketing in its industry and became a truly global enterprise by marketing its educational toys in the same fashion in more than 100 countries.

Recently, however, Lego has encountered stiff competition from look-alike and lower priced rival products from Japan, the United States, and other countries. In the United States, where the competition has been the fiercest, Tyco, a leading competitor, began putting its toys in plastic buckets that could be used for storage after each play. This utilitarian approach contrasted with Lego's elegant see-through cartons standardized worldwide. But American parents seemed to prefer the functional toys-in-a-bucket idea over the cartons. Seeing a potential for serious damage, Lego's alarmed U.S. management sought permission from Denmark to package Lego toys in buckets. The head office flatly refused the request.

The denial was based on seemingly sound arguments. The bucket idea could cheapen Lego's reputation for high quality. Moreover, the Lego bucket would rightly be seen as a "me too" defensive reaction from a renowned innovator. Finally, and perhaps most important, buckets would be a radical deviation from the company's policy of standardized marketing everywhere. Even U.S. consumer survey results comparing buckets favorably with cartons

weren't considered a good enough reason for a change from the global concept.

Two years later, however, headquarters in Billund reversed itself. The impetus was a massive loss of U.S. market share to competitive goods sold in buckets. Soon after, the American subsidiary began marketing some of its toys in a newly designed bucket of its own. Now, to the delight of many in Billund, the buckets are outselling the cartons, and the share erosion has reassuringly halted. (Last Christmas the bucket was introduced worldwide and was a smashing success.) An observer of Lego's about-face in the United States attributed the two-years-late response to automatic piloting on the part of its global marketers.

The Lego story highlights the principle adhered to by some, but ignored by many others, that international conformity to global standards may have to be sacrificed to respond to shifting conditions in particular markets. As one Lego executive put it ruefully, "While kids will always be alike around the world, parents who buy the toys may change their behavior."

Improving the Process

The pitfalls I have examined can all be traced to shortcomings in a global program's decision-making process. But the winners in my sample show that such traps can be avoided. Analysis of them leads to the following observations on ways of upgrading the process and the decisions that result from it.

☐ Market research helps a global marketing program in two ways: by influencing decisions to more accurately reflect the commonalities as well as the differences among subsidiary markets; and by winning support for the program in local organizations when research results are especially encouraging.

Useful research is multisite in geographic coverage and uniform in methodology. The multisite criterion ensures enough local diversity to make the findings valid for the program's international scope. Needless to say, a global marketing program doesn't have to be tested everywhere. Some companies find the inclusion of at least one major subsidiary market and a few others considered representative of the rest sufficient not only for geographic diversity purposes but also for building internal credibility for the results. Uniform methodology, on the other hand, ensures comparability of international research data, which is so often a problem for global marketers. "Without similar methods," one experienced executive noted, "the local organizations can kill a good global program with their own research."

☐ Local initiative and decision making are often the

keys to a program's long-term success. To avoid sterile uniformity at one extreme and a free-for-all at the other, global marketers have to delineate early on the few standards that are essential to attaining a program's objectives and the many that are not. They must insist on compliance with the essential standards.

Strike a balance between central control and subsidiary autonomy.

But at the same time, local experimentation with the less critical elements should be allowed and even encouraged. Astute marketers will keep an eye on the local experiments and in due course incorporate the successful innovations into an evolving and dynamic set of global standards.

□ Effective follow-up—as important as any prelaunch measure—means identifying common problems hampering implementation, spreading creative solutions found by local units, and winning support for the program over parochial priorities. But these tasks don't get performed automatically; they need to be recognized and assigned.

The responsibility for initiating and directing postlaunch activities must therefore be focused by a central program manager or a management team. The chosen individual(s) should possess not only the international overview necessary to administer the program but also negotiating skills for bypassing organizational barriers and building consensus and support for the project. These skills become particularly useful in cases where globalization demands radical departures in local practices.

□ While the *process* for formulating a program, starting it, and following it through may be driven centrally by, say, program management, decisions on its *content* are best left to the subsidiaries or country organizations. So an ad hoc decision-making mechanism incorporating a number of subsidiaries offers more openness to local input than one centered at headquarters or in a lead market.

To prevent this process from becoming cumbersome, headquarters should limit the group's membership to a few of the larger and more influential subsidiaries and confine its participants to those local marketing managers with deep knowledge of the issues and the organizational weight to see decisions through to implementation. The experience of a growing number of companies employing such ad hoc mechanisms suggests, not surprisingly, that their effectiveness improves as the participants get practice working together on issues of concern to most member countries. That experience also suggests that thorny problems are best left for resolution after the group has established a track record of successful decisions.

□ Flexibility should be built into a global program's implementation. That means a willingness on its sponsors' part selectively to sacrifice global standards when local conditions so dictate or to leave open an exit door when local management argues against adoption of a program. In the absence of flexibility, standardized marketing risks becoming an obstacle to competitive advantage.

But what to do in those frequent cases when global marketers and their subsidiary colleagues differ on the standards appropriate in a certain market? A number of companies in my study have a "facts-over-opinions" policy to get around this potentially volatile problem. A subsidiary gains exemption from having to conform in part or altogether if, and only if, careful research confirms its doubts. By letting facts decide each case, the policy helps focus the attention of both sides on the substantive issues and clears the debate of mere opinions—which are so often colored. Implementation of the marketing program then proceeds in an informed but flexible fashion.

Isolationism in a Global Economy

MURRAY WEIDENBAUM

growing paradox facing the United States is the simultaneous rise of a new spirit of isolationism amid the increasing globalization of business. Viewed independently, each of the two trends seems to make sense. In juxtaposition, however, isolationism amid globalization is simply unachievable.

The end of the Cold War brought on a widespread expectation that the United States could safely cut back its military establishment. Government leaders could shift their attention from foreign policy to the domestic problems that face the American people. That simple approach was not bound to last.

Many recent disturbing events overseas—in Haiti, Somalia, Bosnia and China—remind Americans that we still live in a dangerous world. It does not make sense to dismantle our military establishment.

But, in a far less dramatic way, it has become clear that the rest of the world is going to have an increasingly powerful impact on American business. History tells us that trying to shut ourselves off from these "foreign" influences just does not work. When imperial China tried to do that some 500 years ago, it rapidly went from being the world's most advanced and powerful nation to a poor backwater.

The rapidly growing global marketplace is a source of great actual and potential benefit to American entrepreneurs, workers and consumers. Those who identify with the change are likely to be the winners; those who resist will lose.

The global marketplace has rapidly shifted from just a simple-minded buzzword to complex reality. International trade is growing far more rapidly than domestic production, to a point where companies hardly have a choice about participating. Six basic points illustrate why.

1 *Americans do not have to do anything or change anything to be part of the global marketplace.* Even if a business does not export a thing and has no overseas locations, its owners, managers and employees are still part of the global marketplace. The same goes for its suppliers. The issue has been decided by technology. The combination of fax machines, universal telephone service (including cellular), low-cost, high-speed copiers and computers, and speedy jet airline service enables money, goods, services and people to cross most borders rapidly, if not instantly. And that goes especially for what is the most strategic resource—information.

BRIEFCASE

There has been a marked shift from military to economic competition since the end of the Cold War. This means that the business firm is now the key to global economic competition. Governments, to be sure, can help or hinder, and in a major way. But they are, at best, supporting players in this new global marketplace.

ILLUSTRATIONS: SHANE KELLY

A dramatic example of the ease of business crossing national borders occurred during the Gulf war. On the first day of the Iraqi attack on Kuwait, a savvy Kuwaiti bank manager began faxing his key records to his subsidiary in Bahrain. By the end of the day, all the key records had been transferred out of Kuwait. The next morning, the bank opened as a Bahraini institution, beyond the reach of the Iraqis. Literally, a bank was moved from one country to another via a fax machine.

American businesses are no longer insulated because of vast distances from other producers. Every American is subject to competition from overseas. If that force has not hit a region yet, it probably is on its way.

most of their assets overseas: Citicorp (51 percent), Bankers Trust (52 percent), Digital Equipment Corp. (61 percent), Chevron (55 percent), Exxon (56 percent), Mobil (63 percent), Gillette (66 percent), and Manpower Inc. (72 percent). Increasingly, U.S. firms are establishing factories, warehouses, laboratories and offices in other countries. One-half of Xerox's employees already work on foreign soil.

A recent survey of American manufacturing companies showed that becoming an internationally oriented company usually pays off. Sales by firms with no foreign activities grow at only half the rate of those with foreign operations. Firms with international activities grow faster in every industry—and profits are higher.

A decade from now, Southeast Asia will be one of the major economic regions of the globe, competing for world markets with Japan, North America, and Europe.

2 Employees, customers, suppliers and investors in U.S. companies are increasingly participating in the international economy. Large numbers of American companies have deployed

3 The transnational enterprise is on the rise. It is more than just choosing where to locate a manufacturing or marketing operation. The larger business firms operating in several regions of the world have been setting up multiple locations for decision making. For those domestic firms that sell goods or services to other American companies, increasingly their customers are located in one or more decentralized divisions, some of which are now based overseas. That works two ways for Americans. Du Pont has shifted the headquarters of its electronic operation to Japan. Germany's Siemens has moved its ultrasound equipment division to the United States.

Cross-border alliances have become commonplace. New international business relationships have arisen: joint ventures, production sharing, cross-licensing, technology swaps and joint research projects.

Increasingly, the successful business looks upon its entire operation in a global context. It hires people, buys inputs and locates production, marketing and decision-making centers worldwide. An example may help convert theory to reality. Here is a shipping label used by an American electronics company: "Made in one or more of the following countries: Korea, Hong Kong, Malaysia, Singapore, Taiwan, Mauritius, Thailand, Indonesia, Mexico, Philippines. The exact country of origin is unknown."

ASSETS OF AMERICAN COMPANIES DEPLOYED OVERSEAS

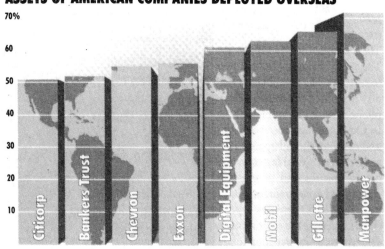

4 The rise of the global marketplace provides vast new opportunities for Americans to diversify their investments. Southeast Asia is currently the fastest-growing part of the world. Any observant visitor will see that the 8 percent real growth that they report is no statistical mirage. Each of those economies is booming.

Government policy in Southeast Asia welcomes foreign investment. While these present or former totalitarian countries move toward capitalism, the United States has been expanding government regulation of business. It is not surprising that so many American companies are expanding overseas. Examples include the energy company exploring in Kazakhstan, the mining enterprise moving to Bolivia, and the medical devices firm setting up a laboratory in the Netherlands.

Overseas risks may be great. Even the most experienced China experts do not know what will happen after Deng Xiaoping. The tremendous amount of income and wealth created by Deng's economic reforms is the best guarantee of their being continued. But, the acceleration of misunderstandings between China and the United States is a dark cloud on the political as well as economic horizon.

A decade from now, Southeast Asia will be one of the major economic regions of the globe—along with Japan, North America and Western Europe. Potentially, those economies are both customers and competitors for American companies. The level of technology is high in Taiwan, Singapore and Malaysia. Intelligent and productive workforces are available in substantial quantities. The 1.5 billion people in Southeast Asia constitute the major new global market.

5 *Despite the military and political issues that divide Western Europe, the economic unification is continuing full bore.* With a minimum of fanfare, Sweden, Finland and Austria are entering the European Union. The six-nation European Common Market became the 12-nation European Community and now is the 15-member European Union.

Fifteen member-nations are not going to be the end of the line for the European Union. The entrance of Austria is strategic because Vienna is a major gateway to Eastern Europe. Hungary, Poland and the Czech Republic are anxious to develop closer economic and business relations with Western Europe. They can become low-cost suppliers, low-cost competitors—or both.

The most important positive development in Europe in the coming decade will be the new

economic strength of the largest member—Germany. A visitor is struck by the substantial amount of physical investment that the national government is making in the recently liberated Eastern provinces. That is bound to result in a strong and newly competitive region.

6 *The American economy is still the strongest in the world and our prospects are impressive.* In many industries, American firms are still the world leaders. U.S. firms rank No. 1 (in sales volume) in 13 major industries—aerospace, apparel, beverages, chemicals, computers, food products, motor vehicles, paper products, petroleum, pharmaceuticals, photographic and scientific equipment, soap and cosmetics, and tobacco.

What about the future? Nobody can forecast which specific technologies will succeed in the coming decade. But the prospects for American companies being in the lead are very bright. There is a special reason for optimism.

In the 1990s, America will be benefiting from the upsurge of industrial research and development during the 1980s. For the first time in more than half a century, the magnitude of company-sponsored R&D exceeded the total of government-financed R&D. That primary reliance on private R&D continues to this day.

Few people appreciate the long-term impact of that strategic crossover. The new and continued dominance of the private sector in the choice of investments in advanced technology makes it more likely that there will be an accelerated flow of new and improved civilian products and production processes in the years ahead. A progression of innovation may be forthcoming comparable to the advent of missiles and space vehicles following the massive growth of military R&D in the '50s and '60s.

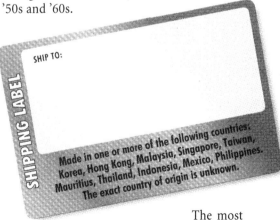

The most basic development since the end of the Cold War has been missed by all observers and analysts—because it is so subtle. During the Cold War, the two military superpowers dominated the world stage. It is currently fashionable to say that, in the post-Cold War period, three economic superpowers have taken their place— the United States, Japan and Germany. That is technically accurate but very misleading.

During the Cold War, government was the pace-setting player on the global stage. Government made the strategic decisions. Businesses were important, but they were responding to government orders, supplying armaments to the superpowers. In the process, of course, business created substantial economic wealth. But the shift from military to economic competition is fundamental. It means that the business firm is now the key to global economic competition. Governments, to be sure, can help or hinder, and in a major way. But they are supporting players, at best.

The basic initiative in the global marketplace has shifted to private enterprise. Individual entrepreneurs and individual business firms make the key decisions that will determine the size, composition and growth of the international economy. That makes for an extremely challenging external environment for the competitive American enterprise of the 1990s as well as for U.S. public policymakers.

Murray Weidenbaum is chairman of the Center for the Study of American Business at Washington University in St. Louis.

Hot Markets Overseas

Roberta Maynard

In Ginny Hall's view, nearly every international market is hot. From her two-person business, Hall & Hall Global Trading, in Colorado Springs, Colo., she has been busier than ever arranging for the sale of goods around the world: chicken to Egypt, sugar to Russia, and American blue jeans to just about everywhere. In business only five years, Hall already has commercial ties in 45 countries.

In those five years, she notes, a major change has taken place: More people want more things, and those would-be consumers have the money to buy them. "Everything American is in demand," she says, "including beet sugar, butter, beef, veal, canned goods, turkey, cigarettes. Fertilizer and portland cement, too."

Like many international traders, Hall has been successful in traditional markets, but she has also discovered extraordinary opportunities in what are called the world's emerging markets.

These dozen or so countries, many with large populations, are enjoying explosive economic growth. Most are moving toward democracy, and most are transferring industries from public to private ownership and reducing tariffs and other barriers to imports. In all, they promise to become powerhouse markets for U.S. goods in the decades to come.

Last year, the federal government identified the top 10 emerging markets for U.S. exports and investment. They are the Chinese Economic Area, which includes China, Hong Kong, and Taiwan; India; Indonesia; South Korea; Argentina; Brazil; Mexico; Poland; Turkey; and South Africa.

The gross domestic product of these countries, with half the world's population, totals more than $2 trillion, about one-fourth the GDP of the industrialized world. In 15 years, the emerging markets' GDP should rise to about half the industrial world's GDP, according to the U.S. Department of Commerce.

The Commerce Department forecasts that opportunities for U.S. trade are likely to increase dramatically as these big emerging markets (BEMs) increase purchases of capital equipment, including industrial and farm machinery, electric-power transmission and transportation

equipment, and high-technology products. Here is a sampling of these hot markets:

Chinese Economic Area (CEA). Made up of China, Hong Kong, and Taiwan, it's the biggest emerging market, with the world's seventh-largest economy.

China alone has a population of 1.2 billion and has enjoyed an annual economic growth rate of 13 percent the past two years.

Asia generally is poised to become the epicenter of future global investment activity, according to a survey by Ernst & Young, the New York-based professional-services firm. Ernst & Young foresees substantial investment growth in India, Indonesia, Thailand, and Malaysia, as well as in the Chinese Economic Area.

Ohio Electronic Engravers Inc., which manufactures heavy equipment for electronic printing, is already reaping the benefits of sales to the BEMs. Five years ago, the Dayton, Ohio, company had sold five of its units in China. Since then, it has sold 52 more at a cost of $400,000 to $900,000 each.

South Africa. Its population of 39 million (9 million more than in California) has a pent-up demand for American goods in the wake of the lifting of sanctions in 1991.

Import growth sectors during 1993-94 include machinery (computers, appliances, and office machines), up 14 percent; telephones, 35 percent; electrical products, 20 percent; compact discs, cassettes, and related media, 30 percent.

India. It has a low average per-capita annual income but a growing middle class. An estimated 200 million Indians now have annual incomes comparable to those of middle-class Americans.

In 1993, the Indian government approved $1.1 billion in U.S. investments, up from $20 million in 1990. Also in 1993, U.S. exports to India increased 44 percent over the previous year.

FloWind Corp., of San Rafael, Calif., is benefiting from India's need for power-generation equipment. The company recently signed its first Indian contract, involving a $29 million sale of wind-energy equipment and technology. Harold F.

Koegler, FloWind's president and CEO, expects sales to India to grow to $90 million in 1996.

Poland. While some Americans have experienced difficulty exporting in this former Soviet bloc country, others have enjoyed success. For example, Ginny Hall, the export trading company owner, has found Poland "wide open, with a lot of privatizing going on." The demand there is for many of the goods she handles, including basics such as sugar, tires, and housing components.

Other hot prospects are hotel and restaurant equipment, furniture, and pollution-control equipment.

Though the United States is not a principal trading partner of Poland, U.S. exports to Poland increased from $400 million in 1990 to $900 million in 1993. They are projected to reach $7 billion by 2000.

Turkey. Total imports are expected to grow an average of 15 percent annually through 2000, to about $120 billion. The promise of growth prompted U.S. entrepreneur Robert Stevenson to enter the market through a joint venture a year ago.

Stevenson is president of Eastman Machine Co., in Buffalo, N.Y., which makes equipment for the apparel industry. Turkey's strategic location has made it a distribution point for goods heading to Europe, Asia, and the Mideast, Stevenson has found.

Argentina. South America's richest country enjoyed GDP growth of nearly 24 percent from 1990 to 1993. During this period, its total imports increased 400 percent to $16.8 billion as the government eased trade barriers.

A world leader in privatization, Argentina has placed nearly all of its major public-sector companies in private hands, including the nation's airlines as well as its natural-gas, oil, insurance, and electric-power companies.

Emerging markets figure prominently on individual states' export-priority lists, too. Iowa, for example, has been focusing on Latin America, Japan, and the rest of Asia as potential markets for its farmers' grain, soybeans, corn, cattle, and pork—but also for medical products and other high-tech goods.

"Small manufacturers are emerging here as a new business arena as a result of 10 years of downsizing," says Ronald Manning, director of the Small Business Development Center in Ames, Iowa.

Oregon's proximity to the Pacific Rim gives it an edge in the booming environmental market there. Of the four countries Oregon targets for export promotion, three are in Asia. Three of the countries it targets are emerging markets: South Korea, Taiwan, and Mexico; the fourth is Japan.

"If you look at environmental services, most countries in Southeast Asia will be really good markets," says Sunun Setboonsang, international trade development officer in Oregon's economic development office. "Years of very strong growth have left behind very polluted areas that need help with air and water." This is especially true of Thailand, Malaysia, and Indonesia, known as the "little dragons." Consumer goods as well as agricultural and forest products are also in demand, says Setboonsang. "For these, the buying power in Asia is enormous."

The strong interest in emerging markets by no means suggests that industrialized countries can't continue to be lucrative markets for U.S. goods.

In just one evening last month, trader Ginny Hall received 23 orders from Europe. She is selling large volumes of used jeans in Italy and Greece, sometimes shipping as many as four 20-by-40-foot containers a month. She buys jeans for as little as $1.95 a pair and sells them for up to $80.

In 1993, governors from 27 states made more trips to Germany than anywhere else, according to the National Governors' Association, in Washington, D.C. Of 81 trips abroad made for investment and export promotion and related purposes, 17 were to Germany, followed by 12 to Mexico and eight to Japan.

A recent Coopers & Lybrand survey of 428 small and midsize U.S. companies shows that more than 40 percent of those targeting new countries for export are planning to enter the Pacific Rim. But almost as many, 39 percent, plan to expand activities to European countries. The United Kingdom, France, and Germany were the top three named.

> "**E**verything American is in demand."
> —Ginny Hall, International Trader

In truth, there can be no definitive list of hot markets because no product or service does well everywhere. Any business thinking about exporting to or investing in any country—emerging markets or otherwise—should evaluate each market separately. Here are a few sources of market data:

State international trade offices. Check with your state economic development department for details.

Private firms. Dun & Bradstreet, for example, has just introduced Global Scope—detailed, customized reports on the largest, fastest-growing markets. The cost per report is $149. For details, call 1-800-999-3867, Ext. 6514.

U.S. Department of Commerce. It is co-sponsoring seminars on the big emerging markets in several cities this summer.

The cities include Cleveland, June 8; Chicago, June 13; Los Angeles, June 15; New York, June 20; Denver, June 30; Atlanta, July 20; Miami, July 26; and Orlando, July 27.

A second round of seminars at different locations is planned for the fall. Each one-day seminar, geared toward senior-level executives, costs $179.

For more information, call 1-800-336-4307.

Also this summer, the Commerce Department plans to offer a new book on emerging markets. And by July, BEMs will have a home page on the Internet.

U.S. Chamber of Commerce. It has announced a new system to enable small and midsize businesses to buy, sell, and invest in markets around the world by using their personal computers. IBEX will be marketed through the national Chamber, local chambers, and trade associations.

Full-scale distribution is slated for September. For information, call the Chamber at (202) 463-5460.

A Whole New World

*The Internet offers an easy means of extending your market outside the U.S.—
but there are some hurdles to overcome*

Peter Krasilovsky

As the Internet and online services begin to attract users around the world, many marketers are taking advantage of the Net's global reach. Major global marketing activities already underway on the Internet range from automakers (General Motors) to direct-mail companies who put their catalogs online (L.L. Bean) to global wine shippers (Virtual Vineyards). Even new-fangled lottery and gambling companies (Liechtenstein's InterLotto) have gone onto the Net, taking advantage of cyberspace's trivialization of national boundaries.

For some of these companies, the global market has largely been a hit-or-miss affair. They put their content up in English for the American market, and if any international users stumble across it and end up buying something, so much the better. Such orders can be gravy for U.S.-focused marketers. CompuServe's pioneering Electronic Mall, for instance, reports that 40 percent of some merchants' sales come from CompuServe's 1.8 million overseas members, who are largely attracted to merchandise that previously had been available only in the U.S. Given the weak U.S. dollar, non-American buyers have often gotten excellent bargains in the process.

Other marketers have made a strategic decision to dive into the global market with both feet, realizing they can use the Net and/or online services to:
• reach new customers outside their home countries
• support existing customers who reside abroad
• build global brand awareness

These marketers may identify their best potential international markets, and then take extra steps to provide country-specific content and services, ideally in the native language of that country. They may also provide local sales support and, where applicable, bill in local currencies.

Marketers may also decide to go with an online service such as CompuServe, Europe On-line, America Online (AOL), or Microsoft Network in Europe, or services such as NiftyServe or PC Van in Japan. Although such services are not available to the entire Web community, the simple fact that they represent discrete, closed environments means there's less chance that a company's message will get lost in the shuffle. Moreover, online services can form "partnerships" with a marketer, helping to perform transactions and other services.

The Best Countries

For the most part, marketers have zeroed in on the countries with the largest potential Internet/online populations. The four "core" countries for such marketers are generally considered to be Germany, the United Kingdom, France, and Japan. Together, these countries represent 92 percent of the non-U.S. Internet/online home subscriber base of 5.355 million. Due to their size, per capita income, and interest in information services and technological capabilities, these countries are likely to continue to dominate the global marketplace for online services and Internet access.

A more ambitious list of countries would also include many of the "second tier" countries, including the Netherlands, Scandinavian countries, Australia/New Zealand, and Italy. Indeed, the Scandinavian countries are considered to be the most Internet-intensive, on a per capita basis, in the world. There are currently more than 150,000 online

From *Marketing Tools*, May 1996, pp. 22, 24-25. © 1996 by American Demographics, Inc. Reprinted by permission.

subscribers in these markets.

The chart on Global Reach by Simba Information estimates the number of home-based online and Internet subscribers at the end of 1995. There are many more Internet "users" in each of these countries, of course, but most of them are institutional users that would not be ideal for marketing purposes.

How fast might these markets grow? Inteco Research estimates that there will be more than 10 million subscribers in Germany, the U.K., and France by the year 2000. Worldwide—outside the U.S.—Simba Information predicts there will be almost 21 million Internet/online users by that time.

Despite these encouraging numbers, sure-fire opportunities for Internet and on-line marketing outside the U.S. have occasionally been overstated. This is largely due to misreads of local situations. Just as turn-of-the century shoe salesmen looked at China and saw a faceless country with the theoretical potential to sell "a billion pairs of shoes," today's marketers have sometimes gotten caught in the hype of "universal" Internet access.

Executives may get excited, for instance, by exchanging personal e-mail with, say, a citizen of Germany, South Africa, or New Zealand—without stopping to think that their correspondent may only be a student using university facilities. And students aren't always the best sales prospects. The reality of the international market for the Internet and online services depends on each country's economic, technical, cultural, political, and regional dynamics. Outside of the "best" nations, many countries remain technologically underdeveloped and have a low-income citizenry. Subsequently, they do not have significant phone penetration, much less a sizeable base of PC and modem owners.

Other countries have acceptable phone and PC/modem penetrations, but the costs of being connected to the phone system are so high that it sharply impacts casual uses such as surfing on the Internet. Even advanced countries, like the United Kingdom, sometimes have sky-high

Figure 1: *America Online goes global*

Figure 2: *Compuserve with a Continental flavor*

phone connection rates that can run over $3.50 per hour. Connection fees can be even more burdensome outside of metro areas, where long-distance calling and data surcharges can run as high as $16 per hour. When such costs are imposed on top of Internet/online provider fees—and Value Added Taxes as high as 25 percent—going online quickly becomes an expensive proposition for the average consumer.

Depending on the country, the global marketer may also run up against governmental restrictions on commerce. In France, for instance, there are laws against providing encrypted content. In Germany, it is against the law for credit-card companies and direct-marketing firms to gather certain types of data on potential applicants—a precaution taken by the country to prevent the massive abuses of centralized information experienced during the Nazi era. These types of restrictions, and underdeveloped banking systems, have limited credit-card and direct-mail usage in many countries. Subsequently, marketers outside the U.S. sometimes have to find marketing and collection alternatives.

Qu'est-ce que c'est, "l'Internet?"

Finally, there is the problem faced by any new medium in any country—getting recognition. Given the cyberspace hype in the U.S., it may be surprising to learn that familiarity with the Internet among the mass audience overseas is still very low. Affluent, information-intensive residents are catching on to the Internet and online services in the "best" countries. But mainstream consumers remain clueless.

For instance, 35 percent of U.K. PC owners were unaware of online services, as were 36 percent of French PC owners, according to a 1995 Inteco study. Where residents of these countries have heard about the Internet and online services, it was often in association with news stories chronicling high charges associated with teenager abuse, and/or bulletin boards and chat lines run by child pornographers, neo-Nazis, and other anti-social groups. Obviously, some consumer education on the more beneficent aspects of the Information Superhighway are in order.

It won't be easy. One challenge in getting the word out is that many markets lack classic venues, such as malls and computer stores, in which to demonstrate the services.

Some marketers have found fairly good alternatives. The online services in Europe are now demonstrating their products in such untraditional outlets as book stores, food stores, record stores, and even Nike sneaker shops. For instance, AOL Germany is demonstrating its service and distributing its software via a number of Tower Records outlets in Germany. In exchange, AOL is hosting Tower's huge 100,000 title catalog online. Trade and computer shows are also being used for demonstrations.

Vertically integrated companies that have both online/Internet services and retail outlets are in an even better position to provide such demonstrations. Tokyu, a Japanese trading company with cable TV holdings, has used its downtown Tokyo department store to set up an "Internet Media Shop" where customers can see the Internet in action, and use it themselves, free of charge. Marketers may consider setting up partnerships with such vertically integrated companies.

• • • • • • • •
Global Reach

Home-based online and Internet users as of late 1995

Country	Online Subscribers	Internet Subscribers
Japan	3,400,000	200,000
Germany	1,200,000	150,000
U.K.	265,000	100,000
France*	40,000	50,000
Netherlands	30,000	50,000
Australia	70,000	100,000
Sweden	10,000	100,000
Italy	33,000	60,000

*excluding 6.5 million Minitel users
Source: Simba Information

For companies that hope to extend their markets beyond the U.S., the Internet and online services can represent an easy way to get started, and/or to reinforce other efforts. If the decision at company headquarters is to "go for it," however, make sure to do it right: treat every country as a unique market and develop "partnerships" where they would be helpful. The dangers of not providing country-specific content have become too quickly apparent to marketers, who have found that jokes go flat, inside references are unappreciated—and services are underused.

Peter Krasilovsky is a senior analyst with Arlen Communications Inc., a leading new media research firm in Bethesda, Maryland. He is also editor of Find/SVP's Interactive Consumers, *the monthly primary research report. Readers may e-mail him at Pkras@aol.com.*

⎯ MORE INFO ⎯

Arlen Communications Inc., Bethesda, MD; (301) 656-7940

Inteco Research, Norwalk, CT; (203) 866-4400

Simba Information, Wilton, CT; (203) 834-0033 ext. 171. Peter Krasilovsky's new report, "International Opportunities: 1996," may be obtained by calling this number.

Glossary

This glossary of marketing terms is included to provide you with a convenient and ready reference as you encounter general terms in your study of marketing which are unfamiliar or require a review. It is not intended to be comprehensive but taken together with the many definitions included in the articles themselves it should prove to be quite useful.

Advertising　Efforts to stimulate sales through the use of mass media displays, direct individual appeals, public displays, give-aways and the like. Although advertising can take many forms, the particular mix of such forms which gets the best results for either a product category or an individual company is often developed to a high level of efficiency. *See* Marketing Mix, Promotion

Anti-Dumping Tariff　A tariff penalizing the sale of imported goods at a price lower than they sell for in their country of origin. *See* Imports

† **Barter**　The exchange of goods or services between two parties without resort to money. A practice which is becoming more common in international trade.

Brand　An identification, name or symbol used to differentiate the products of one company from its competition. A brand may actually consist of any set of individual product characteristics which the consumer associates with only that single product, product line or selling company. *See* Brand Differentiation, Brand Image, Brand Name

Brand Differentiation　The degree of consumer discrimination between products on the basis of product brand, or the ability of a company to promote such discrimination.

Brand Image　The quality and reliability of a product as perceived by consumers on the basis of its brand reputation or familiarity.

Brand Name　That part of the brand of a product which can be and is communicated as a name or equivalent product identification. The brand name is usually that element of a particular brand which triggers the brand consciousness within the consumer.

Buyers Market　A condition of a market in which supply exceeds demand, thus putting downward pressure on prices. *See* Sellers Market

Capital Goods　Equipment, machinery or tools which are used in the production of, or facilitate the eventual production of, other goods. In general, they are comprised of that portion of industrial goods which are not consumed in the normal course of business.

Caveat Emptor　"Let the buyer beware." A principle of law meaning that the purchase of a product is at the buyer's risk with regard to its quality, usefulness and the like. The laws do, however, provide certain minimum protection against fraud and other schemes.

Channels of Distribution　The various means employed by a company in distributing its products through wholesalers, distributors, jobbers, retailers and the like. *See* Distribution

Competition　The contest by two or more parties for the business of a third party. It is the act of securing business through offering the most favorable deal to one's customer.

Consignment　An arrangement in which a seller of goods does not take title to the goods until they are sold. The seller thus has the option of returning them to the supplier or principal if unable to execute the sale.

Consumer　The final buyer or user of a product, good or service. Commonly used in reference to individuals rather than industrial, institutional or other classes of consumers.

Consumer Advertising　Advertising which is directed at the final purchaser of goods or services.

Consumer Behavior　The way in which buyers, individually or collectively, react to marketplace stimuli.

Consumer Goods　Those goods which are produced for direct use by individuals and households. *See* Capital Goods, Convenience Goods, Industrial Goods, Shopping Goods, Specialty Goods

Convenience Goods　Consumer goods which are purchased at frequent intervals with little regard for price. Such goods are relatively standard in nature and consumers tend to select the most convenient source when shopping. Convenience goods include tobacco, drugs, newspapers and some grocery items. *See* Shopping Goods, Specialty Goods

Cooperative Advertising　Advertising of a product by a retailer, dealer, distributor or the like with part of the advertising cost paid by the product's manufacturer.

Copyright　A statutory right granted to the creator of a published or artistic work protecting the exclusive prerogative of reproduction for a specific period of time. A relatively simple and inexpensive process, works copyrighted in the United States are afforded reciprocal protection under a copyright agreement.

Demand　In general, the need or desire for individual or collective products within a marketplace. *See* Law of Supply and Demand, Supply

† **De-Marketing**　The use of marketing techniques to discourage consumption of a particular product or service. For example, when a utility company encourages consumers to turn off lights.

Demography　The study of human population densities, distributions and movements.

Direct Mail Promotion　Marketing goods to consumers by mailing to them unsolicited promotional material.

Direct Selling　A manufacturer's sales efforts directed to the final purchaser or consumer.

Discount　The reduction in the price of an item, usually given in return for some benefit such as prompt payment or quantity purchase. It also refers to the difference between a bond's (or other item's) selling price and its face value when it is selling below face value.

Discount House A retail company which sells goods at prices below those generally prevailing, usually relying on selling large quantities in order to pay overhead expenses and generate sufficient profit.

Discretionary Income That portion of disposable income, either of an individual or of a nation as a whole, which remains after paying for necessities.

Disposable Income That portion of income, either of an individual or of a nation as a whole, which remains after payment of personal taxes to the government.

Distribution The ways by which a company gets its product to the point of purchase by the final consumer. In statistics, the way in which a set of numbers tends to be more or less concentrated in different ranges or categories. Perhaps the most widely known distribution is the classical bell shaped curve, with the largest concentration of numbers at the mid point. *See* Channels of Distribution

Distributor In general, any person or organization performing the function of product distribution. The term usually excludes retailers but includes wholesalers and dealers who sell to either retailers or industrial consumers.

Dual Distribution The selling of products to two or more competing distribution networks, or the selling of two brands of nearly identical products through competing distribution networks. An example of the first case is found in the petroleum industry which sells to independent dealers as well as captive retailers. An example of the second case is found in the marketing of products under private label which are also being sold as nationally advertised brands. *See* Channels of Distribution, Distribution

Dumping The act of selling large amounts of goods or securities without regard to the effect on the marketplace; or the selling of imported goods at a price lower than that charged in the country of origin. *See* Anti-Dumping Tariff

Durable Goods Products that continue in service for an appreciable length of time such as automobiles or major household appliances. *See* Non-Durable Goods

Exports Goods produced within a country and subsequently sold in another country. *See* Imports

Fair Trade Laws (Fair Trade Acts) Statutes which exempt price maintenance agreements between manufacturers and distributors for certain trademarked items. While the use of fair trade agreements is diminishing, the absence of this special legal status would put such agreements in direct conflict with the restraint of trade provisions of the antitrust laws.

Franchise The right to distribute a company's products or render services under its name, and to retain the resulting profit in exchange for a fee or percentage of sales.

Free on Board (FOB) Delivered, without charge, to a specific location where ownership changes hands at the expense of the buyer.

Freight Absorption Payment of transportation costs by the manufacturer or seller, often resulting in a uniform pricing structure.

Imports A country's buying of goods or services which are manufactured or produced in some other country.

Industrial Goods Those goods which are destined for use in, or consumption by, commercial businesses. The industrial goods market generally exhibits more uniform and rational buying patterns than the consumer goods market. *See* Capital Goods

Inventory An asset composed of goods held for sale or raw materials and semi-finished goods held for use in their production.

Inventory Profit Profit made by a company because it had inventory on hand during a period of rising costs and prices. If a company increases its selling prices as soon as its costs increase, it will realize more than its normal profit on the on-hand inventory which it purchased at historically lower costs.

Inventory Turnover Rate The rate at which inventory is fully replaced each year. It is normally determined by dividing the cost of goods sold during the year by the average inventory level during the year. Also called stockturn rate.

Invoice A detailed statement of goods or services provided, usually including a request for payment.

Jobber One who buys from wholesalers and sells to retailers to eliminate the necessity of one-to-one contact between each wholesaler and retailer. Sometimes used synonymously with wholesaler.

Law of Supply and Demand Those laws, generally relating to economic theory, which describe the behavior of prices through an understanding of such factors as the economic structure, the nature of products, and specific combinations of the supply and demand levels for products.

Life Cycle The phases through which a product or business passes during its viable life. There are four generally accepted life cycle phases: (1) development, 2) growth, 3) maturity, and 4) decline. The duration and intensity of each phase depends upon the characteristics of each product or business.

Logo The symbol or trademark which a company uses to identify itself such as on letterheads, signs or advertising.

Loss Leader An item which a manufacturer or retailer sells at or below cost in order to either achieve greater market penetration or attract purchasers for other products in the product line.

Market The potential buyers for a company's product or service; or to sell a product or service to actual buyers. The place where goods and services are exchanged. *See* Marketing, Marketplace

* **Market Analysis** A sub-division of marketing research which involves the measurement of the extent of a market and the determination of its characteristics.

Marketing The total effort of a company in directing products from manufacturer to final consumer including advertising, selling, packaging, distribution, market research and other such functions.

* **Marketing Budget** A statement of the planned dollar sales and planned marketing costs for a specified future period.

† **Marketing Concept** A company belief that the best way to be successful is by identifying the needs and wants of a particular market segment and developing and implementing marketing strategies to satisfy those needs in ways that are more efficient than the competition's.

* **Marketing Management** The planning, direction and control of the entire marketing activity of a firm or division of a firm, including the formulation of marketing objectives, policies, programs and strategy, and commonly embracing product development, organizing and staffing to carry out plans, supervising marketing operations, and controlling marketing performance.

Marketing Mix The elements of marketing: product, brand, package, price, channels of distribution, advertising and promotion, personal selling, and the like.

* **Marketing Planning** The work of setting up objectives for marketing activity and of determining and scheduling the steps necessary to achieve such objectives.

Market Orientation A marketing philosophy which emphasizes the dynamics of the marketplace (particularly customer needs) as opposed to the product. *See* Product Orientation

Market Penetration Typically, market penetration refers to the advancement of one's products or services into a particular marketplace or market segment. *See* Market Share

Marketplace In general, the place where the business of a market is conducted. It is the place or circumstances where the buying and selling of goods and services occurs.

* **Market Potential (also Market or Total Market)** A calculation of maximum possible sales opportunities for all sellers of a good or service during a stated period.

Market Research The generation of empirical and statistical information concerning consumers or purchasers. Market research seeks, for example, to determine how purchasers behave and how they perceive the various characteristics of products.

Market Segment A group or segment of consumers who share some characteristics in common, such as age, sex, income, education, occupation, marital status or geographic location. A company usually directs its marketing effort at specific market segments.

Market Share A product's sales as a percent of all sales of similar products. Market share may also apply to a group of products or to a company in relation to its industry.

Market Skimming Exploiting only the prime market segment of a product's or company's marketplace which is either the most profitable, the least costly to reach, or requires the least amount of available resources.

Market Stimulation The act of increasing sales through the introduction or augmentation of an element of the marketing mix.

Mark Up As it relates to retail selling it is the retailer's expected margin expressed as a percentage of selling price (selling price minus cost divided by selling price). It differs from gross margin in that the latter is an achieved percentage of gain while the former is an intended percentage of gain.

† **Mass Marketing** Utilizing marketing strategies to attract as many customers from all market segments as possible. Usually involves the mass-production and mass-distribution of a single product; some toothpastes and laundry detergents are examples.

Mass Media Advertising The use of any advertising media whose audience consists of the general population such as with radio, newspaper or television advertising.

Middleman A person or business which buys and sells between manufacturers and consumers or similarly brings together two complementary interests.

Missionary Selling The initial sales efforts by a manufacturer into virgin markets. Typically, the missionary sales person will receive a salary rather than a commission for services.

* **Motivation Research** A group of techniques developed by the behavioral scientists which are used by marketing researchers to discover factors influencing marketing behavior.

Multinational A company which conducts operations in many countries.

Non-Durable Goods Products that do not last or continue in service for any appreciable length of time. Clothing is an example of non-durable goods.

Obsolescence The decrease in the value of an item which is caused by age, style change or new technology. An item may be obsolete even though it still functions in the way in which it was designed. *See* Planned Obsolescence

Patent A license granted by a government to an inventor giving, for a period of time, exclusive manufacturing rights to the invention. A patent has value and is often included as an asset on a company's balance sheet. In the United States, a patent can be protected for 17 years.

Personal Selling Any form of oral sales presentation or assistance to a customer. Traditionally the cornerstone of selling and promotional activities, it is one of the elements of the marketing mix.

* **Physical Distribution** The management of the move-

ment and handling of goods from the point of production to the point of consumption or use.

Planned Obsolescence Purposely designing obsolescense into a product. This can be achieved either by incorporating periodic changes which are stylistic rather than functional, or by designing a product with a physical life shorter than its useful life.

Point-of-Purchase Advertising The act of promoting a product at the location of purchase. A point-of-purchase display is designed to impel on-the-spot buying by customers. It is used more extensively in marketing consumer than industrial goods, because ultimate consumers are more susceptible to impulse buying.

Predatory Price Cutting The practice of selling goods or services at or below cost. Predatory price cutting may be employed to increase a company's market share or to sell unwanted merchandise. Note, however, that predatory price cutting does not refer to such selling of seasonal or perishable items.

Price Elasticity An economic concept which attempts to measure the sensitivity of demand for any product to changes in its price. If consumers are relatively sensitive to changes in price (i.e., higher price results in a lower demand for a product), then the demand for such a product is elastic. If, on the other hand, changing price does not affect the quantity purchased, then such a product is said to exhibit an inelastic demand characteristic. *See* Law of Supply and Demand

Price Fixing The illegal attempt by one or several companies to maintain the prices of its products above those that would result from open competition.

* **Price Leader** A firm whose pricing behavior is followed by other companies in the same industry. The price leadership of a firm may be limited to a certain geographical area, as in the oil business, or to certain products or groups of products, as in the steel business.

Price Out To calculate the price or cost of a set of actions; or to lower a price in an effort to drive high priced competition out of a market.

Pricing Policies The manner in which a company determines the prices of its goods or services. Three such methods used are: 1) to apply a standard markup to the cost of goods, 2) to maintain prices in line with competition, and 3) to charge what the market will bear.

Primary Market Demand The demand for goods and services in the market for which they were primarily intended.

Product Anything which a company sells. In the narrowest sense product refers to manufactured items. In popular terminology, however, product can also refer to services, securities and the like.

Product Differentiation The ability or tendency of manufacturers, marketers or consumers to distinguish between seemingly similar products. *See* Brand, Brand Differentiation

Productivity The rate at which production occurs (presumably to generate profit) in a given period of time.

Productivity may apply to a laborer, machine, company, industry or even an entire country.

* **Product Line** A group of products that are closely related either because they satisfy a class of need, are used together, are sold to the same customer groups, are marketed through the same type of outlets or fall within given price ranges. Example, carpenters' tools.

* **Product Management** The planning, direction, and control of all phases of the life cycle of products, including the creation or discovery of ideas for new products, the screening of such ideas, the coordination of the work of research and physical development of products, their packaging and branding, their introduction on the market, their market development, their modification, the discovery of new uses for them, their repair and servicing, and their deletion.

Product Market Erosion A decrease in demand for a product or service. Product market erosion might be caused, for example, by the introduction of a similar product which consumers purchase as a substitute.

* **Product Mix** The composite of products offered for sale by a firm or a business unit.

Product Orientation A marketing philosophy which emphasizes the product as opposed to the customer. Such an orientation usually involves efforts to perfect product design, improve production efficiencies, and reduce product cost without heeding the dynamics of the marketplace or changes in the competitive situation. *See* Market Orientation

Promotion The stimulation of sales by inducements or product exposure directed at either the channels of distribution or the final consumer. Promotion can refer to various forms of advertising, trade or consumer discounts, specially advertised discounts or the like. The promotion of a new product might include a combination of several of these. *See* Marketing Mix

Proprietary Product A product which is of such distinction as to be under patent, trademark or copyright protection. Also those products protected by proprietary market positions, such as through strength of distribution channels, production efficiencies, geographic location, etc.

† **Psychographics** Measurable characteristics of given market segments in respect to lifestyles, interests, opinions, needs, values, attitudes, personality traits, etc.

* **Publicity** Non-personal stimulation of demand for a product, service or business unit by planting commercially significant news about it in a published medium or obtaining favorable presentation of it upon radio, television, or stage that is not paid for by the sponsor.

Pull Strategy A marketing strategy whose main thrust is to so strongly influence the final consumer that the demand for a product "pulls" it through the various channels of distribution. Such a strategy is generally accompanied by large advertising expenditures to influence the consumer and relatively low markups to wholesalers and retailers. *See* Push Strategy

Push Strategy   A marketing strategy whose main thrust is to provide sufficient economic incentives to members of the channels of distribution so as to "push" the product through to the consumer. Such a strategy is usually accompanied by high price markups, selective distribution and retail price support by the manufacturer. *See* Pull Strategy

* **Resale Price Maintenance**   Control by a supplier of the selling prices of his branded goods at subsequent stages of distribution by means of contractual agreement under fair trade laws or other devices.

Restraint of Trade   In general, activities which interfere with competitive marketing. Restraint of trade usually refers to illegal activities.

* **Retailing**   The activities involved in selling directly to the ultimate consumer.

* **Sales Forecast**   An estimate of sales, in dollars or physical units for a specified future period under a proposed marketing plan or program and under an assumed set of economic and other forces outside the unit for which the forecast is made. The forecast may be for a specified item of merchandise or for an entire line.

* **Sales Management**   The planning, direction, and control of the personal selling activities of a business unit, including recruiting, selecting, training, equipping, assigning, routing, supervising, paying, and motivating as these tasks apply to the personal sales force.

* **Sales Promotion**   (1.) In a specific sense, those marketing activities, other than personal selling, advertising, and publicity, that stimulate consumer purchasing and dealer effectiveness, such as display, shows and exhibitions, demonstrations, and various non-recurrent selling efforts not in the ordinary routine. (2.) In retailing, all methods of stimulating customer purchasing, including personal selling, advertising, and publicity.

Secondary Market Demand   The demand for goods or services in a market other than that for which they were intended. *See* Primary Market Demand

Selective Distribution   The use of only those means of distributing a product which are either most profitable, easiest to manage or control, or otherwise particularly beneficial or consistent with other marketing, production or financial considerations. *See* Distribution, Market Skimming

Sellers Market   A condition within any market in which the demand for an item is greater than its supply. A market in which the seller maintains a more favorable bargaining position than the buyer. *See* Buyers Market

* **Selling**   The personal or impersonal process of assisting and/or persuading a prospective customer to buy a commodity or a service or to act favorably upon an idea that has commercial significance to the seller.

Services   In general, efforts expended to meet human needs which are primarily direct person to person activities or those activities not associated with the manufacturing or processing of a product, good, commodity or the like.

Shopping Goods   Consumer goods which are purchased only after comparisons are made concerning price, quality, style, suitability and the like. Shopping goods are often purchased infrequently, consumed or used up slowly and are subject to advanced or deferred purchase decisions on the part of the consumer. Such items include, for example, furniture, rugs and shoes. *See* Convenience Goods, Speciality Goods

† **Social Marketing**   The use of marketing strategies to increase the acceptability of an idea (smoking causes cancer); cause (environmental protection); or practice (birth control) within a target market.

Specialty Goods   Consumer goods, usually appealing only to a limited market, for which consumers will make a special purchasing effort. Such items include, for example, stereo components, fancy foods and prestige brand clothes. *See* Convenience Goods, Shopping Goods

† **Target Marketing**   Developing product and promotion strategies for a very well-defined group of potential customers to which a company decides to market goods or services.

Trade Advertising   Advertising directed at the trade which distributes, sells or uses a product.

Trademark (Trade-Mark)   An affixed sign or mark distinguishing articles produced or marketed by one company from those of another. Generally used to protect the goodwill or name of a certain class of goods, trademarks can be registered thus restricting use by others.

* **Ultimate Consumer**   One who buys and/or uses goods or services to satisfy personal or household wants rather than for resale or for use in business, institutional, or industrial operations.

* **Value Added by Marketing**   The part of the value of a product or a service to the consumer or user which results from marketing activities.

Wholesaler   One who makes quantity purchases from manufacturers (or other wholesalers), and sells in smaller quantities to retailers (or other wholesalers). The wholesaler usually handles the products of many different manufacturers and in turn is only one of many suppliers to his customers. Similarly, the wholesaler will operate in a smaller geographic area than the manufacturer but a much larger area than the retailer. The wholesaler will usually rely on a small percentage profit from a large volume of sales, and may be expected to provide various services to the customer which would otherwise not be available.

Sources for the Glossary:

Terms designated by an asterisk (*) were taken from "Marketing Definitions: A Glossary of Marketing Terms," Committee on Definitions of the American Marketing Association.

Definitions for terms designated with a dagger (†) were developed by the Annual Editions staff.

The remaining terms were taken from "The Language of Business" (1975). The complete pocket glossary is available at either single list price or quantity discount price through Cambridge Business Research Inc., 4 Brattle St., Suite 306, Cambridge, MA 02138.

Index

Credits/Acknowledgments

Cover design by Charles Vitelli

1. Marketing in the 1990s and Beyond
Facing overview—New York Stock Exchange photo.
83-86—Photomontages by Lou Beach.

2. Research, Markets, and Consumer Behavior
Facing overview—Photo by Pamela Carley. 96-97—Illustrations by
Terry Allen.

3. Developing and Implementing Marketing Strategies
Facing overview—Photo by Cheryl Greenleaf.

4. Global Marketing
Facing overview—United Nations photo by Y. Nagata.

ANNUAL EDITIONS ARTICLE REVIEW FORM

■ NAME: _____ DATE: _____

■ TITLE AND NUMBER OF ARTICLE: _____

■ BRIEFLY STATE THE MAIN IDEA OF THIS ARTICLE: _____

_____

■ LIST THREE IMPORTANT FACTS THAT THE AUTHOR USES TO SUPPORT THE MAIN IDEA:

_____

_____

_____

_____

■ WHAT INFORMATION OR IDEAS DISCUSSED IN THIS ARTICLE ARE ALSO DISCUSSED IN YOUR TEXTBOOK OR OTHER READINGS THAT YOU HAVE DONE? LIST THE TEXTBOOK CHAPTERS AND PAGE NUMBERS:

_____

_____

_____

_____

_____

■ LIST ANY EXAMPLES OF BIAS OR FAULTY REASONING THAT YOU FOUND IN THE ARTICLE:

_____

_____

_____

_____

■ LIST ANY NEW TERMS/CONCEPTS THAT WERE DISCUSSED IN THE ARTICLE, AND WRITE A SHORT DEFINITION:

_____

_____

_____

_____

*Your instructor may require you to use this ANNUAL EDITIONS Article Review Form in any number of ways: for articles that are assigned, for extra credit, as a tool to assist in developing assigned papers, or simply for your own reference. Even if it is not required, we encourage you to photocopy and use this page; you will find that reflecting on the articles will greatly enhance the information from your text.

We Want Your Advice

ANNUAL EDITIONS revisions depend on two major opinion sources: one is our Advisory Board, listed in the front of this volume, which works with us in scanning the thousands of articles published in the public press each year; the other is you—the person actually using the book. Please help us and the users of the next edition by completing the prepaid article rating form on this page and returning it to us. Thank you for your help!

ANNUAL EDITIONS: MARKETING 97/98
Article Rating Form

Here is an opportunity for you to have direct input into the next revision of this volume. We would like you to rate each of the 42 articles listed below, using the following scale:

1. **Excellent: should definitely be retained**
2. **Above average: should probably be retained**
3. **Below average: should probably be deleted**
4. **Poor: should definitely be deleted**

Your ratings will play a vital part in the next revision. So please mail this prepaid form to us just as soon as you complete it.
Thanks for your help!

Rating	Article	Rating	Article
	1. The Future of Marketing: What Every Marketer Should Know about Being Online		22. Penetrating Purchaser Personalities
	2. The New Gold Rush?		23. The Very Model of a Modern Marketing Plan
	3. The New Marketplace		24. Win the Market
	4. Sensitive Groups and Social Issues: Are You Marketing Correct?		25. What's in a Brand?
	5. Marketing Myopia (with Retrospective Commentary)		26. How to Tell Fads from Trends
	6. Happiness Isn't Everything, Keep Them Coming Back		27. Flops
	7. How to Keep Your Customers		28. Ten Timeless Truths about Pricing
	8. Leader of the Pack		29. Stuck! How Companies Cope When They Can't Raise Prices
	9. Relationship Marketing: Positioning for the Future		30. More to Offer than Price
	10. Service Is Everybody's Business		31. Your Secret Weapon
	11. 'My Lawyer Sent Me Flowers'		32. Retailers with a Future
	12. Learning from Customer Defections		33. Selling the Superstores
	13. Marketing and Ethics		34. Target "Micromarkets" Its Way to Success; No 2 Stores Are Alike
	14. The New Hucksterism		35. The Death and Rebirth of the Salesman
	15. The Frontiers of Psychographics		36. Talk of the Town
	16. Database Marketing: A Potent New Tool for Selling		37. The 'Net Effect
	17. A Beginner's Guide to Demographics		38. First, Green Stamps. Now, Coupons?
	18. The Generations Quiz		39. Beware the Pitfalls of Global Marketing
	19. Making Generational Marketing Come of Age		40. Isolationism in a Global Economy
	20. Scouting for Souls		41. Hot Markets Overseas
	21. Consumer Behavior: Yesterday, Today, and Tomorrow		42. A Whole New World

(Continued on next page)

ABOUT YOU

Name _____ Date _____

Are you a teacher? ❑ Or a student? ❑

Your school name _____

Department _____

Address _____

City _____ State _____ Zip _____

School telephone # _____

YOUR COMMENTS ARE IMPORTANT TO US!

Please fill in the following information:

For which course did you use this book? _____

Did you use a text with this *ANNUAL EDITION*? ❑ yes ❑ no

What was the title of the text? _____

What are your general reactions to the *Annual Editions* concept?

Have you read any particular articles recently that you think should be included in the next edition?

Are there any articles you feel should be replaced in the next edition? Why?

Are there other areas of study that you feel would utilize an *ANNUAL EDITION?*

May we contact you for editorial input?

May we quote your comments?

ANNUAL EDITIONS: MARKETING 97/98

┌───┐
│   **BUSINESS REPLY MAIL**   │
│ First Class   Permit No. 84   Guilford, CT │
└───┘

Postage will be paid by addressee

Dushkin Publishing Group/
Brown & Benchmark Publishers
Sluice Dock
Guilford, Connecticut 06437